THE LOST LEADER
A Study of Wordsworth

By the Same Author

THE LOST LEADER

A Study of Wordsworth

BY

HUGH I'ANSON FAUSSET

'*As long as thou hast not grasped this die-and-become
thou art but a dull guest on this dark earth.*'
GOETHE.

JONATHAN CAPE
THIRTY BEDFORD SQUARE
LONDON

FIRST PUBLISHED 1933

JONATHAN CAPE LTD., 30 BEDFORD SQUARE, LONDON
AND 91 WELLINGTON STREET WEST, TORONTO

PRINTED IN GREAT BRITAIN BY J. AND J. GRAY, EDINBURGH
PAPER MADE BY JOHN DICKINSON AND CO. LTD.
BOUND BY A. W. BAIN AND CO. LTD.

CONTENTS

TO
L. H.

PREFACE

TWO events have during the last twenty years invited a reconsideration of Wordsworth both as a man and a poet —the discovery by Professor Legouis of his relations with Annette Vallon, and the publication by Professor de Selincourt of the original version of *The Prelude*.

It is possible to exaggerate the importance of both these discoveries; for they have only confirmed a change in critical opinion and emphasis which had already manifested itself. It had, in fact, long been recognised that the real Wordsworth was neither the rural simpleton nor the mild pietist whom so many Victorian 'Wordsworthians' cherished; that he was instead a man of violent feelings and violent revulsions, a lonely and a haunted man who knew the beauty that hath both terror and ecstasy in it, but a man, too, with a tough and tenacious mind which eventually dominated his instinctive being and produced what Professor Garrod has called 'the most dismal anti-climax of which the history of literature holds record.'

That abrupt decline of creative faculty from the age of thirty-seven is the fact in Wordsworth's life upon which critics have increasingly concentrated. And rightly so, because in penetrating to its causes we touch the essentials of Wordsworth's personality and the qualities which made him in turn the most original and the most conventional of poets. Yet although many intelligent and interesting explanations of it have been offered from the time of De Quincey to that of Mr. Herbert Read, I cannot help feeling that all of them are partial or fail to go deep enough, because the critics have studied Wordsworth's life rather as an intellectual or psychological problem than as a spiritual event.

It was left to Blake, who never professed to be a critic, to make the simple and profound comment: 'I see in Wordsworth,' he said, 'the natural man rising up against the spiritual man

7

continually, and then he is no poet, but a heathen philosopher, at enmity with all true poetry and inspiration.'

It is, perhaps, too simple a statement to carry meaning to our complex modern minds. But this book is nothing more nor less than an attempt to reveal in detail its truth. For unless we recognise in Wordsworth the spiritual man striving and ultimately failing to be born out of the natural man, we miss equally the real significance of his early fidelity to Nature and the real pathos of his later apostasy.

Wordsworth, in short, was a potential mystic who failed to complete himself at a crucial point, failed to pass from the state of childhood and boyhood when the spiritual is inevitably a condition of the natural to a creative maturity when the natural should be as inevitably a condition of the spiritual. Hence, when his natural forces began to decline, he not only ceased to grow imaginatively, but he began to die. And all his natural faculties, which in his short inspired period had been channels for a life and consciousness which transcended the narrow bounds of self, lost touch with their spiritual source and came to serve, beneath a mask of piety, morality and high principles, the barren needs of a nervous egotism.

To discuss further at this point, however, how Wordsworth went wrong, and what it was in his personality and his experiences which arrested and frustrated him would be to forestall the pages that follow. It is enough here to emphasise the importance for us to-day of trying to understand his failure. For we are in a real sense the inheritors of it. It is not merely, as Professor Beatty has written, that 'he who touches Wordsworth touches an age, and the explanation of Wordsworth involves the explanation of all his contemporaries.' For in Wordsworth's failure is involved, too, the failure of the nineteenth century and the necessity which that failure has imposed upon us to-day of advancing anew from the point at which Wordsworth turned back.

Wordsworth holds a peculiarly significant place among the great poets of the Romantic Movement, because he alone lived long enough to work out in his life and art the new conflict of feeling and thought characteristic of his age. He failed, and lived for forty years haunted by an uneasy conscience, a sense of faded glory, of vision darkened, and deep assurance quenched.

And that failure and the way in which it came about offers, perhaps, a more detailed and informing revelation of the problem of self-adjustment with which the modern consciousness is faced than the triumphant crucifixion of self to life to which the dying Keats submitted. Wordsworth's failure had, indeed, more disastrous consequences than that of any other poet of the Romantic Movement, because it was for so long not recognised as such. To suggest that the fatal Victorian compromise derived from him would be of course a gross exaggeration. And it would probably be truer to say that Wordsworth in middle and old age reflected rather than engendered a temper which the French Revolution and the Napoleonic Wars had made inevitable. There is truth in Morley's contention that 'poetry, and not only poetry, but every other channel of emotional expression and artistic culture, confessedly moves with the general march of the human mind.'

But it is a half-truth, since the great poet has always done more than transform into ideal and imaginative shapes 'a predominant system and philosophy of life.' He has led the march of the human mind, too; he has renewed and restored its virtue, and he has infected it through the depth and richness of his consciousness with a hunger for more creative realisation. Up to a point in his development, Wordsworth was and is such a leader. But his apostasy has sadly weakened the virtue of his leadership. There can, indeed, be few to-day who do not recognise the negative quality of his later life and philosophy.

But there are many who allow this sad anti-climax to blind them to the creative truth on its own level of his early faith. His history seems, indeed, to justify those critics of romanticism who proclaim the folly of believing in man or in Nature, in love or in liberty. This, they can argue with much plausibility, is the kind of sterility to which such credulousness inevitably leads, if it has not previously culminated in sensational catastrophe.

The present reaction against romanticism is very understandable, and so far as it represents a resolute rejection of all abstractions, idealisms, or moralities which are not rooted in reality or which are projections of a sick or selfish egotism, it is right and necessary. The world, indeed, is so stricken with perverse individualism that it may be necessary to secure the physical and collective basis of life before any superstructures of new reality can be built upon it. But the problem of fulfilling the self is no more solved by a return to a collective state than to a state of Nature. To be in all our activities in creative harmony both with Nature and our fellow-men is a necessary condition of all fertile human life. But that is not to be achieved, except at an elementary stage of development, by submerging the self in the mass or denying its demands for unique and ideal expression. The dreams of romantic youth have a reality no less than the facts of life, and the quest of a real maturity involves bringing them into a true relation.

And in this quest there are two factors of growth, neither of which can be sacrificed to the other without a loss of integrity—those of individuation and co-operation, of self-assertion and self-surrender. Each is necessary to man's vital development, and in the ultimate completion of the self in unity with the creative spirit of life, both are reconciled and fulfilled.

To reduce the self to the undifferentiated and generic status of the crowd or of physical nature because its burden has become intolerable, is no less to cripple human growth than to exploit the self perversely. And it is because Wordsworth's life and the inner record of it which his poetry provides in such exhaustive detail offer a remarkable opportunity for the study of the relation between selfhood and selflessness, the spirit of man and the forces of Nature, that I have undertaken this book.

If Wordsworth had been no more than a naturalist, the psychologists could sufficiently explain him. But working in him and in his purest moments possessing him was the creative imagination which Coleridge recognised and did so much to quicken and foster. In such imagination the spirit of man and the spirit of Nature are reconciled. But it is equally unattainable by those who falsely deny Nature whether as intellectuals or moralists, and by those who merely affirm her physically. To discover, in short, how the rational and the instinctive may be creatively harmonised is, it seems to me, the most fundamental problem which faces us to-day. And since the cardinal importance of Wordsworth is that he tried and failed to solve this problem as a man, although he came near solving it in moments of divination as a poet, he has, I believe, a very vital meaning for us to-day.

And my whole aim in this book is to discover something of that meaning. This is its central thread, to which all its biographical, critical, and psychological elements are subordinated and related. I am concerned with Wordsworth's outer life only so far as it reveals and influenced his inner life, and the same is true of his practice and theory as a poet, his political enthusiasms and revulsions, his philosophy and his theology.

No one shows more clearly than Wordsworth that the problem of reconciling the spiritual and the natural man is ultimately a problem of achieving a true individuality. The depth and richness of his consciousness up to a certain point was due to the very limitations of his tenacious individualism.

But because the evolutionary principle in the natural world becomes in man an urge towards self-transcendence which must be progressively satisfied if his creative life is not to be arrested, these limitations proved later his undoing.

In him, therefore, as in every individual, if we probe deep enough, the laws, not only of the phenomenal world which science studies, but of the spiritual world which religion and poetry recognise, are discoverable. To study a personality deeply is, indeed, to study a more essential expression of the nature of life than that with which science has hitherto mainly concerned itself. And just as the man who realises his own organic unity reveals how mankind may become organic, so the man who fails to do so contains within himself all the feuds and conflicts of human society. To explore the causes of his failure is, therefore, to undertake a piece of research into a deadly disease, which is no less important than that of the specialist in the laboratory.

And the disease which Wordsworth strove unavailingly to cure in himself is the disease of the modern world. Human destiny stands to-day at the point which he reached and failed to make a point of departure. We, too, have outgrown the state of Nature and fallen into a state of sin. Some of us would temporise, as he did, clinging to our egotism and its privileges, but concealing the fact beneath professions of morality, humanism, and worldly wisdom. Others would destroy the whole ugly growth that has sprung from the self-centred mind of man through four centuries, and live once again the healthy life of the body in vital association with other healthy bodies.

But neither of these is a true, or to-day even possible, solution of our problem. For both fail to satisfy the needs of the spirit which through the very conflict of body and mind, of self and anti-self, has become ripe for rebirth into a new consciousness and a new world of co-operative individuality. And in tracing Wordsworth's history I have tried to show what that new life of harmonious selfhood involves. I have striven to reconstruct his life from year to year and, in its crucial period, from month to month, from within, until in 1815 the last efforts of self-transcendence ceased, and he was immured in the prison-house of which he had for so long felt the deepening shadows.

For the earlier parts of this record I am, of course, primarily indebted to *The Prelude*, and to Professor de Selincourt's noble edition of the original version. And if readers should complain that I have unduly borrowed from and paraphrased its text, I can only plead the necessity of doing so, if constant quotation was to be avoided, and the fact that, more than most great poems, it lends itself to such treatment. For, if it had been written to-day, much of it might well have taken the form of prose. The generous quotation, in which I have indulged, from the rest of his poetry has been similarly necessary to my endeavour to trace in all its detail the developing pattern of his inner life and thought. And I can only hope that by so doing I may have enriched the meaning of many of his poems by adding to their personal significance.

I owe much, too, to Professor Harper's *Life* and Professor Legouis' *William Wordsworth and Annette Vallon*, and something to Professor Beatty's *William Wordsworth: His Doctrine and Art in their Historical Relations*. But this book is primarily the fruit of two years' absorbed concentration, so far as the distractions of continual reviewing have allowed, upon what Wordsworth wrote himself.

For permission to quote certain lines from the original version of *The Prelude* I am greatly obliged to Professor E. de Selincourt and the Delegates of the Oxford University Press.

H. I'A. F.

THE LOST LEADER
A Study of Wordsworth

PART I

THE STATE OF NATURE

§ 1

WHITEHAVEN is to-day an industrial centre, and the traveller approaching it from inland is warned of what awaits him by the chimneys and pit-heads that stand out against the skyline. But towards the end of the eighteenth century it was still a little port which came suddenly into view from the high ground down which a road ran steeply. And instead of belching chimneys, the hiss of steam, or the clank of shunting coal-trucks, those who approached it on a clear day not only saw with a startling distinctness the white waves breaking against its quays and piers, but heard and smelt the breathing of the sea.

To come thus abruptly upon the sea was for any stranger to the district an exhilarating experience. But for one child who with her brother trod this road for the first time in the 'seventies of that century it was overwhelming. The elemental in Nature spoke so compellingly to the wildness in her heart that she burst into tears. It spoke also to her brother, a boy of seven or eight, and her elder by a year and a half. But if he, too, felt violently, his feeling, far less than his sister's, flowed outward in a selfless and helpless sympathy with life. Instead it was often turned inward through an innate reserve, which, if at times it made him moody, bespoke a strong individuality.

It was this quality which distinguished him both from his younger sister and from his three brothers, and which led his mother to confide to a friend that William was the only one of her children about whose future she was anxious; and he, she added, would be remarkable either for good or for evil. Yet it seems probable that he inherited the hard and tenacious strain in his nature as much from his mother's as from his father's side. The Cooksons had the reputation of being a narrow and unyielding people, although Anne Cookson herself was an exception, as her son was later to testify when he paid a grateful tribute to her simplicity and intuitive wisdom.

She owed these characteristics, however, less to the prosperous Penrith shopkeeper who was her father than to her mother, who was a Crackanthorp, a family which had lived in Newbiggen Hall, Westmorland, for many centuries, and had produced an eminent divine in the reign of James 1. Anne Cookson had married a law agent to Sir James Lowther, named John Wordsworth, who came of a long line of yeomen farmers, attached for generations to Yorkshire and Westmorland. And doubtless William drew something of his obstinacy and much of his sturdy independence from this source.

On the day on which he and his sister Dorothy first saw and heard the waves breaking against the quays of Whitehaven, they had walked over from Cockermouth, a village which lay a short distance inland. And here in a square and solid house that overlooked its humbler neighbours William had been born on 7th April 1770. He came, as has been shown, of a stock which, on both sides, in farming, business and professional work, had cultivated simple living and practical sagacity. And from his earliest years his upbringing was of a kind to confirm the qualities which he had inherited. His father was a prosperous man of business, but the family lived with that thriftiness, blended equally of native caution, self-respect, and a blunt contempt for affectation or display, which even to this day characterises the Northerner of these parts.

And with the healthy discipline of plain living the Wordsworth children also enjoyed a freedom from undue parental interference. We know more perhaps to-day of the ways in which personality can be warped in childhood by the ignorant selfishness of too fond or too anxious parents. William's mother,

> Fetching her goodness rather from time past
> Than shaping novelties from those to come,

might well have smiled at our sermons on the respect that is due to the child. But instinctively she fostered their independence. Like 'the parent hen amid her brood,' she was content to be 'a centre to the circle which they make.' Her habit was to trust her children's nature, to believe their instincts not only innocent but the determining factor in their proper growth. And so she was neither 'selfish with unnecessary cares,' nor 'with impatience from the season asked more than its timely produce.' And her children, instead of being 'attended, follow'd, watch'd, and noos'd,' were left much to themselves and allowed to roam freely in the countryside.

Consequently, William was never in danger of being civilised before his time. He preserved intact those 'motions of savage instinct' which are native to the child, and may prove in time the rich soil of a vital imagination. He knew the savage's fear as he entered in boyish play the dungeon of Cockermouth Castle, the thrill of the hunter as he chased the butterfly through its green courts, the climber's breathless triumph as he stretched for the flowers that waved upon its ruined brow. And underlying and intimately involved in the active play of his primitive instincts was the tidal rhythm of the natural world, of its bleak winds and radiant calms, its wild woods and murmuring waters.

For the essential genius of the child lies in his ability to be passive to life even in his most eager activities. He shares this faculty with the dancer or with the saint, whom Kabir described in one of his poems as one

> Who, ever immersed in bliss, having no fear,
> Keepeth the spirit of union thro'out all enjoyments.

The purest example of this unconscious, yet purposeful, union with Nature is the infant, but it may persist long after infancy. For the 'mute dialogues' which the infant holds 'by intercourse of touch' with his mother's heart, the growing child may in favoured circumstances hold with the heart of the natural world.

And so fortunate was the young Wordsworth that even as an infant he was cradled in Nature's as well as in his mother's arms. The River Derwent passed close behind his home,

> And from his alder shades and rocky falls,
> And from his fords and shallows, sent a voice

that flowed along his dreams. And to this 'ceaseless music through the night and day,' tempering with its steady cadence the human waywardness even of infancy, he was later to attribute some part in strengthening his deepest instinct, his sense of the sustaining rhythm of natural life. It gave him, unconscious though he was of the gift,

> Among the fretful dwellings of mankind,
> A foretaste, a dim earnest, of the calm
> That Nature breathes among the hills and groves.

The River Derwent, however, soon ceased merely to act upon him. For unlike another child, whose life was to be linked with his and who, a year or two later, was to find in the River Otter a perfect counterpart of his own dissolving moods, William at five years of age was as little given to passive dreaming as a young savage. The active principle worked indeed so intensely within him that it not only neutralised timidity; it impelled him to seek out and defy danger, so that no temptation was so dear as that which urged to a daring feat. He loved to challenge the forbidding looks of deep pools, tall trees, black chasms and dizzy crags.

But the satisfactions which he sought were not always so aggressive. More often his was the primitive joy of pure, unreflective being, of a naked participation with the elements as through a summer's day he alternately basked by the side of a little mill-race and plunged into it, or coursed over the sandy fields, leaping through groves of yellow ragwort. Or when wood and hill and the heights of distant Skiddaw were bronzed at sunset, he would stand alone beneath the sky; yet not alone, because merged in the whole animated body of the world about him.

For in the open air the child is by right a savage; his primitive instincts are not exasperated by being bridled and turned inward. They are chastened, indeed, by pain if he disregards Nature's conditions. But by her teaching Nature tempers the child's egoism without inflaming it. He learns in contact with her a lesson of unconscious adaptation. And because the discipline is never separated from positive living, it is positively accepted, while the negative repression of misguided human educators excites a wilful opposition.

Even the predatory instinct, when it is thus linked to wild life and subdued to the rhythm of Nature, is quite devoid of egoism. As a boy of eight Wordsworth would wander half the night among the mountain slopes, oblivious of the frosty wind, as he set snares for woodcocks or hurried eagerly on to examine snares previously set. But if in thought and wish, as well as in act, he was then 'a fell destroyer,' he was as little self-engrossed as a primitive huntsman. Even poaching was a source of spiritual ecstasy heightened and almost sanctified by the moon and stars shining over his head.

At times indeed he may have felt his loneliness and that he was 'a trouble' to their peace. But deeper still was his sense of being overlooked and surrounded by impalpable presences. So that when he yielded to the temptation to steal a bird caught in another's snare, the very universe itself seemed to close in

upon him and invest his guilty conscience. And it was the same
when he went bird-nesting in spring. Nature seemed to approve
his plundering and the daring feats which it involved, if only
by enhancing his sense of unity with her elemental forces. As
he hung above a raven's nest, flattened perilously against a
naked crag,

> With what strange utterance did the loud dry wind
> Blow through my ear! the sky seemed not a sky
> Of earth—and with what motion moved the clouds!

It was only in later years that to the humanised man such
predatory acts were violations rather than affirmations of
Nature. For to the boy the 'spirit in the woods' and hills and
streams was a wild spirit, which had its moods of fury as well
as gentleness, moods which he shared with equal delight,
because he was still almost a pure primitive to whom destruction is as vitally necessary an impulse as creation.

And being thus animated in all his actions, all his physical
experiences were, on an elementary level, spiritual. For him in
his most ecstatic moments there was no such thing as either a
moral or a material universe. There was only a symphony in
which he was a note, a heart with which his own heart beat in
time, a something other than himself which included himself,
streaming through him from some ultimate fount of mystery
and delight.

It was thus that the unconscious soul of the young Wordsworth was 'fostered alike by beauty and by fear,' by the beauty
of Nature's spiritual radiance and the menace of her elemental
power. Whether he expanded in the celestial light which
seemed at times to invest every object of sight with a dream-
like vividness and splendour, or whether the pure force of the
elements overwhelmed him with a feeling of awe and impotence,
he lost in such moments all sense of human separateness.

And because, particularly in the open air, the child obeys the rhythm of a larger life, even sinister and eerie experiences foster his soul's growth instead of straining his nerves. When, for example, William was not yet six years old and his hand could scarcely hold a bridle, he rode with 'honest James' as his guide and guardian towards the hills. By some accident the two got parted and the child was compelled to lead his horse, often stumbling, down the rough and stony moor, until at last he reached the bottom, where in former times a murderer had been hung in chains. The gibbet had mouldered down, but on the turf some unknown hand had carved the murderer's name, which local superstition had preserved by keeping the grass from covering the letters. These letters he read with a sort of horror and when, reascending the bare common, he saw a naked pool that lay cupped in the hills, the beacon on the summit, and a girl carrying a pitcher on her head who forced her way with difficulty against the strong wind, a sense of elemental dreariness immersed him as he looked all round for his lost guide, a sense which he could never forget of something more and less than human, of mysterious depths and wastes at the back of life.

It was, of course, only in later years that he came consciously to measure the significance of such experiences. But the unforgettable impression which they left upon him proves how intensely he lived them, absorbing with his whole being the mysterious breath of the primeval, while his later divinatory powers as a poet were inevitably related to these primitive intimations.

Within the walls of his home, however, he was a primitive under some constraint, who was occasionally moody and could even commit acts of sudden violence, as when he struck his whip through an old lady's petticoat in a family portrait or retired to an attic, after having suffered some indignity, intending to kill himself with one of the foils kept there. But the

proud and passionate depths of his nature were seldom provoked in a house in which he was so little repressed or confined,
and in which there were several brothers near his own age to
draw him out of himself. And above all there was his sister
Dorothy, his chosen companion and playmate.

Their favourite playground was the high terrace at the end
of the garden overlooking the River Derwent and Cockermouth
Castle. Here together they would chase a butterfly, William
like a hunter bounding upon his prey, Dorothy as swiftly
dancing from brake to bush but trembling to catch it for fear
of brushing the dust from its wings. And here amid the closely-
clipt privet and roses which covered the terrace wall they found
the sparrow's nest with its bright blue eggs on which Dorothy
gazed torn between love and fear, caressing their fragile beauty
with her eyes, but fearing to shatter it by a breath.

> Such heart was in her, being then
> A little Prattler among men,

and if it was only in later years that he consciously recognised
how much her trembling responsiveness to life and her ardent
gentleness blessed his childhood, her influence over him was
all the more potent for being unconscious. For no brother
and sister ever completed each other more perfectly; both were
creatures of the wild, the one intrepid, the other exquisitely
shy. And they blended together in a rare chord of tenderness
and daring.

If, then, occasionally within the walls of his home the young
William revealed his passionate nature by acts of angry or
stubborn defiance, ill-temper was unknown to him, because
objectless, in the open air. There he loved whatever he saw,
and even if at times his love was predatory, it was a pure flame
of life. The little world in which he moved satisfied all his
desires. So complete was his happiness that it excluded any

thought or dream of grander or fairer regions. Each day his world seemed divinely created anew for his delight, and he felt its forms and motions in his blood. It mattered nothing that, apart from visits to the Cooksons at Penrith and occasional trips to the seashore, there was a sameness in his days. For monotony is a meaningless word for those, whether child, saint, or artist, who are wholly possessed by the spirit of life.

And the early education which his father gave him was not of a kind to disturb before its time this primal unity of being. For it was his son's memory which he sought to cultivate by setting him at an early age to learn portions of the works of the best English poets by heart. And memory is a primitive and a passive faculty, the least conscious of the mind's activities. And so little was the young Wordsworth given to conscious thinking that it was some years before he was even drawn to books. He had no need as yet to feed his fancy on the wishing-cap of Fortunatus or the invisible coat of Jack the Giant-killer, because he was too absorbed in the real life of Nature to crave miraculous inventions. Later he could write of fairy tales that

> The child, whose love is here, at least, doth reap
> One precious gain that he forgets himself.

But since he was still a note in the harmony of natural life, he had as yet no self to forget. He 'felt, and nothing else,' not as the self-conscious subscribers to the doctrine that 'feeling is all,' but with the integrity of the simple.

And to such, life is miraculous in all its motions. It has no logic because it is all meaning. It is a dance and a song, a rhythm and a mystery. There is joy in its anger and beauty in its scars. It is new-born and immemorial, a dream and a fact. And 'with the gift of all this glory' the growing boy was 'filled and satisfied.'

§ 2

In March 1778, however, his mother died. But so strong and secure by this time was his attachment to Nature that even the loss of one who was 'the heart and hinge of all our learnings and our loves' could not wound a sensibility so firmly rooted and centred in life. Nature was now wholly his mother and his home, and his attachment to her was only deepened by the break up of the home life at Cockermouth which followed his mother's death and in particular by the parting from Dorothy, who was sent to live with cousins at Halifax and later with her grandmother Cookson at Penrith.

She was happy at Halifax. Nevertheless the ten years during which she and William were divided were for her a period of spiritual homelessness during which her attachment to her brother assumed the intensity of a passion, and she dreamed of reunion with all the longing of a lover. He felt the cut less deeply, not only because he was more independent and self-contained, but because from his ninth to his eighteenth year he lived a life which completely satisfied the demands of his nature.

He was sent with his brother Richard to school at Hawkshead, an old market town in the shallow vale of Esthwaite. It stood near the head of a little lake amid green pastures, sprinkled with small farms and fringed on the higher levels with woods. The hills between which it lay were of no great height, but at a short distance to the west and north-west the peaks of Helvellyn, Sca Fell, and Coniston Old Man stood out against the sky.

The town itself was typical of the northern dales in its grey stone cottages huddling together and threaded by narrow winding alleys beneath one of which a mountain beck flowed half-hidden; typical, too, in the common size of its houses, none of which were large, and none hovels, as befitted the democracy of the dale folk.

And amid the cottages and hardly distinguishable from them stood the Free Grammar School to which the clergy, professional and business men, small farmers, and those Westmorland and Cumberland 'statesmen' whose strength of character Wordsworth was later to extol, sent their sons. Here they were taught Latin, mathematics, and the elements of Greek, and since they began their lessons soon after six in the morning, they were free for two hours at midday and from four or five in the afternoon until dusk to employ themselves as they wished.

This liberty was invaluable to Wordsworth. For it meant that his school life in no way curtailed the actively passive communion with Nature which had enriched his childhood. The continuity of his experience was preserved. It was merely extended and diversified at the very time when he was ripe for such extension. With his primitive integrity unspoilt he passed from a domestic into a tribal phase, exchanging for the gentle companionship of Dorothy the rough and tumble of schoolboy packs.

For, unlike the young Shelley or Tennyson, he did not recoil from the crowd. He withdrew from it when he needed to be alone with the primeval in Nature, as we shall see. But in his withdrawals as in his participation in the sports of his schoolfellows he satisfied the same positive need of instinctive communion with life, whether elemental or human. For abnormal as his sensibility was, it was not in the least morbid. He adapted himself to his new surroundings with the ease and assurance of a healthy animal. And if this was in itself proof of an organism that possessed a certain hardness and was without any vulnerable spot, the active companionship in play and adventure which he thus embraced prevented him from being drawn away prematurely from the concrete world into one of self-created abstractions.

His school-fellows, too, were of a kind both to test and

reinforce his native soundness. They belonged to no exclusive class, but were alike only in this that they came from homes in which mental attainments were respected, but in which simplicity was more prized than elegance and character than culture. Like Wordsworth himself they had grown up freely, shut off by no barriers of class convention or undue domestic indulgence from the natural forces of life. From these they had drawn and continued to draw vital inspiration, and from these too, in the painful process of adapting themselves to an impersonal universe, they had begun to learn humility and discretion.

Consequently, 'simplicity in habit' and 'truth in speech' were for them moral instincts rather than moral maxims, while the frugal, but wholesome fare which they received from the old dames in whose cottages they lodged and the unrestricted open-air life which they lived out of school hours ensured health of body as much as the spare diet of Latin, mathematics and Greek ensured health of mind.

The old dame with whom Wordsworth lodged was named Anne Tyson. Homely and plain as her own cottage, she mothered him with the selfless affection of the simple. And before her or a neighbour's peat fire on winter evenings the boys would amuse themselves playing noughts and crosses or games of Loo or Whist with much-thumbed cards, while the rain pelted outside or such a keen frost raged that the game would often be interrupted by the sound of splitting ice on Esthwaite water. The centre of their outdoor sports was a grey stone in the middle of the village square, where another old dame sat offering simple wares to those with pocket-money to spend. And here on mild winter nights they would often continue their games beneath the stars, or in the summer twilight linger on until the old men and labourers who would sit watching them had gone off to bed.

But the little town itself was the least important of their

playgrounds. And in the frosty season after school and sunset, when the cottage windows twinkled through the twilight, the boys would seize their skates and race in rapture to the frozen lake nearby. And there in games of hare and hounds they would hiss along the ice in a pack, flying through the darkness and the cold, and shouting as they went. The surrounding precipices rang aloud with the din of their shrill voices, the icy crags 'tinkled like iron,' while from the distant hills came a melancholy murmur, as the stars sparkled in the eastern sky and in the west the afterglow died away.

It was characteristic of the young Wordsworth to notice this curious alien reverberation, faintly intruding upon the tumult of animal activity, and, as if in answer to it, to break away often from his noisy companions into a silent bay, pursuing as he went the elusive gleam of a star in the ice. Equally characteristic was the experience in which he delighted when after abandoning himself to the rapture of speed, intoxicated by the rush of wind and the sense of the shadowy banks on either side coming sweeping through the darkness, he suddenly stopped short by leaning back upon his heels. Yet still for a moment or two the cliffs continued to wheel by him,

> even as if the earth had rolled
> With visible motion her diurnal round!

It was, however, hardly necessary for him to induce by any such artifice the sense of being

> Rolled round in earth's diurnal course,
> With rocks, and stones, and trees.

For he was so elementally at one with the physical world that he not only moved to its rhythm but, like the savage, he read into it a power of personal volition and purposeful intervention which was in fact his own. The most notable experience of this kind occurred to him, not with his school-fellows in the mild reaches of Esthwaite, but in the holidays at the head of Ullswater, under the frowning crags of Helvellyn.

One moonlight evening he had unloosed a shepherd's skiff, tied to a willow tree, and pushed off from the shore. That he had no right to use it made the act one 'of stealth and troubled pleasure.' Beneath the adventurer's zest was the miscreant's sense of guilt. But at first both heaven and earth seemed only to approve his joy. The lake shone clear in front, and behind the moving boat the small circles plucked from its smooth surface by his dipping oars glittered in the moon until they melted into one track of sparkling light. But after stealing thus quietly for a time through the water, he began to exert himself more actively, and fixing his eyes on a chosen point at the top of a crag that rose up sheer against the horizon, he took it as his line and broke into lusty rowing. His boat went heaving through the water, and then suddenly behind the crag upon which his eyes were fixed,

> a huge peak, black and huge,
> As if with voluntary power instinct
> Upreared its head. I struck and struck again,
> And growing still in stature the grim shape
> Towered up between me and the stars, and still,
> For so it seemed, with purpose of its own
> And measured motion like a living thing,
> Strode after me. With trembling oars I turned,
> And through the silent water stole my way
> Back to the covert of the willow tree.

Disembarking, he went home through the meadows not only sobered, but shaken. It was as if Nature herself, assuming this grim and gigantic form, had risen up to reprove his guilt and

threaten punishment. But the experience went deeper
than this. For so awesome was the impression that for
many days his brain

> Worked with a dim and undetermined sense
> Of unknown modes of being; o'er my thoughts
> There hung a darkness, call it solitude
> Or blank desertion. No familiar shapes
> Remained, no pleasant images of trees,
> Of sea or sky, no colours of green fields;
> But huge and mighty forms, that do not live
> Like living men, moved slowly through the mind
> By day, and were a trouble to my dreams.

By such 'chance collisions and quaint accidents' could Nature
speak unforgettably to him. Actually, of course, it was he
himself who clothed such accidents with purpose, investing the
physical world with moral qualities which were in fact the
reflex of his own emotions, just as when he stopped short on
the ice he invested the banks with movements which were in
fact the reflex of his own sensations.

And in this again he was characteristically primitive. For
the primitive reveals his identity with the natural world not
only by his tendency to lapse into the subhuman and to experience with superstitious awe 'a dim and undetermined sense
of unknown modes of being,' but also by his habit of unconsciously projecting into natural phenomena his own human
moods and purposes.

And the awestruck boy on Ullswater did both. He attributed a punitive will and purpose to the threatening crag, which
also grew in his imagination into a symbol of that terrifying
'otherness' which transcends all powers of human definition
and can in a moment, for those who are sensitive to the
elemental, shatter the illusion of human security which civilisa-

tion has laboriously built up and plunge them into a homeless and a formless void.

No experience, indeed, of the divine can be profoundly real which has not included also an experience of the demonic. And the fact that the young Wordsworth could be thus shocked and haunted by a sense of elemental homelessness is perhaps a surer proof of that primitive absorption in life to which all his later development must be referred than his more familiar experience of Nature as a 'beloved Presence.' For in such moments of listening to 'the ghostly language of the ancient earth' his personal identity was too wholly submerged in an impalpable non-human world for him to humanise, as he ordinarily did, the forces of Nature.

It was seldom, however, that the primeval overpowered him to this degree. Generally the 'Presences of Nature' and 'Souls of lonely places' with which he peopled the sky and earth were rather the kindly, if potentially stern, tutors of a growing boy than shadowy elementals. And years later he could still personify them, exclaiming in a rapture of remembrance that no

> vulgar hope was yours when ye employed
> Such ministry, when ye through many a year
> Haunting me thus among my boyish sports,
> On caves and trees, upon the woods and hills,
> Impressed upon all forms the characters
> Of danger or desire; and thus did make
> The surface of the universal earth
> With triumph and delight, with hope and fear,
> Work like a sea.

Doubtless it was his own imagination which,

> creator and receiver both,
> Working but in alliance with the works
> Which it beholds,

impressed upon the physical world the characters and emotions which he attributed to Nature herself. But such personification, false as it may seem to sophisticated minds, was true enough for him. For he *was* the cave and tree, wood and hill, upon which he looked or in which he moved. He and they grew and breathed together in vital association. The creative spirit which shaped and animated them was for him indistinguishable from the spirit which quickened his heart and senses to triumph and delight and hope and fear. And so in attributing to earth and sky his own emotions, he was merely affirming his instinctive identity with that mysterious life which flowed into and through all forms, and rose and sank in waves of birth and death, of growth and decay, over the surface of the earth.

But although he was thus absorbed in the ocean of life, he was never in danger of being drowned in it, because his days were full of healthy animal activities. Wordsworth's schoolfellows were not preternaturally studious. They were a noisy crew, but they enjoyed the sun and the beautiful vale which was their playground with a pure physical relish, whether they scoured the autumn woods for hazel nuts or with rod and line followed the windings of a stream to its source among the tumbling mountain becks. Sometimes on sunny afternoons they would fly a kite, with hearts uplifted to the fleecy clouds amid which it rode and hands sensing the wind that tugged at the captive cord.

Occasionally, too, they hired horses from the local innkeeper, and, unknown to him, rode as far as Furness Abbey, twenty miles away. Dismounting there and leaving their horses to graze along the smooth green turf, Wordsworth would explore the ancient ruin with its broken arch and belfry and tombs of crusader and abbot. After his long ride through open country he felt with the force of contrast the mystery and sanctity which clung to its mouldering walls, and the timelessness of its 'inland peace.' And one day when rainstorms had

c

made it a less desirable haven and the ivy on the roofless nave dripped as it shuddered in the breeze, a single unseen wren sang so sweetly in the gloom of the old church that for entranced moments everything but its song was forgotten.

But these boys were as happy in their rapid alternations of mood as in their power of complete absorption in the experience of the moment. From perfect quiescence they leapt into reckless activity, remounted their horses, and using whip and spur raced each other down the valley and by a roundabout route scampered homeward. Yet even at such times of exuberant activity part of the young Wordsworth remained passive to the life about him. He felt in the rocks and streams and the still evening air a presence,

> when with slackened step we breathed
> Along the sides of the steep hills, or when
> Lighted by gleams of moonlight from the sea
> We beat with thundering hoofs the level sand.

Such spiritual intimations could hardly haunt the races which they rowed down Windermere to a selected island. But on so spacious an arena false pride and vanity were unconsciously tempered, and rivalry, while it added a zest to bodily effort, left behind no jealousy or disappointment between the victors and the defeated. They shared alike the joy of matched muscles and straining sinews and the reward of contented relaxation which followed. And by thus co-operating truly even in their boyish battles they tended to develop in themselves that quiet independence and modest self-sufficiency which belong to all natural creatures who are equally devoid of arrogance and of diffidence, and who are at harmony both in themselves and with their world.

All their activities were thus tempered and enhanced by the natural world in which they moved as inmates. They took their tone from the season or the hour, racing with the winds, sporting gleefully through half an afternoon of sunshine, and subdued, like the earth itself, beneath the hush of evening. And occasionally on such summer evenings, as they were returning in their boat over the dusky lake from a bay on the eastern shore of Windermere, they would land one of their number on a small island, and leaving him there row off gently while he blew his flute. The plaintive notes intensified the vast stillness upon which they floated, and upon the mind of the boy Wordsworth 'the calm and dead still water lay'

> Even with a weight of pleasure, and the sky
> Never before so beautiful, sank down

into his heart, and held him like a dream.

The same experience of receiving the natural world into himself would come to him when he stood alone at twilight by the side of the glimmering lake and with both hands pressed closely to his mouth mimicked the hooting owls to make them answer him. Often they would, and the vale would quiver with long halloos and screams. But in the pauses of silence, while he hung listening for an answer which did not come, and his whole being lay open to receive, the soft sound of mountain torrents would gently shock his heightened expectancy and their very waters seem to flow deep down into his heart.

In all these boyhood experiences that creative union of activity and passivity, which is native to the infant and the child, was preserved. He drank in 'a pure organic pleasure' from the world about him, because he was organic in himself. In his unconscious intercourse with 'beauty old as creation' he at once gave and received. The two motions were reciprocal and as inevitable as the taking in and giving out of breath by the lungs. By this creative rhythm

> The daring instincts and the brooding powers
> Were mutually sustained.

They conditioned and enhanced each other. The giddy moment stirred the blood and passed, but the physical ecstasy which it engendered quickened his responsiveness to the forms of life about him, so that 'earth and the common face of Nature' spoke to him 'rememberable things.' And occasionally he was so purged by these reckless outgoings from himself, by the tempestuous blisses of healthy boyhood, that he seemed born anew to life and pillowed upon Creation's breast.

But truly many years were to pass before Wordsworth needed to be reborn to life. Few boys can have preserved more vitally

> those first-born affinities that fit
> Our new existence to existing things,
> And, in our dawn of being, constitute
> The bond of union between life and joy.

As he watched the sun 'lay his beauty on the morning hills' or set behind the western mountain, such 'excess of happiness' was his that his blood 'appeared to flow with its own pleasure.' And for him the moon, rising over the sea, always unveiled a new and strange world, a world of shining water over which the eye moved

> gathering, as it seemed
> Through every hair-breadth in that field of light,
> New pleasure like a bee among the flowers.

Thus through all his senses he fed upon life, but with such purity of being that its material substance and his own individual self met together and dissolved in an ethereal fusion. Often, indeed, he was unable to credit external things with external existence, and would sometimes even have to grasp at a wall or tree to prove their actuality. But at this time such a trance condition was not morbid, as it was later to prove. It was simply that in such moments his mind was so completely submerged in pure sensation that it could not perform its usual function of imposing forms upon feeling. Both the external world and himself were dissolved in a sense of immaterial being.

Such experiences, however, were exceptional. Generally his communion with life had a solid and homely basis in 'earth and every common sight.' And the boy divined the glory and freshness in every common sight, because he was an inspired actor in an *'active* universe.' The day was to come when Wordsworth was no longer thus an inmate of the *active* universe, when his local self disputed the will of life. And it was, perhaps, the very completeness of his early instinctive identity with life and the fact that it was so unusually prolonged which prevented him from creating in himself a new kind of wholeness when self-consciousness brought the inevitable division. It is, perhaps, necessary to hate Nature, to see her, like Blake, as the work of the devil, if we are to recover with a difference the love of her which was childhood's instinctive heritage, but which the maturing mind destroys.

Circumstances, however, had conspired to retard the growth of self-consciousness in Wordsworth, and years had yet to elapse before it threatened his well-being. Meanwhile he had laid a basis of natural joy and strength and had established a creative faith which were for long to stand firm against the insidious sappings of mental disillusionment.

§ 3

In his fourteenth year, however, an event occurred from which we may perhaps date the first definite disturbance of the purely instinctive harmony of his being. On the day before the holidays began in December 1783 he climbed to the top of a crag which overlooked the two roads by which the horses that were to carry himself and his two brothers home were to be brought. It was a stormy day, and he sat on the grass half sheltered by a bare wall, with a single sheep on his right hand and a blasted hawthorn on his left. He was restless with anticipation, and as he strained his eyes through the mist that now lifted, now closed, upon the plain beneath, his thoughts were less of the expected horses than of the holiday pleasures of which they were the heralds.

Within ten days of his return home, however, his father died, and as he followed his body to the grave, the event, with all the sorrow that it brought in such abrupt contrast with the pleasures which he had so impatiently anticipated, seemed 'a chastisement.' For the first time, perhaps, he felt how unconcerned life could be with his own hopes and desires, and although he humbly accepted the corrective, the shock which he received was such that years afterwards the sound of storm and rain beating on the roof at night or of trees creaking in the wind would renew an inward agitation. The sense of a power in life that implacably overruled all the little schemes of men would return to him, and with it the lonely crag, the single sheep, the blasted tree, the mist advancing in strange shapes, and 'the bleak music' of an old stone wall.

In childhood, he was later to remark, nothing was more difficult for him than to admit the notion of death as a state applicable to his own being. For he was then so completely possessed by the spirit of life, that even the loss of his mother failed to startle him into conscious thought. But when his father died that instinctive self-surrender to life which had so enriched his childhood with joy and health was beginning to be leavened by the mind. And the shock of the event quickened the process. For the first time he felt himself deserted and alone, *seeking* the visible world which for so long had come to him unsought. The props of his affections, the unquestioned certainty that Nature cherished him as a mother, were removed. And yet the building stood, as if sustained by its own spirit. He had rooted himself so deeply in Nature that the first activities of the inquiring mind could not, as with those less richly grounded and nurtured, shake his belief in her.

He was for a time obscurely troubled, but became as a consequence more finely responsive to the beauty of the natural world. Instead of grief turning him in upon himself, it gently shocked him into a more exact awareness of objects already loved. A slight fissure had opened between his instincts that affirmed life and his mind that now admitted death. And so, if only by an imperceptible degree, he was for the first time detached from the world about him and recognised its objectivity.

But there was no separation. If he drew away a step from the objects of his delight, he was enabled thereby to focus them more exactly, to perceive minute differences unrecognised before, without weakening the ties of his attachment to the life which all forms expressed. And so his communion with life became more significantly intimate, while the hours of retirement and contemplation grew more frequent and told him more. He began to observe more closely, not, however, as a curious spectator, but as one who refined the influxes of Nature which he still continued to receive. The 'store of transitory qualities' which the seasons brought were no longer merely assimilated by the hungry senses. They were felt in the heart, and the heart's affection differed from the unconscious absorption of the instincts in being penetrated to some extent by the intelligence which had begun its task of discovering order and form in life and in registering the permanent relations of transitory things. To his earlier sense of the creative affinity of all things living was added a growing perception of distinctions. The 'agitations of the mind' were far too gentle for him to be conscious of them. But they had begun to transform his instinctive response to life into 'inobtrusive sympathy,' and to intensify his joy by making him more aware of it.

This did not, however, curtail his powers of surrender to the elemental. And these moods of 'shadowy exultation' were of lasting value to him because, while they engraved no definite image upon his memory, they enriched him with 'an obscure sense of possible sublimity,' which by its very infinitude eluded exact definition, and thereby endlessly incited him, as his faculties unfolded, to the pursuit of a more essential reality.

This sense of the sublime came to him not only in moments when Nature intoxicated or cowed him by the grandeur or the tumult of her forces, but also amid tranquil scenes. And it was then that he began to feel the universal life as a principle of order and harmony informing all things, as 'fitness in the latent qualities and essences of things.' This growing recognition of a palpable order in Nature was another sign of his own un-conscious mental growth. For it is only when the mind has begun to assert itself that it perceives with delight its own orderly purposiveness as at least an element, if not the central element, in the miraculous flux of life.

Wordsworth experienced this delight particularly during the early morning walks which he took before school hours with a much-loved friend round Esthwaite water. Sometimes he would steal out even earlier, before one chimney had begun to smoke or the first thrush to sing. And sitting on some jutting eminence with the valley sleeping beneath him, his whole being would be caught up in a holy calm, in which he seemed no longer to view a world outside himself with bodily eyes, but rather something in himself, 'a dream, a *prospect of the mind.*'

So completely was the actual world possessed by his im-agination and his imagination fulfilled by the actual world, that instead of merely observing it, he *was* it and it was he.

Whether he discovered himself in the objective world, or, as in such moments as these, resolved the whole cosmos into himself, his self-consciousness was life-consciousness. For him there was as yet no object and no subject, but a continual realisation of their identity. He had hardly begun to view the world from a personal standpoint. His vision was still as new every morning and as undulled by habit and routine as life itself.

The 'auxiliar light,' therefore, which came from his own kindled mind and which 'bestowed new splendour' on the setting sun was no wayward, private illumination. It was generated by the same creative force which the singing birds, fluttering breezes, and murmuring fountains obeyed. At moments it might dazzle him with its glory and the external forms of things be dissolved in his inward bliss, but they were never distorted. And when he saw them clearly, they spoke the language not merely of his own mind but of the creative mind to which his own was still submissive.

The hazardous 'progress from our native continent to earth and human life' had, in fact, begun. But he was hardly aware of it. 'The appropriate calling of youth,' he wrote later, 'is not to distinguish in the fear of being deceived or degraded, not to analyse with scrupulous minuteness, but to accumulate in genial confidence.' This he had done and continued for some years to do, if with an increasing tendency to self-analysis.

And if it was Nature which still preserved his imagination whole, books, too, began to nourish it. The life that was in Art was, indeed, always to mean far less to Wordsworth than the life of the fields, the woods, the hills, and the cottages. Why, he was to ask in later years,

> call upon a few weak words to say
> What is already written in the hearts
> Of all that breathe?

Yet he regarded then the inspiration of the written word as only less 'than Nature's self, which is the breath of God.' And often in boyhood he combined the two inspirations, taking some book from his father's library when he went to fish in the Derwent and devouring it, as he lay on the sun-bathed stones, completely lost to his surroundings, until with a start of self-reproach at the thought of the disregarded summer day he seized his rod again.

And this instinctive and almost guilty recoil from the printed word to life governed always his attitude to books, as it dictated his later indictment of a prescribed 'literary' education. The virtue of books depends, as he knew well from his own experience, upon the vital perception which the reader brings to them. Here, too, we must give, if we are to receive. And the child who from tender years is 'garnished out' by his elders, shaped to their pattern, and invested with their 'good taste,' is devitalised. He is robbed of the real experience of life that books should enhance. Thus artificially fenced round by abstractions against the joys and fears of immediate living, he may grow into a prodigy of learning, but his heart is a 'dimpling cistern.' His head may be full, but his being is all hollow. Pent 'within the pinfold of his own conceit,' he has led a life of lies from the beginning, and, unless he can renew the instinctive springs of his being, his life remains a lie.

Such education was exactly the opposite in kind to that which Wordsworth had received. The natural world had been his teacher and its lessons had been neutralised, as little as could be, by the morals and maxims of his elders. And the same freedom had characterised his reading. Here too he had been allowed to range at will

> Through heights and hollows, and bye-spots of tales
> Rich with indigenous produce, open ground
> Of Fancy.

Some modern educationalists have frowned upon the fairy story as likely to pervert the child's respect for fact. But a conscious respect for fact is, in the nature of human growth, a later development and one which is inevitably barren unless it is rooted in a sense of wonder and an imaginative hunger for reality. It is these impulses which fairy stories, however fantastic, nourish, while romances, monkish legends, tales of chivalry and of warlike adventure all satisfy the hidden appetite of childhood for a kind of life which corresponds with its own age. For a child's age is that of the myths, as a boy's is that of the romances, and to seek to impose upon either the habits of mental maturity is to thwart organic growth. For Experience thus to shackle the life of Innocence is, indeed, to dam disastrously the creative current.

But for Wordsworth, who enjoyed the same free roving in literature as in life, dreamers and forgers of lawless tales were a source of creative inspiration. They transported him into a world in which a thought was a deed and it was enough to wish to realise a desire, a world which was 'here, nowhere, there, and everywhere at once.' There the fetters of actuality were thrown off and the limits of time and space. Earth and the elements were like potter's clay for imagination to shape to its own pattern.

For some children, less firmly rooted in life than him, such commerce with the fabulous may, indeed, prove demoralising, nourishing a tendency to indulge in fugitive fancies or morbid terrors. But with Wordsworth, whose reading was always secondary and complementary to his direct communion with Nature, there was no such danger. Instead of inclining him to shrink from the realistic, it merely prepared him for the shocks which actuality would inflict.

In the very week of his first going to school, for example, while wandering alone by Esthwaite water, as twilight was coming on, he saw distinctly through the gloom a heap of clothes. He watched, until the lake grew dark and the stillness heavy, to see if any one appeared to own them. But no one came. Next day the unclaimed clothes drew an anxious crowd to the spot. They dragged the lake with grappling irons and sounded it with long poles, and at last a dead man rose suddenly upright to the surface. His ghastly face might well have terrified an onlooker of any age. Yet, young as he was, the boy felt no 'soul-debasing' fear. And it was not only the beautiful setting of trees and hills and water, so charged with life, which reduced for him the horror of the incident. He was also imaginatively prepared against the crude assault of fact by all that he had read of the grim and the bewitching. His inner eye had seen such sights among the shining streams of fairyland and the forests of romance, where the art of the story-teller had purified them of the sensational and lifted them out of the wounding realm of fact.

The little yellow canvas-covered abstract, then, of the *Arabian Nights*, which had been a precious treasure to him from his early years, had not, as with the young Coleridge, fed a morbid appetite or evoked spectres that haunted him in the dark. And so his craving for the marvellous and fantastic gave way gradually and without any disillusionment before a strengthening love for things that he had seen. This transition from the miraculous to the actual, so painful to the boy or the man who has falsely indulged a romantic fancy, was for him a 'delightful time of growing youth.' For knowledge was 'not purchased by the loss of power.' Rather it seemed to condense such power, and in his reading the sober truth and steady sympathies revealed by less daring writers began to attract him, and words were more consciously regarded for their own sake rather than as incitements to vague, unanalysed rapture.

Consequently at about the age of thirteen he first began to appreciate the charm of tuneful words and ordered phrases.

And in his early morning walks round the misty lake he and
his friend would repeat their favourite verses, savouring them
consciously as well as being caught up by their rhythm and airy
fancies. Doubtless the verses which he loved at this time were
not of a high order. They were more probably the pompous
or lachrymose odes of Mrs. Elizabeth Carter than those passages
from Milton, Spenser, and Shakespeare which his father had
made him learn.

For while the boy's

> wish for something loftier, more adorned,
> Than is the common aspect, daily garb,
> Of human life,

is essential to all creative growth, it inevitably inclines him at
first to love the high-flown. Yet such inability to distinguish
the meretricious from the true is a far healthier symptom in
the young than a precociously cultivated taste. Really to love
the second-rate is of more vital value to youth than to despise
it with conscious superiority. For it is through ardent if
misplaced loves that we grow in real knowledge and being,
while a loveless taste, derived from others and assumed by
those who fear to be convicted of ignorance and error, is barren
because rooted in self-esteem.

However untutored and inordinate, then, Wordsworth's
love of Mrs. Carter's odes may have been, it nourished the
creative impulse in him. And gradually as he became more
conscious of the formal quality of art, it fostered in him the
desire to shape and arrange as well as to express. Thus his
critical faculty developed in intimate association with his
creative sense rather than as an instrument of destructive
analysis. And poetry opened out before him, not as an enclosed
garden, still less as a bookish retreat, but as a delicious holiday
world, full of music, incense, festivals, and flowers, in which,

as he became a more familiar intimate, he detected more and more rational order and distinctive design.

He pursued, in fact, the same path of organic development in his experience of the natural world and of the great Nature that exists in the works of imaginative men. For him the two were voices of the one spirit. His growing sense of life in poetry enhanced his sense of poetry in life. And although he was at the time far too engrossed in the experience of this unity to explain it, he expressed it finely later, when he exclaimed —

> Visionary power
> Attends the motions of the viewless winds,
> Embodied in the mystery of words:
> There, darkness makes abode, and all the host
> Of shadowy things work endless changes, — there,
> As in a mansion like their proper home,
> Even forms and substances are circumfused
> By that transparent veil with light divine,
> And, through the turnings intricate of verse,
> Present themselves as objects recognised,
> In flashes, and with glory not their own.

The 'glory not their own' was the same dream-like vividness and splendour which had invested for him the natural world. Words now no less than things evoked for him this unearthly radiance, and continued to do so while he became more conscious of their distinctive forms. But if, as seems probable, his new sense of the charm of ordered words coincided with his first attempts to write verse himself, the first poem in which he described his boyish adventures and the scenery of the country was inevitably little more than a composition in the manner of Pope whose versification set the standard for school exercises.

Yet even in the schoolroom he was more favoured than

most poets have been. For his headmaster, William Taylor, was no arid pedagogue, but a young man who had tilled the soil before he took to teaching, who loved the poets and whose homely culture was rooted in the countryman's simple feeling for his kind and for the valley and hills amid which he had been reared. The fact that he died while Wordsworth was still at school was a real loss, but it served too to impress poignantly the image and the essential goodness of the man upon the boy's memory.

And while he was thus favoured in his schoolmaster and school-fellows, in the habitual grandeur which surrounded him and in an unhedged world of poetry and romance, he was equally fortunate in living in a neighbourhood rich in more than 'the ordinary human interests.' Hawkshead, as a small and remote town encircled by mountains, commanded a region to which such people as retired highwaymen or ruined men of the world had until recently resorted for concealment when fleeing from justice or to nurse their despair. Wordsworth heard their stories from his old dame, who knew all the legends of the neighbourhood and doubtless embellished them. And these

> tragedies of former times,
> Hazards and strange escapes,

excited in him a sense of the darker drama of human life which corresponded with his feeling of the terror which lurked in natural beauty. The

> images of danger and distress,
> And suffering among awful Powers and Forms,

which rose in his mind as he listened to his homely story-teller or remembered her tales in his walks among the crags and woods, deepened his innate sense of the mystery that was man.

For while for the town-dweller man tends to become dwarfed and vulgarised by the crowded contact of the streets, he could still be, for the young Wordsworth, the hero, villain, or victim of a romantic legend. Something of the mythically sublime or desolate yet clung to him and he moved in a world still charged with supernatural reality.

But if the bygone stories which his old dame told him fed his romantic instinct, the roads about Hawkshead were also an open school in which he could unconsciously study human nature at first hand. And it was a human nature which, though humble, conformed to no approved or conventional pattern. Shepherds were the men to whom he was most drawn at first, and he found in them, without of course as yet appraising them morally, a natural sagacity and kindliness, and a simple dignity bred of a life

> Intent on little but substantial needs,
> Yet rich in beauty, beauty that was felt.

But on the roads he often fell into talk with more widely-travelled men, with old beggars on their regular weekly round, or with packmen and pedlars.

So early began a lifelong habit, and those who see in its later manifestations a sort of morbid inquisition would do well to remember that it had its roots in the familiar and certainly unmorbid comrade instinct of boyhood. The young Wordsworth had begun to be curious about human life, but his curiosity was so grounded in real community of feeling for the original characters whom he met that he was hardly conscious of it. And it was because he thus feelingly identified himself with the men and women whose natures and histories he later consciously explored that his psychological discoveries were to be enriched by such imaginative insight.

Meanwhile, although he was still boyishly indifferent to the problems and pathos of human life, he learnt more of humanity from these travellers and vagrants than any book could have taught him. For he absorbed its living essence. Of his comradeship with one of these he was to write later in *The Excursion*. He was a pedlar who in his wanderings had come close to the heart of wild nature and of his fellow-men, and who through years of unhurried and solitary tramping had pondered much upon life's meaning. He was drawn to the young Wordsworth by a thoughtfulness in his face unusual for one of his years. And the boy returned his affection. Often in the holidays they rambled together through the woods. As they walked or stopped to rest the old man would tell of the things which he had seen with that vividness and veracity which belong to all stories taken directly from the book of life. Addressing himself as much as his young listener, he would argue points in the philosophy which he had constructed out of his own experience, or sing old folk songs that he had learnt as a child.

In such men as these Wordsworth first unconsciously discovered 'the Poets that are sown by Nature,' and began to learn

> the lesson deep of love which he,
> Whom Nature, by whatever means, has taught
> To feel intensely, cannot but receive.

In humble, unself-conscious men such as this pedlar, 'to feel intensely' was indeed to love. And although at the time the listening boy could not have explained the satisfaction which he found in the person and the talk of this simple man, could not know that the charm of his companionship lay in the fact that he was both experienced and innocent, a man in knowledge and a child at heart, it was, perhaps, from his converse with such men that he first derived the idea of his own vocation in life and first recognised, however dimly, that to walk the country roads might educate a man more deeply than any other path

D

    in those passions and feelings
    Essential and eternal in the heart,
    That 'mid the simpler forms of rural life,
    Exist more simple in their elements,
    And speak a plainer language.

Nor did he owe to these pedlars and vagrants of his boyhood any later tendency to idealise unduly the rural character. For many of them were far from being models of piety. The important thing was that they were 'characters' in the old sense of the word, flawed but original beings whose very eccentricities proved that they had lived a life of their own.

Such a one was old Daniel, a ninety-year-old pilferer, who had become obsessed with avarice, and who, setting out early every morning hand-in-hand with his little grandson, would steal anything, however valueless, that he chanced upon, and make his companion his accomplice. Neither were responsible for their actions, although the vacant, doting face of the old man would assume a look of sly cunning as his eyes fell upon some trivial quarry such as the carpenter's shavings or a turf at an old woman's door.

Wordsworth loved this old man and his boy, as he might have loved two actors in a morality play. For old Daniel, too, in his own way, was a poet sown by Nature. He was a real actor in the drama of life, and, as such, a teacher who revealed more directly than a score of ethical treatises how human nature might become twisted. To this pathetic caricature of greed had old Daniel's early lust for pleasure and later miserliness come! 'No book,' wrote Wordsworth in years to come, 'could have so early taught me to think of the changes to which human life is subject; and while looking at him I could not but say to myself—we may, one of us, I or the happiest of my playmates, live to become still more the object of pity than this

old man, this half-doating pilferer.' Yet despite the precocious
gravity of his looks it is doubtful whether the boy actually said
any such thing to himself. Rather the figure of old Daniel was
deeply engraved upon his memory. The lesson it impersonated
was abstracted, if imperfectly laid to heart, later.

And so it was with all the diverse human beings with whom
he mixed on terms of easy intimacy throughout his boyhood.
They quickened unconsciously his sense of his common
humanity and also his perception that every individual was
essentially uncommon and unique; whether it was the angler
whom he followed up to the source of the River Duddon
beyond the hills, and after fishing with him all day in pelting
rain rode home on his back, or the Irish lad, employed by a
strolling conjuror, whom he took to see a favourite spot on
Esthwaite water, commanding a beautiful view of the island
below, because he was eager to see the boy's face kindle with
pleasure at the sight.

Such acquaintances were simple yet distinctive, and the
knowledge they imparted was real and fertile. It came, not
from a detached mind, but from their whole being. It was
transmitted, not merely by words, but by glances or gestures,
by a touch of the hand or an inflection of the voice, by the
wrinkles on the face, the light in the eyes, or the lines of the
body.

And so the young Wordsworth learnt from them as he
learnt from Nature, extending his knowledge without weakening his instinctive ties with all living things. And if the pedlars
or vagrants of the neighbourhood quickened his sense of the
strange, dramatic, or grotesque in human affairs, the plain
dale folk amongst whom he lived personified the staunch and
the constant.

It has been complained that in his poetry he later senti-
mentalised these folk. And he himself was to forestall the
charge when he wrote —

>   call ye these appearances—
> Which I beheld of shepherds in my youth,
> This sanctity of Nature given to man—
> A shadow, a delusion, ye who pore
> On the dead letter, miss the spirit of things,
> Whose truth is not a motion or a shape
> Instinct with vital functions, but a block
> Or waxen image which yourselves have made
> And ye adore! But blessèd be the God
> Of Nature and of Man that this was so;
> That men before my inexperienced eyes
> Did first present themselves thus purified,
> Removed, and to a distance that was fit:
> And so we all of us in some degree
> Are led to knowledge, wheresoever led,
> And howsoever; were it otherwise,
> And we found evil fast as we find good
> In our first years, or think that it is found,
> How could the innocent heart bear up and live!

Fortunate, indeed, was the lot of one before whose young vision the common man was 'ennobled outwardly,' and whose heart was

>   early introduced
> To an unconscious love and reverence
> Of human nature.

And if, in consequence, the young Wordsworth was to be too credulous of human nature and to pay later for his happy blindness to 'vice and folly, wretchedness and fear,' his belief in and admiration for the dale folk was never misplaced. He erred, as we shall see, not in the moral qualities which he attributed to them, but in seeking to solve his own more complex spiritual problem in their simple terms.

We do not doubt that his faith in them and his admiration for their moral qualities was justified. For he knew them familiarly in the fields and their cottages. He heard their Bible reading and their homely talk. He felt their essential goodness and patience, their kindliness and strength of character. Above all he felt wild Nature as the undertone of their lives, the more potent for being implicit, although occasionally openly proclaimed, as by the farmer who, when walking with him and talking of everyday things, said suddenly with great spirit and a lively smile, 'I like to walk where I can hear the sound of a beck!'

Nevertheless, for one who was not a peasant and who was to shape his manhood under very different circumstances, the ultimate demands of life could not be met as these men and women met them, suggestive and admirable as their integrity was. Already, indeed, in his later school days he had begun healthily to assert himself. As a child he had been almost wholly passive to Nature, although even in this period a certain irreducible core of individuality existed in him, possessing and making its own the outside world, even while it was being possessed. And this active, originating tendency gradually grew stronger, until towards the end of his school days at Hawkshead he began to feel his own separateness. More and more he tended to mould and define the impressions which he received from Nature, to contemplate the universe of which he had before only felt and reflected the inspiration. The rough-and-tumble of a hardy school life had strengthened a naturally independent temper, and in learning to stand up for himself he had learnt, also,

> to keep
> In wholesome separation the two natures,
> The one that feels, the other that observes.

The inward division, which is a condition of all self-conscious life, had begun in him. But far from endangering his growth, it was for many years necessary to it. For only by way of self-consciousness can the creature grow into the creator.

And at seventeen the feeling nature in Wordsworth was still infinitely more powerful than the critical. He took far more pleasure in perceiving affinities than in observing differences. If he had begun to know himself as a separate and singular individual, the knowledge did not incline him to detached analysis. Rather

> From Nature and her overflowing soul
> I had receiv'd so much that all my thoughts
> Were steep'd in feeling; I was only then
> Contented when with bliss ineffable
> I felt the sentiment of Being spread
> O'er all that moves, and all that seemeth still,
> O'er all, that, lost beyond the reach of thought
> And human knowledge, to the human eye
> Invisible, yet liveth to the heart,
> O'er all that leaps, and runs, and shouts, and sings,
> Or beats the gladsome air, o'er all that glides
> Beneath the wave, yea, in the wave itself
> And mighty depth of waters. Wonder not
> If such my transports were; for in all things now
> I saw one life, and felt that it was joy.
> One song they sang, and it was audible,
> Most audible then when the fleshly ear,
> O'ercome by grosser prelude of that strain,
> Forgot its functions, and slept undisturb'd.

The one life was in himself and in everything which flowed into that self through the channel of his senses. It was he who recognised and exulted in the unity of life through being at unity in himself. So perfect was the unity of his being in its most ecstatic moments that no single faculty asserted itself beyond another. He was not conscious of hearing or seeing. All his faculties fused indistinguishably in the song of life of which they were at once the active organs and the passive recipients. The part fulfilled itself in the whole; the body in the pure intensity of its being became a living soul.

§ 4

Up to the time, then, that Wordsworth left school every circumstance might seem to have worked for his peculiar benefit and enhancement, and to have justified, in his own youthful experience at least, his later conviction that

> A gracious Spirit o'er this earth presides,
> And o'er the heart of man.

Yet it is clear that he owed this quite as much to his own native endowment and adaptability as to good fortune. For those who write of environment as a fixed factor in human development fail to realise that each one of us conditions our environment by the manner in which we react to it. The same circumstances of upbringing may make a timid recluse of one and a public rebel of another, and a boy less resolute and physically robust than Wordsworth might well have reacted very differently to the loss of both his parents, the break-up of his home, and the rough-and-tumble of a village school. And it was primarily because Wordsworth so actively responded to life that everything worked for his own good.

Ultimately, as we shall see, the element of hardness, stubbornness, and even uncouthness in him which preserved him from the suffering that is the fate of more sensitive natures, restricted his development. But throughout his boyhood it armed his spirit against premature injury, saved him from those negative recoils from life into the wounded self which prematurely disturb the unity of the growing organism, and enabled him to derive positive enrichment from everything which crossed his path.

Nevertheless, although his happy fate was essentially in himself, the circumstances of his upbringing, as has been sufficiently shown, were peculiarly suited to his needs and temperament. They had ensured the harmonious unfolding of his instincts, and that is the preliminary condition, so seldom granted, of all true education. Looking back, indeed, on his life at Hawkshead, his only memories were to be of 'pleasures lying upon the unfolding intellect plenteously as morning dewdrops—of knowledge inhaled insensibly like the fragrance—of dispositions stealing into the spirit like music from unknown quarters—of images uncalled for and rising up like exhalations . . . of Nature as a teacher of a truth through joy and through gladness, and as a creatress of the faculties by a process of smoothness and delight.'

And so strong was the tie which he had formed in these years, that not only his future philosophy of life and his poetry, but his choice of a place to pass his days in, was to be determined by 'the local sympathy' thus deeply ingrained. As he bade farewell to those 'dear native regions,' he vowed that wherever he might be led, his soul would

> cast the backward view,
> The longing look alone to you.

And resting on his oars beneath a thick grove of sycamores on the western edge of Coniston Lake, as the setting sun flushed the crest of the opposite hills, he renewed the vow with heartfelt conviction.

PART II

THE DAWN OF SELF

§ 1

BEFORE going up to Cambridge in October 1787 Wordsworth visited Dorothy at Penrith. She had returned there early in the year from Halifax, where she had been living with kindly relatives since her mother's death. But Penrith was by contrast a loveless world, and it intensified her sense of isolation. Her grandparents were harshly pietistic and conventional-minded, the duties which she was expected to perform in their mercer's shop were uncongenial, and her Uncle Christopher was the only person in her immediate circle who could in any way satisfy her need to lavish her affections.

Under these conditions her heart went out to her brothers, and particularly to William, with an intensity of longing, hope, and regret. 'I can bear the ill-nature of all my relations,' she wrote at this time to her Halifax friend, Jane Pollard, 'for the affections of my brothers consoles me in all my griefs; but how soon, alas! shall I be deprived of this consolation, and how soon shall I then become melancholy, even more melancholy than before! They are just the boys I could wish them, they are so affectionate and so kind to me as makes me love them more and more every day. . . . Oh, Jane! when they have left me I shall be quite unhappy. . . . My brother William goes to Cambridge in October, but he will be at Penrith before his departure. He wishes very much to be a lawyer, if his health will permit, but he is troubled with violent headaches and a pain in his side.'

The legal ambition, if it ever existed, was as transient as the physical ailment, and Dorothy was left in the autumn with a renewed image of her adored brother to cherish and a more lamentable sense of 'how we are squandered abroad.'

But to Wordsworth a new world beckoned, which, if it

failed to satisfy his expectations, was full of quickening novelty. For him, as for so many others, even to-day, his first sight of Cambridge, as he drove across a flat plain under a grey autumnal sky, was the long-backed chapel of King's College rearing its pinnacles above the dusky trees. Then a student on the road, striding hastily along in cap and gown, seized his attention and held it as long as he was visible. The coach swung on beneath the castle, over Magdalene Bridge, and drew up at the Hoop Inn.

For a boy, strange to the bustle of towns and reared amid the silence of the hills, it was a thrilling moment. His spirits were at full stretch, his hopes boundless, as he came down from the coach to be surrounded by some of his school-fellows who were in their second or third years and were liberal in instruction and advice. At a leap he had left his boyhood behind. And as he went from shop to shop about his affairs, to his tutor to report himself, and to his tailor for his gown, he seemed already a man of the world. Yet as he wandered about the streets and courts, through vaulted gateways and cloisters, the whole novel spectacle seemed at first to the simple northern villager a dream. Even the buying of new clothes and the powdering of his hair, which gratified a vanity that previously had had nothing to feed upon, gave him a sense of participating in some magical rite to which breakfast and supper parties added the charm of conviviality.

His rooms were in the first court of St. John's, immediately above the college kitchens, from which a murmuring sound constantly issued, while near at hand the clock of Trinity told the quarters. He could hear, too, the pealing of its chapel organ, and when lying in bed could see on moonlight nights a few yards opposite his window its antechapel, where the statue of Newton stood

with his prism and silent face,
The marble index of a mind for ever
Voyaging through strange seas of Thought, alone.

This descriptive evocation, however, came to him in one of the few inspired moments of his middle age, and although it fitted well his youthful preconception of Cambridge as the home of heroes of the mind, this preconception did not survive many weeks of residence. The Cambridge which he quickly discovered would, in fact, have been more aptly described as the home of what Blake called 'single vision and Newton's sleep.'

The academic world at the best of times is not very sympathetic towards the imagination, and although Cambridge has housed more great poets than Oxford, she has, inevitably perhaps, done little to foster their genius. In Wordsworth's time the tone of the university was not very high, and his college was particularly loyal to its mathematical tradition. Apart from Euclid, in whose abstract logic he was soon to find a welcome refuge from intensity of feeling, Wordsworth disliked mathematics, and the practical, common-sense tendency of Cambridge, combined with the pedantry of scholarship, had little in them to attract one who had experienced so much of the inspiration of life.

Admittedly there was a certain intellectual ferment in the Cambridge of his time. Its rational temper showed signs of becoming rationalistic. Unitarianism had begun to raise its head in the privileged enclosure of the Church of England, and William Frend, a Fellow of Jesus, was urging that subscription to the Thirty-Nine Articles should no longer be a condition for the degree of Master of Arts. Echoes, too, of subversive thought had floated over from the Continent; the French philosophers were read, and here and there undergraduates were to be found whose 'mind's simplicity' had been rasped by the barb of Voltaire.

But Wordsworth did not become one of them. His temper was still too simple and instinctive to be attracted by either Unitarian or revolutionary rationalism. And the same disposition made him indifferent to either the narrow logic or the competition of the schools. Their rewards made little appeal to one who had been reared in the school of the Lake Country, and the homely rural characters he had known threw into damaging relief the petty egotism and intellectual conceit of the average don. Such men seemed phantoms 'of texture midway between life and books,' whose eccentricities were a parody of real originality and whose pedantry was the inevitable outcome of knowledge unkindled by imagination.

One, too, who had derived so much joy from co-operating in vital activities could not but dislike the system of competitive examinations which made self-interest the motive force of human endeavour, and so tended to foster jealousy, smallmindedness, and false ambition. Years later, indeed, he was to write to his brother—'I can sincerely affirm that I am not indebted to emulation for my attainments, whatever they may be. I have from my youth . . . cultivated the habit of valuing knowledge for its own sake and for the good that may come, and ought to come, out of it—the unmixed, pure good.'

And although there was in this assertion the pride of a dour independence, which narrowed his knowledge, it was a true self-judgment. And it was typical of his honesty as well as of his indifference to conventional opinion and the favour of his elders that when soon after his arrival at Cambridge the master of his college died, he refused to follow the prevailing custom by fastening a copy of Latin or English verses to the pall which covered the coffin as it lay in the college hall. He could not pretend to be moved by the death of one with whom he was hardly acquainted. And feeling alone in his view could justify such verses.

There were times, however, even in his first year, when he was worried by thoughts that he was not acting fairly by his family in the irresponsible life which he was leading. And his situation was complicated by the fact that at his father's death the Earl of Lonsdale had refused to pay debts owing to his agent and amounting to nearly £5000, of which the family estate almost wholly consisted. For nineteen years, therefore, until in 1802 the next Earl paid them their due with interest, the Wordsworth children lived on prospects, while, until they came of age, they were put in charge of two uncles.

The sense of duty to an uncle, however, particularly when it is tempered by vague financial expectations, will hardly goad a young man to uncongenial activities, and the fact that Wordsworth found himself well in advance of the freshmen of his year in the knowledge which he had acquired at school, encouraged him from the beginning to neglect college labours and lectures, and to read nothing but classic authors who pleased him, and Italian poetry.

But deeper than any accidents of circumstance or inclination was a sense of maladjustment to his new environment, a strangeness of the mind, a feeling that he was not for that hour or that place. It was something more than the discomfort of the ardent student of life amid students of books. It was a conviction, still vague and yet all-sustaining, that he was a being chosen for something not yet defined, that he had been endowed

> with holy powers
> And faculties, whether to work or feel,

and that these powers were ultimately to be used to seize by force of his own mind

> all passions and all moods
> Which time, and place, and season do impress
> Upon the visible universe.

He could not at this time have put his conviction into words. But it was powerful enough to justify, to himself at least, his apparent idleness.

For freedom was the right of a freeman. And instinctively he knew himself to be a freeman, not through great learning or intellectual brilliance, but by virtue of that bond with life which his upbringing had preserved. To continue to honour that bond and to extend and deepen it was far more necessary a duty to him than to please his tutor. And since the one duty demanded a continuance of that positive surrender of himself to experience which had been his habit since childhood, and the other the active but exclusive exercise of the mind, his native genius as well as his inclination disposed him to reject the latter.

It was a choice inevitable to a poet. Yet characteristically enough Wordsworth made no attempt to justify his position either to himself or to others by writing. Here again his independence served him well. For while many a young poet has been driven into immature and wasteful expression in order to excuse his apparent idleness, Wordsworth could wait. Like the oak in February, he knew that his time for putting forth bud and bloom was not yet. The mystery he felt within himself was not ripe for birth in words. It must grow slowly and surely in the fertile darkness of the unconscious. And so averse was he to disturbing this patient process that he instinctively rejected any routine of conscious intellectual effort.

After the first excitement, therefore, of his new surroundings passed, he returned both mentally and socially into his former self, pacing the level fields and roads of the Cambridge country-side in the same spirit as he had ranged the heights of Hawks-head, but with an enlarged recognition of what his peculiar needs were and how they were to be satisfied. For the lovely placidity of the landscape, if only by its contrast with the sterner and wilder north, induced a more conscious activity of the mind, while the petty aims and pursuits of most of his fellow-students and teachers heightened his sense of the value of that experience of the universal which had been so felicitously his own. Amid the hills of the north it had come to him unsought. But here, where apparently so few felt or craved the mystery and the ecstasy of such possession, he began to search for it.

Eagerly he scanned the common face of earth and sky for traces of that divinity which dons and undergraduates had so lamentably lost. Now he turned his mind in upon itself, and pored and watched and listened; now he extended himself outward, passing into all that lay within the circle of his vision, until he felt

> Incumbencies more awful, visitings
> Of the Upholder of the tranquil Soul,
> Which underneath all passion lives secure
> A steadfast life.

Once again his own pulse beat in harmony with the pulse of life and even the loose stones upon the road throbbed to it. He 'saw them feel or linked them to some feeling.' 'The great mass lay bedded in a quickening soul,' and everything which he saw 'respired with inward meaning.'

To say that the 'one Presence' which he recognised as the vital principle 'of the great whole' was his own projected self is not to disprove his belief that it was God. For the essential, as distinct from the local, self of every man is divine. And by those who are in complete harmony with life this real self may be discovered equally through turning the mind inward, away from the surface agitations of consciousness, or by projecting it outward into the objective universe. And it is clear that in both ways Wordsworth joyously affirmed at this time his unity with his creative source. To the transitory moods that passed daily over Nature's face he was as sensitively responsive as water is to the sky or a lute to the wind. Yet this world of storm or of sunshine was not external to him. For by entering into it and absorbing it into himself he made it his own.

And so his detachment from his fellow-students did not trouble him. He could not feel lonely, since he had all life for company. And if some of his acquaintances to whom he confided the secret of his inward ecstasy thought him a self-complacent madman, he could smile at their standards of sanity.

For his acceptance of passing joy was no longer mindless like the child's. He could contemplate the joy which possessed him, could shape and preserve it in the mould of his thought. And so far was he from mere sensational intoxication that even in the strongest workings of his feeling he was now able and eager to mark the minute peculiarities, hid in all exterior forms. Yet with this power of critical discrimination went a direct, virginal vision which broke through the conventional surface-covering imposed by use and habit upon things and perceived them in their native purity. In such moments he seemed to sense the inner life of things, whether it was a stone, a tree, a withered leaf, or the arch of heaven. Beneath or in their outward forms he felt not only the power but the pure Idea of life mystically mated with the Idea which was himself.

Such vision was, of course, directly related to that 'dream-like vividness and splendour' which had invested objects of sight in his childhood. Both sprang from an imaginative innocence. But his mind had now begun to inform without yet corrupting his innocence. Things were not merely 'apparelled in celestial light;' they were charged with incommunicable but significant meaning. They did not merely dazzle his senses, they spoke to his soul, and his soul communed with them. And it was a rational soul of which he felt both the universal power and the unique singleness.

Yet in these 'Godlike hours' of a more conscious inter-communion with the spirit of life, there was no weakening of his instinctive ties. They were the primitive ground from

which all his ideal apprehension sprang. And while his mind
thrilled to the recognition of an ideal principle working in
every form and movement of the phenomenal world, a sense
of power and exaltation pervaded and penetrated at the same
time his physical being. It was no abstract intelligence or
discarnate spirit which affirmed

> What majestic sway we have
> As natural beings in the strength of nature.

Inevitably perhaps, however, after some months of such
solitary and pondered ecstasy, there came a reaction to a less
intensive level and with it a weakening of that deep inner
certainty which had sustained him, and a temporary loss of
simplicity of purpose.

At heart Wordsworth was as sociable as he was solitary.
He had been so at school, and he would always have been so
if circumstances had not warped his nature. It is not surprising,
therefore, that now he began to share in the harmless under-
graduate frivolities which a few months earlier he had scorned.
He needed to relax, and although he was too wise to seek to
share the secret of his deeper pleasures or to invite others into
those caves within his mind where mystery lurked, the sunny
suburbs of his being were open to companionship.

Later, indeed, he was to accuse himself for pursuing trivial
pleasures when he should have been exalting the mind by
solitary study. But, in fact, a nature too precociously solemn
and self-engrossed needed more than most such harmless
relaxation. He sauntered along the streets, and talked un-
profitably into the small hours. He read lazily, galloped
through the country-side, or sailed boisterously on the Cam,
while the stars came out unassociated with any of those solemn
moods which had haunted him on Esthwaite water or Windermere. Sometimes, indeed, the poet in him quickened at the

E

thought of the great men whose ghosts, he fancied, trod the courts and streets. In the hawthorn shade beside the mill at Trumpington he laughed with Chaucer or in the mild meadows hailed Spenser as brother and friend,

> moving through his clouded heaven
> With the moon's beauty and the moon's soft pace.

The young Milton, with his rosy cheeks, keen eyes, and proud carriage, bounded before him as he walked, and once, sitting in the rooms which the poet had once occupied at Christ's, he drank to his memory so enthusiastically that his brain reeled, and to clear it and reach his college chapel in time for service, he had to run like an ostrich through the streets.

Thus, for a time, the pulse of inner contemplation almost ceased to beat, and if, in consequence, his life became superficial, it was pleasantly diversified. In a university really quickened by creative ideas he might, indeed, have recoiled now from such agreeable idleness and applied himself to study. But he could discover nothing behind the mellow buildings but little thoughts and intellectual sterility. There was no 'holy joy' in the knowledge dealt out in lecture rooms, and no healthy sound simplicity in the teachers. The compulsory attendance at chapel services seemed to him a religious mockery, and the real religious spirit, 'primeval in its purity and depth,' the spirit of a selfless devotion to life, which he had divined in the dale folk, was wholly lacking. Amid so many learned heads there were few whose inner heart was anything but trivial. He was surrounded by men who dined well and thought ill.

But it was, perhaps, well that the defects of the university were so apparent. For Wordsworth was in consequence never tempted to compromise with a kind of thought which might have deadened his faculties and corrupted his innocence. The unthinking natures, the easy and pillowy minds with which he consorted, were at least alive. In them the spontaneous affections had not been sterilised. And meanwhile as he dallied with them or browsed in books of his own choosing, his under soul was hushed, as it is good for the soul to be periodically hushed,

> lock'd up in such a calm
> That not a leaf of the great nature stirr'd.

This, too, furthered that process of slow organic growth by which Wordsworth's genius was moulded. Before going up to Cambridge he had stood remote from the life of the world. In Cambridge he experienced a semblance of that world, with its intrigues and pretensions. There he could watch on a small scale a private performance of the eternal drama of life in which convention stifles truth and pompous emptiness wins the applause withheld from true worth. He was thus broken gradually to the hard facts and conflicts of substantial life. His faith in human nature was exposed to no violent and premature shock. Indeed his visionary innocence was so little tempered by realistic knowledge that when eventually the shock did come, the frail armour of experience which it had acquired proved a quite inadequate defence.

§ 2

At the end of his first year he returned to Hawkshead. And as he reached the top of the dreary moor beyond Kendal and looked down once again over Windermere, coiling in the sun like a vast river round islands, headlands, and gleaming bays, the rush of joy which he felt had in it an element of surprised recognition. For the familiar had acquired for him through absence a hint of strangeness. And it was to the discovery of a new country as well as the recovery of an old that he went, as he bounded down the hill-side and hailed the old ferryman.

In an hour the snow-white church of Hawkshead was in view, and his old dame was welcoming him with motherly pride.

Every detail of her cottage and its surroundings was greedily reabsorbed. Like old friends, he greeted each in turn, from the spreading pine and broad stone table underneath it to the brook that ran through the garden. That they should simply exist in their benign unchangefulness filled him with wonder and gratitude, while the face of every neighbour he met was like a book in which he read a much-loved tale. Others he hailed from a distance as they worked in the fields, forgetful of the elegant clothes which rather embarrassed him when he encountered some of his late school-fellows. For the vanity of the gownsman had 'stopp'd the course and quiet stream of self-forgetfulness.'

But when he took his place again at the familiar table and later stretched himself in the bed from which he had heard so often the lashing of wind and rain or watched the moon rock in the boughs of a near-by ash tree, he could hardly believe that he had ever been away. And when next day, companioned as of old by his rough-haired terrier, he set out once again as the sun was setting to make the circuit of Esthwaite water, the joy of these walks came back on him, like a returning spring.

The evening was raw, but his heart was so full of happiness and love that it seemed only the more beautiful for that. He felt his soul as never before to be stripped of all veils and to stand naked, as in the presence of God. A comfort surpassing even what he had already experienced pervaded his heart. He felt invincibly strong and secure, restored and fulfilled. And in comparison his previous mood, buoyant as it had been, seemed one of weariness, so steady, calm, and charged with contemplation was his joy.

It did not matter that when he stopped to think of himself and to measure his merit, there was little that he could remember or approve. The moment was so full of God-given grace that works were of no account, and his very lack of merit and achievement pleased him, because it threw him so blissfully upon the mercy and the shaping will of his Creator. He had no past of achievement to limit his future, which was steeped in bright, undefined anticipation and an assurance that all was and would be well with him and with life. And about this deep and central certainty, like fleecy clouds about the sun, floated milder thoughts of love and of holiday gaiety, large projects too that he would one day realise and so come at last, like the quiet evening, to a peaceful end, having fulfilled his destiny in the world.

As he mused thus, he sat down at the edge of a wood while darkness crept up the mountains; a rippling breeze drew a hoary line across the lake, and in the coppice where he sat, as if life itself drew breath for him to hear, there came at intervals from among the wind-stirred hazel leaves, a sound like the quick pantings of his dog.

And if a year of exile had thus brought him nearer to the heart of Nature's mystery, it had quickened, too, the affectionate insight with which he read the thoughts of plain-living people, of the woodman or the shepherd, or of his grey-haired dame setting out in her Sunday-best to church. More than ever he appreciated her smooth domestic life, her solicitude that never fretted, her gossip and her small activities. Watching and conversing with such people after associating for a year with others of a very different pattern, his heart warmed anew to their integrity. Simple and untalented they might be by the standards of Cambridge, but they were sound to the core. There was no proud flesh in them, no vaunting mind. They were humble and human and whole.

And, as if infected by their example, his own love of life began to flow out more appreciably towards his kind. His primitive response to the elemental in its beauty and terror was increasingly leavened by tenderness and pensiveness, by those qualities which differentiate the civilised from the savage, a regard for human suffering, sympathy for pain, a perplexed knowledge of the burden of the human mystery. The necessary detachment from the blind processes of Nature which the shock of his father's death had initiated but only to intensify his awareness of Nature's forces, had developed now into a more conscious recognition of the distinctively human.

He saw men no longer as trees walking, but as beings unique in the realm of Nature because they could sin and they could pity, could aspire and could despair. The life of the hills and woods might still be often a dream, in which shadow and substance were indistinguishable, but man was an heroic fact, whose natural weakness was a condition of his human strength and whose distinction it was, in some mysterious way, both to be tied to his mother earth and to be free in his own right.

Wordsworth's interest in humanity had begun to awaken, as we have shown, through his association with vagrants and pedlars. But it was rather the strangeness of life than the fineness or pathos of man which then engrossed him. He had fed his own 'private being' on the tales which they had to tell with a boy's happy immunity. For he was too young, then, to 'think into the human heart' or even faintly visualise a world which was 'full of Misery and Heartbreak, Pain, Sickness, and Oppression.' Now, however, as he became more conscious of his own manhood, he began gradually to enter into all that was heartening and distressing in it, and to seek the same active intimacy with the human universe as he had enjoyed and continued to enjoy with the natural. The one intimacy, he found, supplemented and enhanced the other. For if his social frivolities at Cambridge had seemed to have no relation with his deeper being, the gaieties in which he indulged in his first vacation culminated in a moment of illumination which surpassed any which he had yet received.

It was after a night spent in dancing with a crowd of young

people from the dales. For hours his senses had throbbed to
the din of instruments and shuffling feet, the prattle of talk,
glancing forms, and glittering candles, to slight shocks, too,
of young desire that tingled through his veins. The sun had
just risen as he set out to walk the two miles home across the
fields, and it seemed, stepping out from the hot room into the
fresh morning air, the most glorious day which he had ever
known. The sea was laughing at a distance, the mountains reared
like radiant clouds, and in the meadows and lower grounds

> Was all the sweetness of a common dawn—
> Dews, vapours, and the melody of birds,
> And labourers going forth to till the fields.

And it was in this hour that the sense of the mission which
lay before him, felt deeply but vaguely on that first night walk
round the lake after his return, took definite shape, that he
irrevocably recognised and accepted his vocation. His heart
was full to the brim. He made no vows, but vows were then
made for him.

> Bond unknown to me
> Was given, that I should be, else sinning greatly,
> A dedicated Spirit.

But this sudden recognition of his mission in life was essentially
due to no accident of circumstance. He had returned home a
changed being from the wild, unworldly-minded youth who
had gone up to Cambridge. Self-consciousness, in the interval,
had advanced a pace. He was no longer so passive to experience
as he had been or so simply satisfied. His restlessness was a sign
that he had entered that space of life between boyhood and
maturity 'in which the soul is in a ferment, the character
undecided, the way of life uncertain.'

More stable and self-contained as he was than Keats, the

ferment was more gradual. And it had only now begun to affect him. Nevertheless for the first time in his life he felt that there was something about him 'that perplexed the authentic sight of reason.' The singleness of being and of vision which he had always enjoyed, 'the quiet stream of self-forgetfulness' upon which he had floated, were no longer serenely his. A rebel self had awoken in him which at times went its own wilful way. His own mental rhythm was no longer in perfect accord with the deep rhythm of life, just as the clothes which he wore were no longer part of his body, but, because he was vain of them, seemed 'to prey upon' his strength. His mind had become

> A parti-coloured show of grave and gay,
> Solid and light, short-sighted and profound;
> Of inconsiderate habits and sedate,
> Consorting in one mansion unreproved.

And to this mental fermentation was added the first faint stirrings of passion and romantic love, themselves a sign of his changed condition. For the desire to complete the self in another which underlies the sex-impulse proclaims a nature which in the necessary process of growth has become to some degree divided and one-sided.

Yet to this disturbance of his being by self-consciousness he owed, too, the first conscious recognition of what his mission in life should be. To discover in such an enraptured moment the first manifestation of worldly ambition is not, we think, to debase it. It is merely to remark that the conscious desire had awoken in Wordsworth to impress himself upon life. He had in reality been unconsciously impressing himself upon life in the act of accepting it throughout all his boyhood. And even in this hour of conscious dedication he felt that it was the determining spirit of life which made the vows. But for the

first time he knowingly accepted them. His own particular life
was no longer merged in the universal stream. It had a defined
aim, a purposeful centre into which all his unconscious impulses
would be increasingly drawn.

And if self-consciousness had begun to disturb the serenity
of his being, he could still draw deep draughts from the well of
life in moments of mental or sensuous exhaustion, such as
previously he had never known. Then, walking along the
country roads at night, his being listless and quiescent
through excess of feverish activity, his body drank in from
the stillness

> A restoration, like the calm of sleep,
> But sweeter far. Above, before, behind,
> Around me, all was peace and solitude,
> I look'd not round, nor did the solitude
> Speak to my eye; but it was heard and felt.
> O happy state! what beauteous pictures now
> Rose in harmonious imagery—they rose
> As from some distant region of my soul
> And came along like dreams; yet such as left
> Obscurely mingled with their passing forms
> A consciousness of animal delight,
> A self-possession felt in every pause
> And every gentle movement of my frame.

That he should now depend upon bodily and mental exhaustion
to recover fully his selfless identity with life is a significant
fact. For it shows more clearly perhaps than anything else
that 'the long probation' of a divided consciousness which he
was never to outgrow had definitely begun. The false light of
self-centred sense or thought had first to go out before the
invisible and the infinite could possess him.

§ 3

In the autumn he returned to Cambridge. He was young and the world lay before him. So he quitted both rocky Cumberland and its 'frank-hearted maids' with no more than momentary regret. But the hour of dedication was not forgotten, and he lived again much to himself. He read eagerly and omnivorously, if without any settled plan. But, despite occasional twinges of conscience, he was as detached from academic cares and hopes as in his first year. And if later he was to lament

> that overlove
> Of freedom planted in me from the very first,

he was content at this time to luxuriate in 'the still overflow of happiness and truth' which welled up within him, to know that 'the Poet's soul' was his and in the strength of that knowledge to hold firmly to the thought that he would leave behind him some monument in words which posterity would reverence.

The humble awe with which he had previously regarded books and their makers began to melt away before his gathering self-assurance. He even took up some pages which he had written at school and worked at them anew. They described one of those evening walks in his own Lake Country which had brought him so near to the heart of life, and the gradual transformation of the landscape as daylight yielded to twilight and twilight to night. And if the pulse of life beat but faintly in lines loaded with poetic diction derived from his reading, there was a certain originality in the very extravagances of his artifices.

Inevitably his style of writing rather reflected his reading than expressed himself. And it was a curiously mixed style because of the variety of his models. Based structurally upon Dryden's couplet, refined but weakened by Pope and conventionalised by mid-eighteenth-century poets, it owed its texture to the highly decorated poetic diction of Milton. Into this sophisticated, urban mould the simple countryman tried to pour his feelings and sensations and inevitably falsified them in the process. A student of life rather than literature, he had not yet learnt the power there is in words to stultify as well as to reveal. His inner knowledge, as he was to write later,

> was oft in depth
> And delicacy like another mind
> Sequester'd from my outward taste in books.

Yet even here his close contact with Nature sometimes supplied him unconsciously with a standard of truth. He knew, for example, from what he had seen with his own eyes, that the imagery of Macpherson's *Ossian* was spurious, because in Nature he found everything distinct but nothing isolated, while in Macpherson everything was insulated and so deadened, but nothing distinct. But if he was armed by experience against pseudo-romantic vagueness, he was far less critical of the flat clarity of pseudo-classical elegance, which he had cultivated in his school-exercise, and which was the fixed convention of his time. Being, therefore, 'a better judge of thoughts than words,' and not realising that a style appropriate to didactic or sententious thought was inapplicable to vivid sensations, he could only satisfy his sensationalism by indulging in fanciful epithets and far-fetched figures beyond any of his predecessors in a grotesque attempt to infuse life into unreal abstractions.

Nevertheless impervious for the most part as the decorated couplets which he used were to any intimacy or depth of feeling, they did not prevent him from filling his lines with many vivid descriptions of Nature, which revealed singular powers of exact observation. Not for nothing had he so avidly studied the 'minuter properties' of loved objects. And so the verses which he wrote, despite all their preoccupied abstractions, abounded in images which betrayed a young poet with abnormally acute senses and one, too, in whom romantic feeling had only to gather strength to dissolve the network of pseudo-classical conventions which entangled it and unite at a deeper level the nature 'that feels' with 'the other that observes.'

But his chief and ruling business was still to love and to enjoy, not to write poetry. And throughout the winter, whenever possible, he would wander up and down the avenue of tall elms and the side walks at the back of his college, until at nine o'clock the porter's bell called him in. There was a single ash tree, wreathed in ivy, of which the seeds hung in yellow tassels, under which he particularly loved to stand, looking up at its exquisite tracery beneath a frosty moon, while tranquil visions 'of human forms with superhuman powers' supplied the need which deans and tutors had failed to satisfy.

Rich in visionary rewards, however, as all this solitary communion was, there was a danger in it. And at times he felt the need of liberating 'a mind beset with images and haunted by itself.' The usual avenues of escape were closed to him. But he found an unusual but satisfying substitute in the study of geometry. His knowledge of the subject was only elementary, but it was sufficient to introduce him into a world which corrected any tendency to emotional diffuseness by its austere order, which balanced a too luxurious self-engrossment by its strict impersonality, and which lifted him above the flux of life on to a plane of static symmetry.

The order of geometry might be unreal compared to the spiritual logic which in his most inspired moments he had divined within the flowing forms of Nature. But it was never in danger of being submerged in the flux. And as he meditated upon its 'simple, pure proportions and relations,' he often drew

A pleasure calm and deeper, a still sense
Of permanent and universal sway
And paramount endowment of the mind,
An image not unworthy of the one
Surpassing Life, which out of space and time,
Nor touched by welterings of passion, is
And hath the name of God.

The relation between this independent world constructed out of pure intelligence and the world of Nature, so baffling in its creative excess and variety, remained obscure. The abstract framework of the one failed to hold the concrete content of the other. Yet the mind of Euclid in its precise and ordered self-sufficiency seemed a reflection, if but a pale one, of the mind of Life, of that Reason which, though it underlay and mysteriously worked in the phenomenal world, must surely exist somewhere in its own right and act according to its own inherent laws and essential ideas.

Wordsworth was eventually to fail because he could not realise in his own being this creative Reason, which is not subservient to the bodily senses, but uses them as its organs. And the appeal of geometry to him is interesting, both because it affords further proof that his mind had begun to work independently and because it foreshadows his later attempt to extricate himself from 'welterings of passion' by clinging to Godwinian rationalism.

Euclid, however, no more than Godwin, could long prove a God to one who often felt so ecstatically the God within himself. The problem which demanded solution was how to realise the God within the self instead of mistaking the self for God. But apart from a certain intermittent uneasiness and an occasional 'melancholy from humours of the blood' he was still blissfully unaware that any such problem existed. And even his melancholy was a source of pleasure, a sensation to be exploited or actually induced. For happiness is apt to grow monotonous unless its expression is varied. And beneath autumnal skies and the pensive moods that went with them he felt only more luxuriously the unquenchable spring in his blood.

§4

He spent the summer vacation of 1789 roaming about Dovedale, the Yorkshire Dales, and his own native fells. But it was chiefly notable for the brief reunion it brought with Dorothy. In the previous December her unhappy servitude at Penrith had been ended by the marriage of her favourite uncle, the Reverend William Cookson, who took her with him to Forncett, near Long Stratton, in Norfolk. 'Almost mad with joy,' she had stopped on her way there for a few hours at Cambridge, where she had walked about the courts and backs with William. But although she was now reasonably happy in devoting herself to gardening, raising poultry, and teaching the village children, she longed ardently for 'the day of my felicity, the day on which I am to find a home under the same roof as my brother.' For her future, she had come to feel, must be linked with his. And for six years she was to await with the fondest anticipation the realisation of her dream.

The few weeks which she spent with her brother at Penrith in the summer of 1789 confirmed the plan upon which her heart was set, proving as they did that her instinct had been right, that they were, indeed, made for one another. The years which had separated them had not weakened their deep sense of affinity, while the fact that they had not grown up together as brother and sister in the familiar intercourse of a home gave to their reunion an element of wonder and strangeness, a joy, as Wordsworth later described it,

> Above all joys, that seemed another morn
> Risen on mid noon.

After such long separation Dorothy seemed 'a gift then first bestowed.' And the singular ardour of their attachment in the years to come can only be rightly understood in the light of this separation. It not only differed from the normal attachment of brother and sister in intensity of feeling, but it had in it an element of romantic love. Doubtless neither consciously recognised the fact, but unconsciously they betrayed it.

They were both abnormally passionate beings, and in both of them passion was eventually to prove a destructive force because it was turned back upon the self and denied full creative satisfaction. Already in Dorothy its force was at once concealed and revealed behind a wild shyness, in her brother behind a certain dour reserve. His feelings in particular flowed in a deep but narrow channel. Perfectly self-sufficient as he had been, he had hitherto lived in a sexless universe. But now he was beginning to be aware of women as different from himself, as disturbing, too, and desirable. And dimly conscious of a certain uncouthness in himself, he was a little uneasy in their company and inclined to defend his male integrity against their advances.

But his sister, who was also half a stranger to him, offered him the charm and the stimulus of devoted womanhood, without endangering his masculine independence. It was natural, therefore, that he should feel towards her as something more than a brother and less than a lover, while she who had so little opportunity of giving her heart to another with that eager self-forgetfulness which was the lovely necessity of her nature, could hardly have offered a lover more than she offered him.

This summer of 1789, then, was as rich in promise as in fulfilment for the brother and sister who renewed a mutual joy, so long withheld, in walks along the banks of the River Emont, or who, climbing about the ruins of Brougham Castle with thoughts of Sidney and his *Arcadia*, 'gathered with one mind' the far-stretching landscape, or, lying on some turret's head in the heat of the day, listened to the tufts of grass and the harebells whispering in the breeze.

On some of these walks they were accompanied by a friend of Dorothy's, a girl of about her own age, who as a child had attended the same dame's school at Penrith as Wordsworth. Years later when she had become his wife, in a marriage of placid affection, he was to associate these walks with the first kindling of his affection for her. But it is safe to say that at the time she did little more than enhance

> By her exulting outside look of youth
> And placid under-countenance,

the joy that darted from Dorothy's wild eyes and the rapture of life's morning hours.

Very different, indeed, was the emotion which he experienced as they climbed together the high hill beyond Penrith, where as a boy the mouldering gibbet had affected him with an obscure terror and 'a visionary dreariness.' Now over the waste

> Of naked pools, and common crags that lay
> Exposed on the bare fell, were scattered love,
> The spirit of pleasure, and youth's golden gleam.

The sun of love had risen, and for a short reckless season was to cast out fear.

PART III

THE FALL

§ 1

WORDSWORTH had gone up to Cambridge, like so many young men in those days, with the idea of later taking Orders. His family still supposed that this was his intention, and even Dorothy had not yet abandoned the idea. Yet he himself must have known that the vocation which he had so clearly recognised a year earlier at Hawkshead could never be reconciled with the Ministry of a Church which was then as uninspired in its doctrine as the academic world in its learning.

His relations, however, must have been disagreeably surprised when he decided to devote the long vacation of 1790, not to the hard study expected of a third-year student, but to a walking tour abroad. He felt a little guilty himself, but youth, he determined, must be served.

The lure of the open road, of mountain scenery, and of Europe, particularly France, which seemed to be breaking out into new life, was too strong. But it was the new country which drew him rather than the new ideas. For although even Cambridge had recently been thrilled by the fall of the Bastille, and its Vice-Chancellor had actually hailed the event as 'a subject of triumph and congratulation,' Wordsworth himself took as yet no ardent interest in revolutionary politics. By temperament and upbringing he had inevitably no sympathy with social privilege, but the Liberty he believed in was primarily the freedom he himself enjoyed to feel and think and act from a vital impulse.

Certainly the France which he visualised as he planned his journey from Calais to the Alps was a place of new adventure, but he was hardly conscious that she was

> standing on the top of golden hours
> And human nature seeming born again.

So little, indeed, was he concerned with the politics of the hour, or for that matter with the cathedrals or art galleries which attracted the ordinary tourist, that he arranged to make for Switzerland by as direct a route as possible without turning aside either to Paris, Amiens, or Rheims. The only exception which he made was the Grande Chartreuse, and this less for the antiquity and religious interest of the monastery than for its magnificent natural setting.

His companion was a college friend named Robert Jones, a Welshman and a nature-lover like himself. They landed at Calais on 13th July 1790, the day before the king was to swear fidelity to the new Constitution, and so rapid was their progress that in two weeks they had reached Chalon on the Saône.

They had chosen a happy moment to cross France. The Revolution was in its earliest phase, and if the flowers and garlands on windows and triumphal arches were already withering as they went south through the hamlets and villages, the joy and excitement which possessed the people showed no signs of abatement. Everywhere they sensed cheerfulness and benevolence. The whole nation, it seemed, was in flower, and its gaiety and courtesy was like a spring fragrance. Among the vine-clad hills of Burgundy beneath the evening star they witnessed dances in celebration of the new-won Freedom which were prolonged far into the night, and with a merry crowd of travellers, many of them delegates who had been to Paris to celebrate the fall of the Bastille, they sailed down the Saône and the Rhône between high rocks and woods, orchards and smiling farms. All hearts were open, and if the solitary pair of Englishmen, whose coats were of the same piece to make them lighter and who carried their bundles tied up in handkerchiefs on their heads and an oak stick in their hands, excited a general smile, their singular appearance only confirmed the prevalent idea that the English were pioneers in the cause of Liberty.

Wordsworth was deeply affected by the conviviality and expansiveness. Yet it is doubtful whether even now he began to interpret it as a rebirth of human nature. More than most poets he had the faculty of surrendering himself to experience in the moment and only later and by slow degrees contemplating the experience which had sunk deep into him and informing it with thought. Moreover, he was moving rapidly at this time, intent on the mountains and lakes which beckoned him and pleasantly bewildered by the rush of strange impressions.

Yet although neither *Descriptive Sketches*, written, for the most part, two years later and reflecting the dissolving mood of that time, nor the account given in *The Prelude*, are reliable records of what he actually experienced, there can be little doubt that this journey across France had an immediate, as it had a lasting, effect upon him. Hitherto, despite the sensational intensity of his surrender to Nature, he had preserved a certain aloofness. His ecstasies had been solitary. He and the universe shared them together. But now in a warm, expansive atmosphere, his austerity and his reserve began to melt. The careless sociability in which he had rather guiltily indulged in his first year at Cambridge and his first vacation at Hawkshead, seemed in France to be consecrated by a Cause. Human dignity counted less here than human brotherhood, and the self-contained integrity, the moral gravity of the lonely shepherds of the north were almost forgotten in a world momentarily kindled by a flame of communal enthusiasm.

Certainly if he had not crossed France just at this time, he might never have surrendered so fervently as he later did to the revolutionary impulse or clung so long to his belief that mankind was about to realise a new and lasting brotherhood.

It was not, however, as a student of the Revolution, which was hardly yet recognised as such, but as an avid explorer of

the natural world, that he visited the Convent of Chartreuse.
Yet by chance the Revolution did intrude upon its 'soul-
affecting solitude.' For the peace of the convent was disturbed
by the presence of a regiment of soldiers. Its confiscation had
not yet in fact occurred. But the threat of it was obvious, and
little as Wordsworth was concerned at the time with political
implications, he was unpleasantly 'startled at the gleam of
arms.' He felt then only a sense of profanation and uneasiness.
But years later, as he recollected that moment in tranquillity
and the sadness of after-knowledge, he characteristically
examined his instinctive reaction, and discovered in it the
conflict of two voices in himself. One of these cried,

> Honour to the patriot's zeal,
> Glory and pride to new-born Liberty,
> Hail to the mighty passions of the time,
> The vengeance and the transport and the hope,
> The gay or stern delight of this big hour!

The other voice, and it was the deeper, murmured, 'Spare
this convent. For it symbolises something permanent within
the transitoriness of life, a tradition which may link the future
to the past, and a religion in which the peasant is, in a profounder sense than levelling democrats know, the equal of the
king. If it has become corrupt, let it be redeemed rather than
destroyed, not only for the sake of the faith and meditation
which its rule might foster, but for its majestic setting
amid the crags which must surely transmit a lofty impulse
and teach man

> To think, to hope, to worship and to feel,
> To struggle, to be lost within himself
> In trepidation, from the blank abyss
> To look with bodily eyes and be consoled.

And in fact at the time it was the violation by the military of Nature's grandeur rather than of religion's sanctities which distressed him. As he had issued from the dark woods of Vallombre and gazed up at the rock-bound convent, he had been deeply impressed by the crucifix which at each corner of it stood out against the sky. And characteristically he attributed to the winds a reverence for the cross, and it shocked him that impious men should threaten what 'the storm full surely reverenced.'

The idea was naïve, and reflected a credulity in his worship of Nature for which he was to pay bitterly enough. So ecstatically sure was he of the

> imaginative impulse sent
> From these majestic floods—these shining cliffs,

that he could hardly credit Nature with destructive force, nor did it strike him that the imaginative impulse which the cross symbolised was almost as alien to the indifferent elements as to the predatory soldiery.

To suggest, however, that this first impact with the darker side of the revolutionary movement caused Wordsworth either to affirm in words his faith in Nature or to question his awakening hopes for man, would be misleading. He was too joyously alive to do either, and so absorbed in the new earth that he explored as to be largely indifferent to human concerns. Nevertheless, he left the Convent of Chartreuse with rather less assurance of human benevolence than he approached it, and hastened on to Switzerland.

Aiming rather at lakes than cities or mountains, and as avid for new scenes as a bird of prey, he hurried through enticing villages, yet not too rapidly to feed his senses upon

> Calm huts, and lawns between, and sylvan slopes,

to feel the patriarchal simplicity of the pastoral life

> Where solitary forms illumin'd stray
> Turning with quiet touch the valley's hay,

or to halt enchanted by the spectacle of the sun breaking from
the clouds after a storm,

> Eastward, in long perspective glittering, shine
> The wood-crown'd cliffs that o'er the lake recline;
> Wide o'er the Alps a hundred streams unfold,
> At once to pillars turn'd that flame with gold.

It has been argued that because Wordsworth in his later
Descriptive Sketches borrowed extensively from the Alpine
pictures of Ramond de Carbonnières, a French traveller, his
own impressions on this tour were far from vivid. But it is
more reasonable to suppose that they were too crowded to leave
a precise impression upon his memory. His mood, too, was
one of emotional exaltation which was hardly conducive to
exact observation, and which outran at times even the capacity
of the Alps to stagger the soaring mind, so that the first sight
of Mont Blanc proved less awe-inspiring than his imagination
had conceived it.

It was, indeed, typical of Wordsworth, until his instinctive
powers began to fail, that he absorbed in the process of
observing. He hardly appreciated the Swiss landscape in terms
of form and colour. Its beauty had for him a power as sweet
and gracious as virtue or goodness, love or the remembrance
of a noble deed. It expressed something, in short, which found
an answer in and enriched his whole being. Whatever he saw
or heard or felt was

> but a stream
> That flowed into a kindred stream; a gale,
> Confederate with the current of the soul,

> To speed my voyage; every sound or sight,
> In its degree of power, administered
> To grandeur or to tenderness—to the one
> Directly, but to tender thoughts by means
> Less often instantaneous in effect.

And because he so deeply assimilated natural beauty it fertilised him. He might later, in misguidedly attempting to write a descriptive poem, have to depend upon Ramond de Carbonnières for pictorial details of the route which he had taken. But his visual memory was only weak in proportion as his imagination was strong. Whenever that was quickened, and what he saw was not only associated with strong emotion and sensational delight but became vitally fused with himself, he could never forget it. For then no mere external images were engraved upon his memory, but the creative life which formed such images passed into his being, so that he could continually recreate the image from its vital source within himself and discover in it more and more of meaning and significance.

If, then, his impressions were generally too hasty to be visually vivid, his unique experiences were vital in a deeper sense, as the following experience will suggest. At one point in their journey through the Simplon Pass he and his companion lost their way, but fortunately met a peasant who directed them not upwards but downwards, telling them that they *had crossed the Alps*. To any one but Wordsworth the words might seem ordinary enough. But on him their effect was potent and instantaneous. His whole being was dilated. A sense of life's inmost reality, of its pure creative power, possessed him,

> That awful Power rose from the mind's abyss
> Like an unfathered vapour that enwraps,
> At once, some lonely traveller.

It seemed at once to well up within him and seize him from
without. He was

> lost as in a cloud,
> Halted, without a struggle to break through.

Years later, when he was engaged in his great task of consciously analysing and interpreting his past experience, he was
to discover in this moment a revelation of the working of
Imagination and of all that it implied of fusion between God
and man. But at the time he only knew an 'access of joy,' with
a deep undertone of awe, beyond anything which he had yet
experienced. He seemed for the moment pure spirit without
stain of sense, an elemental amid the elements.

Yet the immediate reaction from this ecstatic moment was
one of dull and heavy slackening. And in that aftermath of
intoxication, that servitude to the ebb and flow of instinctive
life, he might, had he been able to see the future, have read the
shadows of his destiny.

Amid the gloomy and giddy grandeur, however, of the
descent into Italy his melancholy passed, while the sense of
infinity returned. But the valleys, when he reached them,
induced a softer and more luxurious mood. Significantly,
perhaps, the only region in which he had lingered for three days
was that near Neuchâtel, of which Rousseau had written so
meltingly. And something of Rousseau's delicious languor
affected him as he watched the dark-eyed maids tending their
garden plots by Lake Como, 'bosom'd deep in chestnut
groves,' or followed the shadows as they travelled from the
surface of Lake Maggiore up the side of the hills, while part of
a village lay in shade, part in bright sunshine.

In the brief intervals between days of strenuous activity
Nature even breathed 'o'er the failing soul voluptuous dreams,'
the more satisfying because they were intermingled with
'something of stern mood' and a sense of drowsing vigour.

Such a blending of the austere and the voluptuous must have been his when, through an error in reading the time, he so far forestalled the sunrise that he spent most of a warm summer night in the open, stung by insects, listening to the cry of unknown birds and watching the dull red image of the moon, bedded in the lake and changing its form like an uneasy snake. And in a letter which he addressed to Dorothy the voice of the Rousseauist was first definitely heard. 'My spirits,' he wrote, 'have been kept in a perpetual hurry of delight, by the almost uninterrupted succession of sublime and beautiful objects which have passed before my eyes during the course of the last month. . . . At the Lake of Como, my mind ran through a thousand dreams of happiness, which might be enjoyed upon its banks if heightened by conversation and the exercise of the social affections. Among the more awful scenes of the Alps I had not a thought of man, or a single created being; my whole soul was turned to Him who provoked the terrible majesty before me. . . . I have thought of you perpetually; and never have my eyes burst upon a scene of particular loveliness but I have almost instantly wished that you could for a moment be transported to the place where I stood to enjoy it. . . . I am a perfect enthusiast in my admiration of Nature in all her various forms; and I have looked upon, and, as it were, conversed with, the objects which this country has presented to my view so long, and with such increasing pleasure, that the idea of parting from them oppresses me with a sadness similar to what I have always felt in quitting a beloved friend. . . . I feel a high enjoyment in reflecting that perhaps scarcely a day of my life will pass in which I shall not derive some happiness from these images.'

The enthusiastic idiom of his letter was doubtless dictated in some measure by contemporary fashion. Nevertheless it does reveal a new expansiveness. We need not, however, take too seriously the dreams of happiness, 'heightened by conversation and the exercise of the social affections.' Possibly the churlish manners of the Swiss innkeepers dictated these dreams as much as Rousseau. For he had to confess that despite his wish to believe that a landscape so beautiful must generate amiable manners in its inhabitants, the Swiss compared ill with the French, whose 'politeness diffused through the lowest ranks had an air so engaging that you could scarcely attribute it to any other cause than real benevolence.'

But although the awakened political and social spirit of the time, and the expectancy of the nations had begun to affect him, he was touched, fatally indeed, as was soon to appear, but not yet with any intimate concern. In his primitive independence he still scarcely belonged to the household of social life, so deep was his affinity with the wild elements of Nature. He seemed to move among men as a bird moves through the air or a fish through the water.

> I needed not that joy, I did not need
> Such help; the ever-living Universe,
> And independent spirit of pure youth
> Were with me at that season, and delight
> Was in all places spread around my steps
> As constant as the grass upon the fields.

§ 2

He was back in England in time for the Michaelmas term at Cambridge, and in the Christmas vacation visited Dorothy at Forncett, beginning there that pacing of the country roads which was to occupy so much of his time for half a century. 'We used to walk,' Dorothy wrote, 'every morning about two hours; and every evening we went into the country at four or half-past four, and used to pace backwards and forwards till six. Unless you have accustomed yourself to this kind of walking, you will have no idea that it can be pleasant; but I assure you it is most delightful.'

In January 1791 he took his degree. Dorothy informed her friend Miss Pollard in a letter that he had lost his chance of a fellowship through refusing to study mathematics. But in fact he had refused to study anything in the curriculum with any regularity. The only fellowship to which he aspired and for which he had studied was a fellowship with life. In Dorothy's words—'William has a great attachment for poetry . . . which is not the most likely thing to produce his advancement in the world. His pleasures are chiefly of the imagination. He is never so happy as when in a beautiful country.'

Nevertheless it was to the town that his vague and vagrant desire to extend his experience of life next took him. For in February 1791 he went to London. The few brief visits which he had paid it from Cambridge had not shattered the country lad's dream of it as a city of romance. In a few weeks, however, the dream had vanished, crushed beneath a crowd of bewildering facts.

Yet the facts, for a time at least, were breathlessly exciting. Amid the bustling and sordid traffic of the streets, the medley of colours, lights, and forms, the endless stream of men and movement, he felt the quivering pulse of life. Here were coaches dashing by with loud blowing horns, sturdy draymen, glittering shops and secluded alleys, shrill vendors and crude advertisements. Sometimes he plunged into the rapid current and was 'whirled about by the vortex of its *strenua inertia*,' and sometimes he was 'thrown by the eddy into a corner of the stream,' where he lay 'in almost motionless indolence.'

He was drawn to the theatre in which he saw Mrs. Siddons act, and from melodramas to the even cruder entertainments of rope-dancers, dwarfs, clowns and conjurors. He heard Burke, who had published only a few months before his *Reflections on the Revolution in France*, speak in the House of Commons, but at the time found him rather tedious. His impressions, indeed, for the most part were superficial. For he was not attuned to the pitch of the town. He could not adapt his slower rural rhythm to its rapid counterpoint, and although the excitement he felt was pleasurable, it was also distracting.

And yet there were moments even here when his strange visionary faculty awoke, and at the sight of some unusual face emerging from the crowd he seemed to look into the heart of life, had glimpses of

> the things which I had shap'd
> And yet not shaped, had seen, and scarcely seen,
> Had felt, and thought of in my solitude.

That strange sense of moving in a dream, which had alarmed and intoxicated him as a schoolboy, of the actual dissolving into the real or maybe the phantasmal, would come upon him. And he would search the face of every passer-by with a baffled, wondering gaze,

> oppress'd
> By thoughts of what, and whither, when and how,
> Until the shapes before my eyes became
> A second-sight procession, such as glides
> Over still mountains, or appears in dreams;
> And all the ballast of familiar life,
> The present, and the past; hope, fear; all stays,
> All laws of acting, thinking, speaking man
> Went from me, neither knowing me, nor known.

In such a mood of imaginative absorption the sudden sight of a blind beggar, propped up against a wall, with a written paper on his chest explaining his story, affected him much as the face of the Buddha might a devout worshipper. The beggar's label became in that moment a symbol of the utmost which man can know both of himself and the universe, while his fixed look and sightless eyes seemed to admonish as from another world.

One less self-engrossed than Wordsworth might have sought to penetrate to the personal history which lay behind the face, to discover the pathetic meaning of that particular life. But for him it remained only a strange mask which excited by its brooding impassivity a thrilling sensation of the infinite.

Youth is necessarily too intoxicated with life to be patiently humane, and Wordsworth's feeling for his fellow-men was not yet, nor indeed was ever to be, completely disinterested. All that comedy of character which lies between the simply human and the superhuman was a closed book to him.

Inevitably, therefore, the city impressed him most by night when the great tide of human life stood still and he enjoyed, as at Hawkshead, but with a sense heightened by the riot of the daytime, an uninterrupted union of solemn silence and himself.

His condemnations of city life belong to a later time, but they were based to some extent on what he saw and felt now. The townsman, he then claimed with much justice, through the press 'of self-destroying, transitory things,' never developed that under-sense of greatest among least which enables a man to perceive every part and detail in relation to a felt whole. And he attributed this capacity in himself to the habitual influence on his mind of the fixed grandeur of mountain outlines combined with the constant change and gradations of light upon their surface.

But although the fellowship of mountains may well deepen a perception of the absolute, it tends also to foster an in-flexibility which is fatal to a true fellowship with man. And Wordsworth added little to his real knowledge of life by the four months which he spent in London because he remained, for the most part, blinded by his own rural virtues and rural prejudices. Reserved and 'wholly free,' as he too easily assumed, 'from dangerous passions,' he walked the streets, and the only incidents which really penetrated his being were those that appealed to or shocked his rural sensibility. One of these was the spectacle of a cottage child sitting on the bar of a theatre, surrounded by spectators who had come out to drink, but in his innocence wholly immune from the oaths and indecent talk about him. So deeply was Wordsworth impressed by the scene that this child became for him later a deathless symbol of that pristine purity which the years corrupt. Another scene with a similar appeal which remained in his memory because it touched his heart was that of a workman nursing a sickly baby in an open square.

And it was only such reminders as these of his native cottagers and of those uncorrupted domestic virtues which were dear to him, that really passed 'beyond the suburbs' of his mind. London, in short, deepened his existing attachments, rather than added anything to his real experience of life. His inner calm and complacency was as little affected by its turmoil as a deep pool by the wind that ruffles its surface. And although he was bewildered by the 'foolishness and madness in parade,' it added little or nothing to his knowledge of human nature or of the instability of men and women in the mass.

In May he joined his friend Jones at his home in the Vale of Clewd in Wales, staying with him until September and enjoying a walking tour through the Welsh mountains. But it is through his correspondence with another college friend, William Mathews, that we gain most light upon his temper at this time. The vein of ponderous skittishness which appears occasionally in these letters was probably traceable to *Tristram Shandy* and the *Spectator*, which he was engaged in reading. But the wilful recklessness strangely combined with sententiousness were self-revealing.

'The truth of the matter is,' he gaily confessed, 'that when in Town I did *little*, and since I came here I have done nothing.

A miserable account! However, I have not in addition to all this to complain of bad spirits. That would be the devil indeed. I rather think that this gaiety increases with my ignorance, as a spendthrift grows more extravagant the nearer he approximates to a final dissipation of his property.'

He was not, perhaps, as reckless in fact as he liked to appear. At least he was prudent enough to reject a wild proposal that they should travel, made to him by Mathews, who was discontented with his work as a teacher. And he even went so far as to lecture him on the duty of sons not to cause their parents anxiety, as if he himself had never taken a holiday in Switzerland in face of his family's disapproval. The self-complacence of the later moralist is, indeed, curiously evident in his manner of lecturing his friend, as when he wrote, 'I should not be able to reconcile with my ideas of right, the thought of wandering about a country, without a certainty of being able to maintain myself . . . being indebted for my existence to those charities of which the acceptance might rob people not half so able to support themselves as myself. It is evident that there are a thousand ways in which a person of your education might get his bread, as a recompense for his labour, and while that continues to be the case, for my own part I confess I should be unwilling to accept it on any other conditions.'

Admittedly Wordsworth's position differed from that of his friend. He still had a small sum of money sufficient for his immediate needs and hopes of more if the Earl of Lonsdale paid his debts. He had, too, the justification of an inward certainty that he was destined to be a poet and the instinctive feeling which went with it that, in Keats' later words, 'nothing is finer for the purposes of great productions than a very gradual ripening of the intellectual powers.'

Nevertheless there was something both sublime and ridiculous about his readiness to hold up 'hope and industry' as watchwords to Mathews, while he himself was agreeably idling in Wales, touching up, indeed, in odd moments, the lines *An Evening Walk*, which he had worked on at Cambridge, and meditating another descriptive poem on his tour in Switzerland, but resolutely refusing to accede to his Uncle William's request that he should study Hebrew as a preliminary to taking Orders. On the surface he did, indeed, blame himself for his lack of learning and application. But at heart he was complacent, and determined above everything not to be tied.

And so, although he spent some of the autumn of 1791 at Cambridge, it was Italian and Spanish which he read, and not Hebrew. And early in November, despite all his exhortations to Mathews, he had decided to indulge again in foreign travel. He excused himself by suggesting that he could combine travel with study. But he was honest enough to confess that he expected 'considerable pleasure from my sojourn on the other side of the water, and some little improvement, which God knows I stand in sufficient need of.' And he continued—'I am doomed to be an idler through my whole life. I have read nothing this age, nor indeed did I ever. Yet with all this I am tolerably happy. Do you think this ought to be a matter of congratulation to me, or no? For my own part I think certainly not.'

It was necessary, perhaps, to assume contrition before the friend to whom he had preached. But at heart he felt little. He was happy. Life beckoned to his restless blood. If all else failed, he could, as he promised his uncle, study Hebrew on his return. But to Mathews he wrote—'What must I do amongst that immense wilderness, I who have no resolution, and who have not prepared myself for the enterprise by any sort of discipline amongst the Western languages, who know little of Latin, and scarce anything of Greek? A pretty confession for a young gentleman whose whole life ought to have been devoted to study. And thus the world wags. But away with this outrageous egotism.'

Away with it he never wholly could. But the year which lay ahead of him was to destroy for ever the possibility of such flippant self-esteem.

§ 3

Wordsworth crossed to France on the night of 26th November 1791. His intention was to go to Orleans and spend the winter there learning the language and thereby qualifying himself for the office of travelling companion to some young nobleman, if meanwhile no other means of livelihood offered itself. Such at least was his plan as Dorothy reported it; and after spending two days at Rouen and five at Paris he reached Orleans on 6th December.

Even a week's experience was, however, sufficient to convince him that the France to which he had returned was no longer the light-hearted, festive Eden through which he had passed a year before. The expansive emotions of that time had crystallised into a practical challenge. A week earlier Robespierre had returned to Paris, and the National Assembly had addressed a firm declaration to the Foreign Powers that it required the same freedom from interference as it was ready to offer them, and that those who continued to favour hostile preparations would do well to 'calculate what result may follow the awakening of nations.'

Wordsworth attended a rather tempestuous sitting of the Assembly, and although the Revolutionary Power had by its capable moderation justified hitherto the hopes of those who believed that Liberty might be leavened with Justice, he may well have felt, for the first time, the threat of popular violence. His interests, however, were not yet political. Doubtless he knew that the Constituent Assembly had begun the new organisation of Society, abolishing feudal and clerical privileges and curtailing the king's power, that it had set on foot reforms of the judicial system and the nation's finances. But

G

in all this it had acted so temperately that many of the nobles had actually collaborated with it in renouncing their least defensible rights.

The Legislative Assembly which had succeeded the Constituent in October was, indeed, clearly a more extreme and inflammatory body of men. But the spirit of its declarations was lofty, and it had yet to meet the opposition both at home and abroad which was to test the purity of its idealism.

It was easy, therefore, for Wordsworth, staring and listening with a stranger's ears or sitting amid the ruins of the Bastille, to indulge in a 'pleasant exercise of hope and joy,' to feel the bliss of being alive and young in times

> In which the meagre, stale, forbidding ways
> Of custom, law, and statute, took at once
> The attraction of a country in romance.

Yet in Paris, at least, as he later confessed, he both looked for something that he could not find, and affected more emotion than he felt. For he was still a primitive and a solitary at heart, and too content to draw private refreshment from the well of Nature to be really intimately concerned with the world of Man.

But the months which lay before him were to plunge him into experiences that destroyed for ever the unity of his being. The 'long probation' was now veritably at hand. Nature could no longer protect the spoilt child, whom she had nourished through years of quiet retirement, from the convulsions of manhood. The passions and the hopes of men called to him, and the love of woman, that love which, in the words of a later poet, 'sells the proud heart's citadel to Fate,' and is

> a breach in the walls, a broken gate,
> Where that comes in that shall not go again.

Wordsworth could not but yield to the expansive forces of the time and the urge of his own ardent youth. He gave himself, and in giving lost that happy singleness of being which had been his since childhood and which, because later he recoiled in terror from his giving, he could never renew.

It has been said that he went to France as an enthusiastic student and in some sense disciple of Rousseau. Yet this again is probably to antedate his development. We have, indeed, remarked the tones of the Rousseauist in the letter which he sent to Dorothy from Switzerland. But they were then little more than an affectation, and there is no evidence that in the year which followed he had become engrossed either in social philosophy or public events. Rousseau, indeed, was only likely to appeal deeply to him after events had profoundly quickened his interest in humanity and thrust upon him the problem, which he was to struggle henceforth to solve, of reconciling Nature and Man.

But when he set out for France that problem had hardly yet presented itself at least to his conscious mind. He had, as we have seen, begun, in his first Cambridge vacation, to feel more human-hearted towards individuals among his own dale folk. But this did not imply any interest in man in the mass. And never having left Nature himself, the necessity of returning to her which Rousseau preached so eloquently only acquired the force of a gospel when he shared the daily life of a nation which was desperately striving to throw off the disease of inward division which had struck to its vitals.

Then, indeed, as he read the pamphlets which poured from the Press or listened to the talk and debate of revolutionary clubs, he inevitably became a disciple of Rousseau as one who seemed to offer to mankind a return to the kind of instinctively happy life which he had enjoyed himself. The delusive simplification of life which Rousseau preached and his conception of civilised people as corrupt corresponded so exactly

with Wordsworth's own upbringing among simple dalesmen
and his discovery of their moral and human superiority to
Cambridge dons, that he failed altogether to perceive that
Rousseau was diseased himself.

What Rousseau wrote about the beauty of a state of Nature
and the primitive virtues, Wordsworth had lived, while the
dynamic but dangerous catchwords of the Revolution,
'Liberty, Equality, and Fraternity,' 'seemed nothing out of
Nature's certain course,' because at Hawkshead he had
experienced them all.

Rousseau's gospel of Nature was, in fact, a sentimental
perversion of the instinctive life which Wordsworth had
enjoyed. It was the gospel of a sick man seeking self-escape
in a soft, idyllic, and sociable landscape, who would have
shrunk from the stern benignity of Hawkshead. But his
feminine longing to dissolve the self into life, if as fatally one-
sided as the exclusive assertion of the masculine will against
which it was a reaction, did at least breathe union and enchantment. And since it was sustained by remarkable powers of
rationalisation, it seemed the more convincingly to Wordsworth a philosophy confirmed by his own most entranced
experiences, even while it invited him to yield himself emo-
tionally and sensationally to life as he had never done
before.

But Rousseau was at most only a secondary factor in the
situation. For it was inevitable that Wordsworth should, in
Keats's words, be 'imperceptibly impelled by the awakening of
the thinking principle' within him into that state of divided
consciousness of which Rousseauism was both an expression
and a delusive solvent. We have already remarked the first
symptoms of this inevitable fall from primitive unity, surprising only in their being unusually delayed. France did but
accelerate the process, inviting a sudden surrender to
sensational excess, a sudden release of those ardent appetites

which had been absorbed in his earlier ecstatic communion with Nature but which were now to enforce their own particular demands.

It was of course events and human contacts rather than abstract ideas which thus broke his native reserve. And the influence of Rousseau was important only because he deluded Wordsworth into thinking that he was still obeying the creative inspiration of his earlier years. The sensational force of his delusion may be measured by the violence of his later reaction.

§ 4

When Wordsworth reached Orleans on 6th December, he was, had he known it, in a highly inflammable condition. Isolated as he had been for so long from social life and rather glutted by self-communion, he was as likely to fling himself, at the bidding of circumstance, into friendship, or into love, or into the Revolutionary Movement. The woman drew him first; she led him to the friend, and the friend sealed his devotion to the Revolutionary Cause.

He found humble lodgings at Orleans with a hosier, a violent opponent of the Revolution. But in searching for them he made the acquaintance of a very agreeable family with whom he would have liked to stay had his means allowed it. The head of the household was a Monsieur Augustin Dufour, and it included a visitor, a young lady of twenty-five, named Marie Anne Vallon. Wordsworth's acquaintance with the family ripened so quickly that he was soon regularly spending his evenings with them. He was anxious to improve his French; Annette, as she was familiarly called, offered her help, and soon the study of the language which he had originally offered as an excuse for indulging in the pleasures of foreign travel became itself a pleasure that surpassed all others.

Annette Vallon was the youngest child of a surgeon with
Scottish blood in his veins. She had been born at Blois. Her
father had been dead for some years, and since her mother had
married again, she shared with Wordsworth a certain independence from the ordinary family ties, although a brother,
Paul, a witty and sociable notary clerk, lived also at Orleans.
On the father's side at least the Vallon family were liberal-
minded. Annette's eldest brother had been named Jean
Jacques, and they had approved the opening phases of the
Revolution. Stronger, however, than their sympathy with
liberal ideas was an ingrained bourgeois respectability, and they
were already beginning to recoil from the Republican Movement.

But Annette at the time was little concerned with politics,
and the generous temper which both she and her brother Paul
may have inherited from their father found expression rather in
her personal relationships. She was an unconscious Rousseauist
in so far as for her at the moment feeling was all. She talked
eagerly and laughed readily and tears came easily to her eyes.
And if she was too much at the mercy of her sensibility, her
lack of reserve had a particular charm for a young man, her
junior by four years, whom reserve had for so long locked
within himself. All his native hardness and shrewdness was
softened in her presence. He felt in her glance and in her
movements, in the vibrations of her voice, the spirit which in
an innocent obedience to the will of life gives itself and invites
another to give that so he may receive.

And to Wordsworth, who had hitherto only given himself
to hills and woods and winds, the call was irresistible. The
ardent force accumulated through years of instinctive communion with life was suddenly focussed upon a young
woman who seemed the pure image of the Nature which he
loved, no longer awesome or elusive, but warm and near and
palpable.

He beheld
A vision, and he lov'd the thing he saw.
Arabian Fiction never fill'd the world
With half the wonders that were wrought for him.
Earth liv'd in one great presence of the spring,
Life turn'd the meanest of her implements
Before his eyes to price above all gold,
The house she dwelt in was a sainted shrine,
Her chamber-window did surpass in glory
The portals of the East, all paradise
Could by the simple opening of a door
Let itself in upon him, pathways, walks,
Swarm'd with enchantment till his spirit sank
Beneath the burthen, overbless'd for life.

For the first and last time in his life he was completely possessed by love for a woman. The inmost defences of his selfhood went down before the rapture that seized him. He was blindly infatuated as only those who have jealously and austerely guarded the shrine of their being can be, when life compels them at last to fling open the doors. And beneath the overtones of romantic exaltation he felt the throb of sensuous desire.

Nature, indeed, in the mild and fertile valley of the Loire, seemed less concerned to discipline her devotees than in the vale of Hawkshead. Its rich orchards and wheatfields and soft airs invited a luxurious relaxation, while the old royal castles, châteaux, and great cathedrals which dotted the landscape transported the wanderer into a romantic past where dreams of chivalry mocked a niggard prudence, and self-regard was dissolved in knightly adoration.

The poet in Wordsworth inevitably awoke to action with the lover, and it is from the *Descriptive Sketches* which he began to compose during walks on the banks of the Loire that we can best appreciate, despite much artificial diction, how completely the moral strain in him was now submerged in sensational delight, in the delicious languor, too, of a fever which stole through all the fibres of his being, 'binding the charmed soul in powerless trance.'

It was not, indeed, primarily of Switzerland that he thought when he wrote,

> Slow glides the sail along th' illumined shore,
> And steals into the shade the lazy oar.
> Soft bosoms breathe around contagious sighs,
> And amorous music on the water dies.

The voices that stole down the 'enchanted woods' of his poem, the soft winds that whispered joy, still more the dark-eyed maids that tossed their ringlets in the dance, were but emanations from Annette. From her, too, those forms took shape,

> that, in thy noon-tide shade,
> Rest, near their little plots of wheaten glade;
> Those steadfast eyes, that beating breasts inspire
> To throw the 'sultry ray' of young Desire;
> Those lips, whose tides of fragrance come, and go,
> Accordant to the cheek's unquiet glow;
> Those shadowy breasts in love's soft light array'd,
> And rising, by the moon of passion sway'd.

Wordsworth who had prided himself so delusively upon his temperate blood, was powerless against the sudden onset of so intoxicating a desire. It transformed him into a being for whom discretion was no longer a virtue nor self-security a condition to be prized. Within a few weeks he and Annette were lovers in the fullest sense, and when she left Orleans for Blois in the spring of 1792, she was with child.

Some years later, in his *Vaudracour and Julia*, Wordsworth

was to excuse the 'perilous weakness' into which he was thus 'tempted to decline' with a stilted solemnity that could not conceal his sense of shame and embarrassment. But the horrified moralist who then denied the reckless necessity of his impulse, begging the reader neither to speak nor think of his action as the effect

> Of some unguarded moment that dissolved
> Virtuous restraint,

cast no shadow upon the first transports of the young lover, who accepted and exulted in his self-surrender as something for which all his life had been a preparation. As soon would he have read evil into the budding boughs of spring as into a rapture so compelling and so fulfilling. For he could not know that this passion which possessed him so feverishly was in truth a fallacious spring, and that in snatching too hastily at its blossom, he precluded love from ever coming to true fruition in his experience.

And it was only when in the spring of 1792 he followed Annette to Blois, where she was more subject to her family and the conventions of a smaller town, that he began to feel the difficulties of the situation into which he had been so deliriously drawn and to chafe at the necessity for concealment. And for a time even these difficulties served rather to intensify and consecrate his desire than to fret his mind. For since barriers had to be surmounted, he could dramatise himself as a Romeo, cruelly fated to meet his Juliet only by stealth, 'momentous but uneasy bliss!' Those stolen interviews by night, 'accomplished with a ladder's help,' and curtailed so poignantly by 'the lark's note heard before its time,' helped to preserve the illusion that he was moving, not in a realm of fact, but in one of romance.

And at Blois it was even easier than it had been to accept such romance as 'nothing out of Nature's certain course.' For

there he not only surrendered his heart to the popular movement, but he made a friend who by his nobility and generosity
of mind convinced him of the justice of such a surrender.

§ 5

The friend who so deeply influenced Wordsworth's attitude
to the Revolutionary Movement was one of a group of officers
stationed at Blois, almost all of whom were eager to restore the
old regime, even if it involved seeking aid from foreigners.
They welcomed Wordsworth because he was a foreigner, and
while deploring his candid condemnation of feudal privileges
and his approval of government by the people for the people,
they tolerated such views in him as being merely typical of a
mad Englishman.

They served, however, to open Wordsworth's eyes to the
bitter reactionary temper of the Royalist party, and to intensify
by opposition his own liberal enthusiasm. And the apparent
meanness of their motives was thrown into particularly
damaging relief by the one officer among them who favoured
the Revolutionary Movement, a captain in the 32nd Regiment,
named Beaupuy.

Fifteen years older than Wordsworth, he came of an ancient
noble family. On his mother's side he was a descendant of
Montaigne, and it was to her that he and his five brothers owed
their sympathy for the literature and the philosophy of the
eighteenth century. But while his zeal for liberty and human
brotherhood was grounded in a study of principles and of
history, it was also the inevitable expression of a very pure and
courageous nature. Intense as his convictions were, he was
devoid of all fanaticism. Because his faith was both reasoned
and humble, the pride of others, the scorn and hostility of his
fellow-officers, never provoked him to anger. His nature
breathed the more sweetness, the more it was insulted, and the

graciousness which proved him a natural aristocrat disproved more powerfully than any arguments the pretensions of an artificial aristocracy.

To the humblest he was courteous without a hint of condescension and with a kind of radiant joy in the felt fact of his common humanity. And because his belief in the principle of human equality was not a vague theory nourished by envious egotism, but grew out of a loving respect for the rights of every personality with which he came into contact, he valued equally all that made men unique and all that bound them together. Consequently, while he loved the poor for the virtues which sprang from their submissiveness, he was alive also to their lack of knowledge and capacity. And while he deplored the false pride and selfishness of the rich and ardently supported the movement which would deprive them of their privileges, he felt no personal hatred for his opponents.

Such a man was ideally and fatally formed to confirm Wordsworth's belief in the Revolutionary Movement. For Wordsworth was never really at home with abstract ideas. He needed a fact to fasten his affections to,

> giving thus unto events
> A form and body.

Beaupuy provided such a form and body, and one so luminous and serene, that it compelled Wordsworth to dismiss as ignoble any lurking doubts and fears of a land that swarmed with passions, like a plain devoured by locusts. In Beaupuy he saw the justification of every dream of human perfectibility. And disregarding the culture and the breeding of which his friend was the rare flower, he regarded him as the pattern of the emancipated man whom Nature intended and the Revolution, by co-operating with Nature, would bring to birth. By thus delusively confirming his vague enthusiasm at a moment when events might otherwise have shaken it, Beaupuy was destined to influence him more decisively than any other man, except Coleridge.

And ironically enough it was the very temperance of the man which made him so potent an advocate of a cause which contained within it the seeds of a fatal excess. A violent one-sided radical would have aroused all the caution and shrewdness which only lay dormant in Wordsworth at twenty-two. But as he listened to Beaupuy extolling the rights of man or condemning ancient prejudice, the rival claims of the individual and society were lifted out of the temporary arena, where the conflicting passions of the crowd pressed upon and confused his mind. Liberty and Humanity were transformed from the catchwords of the demagogue into eternal principles, while the bewildering events of the moment took their inevitable place in the perspective of history and of thought.

And Beaupuy's idealism was so convincing because it harmonised more perfectly even than Rousseau's with Wordsworth's own previous social experience. Reared in a district where no one received respect for wealth or blood, he felt with particular force the truth of Beaupuy's description of the life of courts and of the nobility as

> A light, a cruel, and vain world cut off
> From the natural inlets of just sentiment,
> From lowly sympathy and chastening truth.

The world-democracy of which Beaupuy dreamed and talked seemed in fact to Wordsworth to be already epitomised in the democracy of the Lake Country. And while doubtless Beaupuy widened his social outlook beyond a provincial range by turning his mind to the abstract problems of society and the facts of history, Wordsworth still remained a provincial at heart. The new world which was being born would simply realise the ancient virtues of Hawkshead. And as Beaupuy propounded his vision of that world, in which man, no longer blinded by false desires, would cast off the chains of oppression and build true Liberty on firm foundations, the complexity of the problem, the peril of unleashed passions, the fact that knowledge and constructive ability as well as humanitarian enthusiasm were required of the builders, the unregenerate will of mankind in the mass—all faded from his mind. He remembered only the virtues of his northern dalesmen and

> saw in rudest men
> Self-sacrifice the firmest, generous love
> And continence of mind, and sense of right
> Uppermost in the midst of fiercest strife.

And since the common man had also shown such virtues in all the heroic moments of history, they were surely a necessity of his nature as they were of Beaupuy's, were in fact the qualities by which he proved himself a true child of Nature.

It was easy thus falsely to simplify man, Nature, and history in Beaupuy's presence. For Beaupuy was a whole man. He was a true child of Nature in the sense that he was organic. His moral being was so pure that he had no need to deny any proud part of himself. That ceaseless struggle against his own imperfections without which the average man cannot hope to bring to birth within him the soul which makes him truly human, was hardly noticeable in Beaupuy. Doubtless he had waged it, but he had achieved such victory over himself that selflessness and moral stability had become literally a second nature to him. As such they seemed effortless and instinctive, and deluded such a young and eager onlooker as Wordsworth into the belief that they were the birthright of every man who was allowed to live his life 'according to nature.'

But such men, particularly of Beaupuy's rank in intelligence and knowledge, are exceedingly few. And it was as misleading to generalise from him as from the humble shepherd of the dales, or even from the past conduct of men in inspired moments of self-devotion to a cause. The fact that most men had fallen away from the unity of Nature into arrogance, greed, and self-will was, indeed, apparent enough in the France of 1792, and could even have been discovered in the faces and speeches of many of the 'Society of the Friends of the Constitution,' a Revolutionary Club at Blois whose meetings Wordsworth attended. But Beaupuy attended them, too, and in the serene radiance of his presence the envies and hatreds of lesser men, masked as they were by the language of idealism, were easily overlooked.

And so as Wordsworth walked with his friend in the wide forests of the neighbourhood, he could believe that it was Nature which was 'standing on the brink of some great trial' in which she would be gloriously vindicated rather than Man, who was to be weighed in the scales of a too easily assumed perfectibility and found wanting.

Occasionally, indeed, his too facile faith in the creative will of the popular party was tested, as it had been at Chartreuse, by the spectacle of rudely dismantled convents, while he could not help being touched to sentimental regret by the many picturesque reminders of the past glories of the French Kings and the Feudal Ages. Beaupuy did not share such regrets, and at times Wordsworth found himself rebelling against the Quakerish single-mindedness of his friend.

But the charm of the past counted for little against the promise and even more, perhaps, the miseries of the present. For wherever he went he saw the poverty and degradation which the old regime had countenanced. And when at the sight of a hunger-bitten girl Beaupuy would say in agitation, 'It's against *that* that we are fighting,' the deep love of the peasant which was so intimately Wordsworth's through his upbringing

as to be almost self-love, would rise up within him and consecrate a cause which promised the speedy end of such in-
human destitution. All feelings for the past were swallowed
up then in his hopes for the future, and in the belief which
Beaupuy so zealously, yet temperately, fostered that soon

> we should see the earth
> Unthwarted in her wish to recompense
> The meek, the lowly, patient child of toil,
> All institutes for ever blotted out
> That legalised exclusion, empty pomp
> Abolished, sensual state and cruel power,
> Whether by edict of the one or few;
> And finally, as sum and crown of all,
> Should see the people having a strong hand
> In framing their own laws; whence better days
> To all mankind.

At the end of July, however, Beaupuy left with his regiment for
Alsace, never to return. He went at the exact moment when
the Revolutionary Movement was about to pass into its
extreme phase. On 10th August, as a result of the increased
threat of foreign invasion, the king was dethroned, and early
in September the massacre of prisoners occurred at Orleans
which first clearly exposed the savage forces that underlay the
professions of humanitarian idealism. The effect of this event
upon Wordsworth must have been considerable, if Beaupuy
had not just raised him to a pitch of exalted Republicanism
from which through the years that followed he was gradually
and bitterly to decline.

Earlier in the year, before Beaupuy's influence had come
into play, he had, indeed, uneasily remarked that 'the approaching summer will undoubtedly decide the fate of France.' But
Beaupuy's selfless courage had made fear seem disloyalty to

the New World and the New Man that were to be born. And so, although he was grieved in particular by the massacre of the Swiss Guards, he regarded the incident as a lamentable but ephemeral lapse, or rather, perhaps, as a cruel birth-pang which was past and to be speedily forgotten in the joy of the New Earth that had sprung to life. The defeat, too, of the Prussians at Valmy a fortnight later made it easier to think that the heavens condoned the offence.

Yet although Beaupuy had given to his instinctive faith just that rational and personal verification which it needed to become a real conviction; and although in consequence he held to it with a characteristic tenacity that even the worst acts of violence could not for a long time shake, his friend's departure coincided with the peak of his romantic intoxication, and from that time the prudence, which was such a strong element in his make-up, gradually reasserted itself against the wild impulse for self-dedication.

The ecstatic hour was over, and the first sign of it was the anxiety which began to shadow his love for Annette. Ever since he knew that she was with child his bliss must have been 'uneasy.' But in the new world of Beaupuy's vision illegitimacy seemed rather a natural virtue than a social disqualification. There was even something heartening in the fact that their love challenged the old order. But with Beaupuy's going he was less able to view his personal feeling and his personal problem in the light of the future freedom of mankind. It was not only that the ambiguity of his standing chafed and humiliated him as a lover who wished to claim his mistress in the eyes of the world, and that it placed her in a trying position at the very time when everything should have been easy for her; but at heart, despite all his Revolutionary enthusiasm, he regarded marriage much as his old dame and her like at Hawkshead did, as a necessary institution and the seal of respectability.

Yet although Annette was already making preparations for her infant's arrival, he held back from marrying her until circumstances were more propitious. And certainly they could hardly have been less so. For Annette's family no longer favoured the Revolution, and were unlikely to welcome an alliance with a young foreigner of unknown origin and prospects who did. Wordsworth himself was nearly at the end of his resources, and was as disinclined to bind himself to a profession as when he set out for France.

He had, indeed, written to Mathews in May that he intended to take Orders in the approaching winter or spring. But in the same letter he had suggested that they should engage together in any literary plan, 'which may have the appearance of producing a decent harvest.' He had in fact been living from moment to moment, buoyed up by the inspiration of first love, of Beaupuy's friendship, and his hopes for man. But now as that inspiration began to fail he was no longer capable of the recklessness which had thrown him into Annette's arms. He could not marry her, he argued, without appealing to his guardians for money. And distressed as they already were by his apparent irresponsibility, they were certain to make it a condition of any advance that he should bind himself to a profession.

And that bondage he still refused. Deeper in him than his love for Annette was his sense of his poetic mission and the independence necessary to it. It may even have been that already he unconsciously realised that to tie himself to Annette by marriage would be fatal to the unfolding of a more essential self than that which was still enslaved by her vivacious charms. He was not of course aware of any such selfish motive. He believed that he longed ardently to marry her, and that he would do so as soon as the worst obstacles were removed. But he could have married her secretly, if necessary, as he had loved her, to ease her mind, without immediately adding to his

H

obligations. And it was probably at bottom his ingrained instinct for self-preservation which prevented him now, as at other danger points in his life, from sacrificing prudence to generosity.

In August Annette decided to return to Orleans. Her condition was so advanced that it could no longer be concealed, and she naturally preferred to move to a town where she was little known. Wordsworth followed her early in September, and was there during the massacre of the prisoners. He did not wait, however, for the birth of the child, but at the end of October left Orleans for Paris. Doubtless he wished to escape from the burden of his personal feelings which could find no active expression. And in Paris, where the Tuileries had been lately stormed and the king and queen were imprisoned, where the Revolution had entered on its third legislative stage with the opening of the Convention, and the Republic had been declared, he could forget his private anxieties in his public hopes and the general excitement.

Yet as he lay in bed in a high room near the roof of his hotel, reading by candle-light, even these began to tremble before the deep disquiet in himself. The 'fear gone by' pressed on him 'like a fear to come.' At a distance the September massacres became a substantial dread, and the violent revolutions instead of the heroic endurances of history haunted his mind. Was it merely through overwrought fancy or a true premonition that he seemed to hear a voice crying to the whole city, 'Sleep no more'? Suddenly the quiet hush of night bristled with dangers and he felt it as rash to sleep as if he was in a wood infested with tigers.

And although next morning his terror seemed fantastic, they received some confirmation that very day by the news of Robespierre's personal triumph over Louvet in the Convention. From this time, indeed, he began to see that the Revolution was no longer a simple struggle between reactionary Royalists and humanitarian 'patriots,' but that a deep split was developing in the popular party itself between the moderates and the extremists.

It seems probable[1] that he actually lodged in the same house in Rue Gretry as Brissot, the leader of the Girondins or Moderate Party, who numbered among his friends many of the most prominent English and American Liberals, and to whom Wordsworth carried a letter of introduction from Charlotte Smith, the novelist. He, it probably was, who enabled Wordsworth a year before to attend a meeting of the National Assembly, and doubtless he profited now by Brissot's inside knowledge of the growing power of the violent Jacobin faction. To this, as much as to his sobering vision, he must have owed his sudden awakening to the fact of the oncoming Terror, his horrified realisation that the September massacres were not an accident but a portent, and that unless the temperate idealists could develop a will-power equal to that of their intoxicated rivals, Liberty, Life, and Death would soon lie in the hands of a mob of ruthless realists.

And before long he knew in his heart that the Girondins would be defeated. Like all who are ready to temporise and to compromise they lacked the force and determination of their fanatical opponents. And Wordsworth felt the fatality of their position the more painfully because he was distressed by his own indecision. He, too, in his relations with Annette, was torn between prudence and recklessness. And although the news which he received in November of the birth of a daughter relieved his immediate anxiety, it only emphasised his responsibility and his uneasiness at evading it. All he could do was to acknowledge the child as his when she was

[1] I owe this fact to the industrious research of Professor James R. MacGillivray.

baptised in the following month, and repeat his promises to
Annette.

He stayed on in Paris to the utmost limit of his resources,
and even felt a wild impulse to make 'common cause with some
who perished,' if only to prove in his person the sincerity of
his wish that those who were reasonable enough to deserve
liberty might come from all corners of the world to save
France from the fanatics who threatened to ruin her. He even
pictured himself as a man of Destiny, a saviour seizing the right
moment to direct forces, already getting out of hand, into the
right channel.

For the fate of nations, he recalled, had so often hung
upon a single person. Man was only weak and violent
through his mistrust and want of hope. Given heroic
desires and circumspection, no cause could fail. And might
not he, with Brissot as his lieutenant, rally the Moderate
Party and form an active centre which would attract to it
all men of good will in whom these lofty qualities only lay
latent and who were ready to respond to firm and inspired
leadership?

For Beaupuy's confidence in the ultimate issue and the justice
of the basic principles of the Revolution was still in the abstract
his. Tyrannic power must always be weak because it was selfish.
It lacked the great sustaining forces of gratitude and faith and
love, which it could not evoke. And surely the purpose of God
could never utterly be perverted or denied. Surely it was
written in the book of life

> That nothing hath a natural right to last
> But equity and reason; that all else
> Meets foes irreconcilable, and at best
> Lives only by variety of disease.

Yet such arguments were no longer as convincing as when he

heard them from Beaupuy's lips. For he was haunted now by
the knowledge of the selfishness not only in the Revolutionary
Party, but in himself. How was he by 'the virtue of one
paramount mind' to abash the impious, quell outrage and
bloody power, and clear a passage for just government when
his own mind was torn by private indecision and he, too, lived
only 'by variety of disease'?

Both his impulse, therefore, to join actively with the
Brissotins and his abandonment of the idea were dictated less,
perhaps, by revolutionary zeal than by a sort of reckless desperation with himself. For distracted as he was by the fever of love
and the burden of its consequences he had inevitably lost that
singleness of being which had been since childhood his pride
and pleasure.

Prudence, however, and necessity saved him at least from
making 'a poor mistaken and bewildered offering' of himself
on the altar of his own distraction, and Dorothy, although
still ignorant of his private complications, was yet right in
thinking that he was 'wise enough to get out of the way of
danger.' And this, early in January 1793, he did, when he
returned to London.

Yet if thereby he escaped sharing the fate of the Brissotins
who went to the guillotine in the following autumn, his life
in more than a physical sense had come under the shadow of
death. For in France he had lost his integrity and entered the
path of compromise. Deep down within him he felt that he
had been false to his truer and purer being. If he could have
candidly faced the fact and humbled himself before it, he might
have expelled its poison from his blood. But although inwardly humiliated, he was not humbled. And so the furies of
perplexity, shame, and remorse were already on his track.
Through the next few years they were to infest his nights and
days. And by resisting and suppressing them he was to
strengthen the defensive egotism which had saved him

indeed from returning with the Brissotins 'to the breast of Nature,'

> With all my resolutions, all my hopes,
> A Poet only to myself, to men
> Useless,

but which was to curtail sadly his development both as a poet and a man.

PART IV

THE STATE OF SIN

§ 1

WORDSWORTH'S immediate intention on returning to London was to come to terms with his guardians, as he had promised Annette, and to publish his two poems, *An Evening Walk* and *Descriptive Sketches*. The latter might at least do something to justify, in his own eyes, if not in his guardians', his claim to poetic privileges. They were hastily printed, and appeared probably before the end of February 1793, without, however, bringing their author either the money or the fame for which he had hoped.

But meanwhile events had moved fast in France. On 21st January the king had been beheaded. Yet still the Revolutionary leaders in their declarations and some of their acts seemed to be guided by humanitarian and liberal ideals, while there were many examples of noble self-sacrifice and devotion. On 1st February, however, France, provoked beyond endurance by foreign hostility, declared war on England and Holland, and on the 11th England declared war in return.

Wordsworth was later to claim that this event shook his moral nature to its foundations, that it threw him for the first time 'out of the pale of love,' and soured and corrupted his feelings upward to the source. Yet he admitted that he had not doubted that this day would come, and despite his absence from England he must have known that English feeling, inflamed by Burke, had become very hostile and French resentment of foreign interference very pronounced. But he had clung, in defiance of his gloomier premonitions, to his belief that the Revolution was an organic movement which would advance inevitably, and without any serious relapses, to its final fulfilment; and his very preoccupation with the perils of internal faction had blinded him to external developments.

Consequently the shock, if not so immediate in its effects as he later suggested, was profound. He felt

> The ravage of this most unnatural strife
> In my own heart; there lay it like a weight
> At enmity with all the tenderest springs
> Of my enjoyments.

It was not merely that the French had been driven to dishonour the cause of Liberty with 'fire and sword,' that his dream of a new world emerging pacifically and persuasively from the crust of the old was, temporarily at least, shattered. What amazed and horrified him was the fact that England was now ranged openly against the Revolution. For in her his deepest instincts were rooted, and even while he was indulging in his wildest dreams in France he had written to Mathews — 'You have the happiness of being born in a free country, where every road is open, and where talents and industry are more liberally rewarded than amongst any other nation of the universe.'

His very blindness to the dangers implicit in the Revolutionary Movement from the start was in a large measure due to his assumption that the 'Liberty' which the French patriot preached was only a loftier extension of the liberty which the Englishman enjoyed as a native right, that Rousseau was only a more fervent and mellifluous Shaftesbury, and that the new world would be the child of Gallic ardour and English moderation.

And now the country which had been the pioneer of Liberty and which by her sympathy might have tempered the violence of French fanaticism, had joined the reactionary forces. Remembering Beaupuy he could not but hate his country and even rejoice in its defeat in battle. And yet the necessity made him wretched. He could argue that such apostasy from an ancient faith was really conversion to a higher creed. But his love of England was something other than an abstract appreciation of her history. It was a love of her mountains and woods, of her fields and lakes, and of the staunch manhood and womanhood which she nourished. It was the love of a son for a perfect mother, the love of a plant for the soil in which it has grown.

Loving thus, as he did, the sight of a village steeple, the gratification of feeding on the day of vengeance yet to come when he sat in the congregation, like an uninvited guest, and heard prayers offered up for victory, was bitter enough. And it was the more bitter because at heart he had ceased to be sure that France would realise the 'higher creed' which she had so enthusiastically professed. In a sympathetic world she might have done so. But a hostile world had already driven her to deny her higher self, dragging her down to its own self-interested level where her violence seemed to justify the opposition which had engendered it.

The declaration of war, then, between England and France so intensified the warfare between the positive and negative impulses in Wordsworth himself that it reduced him almost to a state of inner chaos. He felt like a leaf torn from a tree and tossed about by whirlwinds. Not only his most tenacious instincts as an Englishman were opposed to his most ardent hopes for mankind, but his problem as a lover and a father was greatly complicated.

The war, so long as it lasted, separated him from Annette. If he had been single-minded in his intention to return to marry her, this enforced delay would not have been so painful. But, as it was, it prolonged for month after month the tortuous conflict between his desires, his conscience, and his caution, of which he was only beginning to be aware, but which, as time and distance cooled his ardour, filled him with increasing shame and remorse.

Nor could he look for any sympathy from his family with

the exception, of course, of Dorothy. To her he had confided everything on his return, and she had at once adapted the domestic idyll of which she had so long dreamed to the new circumstances, grafting on to the retired life in a small cottage, which she and William were to share together as 'the happiest of human beings,' a wife and child who would enhance the charms of the roses and honeysuckle with which it was to be wreathed.

But although she wrote affectionately forthwith to Annette, she hesitated to impart the facts to her clerical Uncle Cookson, as her brother had suggested she should, and Annette agreed with her that they should be concealed as long as possible. This must have been a sore disappointment to her, since her lover had promised on parting to come to terms with his guardians without delay. But she neither complained nor reproached and she insisted that, although her 'distress would be lessened were we married,' he was to run no risks.

Nevertheless her long and frequent letters could not but torture Wordsworth. For to him their reiterated appeal— 'Come back and marry me'—must have been in itself a reproach, although it was accompanied by expressions of perfect confidence 'in the unalterable feelings of my dear William,' and assurances that 'I cannot be happy without him, I long for him every day.'

The very reasonableness, however, of such letters, in which there was no explicit blame and no appeal for anything but himself, must have intensified Wordsworth's sense of the false position in which he stood. And if in their manner they sometimes reflected the languishing sentimentality of the novels of the time, they spoke only the more movingly to one whose romantic sensibility was still adolescent and who was still too much involved in the fond and generous nature of their writer to criticise their style.

Thus Annette would tell him how as she held his daughter,

Caroline, 'Her little heart often beats against mine; I think I am feeling her father's.' And again and again she described how, when alone, she dreamt that 'William was going to walk in, how she stood ready to throw herself in his arms, to have her tears dried by him, before she brought him to their daughter.' And then how bitterly she awoke to cold actuality. 'I do not see him, my child's father; he is very far from me.'

Only a callous nature could have failed to suffer deeply with the writer of such letters. And despite the doubts which had begun to whisper in his heart Wordsworth was still as much in love with Annette as he was with the Revolutionary Cause. Moreover, as he wrote later in *Vaudracour and Julia*, he

> Was of a loyal spirit, a conscience nice
> And over tender for the trial which
> His fate had call'd him to.

He had, in fact, nothing of the light lover in him, and yet outwardly he was acting just as any unscrupulous Lothario would. It is not surprising, therefore, that with every month that passed he paid for his self-love with more and more of self-hatred, and that his sensitiveness both to his own position and Annette's became increasingly morbid. As he was to write in *The Excursion*,

> For, like a plague, will memory break out;
> And, in the blank and solitude of things,
> Upon his spirit, with a fever's strength,
> Will conscience prey,—Feebly must they have felt
> Who, in old time, attired with snakes and whips
> The vengeful Furies. *Beautiful* regards
> Were turned on me—the face of her I loved;
> The Wife and Mother pitifully fixing
> Tender reproaches, insupportable!

> Where now that boasted liberty? No welcome
> From unknown objects I received; and those,
> Known and familiar, which the vaulted sky
> Did, in the placid clearness of the night,
> Disclose, had accusations to prefer
> Against my peace.

Yet although Annette's letters thus worked upon him, feeding that pity for forsaken women and afflicted lovers which was to haunt him for years and which he was to pour into so many of his poems, it was only when the war cut the last thread of their contact and even the relief of protesting his love and loyalty in letters was forbidden him, that desperation triumphed over hope. For then he was left wholly alone with his guilt and sorrow and dubious loyalty. He was an outcast from his family. For Dorothy had at last spoken to her uncle, with results as depressing as she had expected. He was separated equally from his own country and the France of his hopes. And an unbreakable silence had fallen between him and the woman whom he had loved and wronged.

Fortunately, however, London offered him some distraction and some proof that he was not the only 'ingenuous youth' in whose mind 'change and subversion' were at work. The publisher of his two poems was Joseph Johnson, whose shop was a favourite meeting-place of republicans and free-thinkers, among them Paine, Horne Tooke, and Godwin, whose *Enquiry concerning Political Justice* appeared in the same month that war was declared between England and France.

It was doubtless here that Wordsworth began to associate with other young Radicals and to imbibe that rationalism and necessitarianism which he was to use as a temporary prop during the earlier phase of his disillusionment.

Yet he did not succumb at once to Godwin's conception of a world in which abstract reason would ensure an abstract good.

For he was still a lover, if a tormented one, and although he could obtain some relief from his feelings by discussing Godwinism in Johnson's shop, he could not yet deny his feelings to the point of embracing it as an adequate philosophy. Instead between February and July he devoted himself to a task which enabled him to express his feelings positively and to lighten the burden of his impotence.

Early in 1793 a celebrated churchman, Bishop Watson of Llandaff, published a sermon on *The Wisdom and Goodness of God in having made both Rich and Poor*, to which he added a lengthy appendix in defence of the British Constitution and attacking both the ideas and the violent acts of the French Revolution. His pamphlet had the more success because he had been known previously as a broad-minded prelate and in consequence spoke for a great number of his countrymen who were liberal in theory and so long as their privileges were not seriously threatened, but whom the execution of Louis xvi had transformed from tepid sympathisers into frightened reactionaries.

For Wordsworth, therefore, he embodied the apostasy of the English nation from what he believed to be its traditional liberalism. And in composing a long reply to him he satisfied his deepest need, at once justifying his apparent disloyalty to his own country and reaffirming his faith in the Revolutionary Cause. Nothing which he ever wrote on the Revolution had the candour, conviction, and passionate eloquence of this tract. For it represented the last desperate assertion of his youthful faith over his growing doubt. And the self-interested sophistries of the turncoat bishop represented doubt in its most ignominious form.

In attacking such doubt he could forget his own deeper misgivings and excuse the violence which secretly alarmed him, claiming that Liberty was unfortunately 'obliged to borrow the very arms of Despotism to overthrow him, and, in order to reign in peace, must establish herself by violence. She deplores such stern necessity, but the safety of the people, her supreme law, is her consolation.' As to the appropriation of Church property he reminded his opponent that for the most part, 'with a servility which has prejudiced many people against religion itself, the ministers of the Church of England have appeared as writers upon public measures only to be the advocates of slavery, civil and religious,' and suggested that his sorrow for the French higher clergy 'will be diminished by recollecting the unworthy motives which induced the bulk of them to undertake the office, and the scandalous acts which enabled so many to attain the rank and enormous wealth which it has seemed necessary to annex to the charge of a Christian pastor.'

The influence of Godwin is apparent in such passages, but the essential tone of the pamphlet as a whole was quite distinct from that of *Political Justice*. It sprang from an enthusiastic faith not in the merely rational mind of man, but in all the simple human instincts, the will to virtue and happiness and kindly self-expression. Wordsworth still clung to his belief in the inherent goodness of man's natural instincts. Hence his ruthlessness towards monarchical and aristocratic privileges and every social institution or convention which thwarted the true unfolding of such instincts. But it was the ruthlessness, not of a political theorist or abstract reasoner, but of a primitive mystic, of one whose sense of the unity of the folk, as they lived close to impartial Nature, was outraged by the selfishly differentiated world of civilisation.

Because his faith had begun to waver, he had, indeed, begun also to rationalise it along the false Godwinian lines. For events in France and his own immediate past were painfully suggesting that human instincts were less to be trusted than the Lake Country had encouraged him to believe. And Godwin equally by rationalising human error and violence and by preaching salvation through rationalism seemed to offer him a way of preserving his faith while altering its terms of reference.

But neither in his *Letter to the Bishop of Llandaff*, nor for some months after its completion, had his faith in his deepest instincts declined so much that he was compelled to cling to Godwinism. Yet it is significant that despite the brave eloquence and generous fire, which he poured into his tract, he neither sent a copy to Bishop Watson nor ran the risk of publication. The risks were real in a time of panic when any act which could be described as seditious was liable to heavy punishment. But Wordsworth was as loath to become a martyr in England as in France, to go to prison with Priestley, Price, and Paine, as to the guillotine with the Girondins. He had written his 'letter' to silence his doubts by a defiant affirmation of faith. Powerless to act, he invoked the power of words.

Yet when he had finished 'performing the oath of his apostleship' in private and his mind and spirits were no longer at stretch, he must have known that only a part of himself had penned this fearless pamphlet. The negative self, which for a short time had been kept in abeyance, reasserted its claims, questioning his deed of faith. And it was perhaps for this reason more than any other that his *Letter to the Bishop of Llandaff on the Extraordinary Avowal of his Political Opinions* remained a secret to the end of his days.

§ 2

In July he sought another kind of relief, fleeing from London and all its political and intellectual ferment into the country. He went with a friend, William Calvert, and if, as seems possible, his overwhelming desire was to escape from all that might remind him of the ominous events of the day and return to the Nature of his childhood and youth, the Isle of Wight, to which he first went, was an ill-chosen refuge. For here, through a whole month of calm and glassy days he was offered the spectacle of the English fleet preparing for sea off Portsmouth, while as he walked each evening on the shore, the sunset cannon sounded its menace 'of woe to come' in his ears.

From there, late in August, he and Calvert planned to go from Salisbury over the Plain through the West of England and along the Wye by Tintern into Wales. Their plan, however, was upset by Calvert's horse, which dragged them and their carriage into a ditch. Calvert rode off on the horse and Wordsworth continued the journey on foot alone to the house of his friend Jones in Wales.

It proved a happy accident. For upon this solitary ramble over Salisbury Plain he received imaginative impressions the force of which, he claimed in old age, he had felt to that day. Alone on the trackless downs after so many months of inward conflict he suddenly experienced a miraculous appeasement. The tension relaxed, and he knew once again that influx of power and joy which Nature had vouchsafed to him in the days of his innocence.

But he knew it with a difference. For Nature was no longer all in all to him. Man, his history and his future, had engrossed his thoughts for nearly two years, and the vision which came to him, quickened though it was by the same primeval forces as of old, was one of savage men serving at the altar of elemental Nature. Doubtless the 'vestiges of ancient times,' the mounds and barrows which dotted the dreary plain, suggested this backward flight to a 'dim ancestral Past'; until he saw with startling clearness

> multitudes of men, and, here and there,
> A single Briton clothed in wolf-skin vest,
> With shield and stone-axe, stride across the wold;
> The voice of spears was heard, the rattling spear
> Shaken by arms of mighty bone, in strength,
> Long mouldered, of barbaric majesty.

> I called on Darkness—but before the word
> Was uttered, midnight darkness seemed to take
> All objects from my sight; and lo! again
> The Desert visible by dismal flames;
> It is the sacrificial altar, fed
> With living men—how deep the groans! the voice
> Of those that crowd the giant wicker thrills
> The monumental hillocks, and the pomp
> Is for both worlds, the living and the dead.

But it was no fanciful reconstruction of the past in which he indulged amid the solitude of Salisbury Plain. His experience of these sacrificial horrors was as imaginatively real as his earlier experiences of Nature's elemental terror. It may even be that in this moment of renewed possession by Nature dim atavistic memories surged up through the broken crust of his conscious mind. But it was his recent dread of the coming Terror in France which clothed them with such a vivid reality. Behind 'the sacrificial altar' was the guillotine; and when in another and happier 'waking dream' at Stonehenge he

> Beheld long-bearded teachers, with white wands
> Uplifted, pointing to the starry sky,
> Alternately, and plain below, while breath
> Of music swayed their motions, and the waste
> Rejoiced with them and me in those sweet sounds,

his vision was not simply of the Druids, but of the harmony which should succeed the Terror and the marriage of heaven and earth in the heart of emancipated Man.

During those three days, then, of wandering on Salisbury Plain, Wordsworth not only renewed for the time his sense of unity with Nature, but he discovered that Man and Nature had become far more closely intertwined in his consciousness. He

I

had a new, although still obscure, sense of their relation, a conviction, to quote his later words, that

> Nature for all conditions wants not power
> To consecrate, if we have eyes to see,
> The outside of her creatures, and to breathe
> Grandeur upon the very humblest face
> Of human life. I felt that the array
> Of act and circumstance, and visible form,
> Is mainly to the pleasure of the mind
> What passion makes them; that meanwhile the forms
> Of Nature have a passion in themselves,
> That intermingles with those works of man
> To which she summons him; although the works
> Be mean, have nothing lofty of their own;
> And that the Genius of the Poet hence
> May boldly take his way among mankind
> Wherever Nature leads; that he hath stood
> By Nature's side among the men of old,
> And so shall stand for ever.

This sudden realisation of the intimate connection between the elemental Nature which he loved and the heart and mind of all men, however humble, who were open to her inspiration and her guidance, banished for a time his dejection. He seemed to have sight of 'a new world,' a world less grandiloquently vague than that of which he had dreamed in France, and which was to be found 'in life's every day appearances,' and was fit

> To be transmitted and made visible
> To other eyes, as having for its base
> That whence our dignity originates,
> That which both gives it being and maintains
> A balance, an ennobling interchange

> Of action from within and from without,
> The excellence, pure spirit, and best power
> Both of the object seen, and eye that sees.

He ceased momentarily to be teased by thoughts of man as a political animal, as a Godwinian formula, or a Jacobin. He saw him suddenly simplified, standing in direct relation to the natural world rather than involved in movements and causes, battles, intrigues and bloodshed. He saw him with the poet's reawakened instinct for the universal in the particular, as a distinctive individual, not as that vague abstraction 'humanity' which the Revolution had dinned into his ears.

And his own outlook was correspondingly simplified. He was no longer caught in a net of complex transitory events. He was a poet again communing with eternal realities, one of those dedicated beings who,

> even as Prophets, each with each
> Connected in a mighty scheme of truth,
> Have each for his peculiar dower, a sense
> By which he is enabled to perceive
> Something unseen before.

Vaguely he had felt this five years before when vows were made for him as the sun rose over Hawkshead. But now he received a more distinct conception of what his poetic vocation was to be. He not only felt that 'in some sort' he possessed 'a privilege' and that a work of his,

> Proceeding from the depth of untaught things,
> Enduring and creative, might become
> A power like one of Nature's.

But dimly and gropingly he foresaw that the 'something unseen before' which he was destined to reveal was the relation

of man to Nature, the moral harmony which rewarded
obedience to Nature's ruling, and the discord which resulted
from rebellion.

He had at this time no more than an imaginative glimpse of
a correspondence between the creative spirit of Nature and the
noblest impulses of man. And, as we shall see, it did not
save him from accepting a year or more later Godwin's
unimaginative interpretation of both Nature and man. Nevertheless he had a remarkable prevision of his life-work as a
poet.

Indeed his life-work as a poet may be said to have begun
during these wanderings on Salisbury Plain. For it was then
that he began the first poem which was characteristically his.
It was entitled *The Female Vagrant*, and was published under
that title in the *Lyrical Ballads* of 1798. Later, however, its
thirty stanzas were incorporated with some modification in
Guilt and Sorrow. We cannot say how much of *The Female
Vagrant*, as it appeared in *Lyrical Ballads*, was written before
the end of 1793. That it was at least revised during the following year we know from Wordsworth's own statement, but it is
reasonable to suppose that during 1794 he was chiefly engaged
upon the forty-four stanzas which transformed *The Female
Vagrant* into *Guilt and Sorrow*. These, as we shall see, are in
places distinctly Godwinian, and may even have been suggested
by a reading of Godwin's *Caleb Williams*, which appeared in
that year.

But the original thirty stanzas, although they were dovetailed
into the longer narrative, owed little, if anything, to Godwin.
The Wordsworth who protests implicitly in them against social
tyranny and war is the disciple of Beaupuy rather than of
Godwin, and they constantly reflect his sufferings during the
months which preceded his vision on Salisbury Plain.

The Female Vagrant is, in fact, the first of his poems devoted
to the theme of the deserted woman. He stated many years

later that 'all that relates to her sufferings as a sailor's wife in America, and her condition of mind during her voyage home, were faithfully taken from the report made to me of her own case by a friend who had been subjected to the same trials and affected in the same way.' But this 'sailor's wife' was of the same order as the 'French lady' who was later so astonishingly cited as 'an eye-and-ear witness' of all that *Vaudracour and Julia* did and said. And in reality it was the remorseful lover of Annette who put into this story both his own sufferings and hers.

The cottage 'by Derwent side' with which the woman's story opens and upon which she looks back with such regret was but a variation of Wordsworth's own Hawkshead. It embodied the happy contentment from which he too was a wretched exile. The war which cast her adrift was the war which had separated him from Annette and decreed that 'homeless near a thousand homes I stood.' And it was of Annette and her letters that he was thinking when he wrote,

> Fondly we wished, and wished away, nor knew
> 'Mid that long sickness, and those hopes deferr'd,
> That happier days we never more must view.

His own recent sense of self-stultification, too, spoke in the lines —

> Oh! dreadful price of being to resign
> All that is dear *in* being.

And again, more precisely, in —

> But, what afflicts my peace with keenest ruth
> Is, that I have my inner self abused,
> Foregone the home delight of constant truth,
> And clear and open soul, so prized in fearless youth.

The stanza which preceded these lines defined even more exactly Annette's situation, as he imagined it—

> What could I do, unaided and unblest?
> Poor Father! gone was every friend of thine.
> *And kindred of dead husband are at best*
> *Small help, and, after marriage such as mine,*
> *With little kindness would to me incline.*
> Ill was I then for toil or service fit:
> With tears whose course no effort could confine,
> By high-way side forgetful would I sit
> Whole hours, my idle arms in moping sorrow knit.

Elsewhere he recorded his recent flight from London to Nature and solitude, and surely a moment of respite from foreboding which came to him in the Isle of Wight was remembered in the passage—

> The very ocean has its hour of rest,
> That comes not to the human mourner's breast,
> Remote from man, and storms of mortal care,
> A heavenly silence did the waves invest;
> I looked and looked along the silent air,
> Until it seemed to bring a joy to my despair.

Whether, then, *The Female Vagrant* was composed for the most part when he reached Wales from Salisbury or during the next seven or eight months, is an open question. But that some at least of it was written in 1793 seems from internal evidence very probable. And it is important to emphasise this because it shows how sudden and remarkable was the effect upon his work as a poet of his experience on Salisbury Plain. *The Female Vagrant* is of an entirely different order from *An Evening Walk* and *Descriptive Sketches*. It is, in fact, in the direct line to his later poems. In it for the first time he caught from the 'actual world of our familiar days'

> a tone,
> An image, and a character, by books
> Not hitherto reflected.

And he may even be said to have slowly groped his way back to the mood in which this poem was written after three years spent, partially at least, in the Godwinian wilderness.

Although he employed in it the complicated Spenserian stanza he avoided all the artifices and descriptive excesses which had marred his previously published poems. The language was plain and the narrative direct and dramatically concentrated. And the explanation of this sudden transformation in his writing was that he had found himself through his suffering. The story he told was his own, and there was too much pain in his heart for him to indulge in pictorial eccentricities or literary affectations.

Thus, long before he had developed any theories about poetic diction, life itself as he had experienced it dictated the kind of language which he was later to exalt in theory. And if *The Female Vagrant* was by virtue of its diction the first uniquely Wordsworthian poem, it was also this in its presentation of a humble character, the victim of man's cruelty to man, but preserving in herself a primitive nobility through her acceptance, beneath the 'perpetual weight which on her spirit lay,' of her desolate fate.

Here, indeed, was the first-fruit in poetry of the vision of Nature breathing 'grandeur upon the very humblest face of human life,' which had come to him on Salisbury Plain. But the immediate, though transitory, effect of this vision, if we are to believe the *Lines composed a Few Miles above Tintern Abbey*, was an intoxicated casting of himself upon the Nature which he had loved in youth and lost in France.

'Like a roe,' he wrote five years later,

> I bounded o'er the mountains, by the sides
> Of the deep rivers, and the lonely streams,
> Wherever nature led: more like a man
> Flying from something that he dreads than one
> Who sought the thing he loved. . . .

>   I cannot paint
> What then I was. The sounding cataract
> Haunted me like a passion: the tall rock,
> The mountain, and the deep and gloomy wood,
> Their colours and their forms, were then to me
> An appetite; a feeling and a love,
> That had no need of a remoter charm,
> By thought supplied, nor any interest
> Unborrowed from the eye.

But the love of Nature which he renewed on this memorable day at Tintern was of a different quality to that of his youth at Hawkshead and Cambridge. No longer was it a serene, entranced communion. No longer he 'sought the thing he loved' with an unquestioning certainty of Nature's response to his seeking. He was divided from her at heart, and so could only repossess her by an act of breathless violence. Hence his *aching* joys' and '*dizzy* raptures.' The pain of separateness haunted his longing for unity; it intensified his physical consciousness of pleasure and made his love an appetite that hungered for brief satisfaction before his gnawing conscience, the 'something' which he dreaded and from which he fled, should reawake and sunder him once again from the joy of life. Such was the mood of reckless flight from self which preceded his arrival at the house of his friend Jones at the end of August. And it makes it the more probable that in September he cast aside his prudence and embarked on a perilous adventure.

All the wild and generous elements in his nature had been roused and reinforced during his solitary tour through the West of England. Deliriously he had come to life again after months of living death. To accept again the burden of that deadly doubt and self-hate was intolerable. At any cost he must ease the conscience which was wasting him like an insidious disease. He must break through the wall of silence which encircled him and lay the ghost, that haunted his days and nights, of a forsaken woman, distraught by 'a thousand fears and hopes,' and contemplating, it might be, 'self-slaughter' as 'her only resting-place.' He must redeem his promise. He must return to Annette.

§ 3

In one of her letters Annette had written that she would be comforted even if Wordsworth should come to marry her and immediately return. And in *Vaudracour and Julia* we read that

> Vaudracour
> Persisted openly that nothing less
> Than death should make him yield up hope to be
> A blessed Husband of the Maid he loved.

Admittedly Wordsworth melodramatised his own story in *Vaudracour and Julia*. He did this not only to conceal the fact that it was his own story but to excuse himself. Thus he made Vaudracour a model of 'filial meekness,' which certainly he himself was not, and he drew a sensational picture of the cruel parental opposition which kept the lovers apart. He may, therefore, have equally romanticised his own feelings when he described Vaudracour's feverish passion to wed. Yet we can hardly doubt that this was a true rendering of one side of his nature during these harassing months of enforced separation, and so far as we can test the story, it follows in its main outlines the facts until the time of the lovers' second parting. We read, for example, that 'to conceal the threatened shame,' Julia moved from her home city to another, as Annette moved from Blois to Orleans, that there

>   the Lovers came
>   To this resolve, with which they parted, pleas'd
>   And confident, that Vaudracour should hie
>   Back to his Father's house, and there employ
>   Means aptest to obtain a sum of gold,
>   A final portion, even, if that might be,
>   Which done, together they would then take flight
>   To some remote and solitary place
>   Where they might live with no one to behold
>   Their happiness, or to disturb their love,

that the Youth returned home and

>   There remain'd a while without hint given
>   Of his design,

and that later he was seized and lodged in prison, after which came

>   A silence, half a circle did the moon
>   Complete, and then a whole, and still the same
>   Silence.

If for imprisonment we substitute the war which did imprison him, the parallel between his own story and that of *Vaudracour and Julia* is up to this point almost exact. May we then say the same of what follows? For the Youth regains his liberty (as

Wordsworth regained it in another sense at Tintern); he flies back to Julia, though in danger of his life.   And

> The Lovers thus
> United once again together lived
> For a few days,

until Vaudracour

> Learn'd that a mandate had been newly issued
> To arrest him on the spot. Oh pain it was
> To part! he could not—and he linger'd still
> To the last moment of his time, and then,
> At dead of night with snow upon the ground,
> He left the City, and in villages
> The most sequester'd of the neighbourhood
> Lay hidden for the space of several days.

Professor MacGillivray has recently[1] pointed out that the likelihood that Wordsworth was drawing upon his actual experience when he wrote 'with snow upon the ground' is supported by a record in the *Gentleman's Magazine* of temperature below freezing for several days at the end of October 1793, when he would have been finding his precarious way back to the French coast.

And he has discovered another even more suggestive coincidence. In *The Prelude* Wordsworth was to write that Beaupuy perished in 1793 in the Civil War in La Vendée, whereas, in fact, he fell at the battle of Elz on the Rhine frontier in 1796. The mistake, he suggests, is due to the fact that on 27th October 1793 in La Vendée,

> Upon the borders of the unhappy Loire,

[1] *Times Literary Supplement*, 12th June 1930.

Beaupuy was so severely wounded, that the rumour spread through the country-side that he was dead.

This battle was fought at Château-Goutier, about twenty miles north of the Loire, and in a district through which, being on the straight line from Paris to the Breton Coast and the Channel Islands, Wordsworth would be likely to be passing at the time, if he went to France. Equally likely is it that he passed on to the coast, before the mistake was corrected, while it is hardly possible that a rumour which can have persisted only for a few days and in a limited district could have reached him in North Wales or Cumberland. The fact, too, that he should have received news of his friend's death immediately after his second ignominious flight from Annette would fill the cup of his bitterness to the brim, and provide additional reason for the anguish of mind to which he confessed at the end of the year.

Carlyle's remark in his *Reminiscences* that about 1840, at a dinner-party in London, Wordsworth told him that he witnessed the execution of Gorsas, the first deputy sent to the scaffold, completes the slender chain of circumstantial evidence. But when we add to this the psychological evidence of Wordsworth's mood when he reached Wales at the end of August, and the complete reaction from it which he has suffered when next he clearly emerges from the ambiguous cloud which hangs over these autumn months, it is difficult not to believe that that second painful parting in *Vaudracour and Julia* had its counterpart in actual life.

Somehow, we imagine, Wordsworth contrived to reach Paris in September, to see with grief and horror the execution there, on 7th October, of Gorsas, the first of his Girondin friends to be sent to the scaffold, to struggle on to Blois or Orleans, where he spent a few days with Annette and her baby, and to return to the coast and England after having been warned by a friend that, as a sympathiser with the

Girondins and an Englishman, his life was in immediate
danger.

Whether he set out with the intention of hastily marrying
Annette or simply to reassure her of his fidelity and himself of
her welfare, can never be known. But it is, perhaps, significant
that when Vaudracour fled to Julia, he greeted her with the
words,

> 'All right is gone,
> Gone from me. Thou no longer now art mine,
> I thine; a Murderer, Julia, cannot love
> An innocent woman; I behold thy face,
> I see thee and my misery is complete.'

Or, in the later version,

> 'the conscience-stricken must not woo
> The unruffled Innocent.'

It is hardly, of course, to be supposed that Wordsworth
embarked on such a hazardous adventure to tell Annette that
he was compelled to forswear her. And the above lines may
have been simply a romantic invention like Vaudracour's act
of violence upon one of the ruffians who attacked him.

Yet we have seen that Wordsworth had passed through
months of a kind of self-murder during 1793. He had been
consumed by indecision, and if he set out for France in
September, it was in a desperate attempt to throw off the disease
by positive action. In Paris he witnessed an execution which
must have profoundly shocked him and confirmed his worst
fears. The abyss of the Terror was opening at his feet, and since
his passion for Annette was intimately linked up with his
Revolutionary dreams, it may well be that he reached Orleans
too 'conscience-stricken' to have any heart for love. And to
complete his discomfiture he found on his arrival there a

different Annette from her he had known and who had written such heart-rending letters.

During the preceding March Orleans had lain under a Terrorist regime and among some thirty persons unfairly suspected of participating in a monarchist plot was Annette's brother, Paul Vallon. Fortunately he had escaped arrest by flight, but the event had transformed his sister into a violent opponent of the Jacobins, and the house of the Vallons into a secret sanctuary for numberless persecuted emigrants and priests.

By thus devoting herself to others in worse misfortune than herself, Annette was less and less obsessed by her own trouble. Instead of indulging in sentimental laments, she was becoming a clever and courageous conspirator, to whom, for the time at least, the immediate dangers and demands of the political situation meant more than a distant and indecisive lover.

Under these circumstances it may well have been with Wordsworth as it was with Vaudracour:

I see thee and my misery is complete.

In Paris his hopes for man tottered; Orleans shattered his romantic dream of himself and Annette as lovers who, like a quickened earth, 'breathed in one great presence of the spring,' and whose passion was consecrated by the new dawn in which it had been consummated. The change in her may well have revealed to him the change in himself which for months he had been struggling to deny. And when in *Vaudracour and Julia* he wrote of the few days spent together by the reunited lovers that they were

> Days of dejection, sorrow and remorse
> For that ill deed of violence which his hand
> Had hastily committed,

he may have been recording the actual dejection which he experienced when the reunion achieved at such risk, far from renewing his wavering belief in the necessity of his love for Annette, convinced him that his impulsive surrender to passion had been an act of folly.

But whether this was so or not, his second flight from Annette must have been even more humiliating than the first. For although she had become a Counter-Revolutionary, she still believed that her lover intended to marry her. And as he struggled back to the coast through wintry weather, more deeply self-convicted now than ever of apostasy, numb with grief that Beaupuy, as he supposed, was dead, and fleeing from the onset of the Terror, the exaltations of Salisbury Plain and Tintern must have seemed delusive indeed.

'But here,' to quote from *Vaudracour and Julia*,

> A portion of the Tale may well be left
> In silence, though my memory could add
> Much how the Youth, and in short space of time,
> Was travers'd from without, much, too, of thoughts
> By which he was employ'd in solitude
> Under privation and restraint, and what
> Through dark and shapeless fear of things to come,
> And what through strong compunction for the past
> He suffer'd breaking down in heart and mind.

§ 4

But at this moment when he seemed to have lost everything, to be a craven to himself and an outcast from his kind, something beyond value was restored to him. Dorothy came to keep at bay the accusing image of Annette, to offer him a love which made no demands, which diverted his tormented feelings into a deep but safe channel, and which was to inspire the most mysterious and moving of his shorter lyrics.

On his return to England he probably spent some weeks with William Calvert near Keswick, and with another friend at Armathwaite, in the same neighbourhood. But in the middle of February 1794 at Mill House, near Halifax, he was reunited with Dorothy, and except for seven months in London in the following year, during which, significantly enough, he seems to have descended again to the depths of disillusionment, they were never again separated for any length of time until his death.

Dorothy's affection for her brother was inevitably deepened by her concern over his romantic misfortunes in France. Intensely ardent herself, she divined so well the forces which underlay his reserve, noting and adoring the 'sort of violence . . . which demonstrates itself every day, when the objects of his affection are present with him, in a thousand almost imperceptible attentions to their wishes, in a sort of restless watchfulness which I know not how to describe, a tenderness that never sleeps, and at the same time such a delicacy of manner as I have observed in few men.'

She apologised to her friend Jane Pollard for talking of him so much in her letters, admitting that 'my affection hurries me on, and makes me forget that you cannot be so much interested in the subject as I am. You do not know him; you do not know how amiable he is. Perhaps you reply, "But I know how blinded you are." Well, my dearest, I plead guilty at once; I *must* be blind; he cannot be so pleasing as my fondness makes him.'

Yet she gloried in her blindness, and the hostility of his other relations only heightened her devoted approval. In June 1793 she had written—'I cannot foresee the day of my felicity, the day on which I am once more to find a home under the same roof as my brother. All is still obscure and dark. . . . Oh, Jane, the last time we were together he won my affection to a degree which I cannot describe, his attentions to me were such as the most sensible of mortals must have been touched with.'

And Wordsworth himself in his letters to her abandoned completely his habitual reserve. 'Oh, my dear, dear sister,' he wrote, 'with what transport shall I again meet you! With what rapture shall I again wear out the day in your sight! So eager is my desire to see you that all obstacles vanish. I see you in a moment running, or rather flying to my arms.'

Even when allowance is made for the fashion of the time in parading sensibility, such letters as these suggest an unusually impassioned relationship between a brother and sister. And in *The Female Vagrant* there is a stanza which, except for one line, might well have been written by Dorothy—

> There was a youth whom I had loved so long,
> That when I loved him not I cannot say.
> 'Mid the green mountains many and many a song
> We two had sung, like little birds in May.
> When we began to tire of childish play
> We seemed still more and more to prize each
>   other:
> We talked of marriage and our marriage day;
> And I in truth did love him like a brother,
> For never could I hope to meet with such another.

Probably Dorothy was not consciously in Wordsworth's mind as he wrote these lines. Yet we believe this to be an early example of that unconscious intermingling of his love for her with his remorseful pity for Annette, the forsaken woman, which was to be so miraculously and imaginatively blended in

K

the 'Lucy' poems. And when in the following stanza he wrote—

> To him we turned:—we had no other aid.
> Like one revived, upon his neck I wept,
> And her whom he had loved in joy, he said
> He well could love in grief,

he may well have been transferring into the woman's story his own experience of reunion with Dorothy.

And to this may be added the probable testimony of two other short poems. After spending a short time together at Halifax, Wordsworth and Dorothy went to Whitehaven, and from there to a farm-house, called Windy Brow, near Keswick, in which William Calvert had offered them rooms. They walked the last thirty-three miles of the journey, and Dorothy was exultant. Wordsworth had decided to stay there until he got some employment, which for her opened up an indefinite prospect of shared delights.

For in a letter to Mathews who was travelling in the Mediterranean, having conducted himself more discreetly than his friend and previous counsellor, Wordsworth wrote—'I have done nothing, and still continue to do nothing. What is to become of me I know not. I cannot bow down my mind to take orders; and as for the law, I have neither strength of mind, purse, or constitution, to engage in that pursuit.'

The neat parlour, therefore, which Calvert had kindly set aside for their use, must have seemed to Dorothy to materialise the one which her fancy had so often furnished, and if her brother was hardly 'the happiest of human beings,' he shared her pleasure in calculating for how very small a sum they could live on a diet of milk for breakfast and supper, and potatoes for dinner. And when her aunt, Mrs. Crackenthorpe, reproved her for her unconventional way of life and in particular for rambling about the country on foot, she answered that the character and virtues of her brother were a sufficient protection, and that her right to enjoy his society was long overdue.

It seems very probable that her brother, too, replied to this reproof in verse. In his old age he attributed the poem *To a Young Lady who had been reproached for taking long walks in the Country* to 1805. But since it had appeared in the *Morning Post* in 1802 this was a mistake. Moreover, after 1795 both Dorothy and himself were free from the interference or reproaches of relatives, and the fact that he used the phrase 'Lapland night' which occurs in the last stanza of the poem, in a letter in 1791, also strengthens the probability that it was written at this time.

That the lines were addressed to Dorothy can hardly be doubted. And in them once again we find Wordsworth unconsciously relieving his contrition for the woman whom he had failed to make a wife, by blending her image with what was now the nearer and dearer image of his sister.

> Dear Child of Nature, let them rail!
> —There is a nest in a green dale,
> A harbour and a hold;
> Where thou, a Wife and Friend, shalt see
> Thy own heart-stirring days, and be
> A light to young and old.
>
> There healthy as a shepherd boy,
> And treading among flowers of joy
> Which at no season fade,
> Thou, while thy babes around thee cling,
> Shalt show us how divine a thing
> A Woman may be made.
>
> Thy thoughts and feelings shall not die,
> Nor leave thee, when grey hairs are nigh,
> A melancholy slave;
> But an old age serene and bright,
> And lovely as a Lapland night,
> Shall lead thee to thy grave.

Time was, indeed, to invest with a singular pathos the last stanza of this poem, expressing as it does the exact opposite of what Fate had in store for Dorothy.

But although we must allow for the element of poetic fiction, we cannot doubt that the lines expressed Wordsworth's feelings for her. He had, in fact, discovered in her his ideal of womanhood, and it was an ideal with which, he realised more and more, poor Annette, with her easy, superficial good nature and her French wit and manners, could not be made to conform. She could only enter as a haunting undertone into poetry which was, in fact, a tribute to another.

And in a second poem which, he admitted, was composed at the same time as *To a Young Lady*, the image of Dorothy completely predominated. It was entitled *Louisa—After Accompanying Her on a Mountain Excursion*, and the first two lines, as they appeared before a later revision, would seem also to have referred to Mrs. Crackenthorpe's reproof—

> Though by a sickly taste betrayed,
> Some will dispraise the lovely Maid,
> With fearless pride I say;
> That, nymph-like, she is fleet and strong,
> And down the rocks can leap along
> Like rivulets in May.
>
> And she hath smiles to earth unknown;
> Smiles, that with motion of their own
> Do spread, and sink, and rise;
> That come and go with endless play,
> And ever, as they pass away,
> Are hidden in her eyes.
>
> She loves her fire, her cottage-home;
> Yet o'er the moorland will she roam

In weather rough and bleak;
And, when against the wind she strains,
Oh! might I kiss the mountain rains
That sparkle on her cheek.

Take all that's mine 'beneath the moon,'
If I with her but half a noon
May sit beneath the walls
Of some old cave, or mossy nook,
When up she winds along the brook
To hunt the waterfalls.

The unusual metre which Wordsworth used in these two poems
but seldom elsewhere is, as Professor Harper has pointed out,
the same as that of *Three years she grew in sun and shower*, one of
the mysterious and haunting 'Lucy' poems. And the fact lends
support to our own conviction that 'Lucy' was not the early
unknown love which Professor Harper and others have been
at such pains to suggest, but an imagined being created out of
his real feelings for Dorothy and Annette.

Admittedly the later poems are elegies. But this only
strengthens our suggestion. In 1794 Wordsworth had received
from Dorothy a new revelation of womanhood and a love
which quickened, if it could not yet replenish, the springs of
his being. But his love for Annette still lived, although already
under sentence of death, and mingled with his wondering
delight in the nearness of a sister who in some sense healed
his divided being, because she was still the 'Nature's inmate'
that he once had been. In 1799, however, Annette as a lover
was dead for him, and so the 'Lucy' of the later poems was a
fit subject for elegy. As a living being she was Dorothy, but as
he mourned over her grave he was remembering a love that
had lived only to die and poison the roots of his being.

To this, however, we shall return later, and we have only

discussed the matter here at such length because it is important to realise from the beginning that Wordsworth's love for his sister had even deeper roots in his passionate nature than the love for Annette which it superseded. Unwittingly Dorothy helped to complete his disillusionment as a lover of Annette by the exquisiteness of her spirit and its close affinity to his own.

As day by day he came to love more the wild innocence and deep constancy of his sister's nature, the whole episode at Orleans seemed like a fever, caught in a strange and convulsed country from one who had fatally fascinated him. And it was not only a fever, but a fall. For he had eaten of the forbidden fruit. No longer could he trust his instincts; his conscience accused him of having been 'passion's slave,' and that secret dread of his physical impulses had awoken, which he was to betray when he wrote seven years later to John Wilson that 'some cannot tolerate a ghost or any supernatural agency in it; others would shrink from an animated description of the pleasures of love, as from a thing carnal and libidinous.'

Both Dorothy and Annette, therefore, were associated in his mind with his lost innocence. In the one he loved passionately the instinctively ecstatic being which he himself had been, and, because she was his sister, the only woman whom he could now dare to love without reserve. The other he at once pitied from his heart and shrunk from as the partner in his fall. And it was thus that the two loves became gradually fused in his imagination and were projected later into the ideal form of 'Lucy.'

§ 5

But if in 1794 Wordsworth relieved both his feelings and his conscience by centring his devotion upon his wonderful sister, he found in Godwinism an additional salve for his distress. He had, as we have said, begun to study Godwin a year before, but it was only now that he began seriously to adopt his philosophy.

And the reason was twofold. Godwin helped him to readjust his attitude both to Annette and the French Revolution. The two were, of course, intimately involved. His blind love for Annette and his blind faith in the Revolution had belonged to the same expansive hour. And now his growing sense of shame at remembrance of his surrender to passion coincided with his growing doubt of the Movement which he had so enthusiastically championed. Was it not equally true of himself as a lover and of the Revolutionary leaders that 'the most licentious theories were propounded, all restraints were broken, libertinism was law'?

Yet he clung tenaciously to his belief in Liberty, and Godwin, by championing Liberty in terms of the individual and self-regarding intellect instead of the generic and self-forgetful instincts, provided him with just the philosophy which he needed to preserve this belief and buttress his tottering self-respect. Godwin also championed free love, but on purely rational grounds. Marriage to him was an outworn prejudice, reinforced by religious sanctions which were meaningless to the dispassionate mind. If the marriage was a true one, it needed no binding contract or ceremony, while if it proved to be a false one, such a legal and religious contract merely perpetuated an error and prevented the parties to it from bringing reason to bear upon an irrational act. Moreover, no one could be reasonably held responsible for such irrational acts. For since they were irrational, they were dictated by necessity, by a confused association of ideas which might afflict even a man of the most exemplary habits.

Inevitably such logic appealed strongly to Wordsworth at this time. It helped him to view his love of Annette objectively as an irrational episode which it would be an additional folly to legalise by marriage. It strengthened all that was prudent and self-regarding in him against the pity and shame that gnawed at his heart. Godwin, in short, helped him to harden his heart by asserting his head, and he could even pretend to himself that to do so was a virtue. Just as Annette found in Counter-Revolutionary activity a means of forgetting her forlorn situation, Wordsworth used Godwin as a means of self-justification.

Yet Godwinism was so alien to his nature and upbringing that it is doubtful whether it penetrated beyond the suburbs of his mind until, early in 1795, his faith in the earlier ideals of the Revolution was finally shattered and the possibility of reunion with Annette was finally rejected. Until then he cultivated the doctrines of necessity as a mental antidote to painful feelings, but his heart still cherished the reason of its own for which Godwin had no place in his philosophy.

For the coming of Dorothy had revived in him temporarily the belief in Nature and the natural instincts which the parting from Annette had so deeply shaken. She at least justified his belief and in the beauty of her wild vitality and ardent affection made Godwinism seem the pale phantom of reality that in fact it was. And so although France, attacked from outside, had gone mad and the violence which he had foreseen and dreaded was unchained, his hopes 'did still outlast the shock' and 'were flattered and had trust in man.'

At the same time he inevitably suffered deeply. His thoughts by day and dreams by night were often miserable, and for months and even years after the atrocities of the Terror his sleep was broken by ghastly visions, in which he pleaded hopelessly before unjust Tribunals and was betrayed and deserted in the last place of refuge—his own soul.

Yet he was so reserved that few, perhaps, would have guessed the pain at his heart. For, to quote his own words in *Guilt and Sorrow*—

As one whose brain habitual phrensy fires
Owes to the fit in which his soul hath tossed
Profounder quiet, when the fit retires,
Even so the dire phantasma which had crossed
His sense, in sudden vacancy quite lost,
Left his mind still as a deep evening stream,
Nor, if accosted now, in thought engrossed,
Moody, or inly troubled, would he seem
To traveller who might talk of any casual theme.

And in the very violence of the times the elemental being in him found a sort of inspiration, akin to that which he had felt when the storm drove across the Lakeland hills. Moreover, he was sustained by the conviction that the enormities in France were not, as the reactionaries argued, the fruit of popular government and equalitarian theories, but rather of the accumulated guilt and ignorance of ages. The Terror was not so much a manifestation of the inherent viciousness of the natural man as a ghastly but inevitable purgation for the past sins of unnatural men.

Nevertheless, when on a day of still sunshine late in August 1794, as he was crossing Ulverston Sands, he heard from a chance traveller that Robespierre had fallen, he experienced the first moment of intense happiness that he had known since he ran wild at Tintern. Surely the period of bitter purgation was now over, the Utopia of which he had dreamed might still be realised and eternal justice vindicate her claims. The calm spaciousness of the sands, from which the menacing sea had ebbed almost out of sight and across which he had so often galloped as a joyous and fearless boy, seemed to confirm his sudden wild hope that the day of mad fanatics was over, and that earth would now 'march firmly towards righteousness and peace.' And in the exultancy of the moment he broke into a hymn of triumph, crying, 'Come now, ye golden times,'

> as the morning comes
> Out of the bosom of the night, come Ye!

In the months that followed, however, the 'golden times' showed little sign of responding to his invitation. Certainly the worst of the Terror was over. 'Authority put on a milder face,' and the victory of the young Republic in its defensive wars heartened him, so long as he could believe that it portended the higher victory of justice and reason in an ensuing peace. Whatever justice or reason, too, underlay the prejudice of the opponents of the Revolution was concealed from him by the persecution to which every radical or free-thinker was now exposed in England. With Madame Roland he might lament the crimes committed in the name of Liberty, but these at least had a sort of elemental necessity, while the banishment of such idealists as Muir and Palmer to Botany Bay or the imprisonment of Hardy, Horne Tooke, Thelwall or Priestley, were acts of petty tyranny by those who were too anxious to preserve their own unjust privileges and vested interests to tolerate either candid criticism or constructive ideas.

Yet the fact, now painfully apparent, that the 'throwing off oppression must be work as well of license as of liberty' had inevitably weakened his belief in the readiness of men to reflect the beneficent inspiration of Nature. He had, he realised, approached 'the shield of human nature from the golden side.' Clearly one could not trust merely in man's instinctive or emotional response to the creative forces which governed the natural world. He was capable of error and perversity, and passionate impulse might as often prove destructive as creative.

It was necessary, therefore, to prevent and correct the possible errors of instinctive impulse by Reason, and by

Reason which was no longer most real when, in subordination
to the instincts, she was

>   most intent on making of herself
>   A prime enchantress,

but when she sought to understand and critically direct the
passional self.

And this modification in his view of human nature was
inevitably accompanied by a more restricted and concrete
conception of the new world which was coming into being.
He no longer saw the whole earth miraculously transformed
into a paradise in which men and women sought each other's
good with an effortless love that gushed from the liberated
spring of their essentially innocent natures. The prospect was
narrowed down to one in which selfishness and unreason strove
with kindly impulse and in which constructive helpers

>   Were called upon to exercise their skill,
>   Not in Utopia, — subterranean fields, —
>   Or some secreted island, Heaven knows where!
>   But in the very world, which is the world
>   Of all of us — the place where, in the end,
>   We find our happiness, or not at all!

And before the end of 1794 even this humbler prospect was
closed to him.

The cause of this second and fatal shock to his earlier hopes
was the manifest fact that Revolutionary France was embarking
on a war, not of self-defence with which he could sympathise,
but of conquest. Necessity in fact dictated this change of
policy. For after the fall of Robespierre the Thermidorians
had a starving army on their hands, and the only way to feed it
was to send it beyond the frontiers to feed upon other nations.

To Wordsworth, however, who was not Godwinian enough

to admit that necessity, in Revolutionary politics as in the life
of the individual, might overrule moral responsibility, this
change from self-defence to external aggression seemed a final
denial of the pacific and humanitarian ideals which the Revolu-
tionaries had originally championed. The earlier declaration of
war between England and France had torn him in two. But
this dealt a death blow to all the faith and hope which had
survived that inner conflict. He was, in his own words,
compelled to exclaim

> As Brutus did to virtue, 'Liberty,
> I worshipped thee, and find thee but a Shade!'

And ironically enough it was through despair and disgust
at this necessitarian event that he turned for private consolation
to Godwin's philosophy. What had previously been merely a
secondary support became early in 1795 his only prop. Amid
the ruin of his heart's desires he took refuge in this coldly
abstract structure of the mind. He had already, as we have
seen, come to admit the need of constructive Reason in the life
of instinct. But Godwin offered him an Intellect that was wholly
independent and dispassionate, which regarded, like a privileged
spectator, the convulsions of instinctive and emotional impulse
and explained them to its own perfectly logical satisfaction.

Had he not written in his *Enquiry Concerning Political Justice*
that 'he, who regards all things past, present, and to come as
links of an indissoluble chain, will, as often as he recollects this
comprehensive view, be superior to the tumult of passion; and
will reflect upon the moral concerns of mankind with the same
clearness of perception, the same unalterable firmness of
judgment, and the same tranquillity as we are accustomed to do
upon the truths of geometry?'

To Wordsworth, whose reflections upon the moral concerns
of mankind were now those of a despairing bewilderment, so

superior and assured a standpoint seemed enviable indeed. He had had enough of the tumult of passion, the agony of faith betrayed and hope deferred and love disproved. Inevitably he failed to see that Godwin's detachment from life was fatal to a true understanding and realisation of its meaning. Godwin did at least provide a specious, if sterile explanation of a world in which everything had become morally meaningless. He offered a platform from which those who could accept his self-satisfied logic could view with unconcern the madness of the people, whether reactionary or revolutionary. And in face of the apparent bankruptcy of humanity he seemed to restore to the harassed individual a measure of rational confidence and self-respect.

§ 6

But we must return for a moment to the spring of 1794, when we left Wordsworth reunited with Dorothy at a farm-house near Keswick. His delight in her company was tempered by the fact that he was almost penniless, and when in the early summer it was suggested that he should act as companion to William Calvert's brother, Raisley, who was stricken with consumption, and who offered him also a share of his income, he readily complied and moved forthwith to the Calverts' house at Greystoke, near Penrith. He was also invited to accompany Raisley later in the year to Lisbon, where he was ordered for his health and he learnt that his charge, knowing his return to be uncertain, had left him in his will all his real and personal property subject to a possible legacy to his brother.

This generous act, testifying as it did both to the Calverts' affection and to their belief in his gifts, was very heartening, and it put him, he felt, 'under an obligation of trying to be of some little service' to his fellow-men. Tied as he was to the country, his opportunities were limited, but he wrote to his friend Mathews in London suggesting that they should combine in editing a radical magazine to be called *The Philanthropist, a Monthly Miscellany.*

The tone of his letters to Mathews was almost as magisterial as of old, but while proclaiming that he was 'of that odious class of men called democrats, and of that class I shall for ever continue,' he also severely condemned 'all inflammatory addresses to the passions of men, even when it is intended to direct those passions to a good purpose. I know that the multitude walk in darkness. I would put into each man's hand a lantern to guide him.'

Doubtless the wick of this lantern was borrowed from Godwin, although the oil that fed it was still his own faith in the ability of the multitude to respond to the light and ensure 'the progress of human improvement.' He admitted, however, his ignorance of and probable incapacity for journalism and confessed, too, to be subject to violent headaches, so that he was not unduly disappointed when by November 1794 the scheme had been abandoned.

And meanwhile he had resumed the activity in which he was really fitted to be of service to his fellow-men. He had enlarged *The Female Vagrant* into *Guilt and Sorrow.* His motive, now, was far more mixed than when he wrote the original stanzas which composed *The Female Vagrant.* The experience which had come to him on Salisbury Plain of primitive man emerging from primeval Nature had for the time lost much of its imaginative hold upon him. It had been dimmed by the stress of contemporary political and social thought. And in *Guilt and Sorrow* his conscious aim was to do in verse what he had suggested to Mathews he should do in prose. He set out upon his task not as a disinterested poet, creating life out of his own experience and as his imagination conceived it, but with the intention of 'explaining and enforcing those general principles of the social order, which are applicable to all times and to all places.' And one at least of his immediate objects was 'to expose the vices of the penal law, and the calamities of war, as they affect individuals.'

Guilt and Sorrow was not published for forty years, and then in a modified form. We know, for example, that as originally written it ended with a strong condemnation of legal vengeance and capital punishment, and that its attacks on war and the oppression of the poor by the rich were far more pronounced. Yet even as we have it, it is in parts definitely an indictment of society which conditions the sins of individuals naturally good and then punishes them for crimes for which it is itself responsible.

This explanation of crime and punishment, although it might equally be described as Voltairean or Rousseauistic, is certainly Godwinian, and particularly in its contention that man's moral nature was at the mercy of circumstance, that oppression and injustice could transform even a virtuous man into a criminal and that such a man was not responsible for his actions. The sailor of the poem who in a fit of desperation induced by his sufferings at the hands of society robbed and murdered a traveller, was, we are told, by nature

mild and good;
Never on earth was gentler creature seen.

To this extent the poem may be said to be Godwinian. But its real significance, for the light it throws on Wordsworth at this time, is that this conscious necessitarian doctrine influenced only the scheme and parts of the surface of the poem. Within and beneath these was a deep undertone of genuine, primitive feeling, alien to Godwin's rationalism, and also of moral sensibility which contradicted his necessitarianism.

Those in fact who, like Professor Garrod, assert that 'the dominating conception of the poem is essentially necessitarian' and consider it 'a thoroughly Godwinian story,' are concentrating upon its outline to the neglect of its inner substance. They are making the same mistake as Hazlitt, who described the famous lines in *Tintern Abbey*,

> A motion and a spirit, that impels
> All thinking things, all objects of all thought,
> And rolls through all things,

as perfectly expressing 'the doctrine of what has been called philosophical necessity;' or as Professor Beatty, who agrees with Hazlitt, and multiplies parallels to show that Wordsworth as a poet was constantly paraphrasing either Godwin or Hartley.

But Wordsworth was too real a poet to paraphrase, except in an occasional passage, the ideas which he borrowed from the fashionable thinkers of his time. As these ideas passed through him they were subtly transformed by his imagination and his personal feeling for life. And just as the three lines from *Tintern Abbey* quoted above expressed a mystical realisation of the creative principle immanent in all things which was of a different order from Godwin's abstract doctrine of philosophical necessity, so *Guilt and Sorrow* on a far humbler level reveals Wordsworth expressing his own immediate sense of life and of primitive character in a poem which owes only its plot and to some extent its social and political emphasis to Godwin.

Although, therefore, it may be that Godwin's novel *Caleb Williams* suggested the central idea and character of *Guilt and Sorrow*, it was Wordsworth's own experience which made such a situation real to him.

He, too, in his own eyes, was 'a man previously of the most exemplary habits,' who had committed an act which haunted his conscience. The guilt and sorrow of the sailor were his own. He too was a fugitive from the remembrance of his own fatal passion and his lost integrity. The very path which the sailor pursued 'On the Skirt of Sarum's Plain' had been his, and his had been the desolation without and within. It was his own sympathy for Annette, too, which 'the Sailor's looks expressed,' as he listened to the woman retracing 'her own untoward fate,' and his own inability to relieve her distress which dictated the lines,

> Of Time's sure help to calm and reconcile,
> Joy's second spring and Hope's long-treasured smile,
> 'Twas not for *him* to speak—a man so tried.

Again, in the incident of the gipsy striking his child, he dramatised his own remorse as a father—

> Within himself he said—What hearts have we!
> The blessing this a father gives his child!
> Yet happy thou, poor boy! compared with me,
> Suffering not doing ill—fate far more mild.

To describe *Guilt and Sorrow*, then, as a distinctly Godwinian poem is to miss its essence. For even if one of the apparent motives of the sailor's story is to show that 'sin and crime are apt to start from their very opposite qualities,' it was a fact discovered by Wordsworth in his own experience rather than merely borrowed from Godwin's doctrine of necessity. It was through apparently generous self-abandonment that he himself had fallen into what he felt to be sin. And this problem of sin, of a fall into disunity, was to be his central concern and motive as a poet long after he had cast off Godwin and indeed as long as he remained a poet in a vital sense.

Godwin's rationalising of the problem of sin was, indeed, comparable to that of the modern Behaviourist who, failing to realise its inner significance, can only explain it in terms of

L

external causation. Like his master Holback he regarded Reason as 'merely physical science applied to the behaviour of Man in Society.' And Wordsworth was always too imaginative and introspective to accept such logical generalisations.

Godwin might urge that the superior individual should regard the facts of life with the same detachment as the truths of geometry and that to an emancipated rationalist all moral values were irrelevant prejudices. But Wordsworth's experience denied this. Conscience had become an awful reality to him. And it told him that however prejudiced conventional morality might be, a true life was ultimately moral and that he was suffering because he had in some way sinned against life, and in consequence violated the original harmony of his being.

Godwin's teaching, however, attracted him just because it seemed to offer him an escape from his own painful moral conflict, although in fact this moral conflict disproved the validity of Godwin's contentions and was far too intimately real for any rationalist to argue away. All his previous experience, too, contradicted Godwin's claims that the individual was merely passive to the forces of life. For the whole secret of his early happiness had consisted in a perfect blending of activity and passivity in creative communion.

Although, therefore, he might give mental assent to Godwin's logic and even find in it a temporary refuge from his depression and his remorse, the moment he began to write as a poet his moral and human sensibility reasserted itself, and while the poem might be planned to illustrate a Godwinian thesis, it embodied his own experience. In *Guilt and Sorrow* Godwinism was thus fitted to his own situation and in the process transformed into something else. It is an early example of what was to be Wordsworth's dominating motive as a poet, his absorbed study of himself. For such characters as the sailor and the female vagrant were in reality, like all their successors, imaginative projections of his own experience. In creating them he at once relieved his feelings and analysed them.

Such imaginative introspection was, of course, as alien to Godwin as to the modern psycho-analytical theorist. For Godwin generalised so speciously because he lacked the poet's sense of the uniquely individual and saw life from outside. And Wordsworth only became a professed disciple of Godwin during the year that followed the composition of *Guilt and Sorrow* because amid the ruin of his hopes he lacked the heart to be a poet and could not bear to turn his gaze inward upon himself.

<h2 style="text-align:center">§ 7</h2>

The immediate material difficulties in the way of his dedicating himself to poetry were in fact removed at the very moment when he had lost the faith which was more essential even than independence to creative work. During the autumn of 1794 he remained at Penrith with Raisley Calvert, who was too ill to go, as had been suggested, to Lisbon, and who died in January 1795.

He thus received a legacy of £900, and the cottage life of which Dorothy had so long dreamed was at once realisable. But although eventually this generous gift did, as he acknowledged, clear

> a passage for me, and the stream
> Flowed in the bent of nature,

Nature and all she had once meant to him were for the time so apparently disproved by the events in France that the stream of life seemed frozen at its source. He even disowned the haunts of his childhood, writing to Mathews, 'I begin to wish much to be in Town. Cataracts and mountains are good occasional society, but they will not do for constant companions.' It was, perhaps, the only occasion on which he spoke like Charles Lamb, but his reason was less a love of his fellow-men than a weariness with himself.

In London he could lose himself in a crowd and divert his thoughts from their solitary channel into others less painful and personal, if more superficial. And so to London he went without delay, leaving Dorothy, perplexed but hopeful, at Mill House, near Halifax. And in London he remained, lost to sight, until the following September. The course of his inner life during these veiled months can only be conjectured from the evidence of his condition when he emerged from them. But it seems certain that it was during them that he leant his whole weight at last upon Godwin, that the prop thus tested broke beneath him, and that he was left with the conviction, impotent although it was at the time because 'the prime and vital principle' had ceased to flush 'the recesses' of his being, that every individual must work out his salvation for himself.

We have already suggested that Wordsworth was first attracted to Godwin because there was no place in his philosophy for ideas of guilt, crime, and desert, or for marriage vows or fixed principles. But the need which he now thought to satisfy was of a much larger order. He hoped to renew through Godwinism the faith in Nature and the 'general will' which the latest phase of the Revolution had destroyed. Godwin promised 'to abstract the hopes of Man out of his feelings.' Words-worth's feelings had apparently betrayed him, but Godwin assured him that the only true grounds of hope lay outside the feelings, or rather that 'the human Reason's naked self' might become an object of fervour.

Rousseau had asserted that Man was born free, but every-where he is in chains; Godwin replied that he is born in chains and has never thrown them off, but that the unprejudiced rationalist can count the links in every chain with scientific precision and so discover a new freedom.

The freedom of the individual mind,
Which, to the blind restraints of general laws
Superior, magisterially adopts
One guide, the light of circumstances, flash'd
Upon an independent intellect.

Such a magisterial freedom to explain the blind twitchings of
men in the net of circumstance might seem a poor and selfish
substitute for the universal human freedom of which Wordsworth had dreamed. But it appealed to all that was independent,
individualistic, and narrowly rational in him. And Godwin not
only reasserted the individual liberty which the French Revolution seemed to be crushing. He championed, too, from a
rationalistic standpoint, those ideas of progress which Beaupuy
had infused with humanitarian zeal.

His Utopia was a world composed of enlightened individualists who had cast off the dead hand of tradition, and who
would exercise their reasoning powers dispassionately upon
every matter as it arose. Authority, therefore, of any kind was
to him an evil, since it usurped on the private judgment of the
individual. By thus transferring the grounds of hope from
humanity in general as it was to a collection of private individuals, who would eventually develop their latent powers of
intellectual omniscience, Godwin provided Wordsworth with
a plausible outlet from despair.

In fact, of course, it was no outlet, because his hope was
based on a completely arbitrary reading of human nature.
Rousseau's Utopia was one of humanitarian anarchy inspired
by a mythically benevolent 'general will.' Godwin's was one
of individualistic anarchy directed by a mythically enlightened
'private reason.' And both history and experience taught that
feeling in itself was as unreliable a source of inspiration as the
intellect in itself of enlightenment. Each was at the mercy of
that self-will which Godwin conveniently overlooked. And

only when both were united in that higher power of Imagination, which Blake described as 'the Divine Power in Every Man,' and Spinoza as 'the intellectual love of God,' could they make a man disinterested both in knowledge and action.

There was, in fact, an unresolved contradiction at the very centre of Godwin's teaching, the paradox that man was at the same time a will-less slave to necessity and free to exercise his reason to reform and modify life. This was a parody of the truth that real freedom is to be found through a willing surrender of the private claims of self to the creative demands of life. But Godwin ruled out the will, and in so doing destroyed both the significance of necessity as a creative force and the possibility of directing it from within to high human ends. The Godwinian who believed that morality was simply a matter of intellectual knowledge had in fact no reason to change anything. His interest both in his own conduct and that of others would be purely scientific, and to such a one cruelty would be as reasonable a phenomenon as kindness.

But in truth Godwin's isolated, rational individual was a myth, born of his own defective knowledge of himself and of his disregard of history. And he was a dangerous myth. For if self-will was non-existent in Godwin's theory, it was omnipresent in the world. And the doctrines of 'necessity' and of rationalistic freedom encouraged a man to be a wilful egoist under the assumption that he was a superior thinker. For since he acknowledged no authority, whether moral or individual, outside himself, and since the reason to which he appealed for guidance and justification was merely his own logical faculty, he was entirely self-bound, and inevitably reduced truth to rationalised self-interest.

Before the end of 1795 Wordsworth had discovered this for himself, and begun to embody his discovery in the villain of *The Borderers*. If he had not been seeking to escape from himself, he could, indeed, hardly have overlooked Godwin's ignorance of human nature and ingenuous psychology. But since his own mind was at war with his instincts, he accepted for a few months a philosophy which exalted such a state and even thought to recover his wholeness of faith and action by means of it. He mistook Godwin's cult of egotistic independence for the inner freedom which he desired, and sought in a conceited hardness immunity both from his uneasy conscience and the heart-rending spectacle of a world which mocked his earlier hopes and aspirations. He had ceased to be 'one of Love's simple bondsmen—the soft chain was off for ever.'

In fact, he had only exchanged the soft chain of emotional credulity for the brittle chain of rationalism. But the illusion that he had enrolled himself in the vanguard of the future and was a fellow-labourer with those who would 'enlarge Man's intellectual empire,' and so ensure his ultimate happiness was more easily sustained because the circle of Godwin in which he moved included many with warmer hearts than the Master. Among them was a dissenting preacher, named Fawcett, a generous, original man, and an enthusiastic admirer of the French Revolution, who attracted many intelligent radicals and Wordsworth among them to his Meeting House at the Old Jewry, where he declaimed against war and also 'against the domestic affections.' And once, at least, Wordsworth met in the circle the being who more than any other was to give what Godwin only seemed to give, the breath of a renewing inspiration.

Coleridge himself at this time was almost as sorely perplexed as Wordsworth. He, too, had made a rash promise of marriage, and begun to regret it. He, too, had centred his hopes on a Utopian scheme of society, a colony of 'Pantisocrats' to be established with Southey and others on the banks of the Susquehanna in America. And for him, too, the dream had begun to fade before the hard facts of human nature (in particular Southey's nature), and material difficulties. And meanwhile he had been drugging himself with talk, punch, and tobacco in a little smoky room at the 'Salutation and Cat,' with a kindred hypochondriac, Charles Lamb. In October he was to redeem his promise of marriage to Sarah Fricker, but for the time being he was in his own way as much in flight from himself and his past as Wordsworth.

And although their meeting at this time had little significance, Coleridge must at least have brought to it the sympathy of a poet who had already recognised in *An Evening Walk* and *Descriptive Sketches* 'the emergence of an original poetic genius above the literary horizon,' who had felt 'in the form, style, and manner . . . and in the structure of the particular lines and periods . . . an harshness and an acerbity connected and combined with words and images all aglow, which might recall those products of the vegetable world, where gorgeous blossoms rise out of the hard and thorny rind and shell, within which the rich fruit was elaborating.'

But such contacts could at best only delay for a little while the inevitable disillusionment. For a few months London and its superficial mental activities helped Wordsworth to evade the insoluble problem of his divided inner being. But as its excitements and diversions began to pall, the realisation came starkly upon him that Godwinism in fact solved none of his problems, that it denied his deepest instincts and promised salvation only by excluding all that had once given life its richest meaning. His stricken but still tenacious faith in men and nature had been diverted into a sterile channel.

He could not have analysed the situation at the time so exactly as he came later to do. But obscurely he felt that he had denied, at Godwin's bidding, the Nature in which he was rooted, not for any higher order of Being, but for a limited and self-bound faculty—the mind. And this divorce of reason from feeling brought a worse death in its train than that of emotional despair. For he had been drawn to Godwinism not primarily by a rational impulse, but by a revulsion from feeling. He had suffered so much in his heart that he had felt that he must cut at his deepest instinctive attachments. But having taken Godwin's knife in hand and attempted to probe not only the living body of society even to the heart, but also his own being, he found that his life-blood was draining away.

He had dragged all his passions, notions, and beliefs like culprits to the bar of his mind, and had suspiciously (for at heart he doubted the mind's right to judge in such matters) called upon it to approve or disprove. But the only result had been worse perplexity, a wretched oscillation between belief and disbelief, until finally he had 'yielded up moral questions in despair.' Consequently each way to 'the tree of life' seemed closed to him. If he turned away from Nature with Godwin he found only intellectual sterility; if he sought to return to the Nature which he had loved, he found that he was divided from her by all the heartfelt pains of memory and remorse.

Too hungry for faith to enjoy the barren pleasure of cynicism, the only path open to him, as to so many disillusioned spirits of the time, seemed one of retirement. Perhaps far from the distractions of the town and the moment, healing might come to him and a new light be revealed. Perhaps with Dorothy amid the changeless change of the country-side Nature might quicken him once again, washing away his pain and apathy in her unquenchable fount of joy. Yet even this prospect held no allurement. For Nature can do little for the self-bound man who projects his own unhappy state into all he sees.

And such a man was Wordsworth when he left London in the early autumn of 1795 for Dorsetshire. His condition is plainly revealed in the *Lines Left upon a Seat in a Yew-tree*, which he wrote before the end of the year. He is the youth 'who owned no common soul,' who had been 'led by nature into a wild scene of lofty hopes,' and went forth into the world 'a favoured Being.' And he it was who was wounded, who, 'turning himself away, sustained his soul in solitude with the food of pride,' and who derived a morbid pleasure from tracing in barren rocks 'an emblem of his own unfruitful life' or from remembering, as he gazed on the more distant scene and recognised its loveliness, the days when 'nature had subdued him to herself.'

But perhaps the most significant part of the poem was its moral conclusion—

> If Thou be one whose heart the holy forms
> Of young imagination have kept pure,
> Stranger! henceforth be warned; and know that pride,
> Howe'er disguised in its own majesty,
> Is littleness; that he, who feels contempt
> For any living thing, hath faculties
> Which he has never used; that thought with him
> Is in its infancy. The man whose eye
> Is ever on himself doth look on one,
> The least of Nature's works, one who might move
> The wise man to that scorn which wisdom holds
> Unlawful, ever. O be wiser, Thou!
> Instructed that true knowledge leads to love;
> True dignity abides with him alone
> Who, in the silent hour of inward thought
> Can still suspect, and still revere himself,
> In lowliness of heart.

These lines are of great importance. They portend, indeed, all Wordsworth's later development. The uneasy association of the naturalist and the moralist at the expense of the true mystic, by which he was to solve imperfectly his dilemma, had begun.

For a sensitive ear detects in these lines the very 'pride disguised in its own majesty' which on the surface they reprove.

Outwardly they are a reasoned and feeling plea for humility by one who has learnt the necessity for it. But in the quality of their expression they betray a man who has refused to make that ultimate submission without which there can be no real experience of what humility means.

A man who had had that real experience would not have been concerned with the 'true dignity' of his attitude or with suspecting and revering himself 'in lowliness of heart.' We hear in fact for the first time in these lines, faintly but unmistakably, the patronising moralist who was to intrude so disastrously upon and finally to supersede the creative and divinatory genius.

And it is important to emphasise the fact because the moment of his retirement to Dorset was crucial. Now and during the months that followed he was faced with the real crisis upon which all his future depended. Would he contrive to evade, as he had sought to do in his flight to London and Godwin, the truth of that inner conflict which so distressed and humiliated him? Or would he accept without qualification the fact and the demands of his lost integrity, bowing down before the mystery of life with a willing submission, in which no element of protesting self-esteem remained, and thus committing himself completely to reality?

As a boy and a youth he had so humbled himself to the spirit of life in Nature and known the ecstatic joy of active communion. But that had been an instinctive self-surrender which involved no moral effort. The submission, however, which he was now called upon to make was opposed by his strongest instinct, his tenacious individualism. It meant carrying the painful struggle within him to that extreme point at which new life is born through utter self-abnegation.

Wordsworth was to spend his life in a self-defensive warfare, culminating in barren self-righteousness, because he continued to recoil from this ultimate act of self-surrender which alone could have liberated him. And in the *Lines Left upon a Seat in a Yew-tree* we have the first hint of the false compromise which he was to accept, of the self-deception of the moralist who preaches humility without having really humbled himself. And this recoil from the ultimate demands of life behind the defences of a lofty morality necessitated also that he should henceforth shrink with something of a morbid horror from those physical desires which had become associated in his mind with his fall into sin. To contemplate them not only hurt his conscience; it injured the self-esteem which he wished to re-establish. And this revulsion crippled eventually both his instinctive and his rational being. It made it impossible for him really to recover his sense of the innocence of life, and by poisoning for him the deepest of the natural channels of life, it led ultimately to spiritual impotence.

PART V

THE REVIVAL

§ I

WORDSWORTH and Dorothy went to Racedown in Dorsetshire, in September 1795. The house which they occupied was offered to them by the son of a rich Bristol merchant, to whom Wordsworth had been introduced by a Cambridge friend, Basil Montagu. Montagu had lost his wife, and it was arranged that the Wordsworths should look after his small son, Basil, much to Dorothy's delight, who had thus a double reason for feeling that her existence was no longer 'of very little use.' Wordsworth himself, too, found in the presence and companionship of this child through several years a source of interest and even inspiration.

Racedown was a farm, lying seven miles from the shore of the English Channel. The ground fell away rapidly from the solid but rather gloomy house to the coast, and through the valleys opening to the south the wind brought the scent and the sound of the sea. On the higher ground the trees were stunted and bent to the wind, but in the sheltered hollows that lay along the bed of a small stream winding between the hills, the vegetation was abundant and there were many apple orchards.

The country, therefore, was both wild and domestic, luxuriant and bare. And at first Wordsworth felt a wonderful sense of release greeting

> this gentle breeze
> That blows from the green fields and from the clouds
> And from the sky,

as a friend that welcomed one who had come 'from a house of bondage.' For whatever might be the state of man, the earth remained constant and unperturbed. Its murmuring streams still ran unsullied and might lull him to his rest. He breathed again; and as the clean air flowed into his lungs, his spirit dilated too.

> Trances of thought and mountings of the mind
> Come fast upon me: it is shaken off,
> As by miraculous gift 'tis shaken off,
> That burthen of my own unnatural self,
> The heavy weight of many a weary day
> Not mine, and such as were not made for me.[1]

But the burden was not to be shaken off so easily. Certainly on the surface he was happier, and since Dorothy was in Heaven, he could hardly be in Hell. She saw to it, also, that his days were full of activity, of hewing wood and rooting up hedges, of educating little Basil on Rousseauistic principles, and, of course, of perpetual walks. 'We are never dull,' she wrote. 'Basil is a charming boy; he affords us perpetual entertainment. . . . We have many very pleasant walks about us; and, what is a great advantage, the roads are of a sandy kind and almost always dry. We can see the sea 150 or 200 yards from the door, and, at a little distance, have a very extensive view terminated by the sea, seen through different openings of the unequal hills. We have not the warmth and luxuriance of Devonshire, though there is no want either of wood or cultivation; but the trees appear to suffer from the sea-blasts. We have hills which —seen from a distance—almost take the character of mountains; some cultivated nearly to their summits, others in a wild

---

[1] It may be that these lines and the whole preamble to *The Prelude* from which they are taken were not actually composed, despite Professor Garrod's and Professor de Selincourt's attribution of them to this time, until four years later. But, if so, there can be little doubt that the feelings which Wordsworth embodied in them were as much those which he experienced when he set out from Bristol to Racedown, as when in 1799 he left Germany for England.

state, covered with furze and broom. These delight me the
most, as they remind me of our native wilds.'

Certainly, if all that he had needed was to retrace his steps,
to recover the buoyancy of boyhood with its 'glad animal
movements' and its instinctive ecstasies, Dorothy, by her
'benign simplicity of life' and 'perfect happiness of soul' might
have restored him. For she *was* the Nature which he had loved,
made animate and ardent in a human form. She lived wholly
and intensely in the moment, with all her faculties miraculously
quickened by love. And as she walked so tirelessly by his side,
her wild eyes discovering for him unnoticed beauty at almost
every step, she seemed

> like a brook
> That did but cross a lonely road and now
> Is seen, heard, felt, and caught at every turn,
> Companion never lost through many a league.

But while the sight and sound of a brook can refresh a traveller
on a lonely road, it cannot materially aid him in his journey or
do more than divert him from contemplating his loneliness.
And in a sense Dorothy was a dangerous diversion. For she
encouraged Wordsworth to evade his problem, to look backward rather than go forward, and to think that the purely
instinctive harmony which was so palpably hers might again
be his. In his own later words she

> Maintained for me a saving intercourse
> With my true self; for, though impair'd and chang'd
> Much, as it seemed, I was no further chang'd
> Than as a clouded, not a waning moon.
> She, in the midst of all, preserv'd me still
> A Poet, made me seek beneath that name
> My office upon earth, and nowhere else,
> And lastly, Nature's self, by human love

> Assisted, through the weary labyrinth
> Conducted me again to open day,
> Revived the feelings of my earlier life,
> Gave me that strength and knowledge full of peace,
> Enlarged, and never more to be disturb'd. . . .

Thus, looking back from what he considered the safe haven
of a re-established faith, he described her service to him at this
time. But knowing, as we do, how stultifying that haven was
to prove, it is possible to question whether her loving service
was quite so beneficial to his true self as he argued. For it was
comfortable to regard his inward distress and impotence as
merely a passing distemper to be cured by reviving the feelings
of his earlier life. But it was also a piece of self-deception which
prevented him from becoming truly reconciled with the Nature
in which his roots were so deeply set. And Dorothy, all
unconsciously, fostered his weaker inclination. She, in whom
'guilt was a thing impossible,' helped him to patch up a peace
between himself and life which was no real peace.

But in the early months at Racedown, despite Dorothy's
presence, he was still quite uncreative, occupying himself, so
far as he composed at all, with satires, in the manner of Juvenal,
upon such uninspiring subjects as King George, the Prince of
Wales, the Duke of Norfolk, and the defaulting Earl of
Lonsdale. These, however, he soon abandoned, and informed
his friend Wrangham with whom he had been collaborating,
that he was employed in writing a tragedy, 'the first draft of
which is nearly finished.' A little later he asserted that 'as to
writing, it is out of the question.' And in fact the tragedy was
not completed before the middle or perhaps the end of 1796.
But since it throws considerable light upon the inward struggle
and mental distress which Dorothy was too ecstatically happy
either to understand or to prescribe for, it will be well to
consider it here.

The Borderers is for Professor Garrod the work of a man who had just become 'an out-and-out Godwinian,' a view only possible to one who had failed to enter intimately either into Wordsworth's life or into his play. To M. Legouis it represents the beginning of Wordsworth's revolt against Godwin, and Professor de Selincourt regards it as 'rather an exposure than an exposition of Godwinism.' And so far as it is in any real sense Godwinian at all, they are clearly right.

It is true that in his preface and later notes Wordsworth suggested that the play, like *Guilt and Sorrow*, illustrated a Godwinian idea. 'The study of human nature,' he wrote, 'suggests this awful truth, that as in the trials to which life subjects us, sin and crime are apt to start from their very opposite qualities, so are there no limits to the hardening of the heart and the perversion of the understanding to which they may carry their slaves. During my long residence in France, while the Revolution was rapidly advancing to its extreme of wickedness, I had frequent opportunities of being an eye-witness of this process, and it was while that knowledge was fresh upon my memory that the tragedy of *The Borderers* was composed.'

As with most of Wordsworth's later explanatory comments, this is not quite the truth. As we know, it was only during the two years which followed his stay in France that he became fully aware that generous ideals might apparently produce their opposite, 'sin and crime.' But it is necessary to emphasise the fact, overlooked by such critics as Professor Garrod, that he owed this discovery primarily to his own experience of life and not to a reading of Godwin's *Caleb Williams*. His love of Annette and his belief in Liberty had been generous ideals which apparently and to his deep distress produced their opposite.

M

He may have gone to Godwin for an explanation of the fact, discovering in him one of those 'careful observers' who make intelligible 'the apparently *motiveless* actions of bad men.' But if he adopted for a time Godwin's psychology, the experience to which he applied it was his own, both in relation to the Revolution and to Annette.

The conception, for example, that 'there are no limits to the hardening of the heart' was entirely alien to Godwin, who cared little about the heart and based all his hopes of individual salvation upon the head. But it was a bitter reality to Wordsworth, who was suffering the wretched consequences of denying the heart, not only as a Godwinian but as a tenacious individualist, and who had begun to feel that there *were* no limits to the deadening process.

And in fact not even Oswald, the villain of *The Borderers*, is in any real sense a Godwinian, although at times he talks Godwinism. He is a projection of one side of Wordsworth's dual personality, just as all the other characters embody some phase of his experience. Certainly Marmaduke, originally named Mortimer, the ingenuous youth who is seduced by Oswald's specious doctrine and reduced to despair is more essentially Wordsworth himself than any other character, because he embodies his feeling self. And Professor Mac-Gillivray, in drawing attention recently to the fact that Wordsworth signed his poem *The Convict* with the pseudonym Mortimer, rightly adduces this as additional evidence that the poet saw in the Mortimer or Marmaduke of *The Borderers* a picture of himself.

But in reality the whole play is a myth of himself. The personal *motif* is struck from the very beginning in the lines,

> I have heard
> Of some dark deed to which in early life
> His passion drove him.

The words refer to Oswald. But Oswald represented the intellectual egoist and sceptical realist which Wordsworth had in part become through the deeds of blind enthusiasm and 'unsanctified love' to which passion had driven him in France. And the whole play dramatises the stages by which the Oswald in him, the selfish mind and fear principle, insidiously defeated the Marmaduke, the generous, credulous believer in life and humanity. The old, blind, and good Herbert embodies the Life and Humanity, of which he had begun by doubting and ended by denying the virtue; while Idonea, the old man's daughter and Marmaduke's lover, at once trusting and cherishing life, is the Innocence (Annette's innocence) which Wordsworth felt that he had sinned against as a sensualist. His sin against her he projected into the voluptuary, Clifford, among whose victims was

> A Maiden innocent till ensnared by Clifford,
> Who soon grew weary of her,

and who is supposed to haunt the churchyard where her infant is buried—another example of the wronged and forsaken woman who had already appeared in *Guilt and Sorrow*.

But Marmaduke is also deceived into believing that Herbert, beneath his mask of 'deep and simple meekness,' is planning to hand over Idonea herself to Clifford, and with her compliance. This is, in fact, an invention of Oswald's lying mind, calculated to wound at its most vulnerable point Marmaduke's belief in the inherent goodness of life. And Wordsworth's own revulsion from his passion for Annette, his conception of it as a sin of the senses for which he was primarily responsible, but in which, he felt in his most negative moments, she had wrongly complied, sprang from the rationalistic, life-denying Oswald in himself.

Three years' personal experience, therefore, of mental and

moral disillusionment lay behind Marmaduke's words at the
end of Act i—

> Oswald, the firm foundation of my life
> Is going from under me; these strange discoveries—
> Looked at from every point of fear or hope,
> Duty, or love—involve, I feel, my ruin.

A brief analysis, however, of the rest of the play will reveal
more convincingly than argument the truth of our contention
that in *The Borderers* Wordsworth dramatised the stages by
which he lost his sense of his own and of life's innocence.[1]

Early in Act ii we find Marmaduke protesting to Oswald that
a love of his fellows and compassion for the weak have always
ruled his nature, but admitting, after Oswald has sneered at
sentimental benevolence and youth's instinctive generosity,
that

> there is something
> Which looks like a transition in my soul,
> And yet it is not.

There follows the protracted struggle between the reason of
his heart which tells him that Herbert is good and deserves his
love, and the logic of his head that feeds upon Oswald's lying
tales. He falls into just that agonised perplexity which Wordsworth had known for so long. To Oswald, however, it is
well for all romantic illusion to be shattered, as doubtless
Wordsworth, also, had comforted himself by thinking,
when the self-regarding Oswald in him was in temporary
control. And in the words of Marmaduke to Lacy he confessed, with a characteristic regret for his own damaged
dignity, that

[1] For a fuller treatment with quotations from the dialogue see article contributed by the author to the *Adelphi*, July 1931.

> I have a heart to feel,
> And I have felt, *more than perhaps becomes me*
> *Or duty sanctions.*

Act III records quite clearly his attempt to resolve through Godwinism both his remorse and the problem of a world 'poisoned at the heart.' In the early soliloquy of Oswald we find him analysing his diseased condition, as he must have done so often and as he was to continue doing with deeper and deeper insight through the following years. Meanwhile Oswald's story that Idonea is 'right willing' to become Clifford's mistress completes Marmaduke's disillusionment. He loses all belief in moral values. His heart becomes like a stone.

> I am cut off from man;
> No more shall I be man—no more shall I
> Have human feelings!

Herbert, however, who is of course ignorant of Marmaduke's state or the cause of it, offers him advice which, significantly enough, is in the lofty moralistic strain of Wordsworth's later manner. But to Marmaduke Herbert's words seem only the hypocrisy of a villain. In his heart he still cannot quite believe in Herbert's guilt, as something in Wordsworth could hardly admit that the world and he himself were 'poisoned at the heart.' But the deceived rationalist in Marmaduke assents to the guilt, and he leaves Herbert to die alone on the moor.

Thus had Wordsworth turned his back upon life and sought escape from his wretchedness and sense of guilt in Godwinism. And Marmaduke does the same. For in the play it is now that we have from Oswald those paraphrases of *Political Justice* which have led superficial critics to describe it as a Godwinian tract. Marmaduke, however, having been led to betray his heart to his head, would 'abide the issue' of his act alone.

But Oswald clings to him and combats his inward distress with all the realist's selfish logic. 'My young Friend,' he says (and his words were indeed most intimately Wordsworth's own)—

> As time advances either we become
> The prey or masters of our own past deeds. . . .
>
>   Remorse—
> It cannot live with thought; think on, think on,
> And it will die.

Yet Godwinian thought could not, as Wordsworth had discovered, extinguish a corroding conscience. And the tale which Oswald forthwith tells of his own abandonment of an innocent sea-captain on a desert island only deepens Marmaduke's self-disgust, while it afforded Wordsworth an opportunity of dramatising again the original fall from innocence into sin, which obsessed him. The struggle, indeed, between rationalistic self-justification and a deeper conviction of guilt reaches its climax in the dialogue between Marmaduke and Oswald which follows. Oswald, however, goes on to tell how his sentimental remorse for his act of desertion was cured by a Godwinian philosophy, how he discovered a new and 'salient spring of energy,' through binding himself 'to purposes of reason.' But Marmaduke is too ill at heart to be touched by his vaunting rationalism. Oswald redoubles his persuasions. He describes the entrancing effect of majestic natural objects upon his own 'intellectual being,' and how, in the exultant sense of personal omnipotence which they engendered, he felt raised above all 'the world's opinions and her usages,'

> a Being who had passed alone
> Into a region of futurity,
> Whose natural element was freedom.

But Marmaduke bids him stop. 'I may not,' he says, 'cannot, follow thee.' Nor can all Oswald's scoffs at false shame and the cobwebs of convention move him.

Oswald, therefore, throws off his mask and confesses to his calculated deception, and the horrified Marmaduke is left only with the faint hope that Herbert may still be alive. 'Alive or dead,' he cries, 'I'll find him,' as Wordsworth, fleeing from Godwinism to Dorset, sought to restore the life which he had denied.

This scene, therefore, clearly epitomises in a melodramatic form the crisis of the struggle between Wordsworth's heart and his head, and his rejection of Godwinism. In the next scene we are given still another rendering of the selfish 'desertion' theme, that of the dying Herbert by the terrified Eldred, and in Act v Marmaduke faces his guilt and its consequences with just that imperfect humbling of himself to it which was to be Wordsworth's destiny.

Marmaduke had, indeed, reproved Oswald earlier for not feeling his guilt more deeply, for merely enduring its stigma unchanged instead of suffering it in the deepest sense. 'You ought,' he had said,

> to have seen
> The guilt—have touched it, felt it at your heart
> As I have done.

But he himself, in the moment when he has to face Idonea with the knowledge that Herbert is dead through his act of desertion, qualifies his remorse with an element of self-justification. More true in feeling are his words when Idonea faints—

> *She* is not dead. Why!—if I loved this woman,
> I would take care she never woke again;
> But she WILL wake, and she will weep for me,
> And say no blame was mine—

words which Wordsworth surely wrote with Annette in his mind. And the same personal reference is to be found in Marmaduke's concluding words to Oswald—

> to endure,
> That is my destiny. May it be thine:
> Thy office, thy ambition, be henceforth
> To feed remorse, to welcome every sting
> Of penitential anguish, yea with tears
> When seas and continents shall lie between us . . .
> a wanderer *must* I go,
> The Spectre of that innocent Man, my guide.
> No human ear shall ever hear me speak;
> No human dwelling ever give me food,
> Or sleep or rest: but over waste and wild,
> In search of nothing that this earth can give,
> But expiation, will I wander on—
> A Man by pain and thought compelled to live,
> Yet loathing life—till anger is appeased
> In Heaven, and Mercy gives me leave to die.

If these lines are divested of their melodrama, they may be said to express very accurately the feelings which gnawed at Wordsworth's heart during the early months at Racedown. And although his wound was apparently to heal beneath the ministering hands of Dorothy and the inspiration of Coleridge, deep down the lesion remained. Henceforth it was, indeed, his destiny 'to feed remorse,' to be 'a wanderer over waste and wild' in search of an expiation which he could not find, although he sought to forget his failure in an instinctive surrender to Nature and to conceal it behind a sympathetic study of humble men.

The Borderers, then, like so much that Wordsworth wrote, is autobiographical. Into its fictitious characters he projected himself and his problems, as he was later to do into a host of other characters, actual and imaginary. And its real significance lies in the fact that it reveals as no other extant evidence does (for in *The Prelude* the whole situation was to be modified even in the lines which were borrowed from *The Borderers*), the irresolvable conflict between heart and head, self-contempt and self-esteem, which had torn Wordsworth's being with gathering intensity for three years. It shows the extent to which his heart triumphed in his rejection of Godwinism, but the extent, too, to which it was compromised by his self-regarding mind.

Marmaduke, in short, could not cast off the shadow of Oswald and so regain his innocence. Nor could Wordsworth. For though he abandoned Godwinism he retained as much of the rational egoism expressed in Godwinism as he needed for preserving a wrong kind of self-respect. Consequently *The Borderers* is not merely the product of mental disease, as Swinburne wrote, but a confession of spiritual disease.

How deeply that disease had eaten into his being and how morbidly real to him was his consciousness of sin is revealed again with hysterical intensity in *The Convict*, which he wrote some time after the completion of *The Borderers*, and in which we read—

> His bones are consumed, and his life-blood is dried,
> With wishes the past to undo;
> And his crime, through the pains that o'erwhelm him,
> descried,
> Still blackens and grows on his view. . . .
>
> But if grief, self-consumed, in oblivion would doze,
> And conscience her tortures appease,
> 'Mid tumult and uproar this man must repose;
> In the comfortless vault of disease.

But in the concluding stanza of the poem a sympathetic visitor
assures the convict that

> 'Though in virtue's proud mouth thy report be a stain,
> My care, if the arm of the mighty were mine,
> Would plant thee where yet thou might'st blossom again.'

And in this visitor we may see Wordsworth's growing determination to break from the prison of remorse and to 'blossom
again.'

§ 3

When at Racedown in 1796 Wordsworth saw the spring
return, he was dead to deeper hope. Yet his instinctive being
stirred again. He found a solace in the brooks muttering along
the stones, in the waves kissing the pebbly shore, and in
the woods, interposing their shade, like a sleep, between
himself and his own unquiet heart. And gradually Nature did
more than soothe his pain. The joy of the birds and the lambs,
of plants and insects, began to infect him. Yet his happiness
was not as before; it was enjoyed by stealth and, so to say,
behind the back of his mind and his conscience.

Previous to his disillusionment his intellectual power seemed
to have advanced from stage to stage, hand-in-hand with love
and joy. He had known a natural graciousness of mind. His
thought had been steeped in generous instinct. But from the
time that he left France he had become separated from the
fragrant shore of sentiment and fearless love. For a time he
had justified this separation. And Godwin had encouraged
him to believe that his errand was to sail to other coasts, that
future times would see the man to come parted as by a gulf
from the man of the past.

And so agreeing with Godwin that 'nothing can be more
unreasonable than to argue from men as we find them, to men

as they may hereafter be made' (a true contention, like so many of Godwin's, in a deeper sense than his), he had ceased to feel the inspiration of such past heroes as the Sage, the Patriot, and the Lover. They had been replaced by the hero of the future, the Godwinian rationalist who at once recognised necessity and acted justly. Before the open eye of such Reason even the poets had withered in his esteem, and the poet in himself had withered too. For he had zealously sought to cut off his heart from all the sources of her former strength and to substitute for the 'mysteries of passion' such unreal abstractions as

> the laws of things which lie
> Beyond the reach of human will or power.

At the same time he had come to scan even the visible universe with a merely microscopic eye.

Later he was to admit the necessity of this critical and analytical phase in the growth of true perception. The danger was lest it should become a fixed attitude, lest the mind in satisfying exclusively its inherent love of order and of negative judgment should arrest growth and dry up the springs of life. This danger was implicit in Godwinism just as the danger of mere feeling was implicit in Rousseauism. And Wordsworth, by developing such a critical temper as a defence against his deeper feelings cut himself off from what had been the vital source of his moral power and human affection. And at the same time his vision had been paralysed as a spiritual faculty. It had degenerated into mere detached observance.

Consequently when he began to respond again to Nature at Racedown, his happiness was no more than a

> transport of the outward sense,
> Not of the mind, vivid but not profound.

He no longer forgot himself and his sensations in communion with a spiritual life of which the forms and movements of Nature were a manifestation. Instead he regarded her forms for the conscious pleasure which he could derive from new combinations of them, and was glad to lay his wounded inner faculties asleep.

But it was impossible thus to evade the issue indefinitely. For such transitory pleasures gave no nourishment. And he knew it. Later he wrote that Nature seeks to thwart this tendency to exclusiveness on the part of any of the faculties by summoning all the senses, each to counteract the other and themselves. And on the level of primitive being which he had once known, this was true. But how was a man whose faculties were no longer functioning in perfect harmony with one another but were in fact in perpetual discord to recover the unity which Nature desired and manifested?

This was the problem which faced Wordsworth now and for the rest of his life. And its solution was brought no nearer by those who preached a return to Nature, because the return involved no real healing of their inward discord. Yet Wordsworth himself in his later account of his recovery could only turn from criticism of Godwin's sterile rationalism to an impassioned celebration of the Nature of his boyhood —

> Oh! Soul of Nature, excellent and fair,
> That did'st rejoice with me, with whom I too
> Rejoiced, through early youth before the winds
> And powerful waters, and in lights and shades
> That march'd and countermarch'd about the hills
> In glorious apparition. . . .

On these powers, he wrote, he had waited daily, 'now all eye and now all ear,' but never long without employing the heart and the unfolding intellect. 'Oh! Soul of Nature!' he cried,

> that dost overflow
> With passion and with life, what feeble men
> Walk on this earth! how feeble have I been
> When thou wert in thy strength!

Only such a mystic as Treherne, however, who had really
renewed in himself the innocence of childhood on a new
creative level, could safely invoke such memories of early
beatitude. For Wordsworth it was in some measure a sentimental evasion. Godwin had invited him to press forward to
the future and join hands with the New Men who were to
transform the world by reason. But Godwin's path into the
future had proved a narrow *cul de sac*, and so he recoiled from
it to those wide and pathless wanderings which had blessed his
boyhood and youth with a sense of infinite potency and
well-being.

In those early days when he had felt about him at every step

> The first diviner influence of this world,
> As it appears to unaccustom'd eyes,

he had seemed to worship 'among the depth of things' as his
soul bade him. And in such worship he had gone out from
himself in pure wonder, and the source of all his pleasure had
been 'humbleness and love.' The account which we have
given of his childhood shows that in thus claiming to have
been pleased with 'nothing but humbleness and love,' Wordsworth was to some extent sentimentalising his past. Even in
those years of innocence there was an assertive egoism in him
which in less favourable circumstances might have become
dominant. In the primitive life which he led this egoism was
never inflamed through suppression. It was free to act in
harmony with the elemental forces of Nature and to be
unconsciously disciplined by them. And of the pure moments

of that active communion with life it was true to say that he felt in them nothing but humbleness and love.

Yet if he had examined his boyhood more rigorously, he could not have failed to discover many less enraptured occasions when his own self-will had asserted itself and there was pride in his heart and an element of greed in his pleasure. And as he grew to manhood the contracting force of selfhood had inevitably grown stronger, until the deep conflict between himself and life developed which had now almost reduced him to impotence.

However much, therefore, his childhood seemed in memory ideally moral, it was a profound mistake to think that its conditions could be recovered. The child had humbled himself to life instinctively. It was enough then for him to feel 'and nothing else.' For it was not so much he himself who felt as Life which felt through him. But the moment the conscious mind had really awoken in him he had ceased to be such a channel, and in different degrees perverted the stream of life for his own selfish ends.

It was not, therefore, by any attempted recovery of childhood's selfless feeling, but by participating in a new harmony that the conscious self might regain its lost unity with the creative will of life and feeling and renew its innocence.

To realise this new harmony required, indeed, both moral and rational effort of an intensive order, but it needed to be effort purged of selfish motive. The secret of this regeneration is revealed in the eternal paradox of the mystics that in His Will is our peace and in His Law is our freedom. By offering up the personal self to the spiritual self the being is renewed. Its natural faculties are not denied, but they are spiritually informed and redeemed. The reborn man wills and thinks and feels from a creative centre which is at once in and infinitely beyond himself. And it is thus that he is both utterly overruled and utterly responsible.

And this reconciliation of the moral and the mystical, the personal and the universal will, which has been the essence of all true religion, is also the secret of all true poetry. For in the imagination of the poet the divided faculties are harmonised. He too must submit himself unreservedly to life, must become a channel through which the mystery may unfold its meaning. But he is responsible, too, for crystallising that meaning, for determining what has been determined in him to the last syllable of its significance.

So far then as Wordsworth recoiled from his wretchedness to the ecstatic naturalism of his childhood, he was attempting to evade the burden of a consciousness which it was essential for him to carry forward to real completion. And, as he found, it could not be evaded. Few men, indeed, have been so ineradicably and persistently self-conscious. And although he strove for unity and for some ten years achieved a precarious, but poetically fruitful blending of his own private claims and the claims of life, the self triumphed in the end. And inevitably. For in this matter compromise, for those who have reached such a degree of self-consciousness as Wordsworth had, is ultimately fatal. To go forward grudgingly, with constant backward glances at a state of childhood and of nature which should have been outgrown, is to stand still. To cultivate and deepen the sympathies but never quite to make that final act of self-surrender which transforms personal sympathy into disinterested understanding, is to lose eventually the capacity to understand anything which conflicts with self-interest.

How far Wordsworth went in sympathy in his great creative period we shall see. It was probably to the extreme limit that a man can go short of being reborn into the new life of selfless love. Moreover, we owe to the very bounds which he could not overstep the intense exploration of himself and recreation of moments of freedom on the naturalistic plane which make all his greatest poetry profoundly moving and illuminating.

Doubtless, too, he was right in claiming to be cured of Godwinism and in attributing the transitory effect upon him of such rationalism to the deep roots in Nature which he had formed in boyhood and youth. But had he recovered from something of which his passing attachment to Godwinism was only a symptom? Had he merely humanised his reason and his instincts instead of redeeming them? Was there not a sense, profounder than Godwin's, in which Reason had to deny Nature to affirm her more truly, to transform the fallen natural man into the spiritual man, who was a freeman in the world of Nature, instead of a dependent? And until that transformation was effected, could he rightly claim to be 'a creative soul,' who not only enjoyed visitings of imaginative power as in childhood but was imaginatively integrated in himself?

As late as the spring of 1797 Wordsworth would not himself have laid claim to any real reintegration. At best he had only passed from sickness to uncertain convalescence. But with the coming of the summer an angel descended and troubled the water. And like the first of the impotent folk who stepped into the pool of Bethesda, he seemed to be made whole.

§ 4

Wordsworth was not the man to believe in miracles. But the effect of Coleridge upon him was miraculous. For Coleridge was his true complement. Frailly attached to the natural world, he floated expansively in the spiritual. With an imperfect grasp upon the finite, he hungered ceaselessly for the infinite. His visionary imagination made him almost a stranger in the bounded world of the bodily senses, while through his generous enthusiasms he was at once an inspiration to others and a bewilderment to himself.

Thus he was Wordsworth's perfect anti-self. He supplied his deficiencies, quickening in him all those spiritual centres which were in danger of becoming atrophied through inward conflict. And there was a further subtle tie between them. Both, for opposite reasons, were sick men. Both were consumed by a secret remorse and self-dissatisfaction; Coleridge because his roots in the material world were so insecure, Wordsworth because his spiritual being was bound and hampered by the very tenacity of his physical senses. Each supplied the strength which was lacking in the other. And though for Coleridge, who was more vulnerable to life and who gave more than he received, the relationship bore fruit only for a brief period, for Wordsworth it was persistently fruitful so long as it lasted. So long as he could expand outwards from himself to the sun of Coleridge's belief and admiration, his creative life, although always endangered by egoism, persisted.

It is probable that Wordsworth met Coleridge in March 1797, when he went to Bristol with Montagu for a fortnight. But their real friendship began on an evening in June, when Coleridge, after tramping all day from Taunton, came upon Dorothy and her brother out walking in the neighbourhood of Racedown, and introduced himself with characteristic impetuosity.

The first thing, we learn from Dorothy, that was read after he came was a new poem of Wordsworth's, *The Ruined Cottage*, afterwards inserted in the first book of *The Excursion*, as part of the tale of Margaret. 'All that relates to Margaret and the ruined cottage,' Wordsworth wrote in later life, 'was taken from observations made in the south-west of England.' Yet the theme is, of course, once again that of the 'forsaken woman.' Wordsworth had in fact by this time completely abandoned any idea of marrying Annette and she had doubtless acquiesced, but she still continued to haunt his conscience. Among those, however, who listened to this reading was Mary Hutchinson, who had come to visit Dorothy and spent the whole summer at Racedown. Her cheerful spirits and gentle

N

equability had already attracted Wordsworth, and the fact that he associated her with the days before his Fall marked her out for the wife who would eventually satisfy to perfection his need to domesticate the passions which he would never henceforth cease to fear. And if the coming of Mary Hutchinson had made him, in Dorothy's words, 'the life of the whole house,' the presence of Coleridge renewed in him that belief in his vocation as a poet which had languished for so long.

On the first evening of his visit Coleridge repeated two acts and a half of the tragedy *Osorio*, later entitled *Remorse*, upon which he had been working for six months. And the next morning Wordsworth replied with his *Borderers*. It was a strange coincidence that they should both have been writing tragedies, or rather relieving a morbid impulse in melodrama. Coleridge, in fact, during the previous six months, had been sinking back into the morass of himself. The idyllic life of which he had dreamed so expansively when he moved from Clevedon to the cottage at Stowey had not been realised. He had begun to perceive the error of his quixotic marriage, and the depression and listlessness to which his extreme sensibility exposed him had been deepened by the presence in his house of two friends, Charles Lloyd and George Burnett, in both of whom the disease of romanticism had reached an advanced stage. Increasingly he had languished beneath the 'sort of calm hopelessness,' and sense of ultimate isolation, which always affected him when his desire to diffuse himself into life was baulked. 'All men seemed mad to him,' he had written in *Osorio*, 'in this world he found no fit companion.' And it was of himself that he wrote.

No wonder, then, that he was drawn to Wordsworth, a man secretly stricken like himself, as with his quick sympathy he must have divined, but a man too who revealed not only an intense capacity for feeling but just that gaunt, self-limiting stability which he, and such moody understudies of himself as

Charles Lloyd and George Burnett, lacked. In Wordsworth he felt at once a rock to which he could cling, and behind his reserve a deeply sensitive being towards whom he could expand as he always longed to do.

Both men were haunted by a sense of isolation from life and their fellows. Both had known the experience of being lifted by some tidal force into a dream-world of bliss only to be left derelict upon the shore of actuality. And each had sought a solace for their pains in Godwin and been disillusioned. The Coleridge who listened to *The Borderers* on this June morning was, in fact, projecting 'a book of morals in answer to Godwin.'

Inevitably, therefore, he found the play 'absolutely wonderful.' But its author impressed him even more deeply. 'I speak with heartfelt sincerity,' he wrote to his publisher, 'and (I think) unblinded judgment, when I tell you that I feel myself *a little man by his side*, and yet do not think myself the less man than I formerly thought myself.' And in this tribute we see how perfectly Wordsworth supplied his two needs, his need to give himself in humility, and his need to strengthen and stabilise himself through contact with someone more self-contained and self-defensive.

The need in Wordsworth, which he satisfied, was no less real. Ultimately it was probably a deeper need and it was satisfied more gradually. For Wordsworth was not the man to be transformed in a moment. Indeed, he never was really transformed. But something that had been frozen in him was gradually thawed by the selfless warmth of his friend, while his vision which had been confined to uninspired observation or self-poisoning introspection was roused to life again by a visionary enthusiasm which far exceeded his own cautious bounds. Whether he looked outward or inward he began to identify himself once more with the creative principle in all things. He was in touch once again with the reality that had transcended definition in his childhood, and he brought to it a power of conscious concentration developed in the bitter school of experience.

But this creative renewal came gradually and not at a leap as it did with Coleridge. On that first evening Wordsworth admired *Osorio*, thus giving its author 'great hopes,' but it is safe to say that his admiration had none of the lovable excess with which Coleridge acclaimed *The Borderers* on the following morning. Yet Wordsworth's thrifty restraint was as valuable to Coleridge as Coleridge's boundless bounty was to Wordsworth. Each supplied the other's defect, while Dorothy gave to both the exquisite sympathy and organic awareness of one who still lived and moved in the Eden from which they had been expelled.

But it was because Coleridge was a divided being like Wordsworth himself that he could give something which Dorothy could not. Dorothy in her unspoilt natural wisdom 'welcomed what was given, and craved no more.' She lived wholly in the moment and the particular, never seeking to abstract ideas or general laws from her immediate experience. This perfection of response to the particular and capacity for feeling the ultimate essence of life in any one of its manifestations is the rare gift both of the child and of the spiritually emancipated man. But a deep gulf lies between them. And Wordsworth had descended into it. As we have shown, he had ceased to experience the particular with that singleness of being which made it also the universal. And since it was his mind which had enslaved him, he needed above all a mental liberator. And more perhaps than any other living Englishman Coleridge was fitted for the part.

Imperfectly at home in the world of the physical senses, he roamed ecstatically in the world of pure ideas. He brought the light of that 'Reason' which appeals in all its decisions to itself as the ground and *substance* of their truth, to one whose vision had been darkened by the discursive 'Understanding.'

The region of the purely metaphysical was alien to Wordsworth. His grasp upon the concrete was too strong and his genius lay in his power to divine the metaphysical in and through the physical. But to do this his mind had to become positive. It had to co-operate with his senses in an act of imagination and faith.

And the universal mind of Coleridge, which conceived a world of supernatural harmony and love, put to shame all the petty denials of the practical consciousness. It could not lift Wordsworth's mind to its own sublunary plane. But it could inspire it to affirm once again that life in its essence was good, that beyond and beneath the bitter discord and disillusionments of time there might be a timeless reality in which everything was necessary and acceptable. To quote Wordsworth's own later tribute to his friend —

> O capacious soul!
> Placed on this earth to love and understand,
> And from thy presence shed the light of love,
> Shall I be mute, ere thou be spoken of?
> Thy kindred influence to my heart of hearts
> Did also find its way. Thus fear relaxed
> Her overwhelming grasp; thus thoughts and things
> In the self-haunting spirit learned to take
> More rational proportions.

His description of the change was characteristically temperate. And, indeed, Coleridge's philosophy as distinct from his personality was so acceptable because at this time he was still an ardent devotee of Hartley. Godwin had owed much to Hartley, but he had abstracted from Hartley's system only those elements which he needed to support his own anarchistic rationalism. But it was possible to interpret Hartley very differently, and this Coleridge had done. Stirred by the deep spiritual enthusiasm which animated so much of Hartley's writing and accepting Hartley's own surprising claim to be a supporter, not a subverter of Christianity, he regarded him as a 'great Christian Philosopher.'

Such an interpretation was, in fact, as personal and as misleading as Godwin's, and later, of course, Coleridge was to demonstrate with masterly finality the gulf that lay between such a sensational philosophy and Christian idealism. But for the time being by projecting into Hartley's system his own expansive idealism he found no difficulty in reconciling it with Berkeley's, or at least in believing in both at the same time without any sense of contradiction.

Hence the appeal of his thought to Wordsworth. For though Wordsworth was disillusioned of Godwin, he clung tenaciously to Hartley's belief in sensation as the ground of all thought and the soil of all benevolence. To do otherwise would have been to break with his own childhood and youth. And this he could never do. But Coleridge though apparently grafting his innate idealism upon Hartley's materialism and thus compounding not only 'a mind out of the senses,' but a spirit too, made no such demands at this time upon his friend. He opened up infinite horizons to him without suggesting that such horizons could only be reached and possessed by breaking through the closed circle of associated sensation and thought which Hartley analysed so penetratingly. Thus Wordsworth was able to share his friend's enthusiasm while preserving his matter-of-factness, to enjoy at the same time the raptures of a benevolent idealism and the self-regarding prudence of common-sense materialism.

Yet although Coleridge could never tempt his friend to abandon his native prudence, the change he wrought in him, as a person rather than as a philosopher, was vital. Wordsworth came to see life in 'more rational proportions' because his reason was quickened and enlarged from within. He perceived things in their universal as well as their particular relations because he was infected by the selflessness which in Coleridge was so dangerously developed that he often lost his sense of both personal identity and personal responsibility.

In Wordsworth this could never be. Nothing could ultimately dissolve the hard core of his obstinate selfhood. To that he owed both his virtue and his defects. But since the self-assertive impulse is no less fundamental to life than the self-surrendering, its predominance within limits was not fatal to creativeness. And Coleridge, through fostering by his example and influence the tendency to self-surrender in his friend, redressed the balance which had previously been fatally overweighted. He recognised Wordsworth's one-sidedness, writing of him that 'of all the men I ever knew, Wordsworth has the least femineity in his mind. He is all man. He is a man of whom it might have been said—It is good for him to be alone.'

But to be alone, not with the creative mystery but with his own isolated self, was to be sterile. And Coleridge, in whom feminine receptivity was as much overdeveloped as masculine assertiveness in his friend, fertilised the self of Wordsworth. He enabled him to project himself into life and to receive life into himself to the extreme limit that his ever-insistent and retentive egoism would allow. And ten years of poetic fertility testify to the service which he wrought.

§ 5

Racedown and Nether Stowey lay nearly forty miles apart. And even for such tireless walkers as the Wordsworths and Coleridge, this was a serious bar to the degree of intimacy which they now desired. The Wordsworths, however, were free to move if a house within their means could be found, and Coleridge's enthusiastic account of Stowey as well as his presence there drew them strongly towards it.

Coleridge returned home after a ten days' visit which had transformed three people into 'one soul.' But within a week he was at Racedown again, and carried Wordsworth back with him to Stowey. Wordsworth was captivated by the beauty of the Quantocks, and it was found that a good house could probably be rented on exceptionally easy terms only four miles from Stowey.

Consequently on 2nd July 1797 the Wordsworths came on a visit to the Coleridges which set the seal upon their intimacy. For two weeks they crowded with Basil into the little cottage which already contained Mrs. Coleridge, Hartley, and a maid, and for the second week they were joined by Charles Lamb. Coleridge himself was physically incapacitated by a pan of boiling milk which his wife accidentally spilt over his foot, but spiritually he was reawakened. His sympathies had found an outlet which promised to be as permanent as anything in this transient life can be. And as he watched his guests set out upon one of their wanderings about the wooded hills, Wordsworth's tall, gaunt figure contrasting almost grotesquely with the gipsy smallness of Charles Lamb and of her whom he already called 'my sister,' his heart was full of peace and joy for the gift of friendship which life had brought to his door. And the perfection of the gift lay even more in the opportunity which it afforded for giving than for receiving. It was a joy to acknowledge Wordsworth's strength where he himself was weak, to proclaim that he was 'a very great man, the only man to whom *at all times* and *in all modes of excellence* I feel myself inferior.'

And before the end of the fortnight the Wordsworths had procured the house of which they had heard, a long, low country house named Alfoxden, surrounded by a heavily wooded park, extending far back into the Quantock hills and with a view, to the north-east, of the Bristol Channel. It was to be let very cheaply simply to keep it inhabited during its owner's minority, and on 16th July the Wordsworths moved into it.

Dorothy wrote enthusiastically of the park, 'There is everything there; sea, woods wild as fancy ever painted, brooks clear and pebbly as in Cumberland, villages so romantic; and William and I, in a wander by ourselves, found out a sequestered waterfall in a dell formed by steep hills covered with full-grown timber-trees. The woods are as fine as those at Lowther, and the country more romantic; it has the character of the less grand parts of the neighbourhood of the lakes.'

Truly everything seemed to be conspiring to heal Wordsworth's wounds and open the way to a new life. His reviving spirit had 'great allies' indeed—Coleridge, Dorothy, Nature at her most lyrical, and the soothing domestic promise of Mary Hutchinson. At Stowey, too, was Coleridge's friend and neighbour, Tom Poole, whose staunch qualities reminded Wordsworth of the Westmorland 'statesmen' of his boyhood, and whose success as a business-man showed that radicalism, if it was reasoned and practical, need not prove the false illusion which France had seemed to declare it.

On the day after moving into Alfoxden another radical friend, too, of Coleridge's appeared, and one whose principles had been put to the test of persecution. This was Thelwall, whose activities as an agitator had brought him to prison in the Tower and to Newgate on a charge of high treason, of which, however, he had been acquitted. Like most of those who were rebelling against the vested interests of the Church and the privileged classes, he proclaimed himself an atheist. But his denial of the oppressive God of orthodoxy was the necessary counterpart of his real compassion for the poor and oppressed, whose maimed lives he had described in much verse, poor in quality but kindred in aim to Wordsworth's.

And even in his atheism he was far nearer to Wordsworth than to Coleridge, who had never, even at the height of his enthusiasm for Hartley's materialism, abandoned his belief in the transcendental, who charged Thelwall with 'anti-religious bigotry,' and who was soon to wish that Wordsworth loved and venerated Christ and Christianity more.

Thelwall, indeed, like Poole, must have opened Wordsworth's eyes to the fact that it was possible to be a radical without being a Godwinian pedant. He was, in Wordsworth's words, 'a man of extraordinary talent, an affectionate husband, and a good father. Though brought up in the City, he was truly sensible of the beauty of natural objects.' And as the three friends rambled about the grounds and woods of Alfoxden or the slopes of the Quantocks, while Thelwall passed sentence on the productions and characters of the age and Coleridge extended himself in the ageless realm of metaphysics, Wordsworth may well have felt that he had lost faith too easily in the new world and the new man that was to be born.

Thelwall's visit of ten days, however, had unfortunate practical results. His history and opinions were known, and someone sent word to the authorities that disaffected persons were gathering about Nether Stowey. In that time of panic anything was believed, and admittedly Wordsworth's habit of wandering about at night and looking 'rather strangely at the moon,' or of roaming 'over the hills, like a partridge,' and muttering as he walked, was likely to excite suspicion, which the unusual appearance of Dorothy and Coleridge would tend to increase. Consequently the mother of the heir to Alfoxden was urged to consider her dangerous tenants' credentials, and although Tom Poole guaranteed the respectability of a family which included a canon of Windsor, and insisted that 'Mr. Wordsworth of all men alive, is the last who will give any one cause to complain of his opinions, his conduct, or his disturbing the peace of any one,' notice was served upon him to quit Alfoxden at the end of a year, when the lease expired.

This was a serious blow to Coleridge, who could not

'endure to think of losing' his new friend. And it must have troubled Wordsworth too. But at least it strengthened his conviction that the forces of reaction were contemptible, if the forces of radicalism were dangerous. And a whole year remained in which to consolidate his poetical alliance with Coleridge and re-establish his inner self.

During the late summer and autumn months they were constantly together, Coleridge diffusing his magnetism recklessly, Wordsworth thriftily responding and gradually filling up a reservoir of power. In Coleridge poetry flowered with a tropical speed and luxuriance, but Wordsworth, obeying his own slower rhythm, was not to be hurried into composition, and Coleridge's attempts to draw him into creative partnership failed, both in the famous venture of *The Ancient Mariner* and in a suggested prose rhapsody, to be entitled *The Wanderings of Cain*.

Nor was he unduly disappointed when in December the managers of Covent Garden rejected *The Borderers*. 'There is little need to advise me against publishing,' he wrote; 'it is a thing which I dread as much as death itself . . . privacy and quiet are my delight.' Nevertheless the three weeks' visit to London which he paid at the same time momentarily quickened his creative impulse, if only by deepening his attachment to the country. For it seems probable that *The Reverie of Poor Susan* was composed at this time, the first of his shorter lyrics to be distinctively his own.

But he was not yet ripe for composition. And this was not due so much to inward uncertainty as to his innate caution and foresight. Poetry for him was not only a vocation but a profession which demanded preparation. Unlike Coleridge, who wrote entirely from immediate subjective impulse, he was working out an objective plan. He had already, in his own words, 'carved out work for at least a year and a half,' and it was significant that as a preface to this work he had been writing 'a short essay, illustrative of that constitution and those tendencies of human nature which make the apparently *motiveless* actions of bad men intelligible to careful observers.'

Continuity was an outstanding fact of Wordsworth's whole career. It was not in him to take sudden leaps. He advanced slowly, consolidating his position at each step. And so now he began from where he had left off in *The Borderers*, and the purpose which he set before himself as a poet was not merely self-expression, but a psychological study of human nature. The two were of course intimately involved. For all knowledge of human life depends upon the explorer's degree of self-knowledge. The characters which he creates and interprets are self-discoveries. And of few men was this to be more true than Wordsworth. But he was to be a great poet because his intense interest in himself was more than personal. He could contemplate his past experiences with a certain detachment, while at the same time renewing them imaginatively. And by thus disinterestedly realising his own nature, he achieved a new and significant picture of human nature.

It was for such an achievement that he was now consciously preparing himself. And if his design was in keeping with his native shrewdness and forethought, it was primarily dictated by his desire to escape from morbid introspection. By objectifying his experience and projecting it into the forms of poetry, he ceased to be enslaved by it. Much art, and romantic art in particular, originates in a neurosis. But the true artist triumphs over his neurosis by sublimating it. And thus it was with Wordsworth. He was haunted by a sense of sin which had stultified even his ecstatic communion with Nature. And by dramatising his remorse and objectifying his moral problem, he succeeded in raising himself above it sufficiently to renew again not only his instinctive joy in life, but those moments of super-sensuous ecstasy when the infinite possessed him.

Although therefore the detailed classification which he later attached to his shorter poems cannot be said to represent his original intention, there can be little doubt that a preconceived plan underlay their creation. If they were not yet intended, as he claimed later, to reveal the growth of the individual 'commencing with Childhood, and terminating with Old Age, Death, and Immortality,' he had at least visualised the task of exploring the nature of the individual at three stages of development, those of childhood, youth, and manhood.

This objective study of humanity was also in essence, as we have said, a subjective expression of himself, and its terms of reference emphasise the fact. For it was in the transition from youth to manhood that he had fallen into the abyss of discord and apathy from which he was now emerging. And he rightly felt that the nature of the child might throw considerable light on the process of readjustment upon which he had now entered.

As we shall see, he was as much concerned with the relations of childhood, youth, and manhood to external nature as with their inward characteristics, since a true response to Nature was in his own experience the measure of human virtue. Hence his choice of rustic characters who, living near to Nature, revealed the interplay of the natural and the human with the immediacy which he himself had known.

But there was another reason. As his faith in himself returned, his interest in events in France revived. And Coleridge quickened this interest. We know from *France: an Ode*, and *Fears in Solitude*, written in the early months of 1798, that Coleridge was at this time torn between his ideal belief in freedom and his realisation that men might be 'too sensual to be free.' His position, in fact, was much the same as Wordsworth's had been two years before, while the victories of Napoleon and the war-fever in England made it even less possible to believe that either side were furthering the cause of humanity.

To awake to feeling, therefore, concerning France, was for Wordsworth to open an old wound. Consequently it was the more necessary to divert his feelings from the problems of humanity in general and the dangerous province of European politics and to concentrate them upon the rural individual. For it was possible to contemplate the peasant and the child without losing hope or faith in human nature. And the more virtue he rediscovered in them, the more convinced he became that the earlier ideals of the Revolution had been defeated by men who had broken that bond with Nature which the peasant had preserved. He himself had fallen into sin for the same reason. And by renewing, if imperfectly, his faith in Nature through the peasant and the child he was able to view the Revolution as a wilful aberration rather than a final disaster.

By so doing he turned his back upon the ideas and forces which for good and evil were to determine human development during the next hundred years. He restricted the possibilities of a good life, both for the individual and society within the traditional limits of a rural economy and a primitive stage of development. And inevitably he came to oppose not only the vices of industrialism but the constructive liberalism which these social evils provoked.

It was thus that he became 'The Lost Leader,' denying the creative impulse behind the French Revolution because he was haunted by the nightmare of its destructiveness, instead of striving to purify and establish that impulse, when the conflagration had burnt itself out.

§ 6

But such an issue seemed remote during the early months of 1798, when with Dorothy and often with Coleridge he walked in the wood that separated Alfoxden from the village of Holford, and on the hills above from which they could see the

Bristol Channel and the Welsh coast beyond. Once again the active and passive elements in his nature were vitally balanced. The excessive mental introversion from which he had suffered was being rapidly corrected, and the time had now come when he was sufficiently responsive to life to be able to give himself again in words.

The first of the compositions which were to herald a renaissance in his life and in English poetry was entitled *A Night Piece*. He said later that it was 'composed on the road between Nether Stowey and Alfoxden, extempore.' Yet its delicate descriptive detail does not suggest the extemporary, although doubtless it may have been elaborated from a mental sketch made and memorised at the moment. The probability of this is increased by the clear parallelisms to be found between the poem and entries in Dorothy's *Journal*, describing what they saw on two evenings, 25th and 31st January. And this raises the further question as to how much Dorothy did give to her brother eyes and ears.

Coleridge, who was so much more susceptible to the influence of others and also so much less objective in his vision than Wordsworth, doubtless did owe to her many of the delicate discoveries in Nature which are to be found both in her *Journal* and his *Christabel*. But Wordsworth had already proved in his earlier verse that he possessed unusual powers of minute observance and had later become the slave of this most despotic of all the faculties. It is reasonable, therefore, to suppose that as he and Dorothy rambled in the neighbourhood of Alfoxden they saw in unison or at most collaborated rather than that she taught her brother to see.

What she did eventually help to teach him was to feel the radiant wonder and finality of what they saw together. And doubtless her journal supplemented at times his memory. It may well have done so in the composition of *A Night Piece*. But the interest of this first hesitating shoot of his great creative period lies in the fact that it shows him still to be rather a curious observer of natural phenomena than identified with Nature through that interchange of love 'from earth to man, from man to earth,' which he was to know in 'the hour of feeling.'

He lifted his eyes to the clouded sky, he noted with lively appreciation the illusion that the moon and the stars were being driven across a dark abyss by the wind and then, as the clouds closed over them,

> the mind
> Not undisturbed by the delight it feels,
> Which slowly settles into peaceful calm,
> Is left to muse upon the solemn scene.

Observance and vision, the feeling heart and the meditating mind, were not yet reconciled, although we have a hint here of the manner in which they were to be blended in a poetry which took its origin 'from emotion recollected in tranquillity.'

But for that creative and contemplative process to become effective it was necessary to have a strong originating emotion. And despite Dorothy's vivid example he was not yet capable of responding with his whole being to Nature. He was to return in fact to Nature through human nature to the study of which he could now bring that deep personal feeling which transforms things seen and heard from curious objects of sense to unique inward experiences.

Early in February Coleridge, who had been preaching at Shrewsbury and had been dissuaded from entering the Unitarian Ministry by the Wedgwoods' generous offer of an annuity, was back at Stowey, and for the next three months was constantly at Alfoxden at all hours of the day and night. Wordsworth and he had now planned to combine in a volume which was to consist 'of poems chiefly on supernatural subjects taken from common life, but looked at, as much as might be, through an imaginative medium.' This involved, also, the use of a simple and natural style such as had been common both to the language of poetry and of everyday life, before it had become corrupted by the artifices of poetic diction and the conventions of polite society.

But while they were agreed concerning the necessity of simplifying and vivifying the style of poetry, each approached the supernatural from an opposite direction, Coleridge endeavouring to give 'a human interest and a semblance of truth' to the magical and transcendental, Wordsworth seeking to discover in the things of every day the working of spiritual forces. *The Ancient Mariner*, which was not completed until late in March, and *Christabel*, were the fruit of the one approach; *We are Seven*, *The Thorn*, *The Idiot Boy*, *Her Eyes are Wild* and *Peter Bell*, were some of the first-fruits of the other.

And since Wordsworth was approaching the supernatural through the common and habitual life of men, he was obviously more concerned than Coleridge with the possibility of writing poetry in what he later described as 'the real language of men.' Coleridge, indeed, can never have gone to such literal extremes in this necessary revolt against artificial diction, but he was too generously appreciative of his friend's practice to dispute his theory even when, as was shortly to happen, it was proclaimed in a preface to the contemplated volume. And this was to involve him in much misunderstanding which he was too loyal and possibly too indolent to remove for seventeen years.

We are not, however, much concerned with the problem of poetic diction in this book. For it is not central to Wordsworth's development, but only reflects on the verbal level his deeper confusion of thought concerning the creative virtue of Nature and the natural man, and the relation of the actual to the real.

Fortunately, however, at this time he obeyed his genius rather than his rationalising mind. The simplicity which he

o

achieved was dictated by an inward necessity, not by a theory of diction, just as the power of *association* which his poetry revealed, did not derive from the theories of Hartley, which he had been discussing with Coleridge, but from the imaginative impulse which the faculty of association inevitably subserved.

We know from Dorothy's *Journal* how much the composition of these poems cost her brother in the pains of travail and subsequent exhaustion. They frequently left him tired and ill. And this was not only due to the strain of creative concentration. It was due also to the fact that in many of them he was still probing the wound of his fatal passion for Annette. But Dorothy was always at hand to divert and console, and his days were agreeably divided between contemplation and action. The mornings were devoted to composition, the afternoons and evenings to walking. Often Coleridge went with them, sometimes Tom Poole and their little charge, Basil. And doubtless it was of these walks that he was thinking when he wrote in *The Excursion*—

> Wild were the walks upon those lonely Downs,
> Track leading into track; how marked, how worn
> Into bright verdure, between fern and gorse
> Winding away its never-ending line
> On their smooth surface, evidence was none;
> But, there, lay open to our daily haunt,
> A range of unappropriated earth,
> Where youth's ambitious feet might move at large;
> Whence, unmolested wanderers, we beheld
> The shining giver of the day diffuse
> His brightness o'er a tract of sea and land
> Gay as our spirits, free as our desires;
> As our enjoyments, boundless. From those heights
> We dropped, at pleasure, into sylvan combs;

> Where arbours of impenetrable shade,
> And mossy seats, detained us side by side,
> With hearts at ease, and knowledge in our hearts
> 'That all the grove and all the day was ours.'

In 1798 he was not, indeed, capable of throwing off the self-haunted mood so completely as these lines suggest. He was still often a sick man in mind as well as body. But as he roved with Dorothy 'upon smooth Quantock's airy ridge' or listened to Coleridge chanting 'in bewitching words, with happy heart'

> the vision of that Ancient Man,
> The bright-eyed Mariner,

the burden of his secret self was lifted. Throughout the morning he might have known only the travail of creation, but in the afternoon he was rewarded by a sense of its after-joy. The pain so long pent within him was released in an outflowing music, and he, too, like Coleridge,

> steeped
> In soft forgetfulness the livelong hours,
> Murmuring of him who, joyous hap, was found,
> After the perils of his moonlight ride,
> Near the loud waterfall; or her who sate
> In misery near the miserable Thorn.

In May they ranged further afield, visiting Cheddar and going by way of Wells and Bristol through the valley of the Wye to Thelwall's farm, which lay about forty miles further west. And later in the same month came the youthful William Hazlitt, who had been enchanted earlier in the year by Coleridge's eloquence when he heard him preach in a Shrewsbury Chapel, and who was now to receive a vivid and unforgettable impression of Wordsworth.

Coleridge took him over to Alfoxden soon after his arrival, but Wordsworth was not at home. Two days later, however, he arrived from Bristol at Coleridge's cottage, and it was thus that Hazlitt saw him—'He answered in some degree to his friend's description of him, but was more gaunt and Don Quixote-like. He was quaintly dressed (according to the *costume* of that unconstrained period) in a brown fustian jacket and striped pantaloons. There was something of a roll, a lounge in his gait, not unlike his own *Peter Bell*. There was a severe, worn pressure of thought about his temples, a fire in his eye (as if he saw something in objects more than the outward appearance), an intense, high, narrow forehead, a Roman nose, cheeks furrowed by strong purpose and feeling, and a convulsive inclination to laughter about the mouth, a good deal at variance with the solemn, stately expression of the rest of his face. . . . He sat down and talked very naturally and freely, with a mixture of clear gushing accents in his voice, a deep guttural intonation, and a strong tincture of the northern *burr* like the crust on wine.'

On the day following they went over to Alfoxden, and Wordsworth read aloud in the open air his *Peter Bell*. 'Whatever,' added Hazlitt, 'might be thought of the poem, "his face was a book where men might read strange matters," and he announced the fate of his hero in prophetic tones.' The picture is full of graphic and convincing detail, and although Hazlitt was ignorant of Wordsworth's history, he clearly *saw* it in his face.

Meanwhile the plan of combining with Coleridge in a volume of poetry was soon to be realised. Cottle, a Bristol bookseller, had met Wordsworth at Coleridge's cottage earlier in the year and had been so impressed by the lyrical pieces which he had read to him that he offered at once to publish them. Wordsworth, however, who had only recently brought himself to the point where composition was again possible, refused.

But in April he had gained so much in self-confidence that he invited Cottle to Alfoxden and under the old trees in the park read to him the new poems which he had added so rapidly to his stock. He was now eager to publish, the more so because he and Dorothy were planning to go to Germany for two years when the lease of Alfoxden expired at the end of June, and so was anxious to raise money for the trip.

Cottle repeated his offer, and it was agreed that the proposed volume should be published anonymously and entitled *Lyrical Ballads*, and that it should, with the exception of *The Ancient Mariner*, consist of shorter pieces. It did not appear until the second week in September, when the Wordsworths and Coleridge were about to set out to Germany, but since its contents originated during the first six months of the year, we will consider them, with the other excluded poems, here.

PART VI

FIRST FRUITS

§ 1

BEHIND Wordsworth's poetical activity during these six months there had been, as we have suggested, a controlling purpose. It was to give 'the history or science of the feelings,' and to present ordinary incidents in such a way as to illustrate the working of 'the primary laws of our nature.' He had already, with the philosopher Hartley's assistance, conceived a general scheme of human life which his poetry was both to interpret and to make real, by revealing the vital reaction of individuals to life at certain points in their development.

He had learnt from Godwin's errors that an abstract and rationalistic study of Man was inevitably delusive and unreal, and he had already, under Coleridge's and Dorothy's influence, recovered much of his original capacity for vital experience. Consequently he had come once again into direct contact with reality on a comparatively elementary level, and the poems which he had written dealt with men, women and children who revealed this immediate relation to life, who, in a true sense, suffered whether joy or pain, and whose utterance and conduct, therefore, however apparently irrational, were real and laid bare, as no second-hand knowledge could, the foundations of Truth and Wisdom.

Wordsworth's ultimate intention was to rise from the foundations to the superstructure, to trace the progress of man's powers as self-consciousness supervened upon natural simplicity. But, as we shall see, he could not advance beyond the point at which he himself ceased to progress.

In 1798, however, no second-hand piety had supervened upon the 'natural piety' with which he wished his 'days to be bound each to each,' and he was drawn to a study of simple and submissive people with all the intensified affection of one who had been exiled in a dreary and complex country of the mind and who by sympathising with their deep and direct fidelity to life imaginatively renewed his own youth and innocence.

The 'great and simple affections of our nature' upon which he concentrated in *Lyrical Ballads* were those of the mother, the child, the countryman in middle life and old age, and of himself as he awoke to joy from the long winter of his discontent and apathy in the spring of 1798. But in fact he projected his own experience into each of his subjects. And because he truly identified himself with them, he ceased to rationalise human suffering, as he had in parts of *Guilt and Sorrow*, or to exploit it in melodrama as he had more obviously done in *The Borderers*.

The experiences of which he wrote were felt both in heart and mind. Hence the simplicity and directness of his style. Hence also the blending of deep personal feeling with some degree of impersonal detachment. He no longer fed upon his own private anguish, but used it as a key to unlock the lives and sufferings of others. And this was true even of the feelings which had haunted him most painfully, his pity and remorse for Annette. For with one exception the poems which he devoted to mother-love (*The Thorn*, *Her Eyes are Wild*—originally entitled *The Mad Mother*—*The Complaint of a Forsaken Indian Woman*, and *The Idiot Boy*), dealt once again with the theme of the deserted woman.

But deeply involved in this theme as his feelings still were, he could bring to the subject the degree of detached contemplation necessary to make it objectively real. And so the pain which had previously eaten into his being now flowered into beauty, the beauty of—

> At all times of the day and night
> This wretched woman thither goes;

> And she is known to every star,
> And every wind that blows;
> And there, beside the Thorn, she sits
> When the blue daylight's in the skies,
> And when the whirlwind's on the hill,
> Or frosty air is keen and still,
> And to herself she cries,
> 'Oh misery! Oh misery!
> Oh woe is me! Oh misery!'

The redemptive power of the imagination could not be better displayed than in these poems in which an experience that had so deeply wounded Wordsworth and the bitter theme of undeserved human suffering become forms of beauty, because they are no longer felt as oppressive accidents of time, but as spiritual necessities, timelessly real. And they reveal, too, how intimate is the marriage of the personal and the impersonal in the mystery of Creation. For if the pure poet speaks in such lines as the following, the man who in his own eyes had betrayed Annette speaks too—

> Her state to any eye was plain;
> She was with child, and she was mad;
> Yet often was she sober sad
> From her exceeding pain.
> *O guilty Father—would that death*
> *Had saved him from that breach of faith!*

or

> If his sweet boy he could forsake,
> With me he never could have stayed:
> From him no harm my babe can take;
> But he, poor man! is wretched made;
> And every day we two will pray
> For him that's gone and far away.

And again in the following lines we have a recollection of the actual pain which Annette had suffered when parted from her child, soon after its birth, as she had told Wordsworth in a letter—

> My Child! they gave thee to another,
> A woman who was not thy mother,
> When from my arms my Babe they took,
> Oh me, how strangely did he look!

By such a magical process can imagination at once transform personal feeling, if it be intense enough, into universal experience, and mould conflicting feelings into a living unity; so that Wordsworth could in the same stanza judge himself for forsaking Annette and console himself for being so 'wretched made,' while the pity for her, which must have so often gnawed at his heart, as he walked beneath the stars, becomes the cry of all forlorn and suffering women, whom life and love have betrayed.

But the thought of Mother-love was now no longer necessarily associated in his mind with that of desertion. Imagination had liberated him to this extent from bondage to his actual past. And *The Idiot Boy*, composed almost extempore in the woods of Alfoxden, is instinct with the gleeful mood that possessed him at that time. Wordsworth's humour was characteristic. Judged by urban standards he was humourless, and his occasional efforts to be witty were ponderous. But out of the depths of his dour and reserved being, like a spring from a mountain side, there could gush a stream of ecstatic gaiety. And although to the sophisticated mind *The Idiot Boy* may seem little more than a farcical extravaganza, its gleefulness springs from a deep and elemental source. The 'Good Betty' and her idiot child are of the order of God's fools. Their joy is the inspiration of innocence, while Betty's flustered love and anxiety, despite their apparent absurdities, belong truly to 'the great and simple affections of our nature.'

Wordsworth remarked later that he 'never wrote anything with so much glee as this poem.' And this is very understandable. For the feeling which he expressed here lay outside the bounds of the rational consciousness and all the pains and perplexities that it involved. Betty and her idiot boy might be sub-rational judged by Godwinian standards, but they had the child's spontaneity and purity of response to life. Hence their joy.

> She kisses o'er and o'er again
> Him whom she loves, her Idiot Boy;
> She's happy here, is happy there,
> She is uneasy every where;
> Her limbs are all alive with joy.

Such joy, as Wordsworth knew, was the reward of the pure in heart, whether they had the exquisite sensibility of his sister, or were simpletons like Betty Foy. For they were selfless, and so the same vital music played through them as through the lamb leaping in the meadow or the daffodil nodding by the lake.

And it played through Wordsworth as he wrote, dictating the laughing spontaneity of his poem or the exquisite simplicity of such lines as these —

> By this the stars were almost gone,
> The moon was setting on the hill,
> So pale you scarcely looked at her:
> The little birds began to stir,
> Though yet their tongues were still.

These lines are enough to show how remarkably Wordsworth

had recovered his power to feel Nature with all his senses quickened and purified, and with the fret of the self-conscious mind at times so utterly stilled that he could almost hear the grass growing.

But the *Lyrical Ballads* show that he had recovered, also, his primitive sense of the 'numinous' or 'demonic,' of a power which utterly transcended both actuality and human understanding, and was awesome in its elemental mystery. Even in *The Idiot Boy* the pressure of the supernatural forces is constantly felt, particularly in the wild fancies that pass through Johnny's mind, as he rides 'all silent as a horseman-ghost' beneath the stars. This mingling of domestic simplicity with a strange otherness which transcends all human dimensions was but another proof of the close affinity of Wordsworth's own primitive consciousness with the primitive natures of which he wrote. For behind all the credulity of primitive superstition lies a true and immediate sense of a spiritual world that encircles and permeates the material. And it was because Wordsworth divined such a world that he was a potential mystic, and could make real in his poetry the superstitions of the peasant, as when he wrote in *The Thorn* —

> And all that winter, when at night
> The wind blew from the mountain-peak,
> 'Twas worth your while, though in the dark,
> The churchyard path to seek:
> For many a time and oft were heard
> Cries coming from the mountain head:
> Some plainly living voices were;
> And others, I've heard many swear,
> Were voices of the dead.

The two poems in *Lyrical Ballads* devoted to the affections of the child were *We are Seven* and *Anecdote for Fathers*. The little girl who was the heroine of the former had crossed his path during that memorable journey in 1793 across Salisbury Plain, when he had seemed for a surprised hour to have sight of a 'new world.' And since he had in fact now entered, after long delay, the 'new world' of which he had then but a brief and tantalising glimpse, it was natural that this incident should spring up in his memory, clothed with a particular significance.

But even if the incident did occur as recounted in the poem, it derived most of its significance from his own childhood, of which he later wrote that 'nothing was more difficult for me in childhood than to admit the notion of death as a state applicable to my own being.'

The 'simple child' of the poem, however, refuses to entertain the idea of death, not from any conscious sense of the indomitableness of the Spirit within her, but through the completeness of her physical integrity. She is too instinctively alive for such mental concepts as life or death to have any meaning for her. Or, to put it more succinctly, she *is* life, and therefore she cannot know death. And in refusing to attribute to her any understanding of such a religious notion as 'their Spirits are in heaven,' Wordsworth was a true psychologist. Later in his life, indeed, through his failure to achieve that pure realisation of being on the conscious level which the child unconsciously enjoys, he did tend to ascribe to the instinctive spirituality of the child moral and visionary qualities which it did not possess. But in *We are Seven* his personal needs and regrets did not thus pervert his objective insight.

And in *Anecdote for Fathers* the distinctive nature of childhood and its refusal to rationalise its feelings were no less clearly emphasised. We do not need Wordsworth's own account of the day and the mood in which the poem was conceived to know that it was gleefully written. And, as in *The Idiot Boy*, some at least of his glee was due to the little Basil's unconscious refutation of rationalism. The reason which the child gave for preferring to be at Kilve was, judged by adult and logical standards, quite untrue. But to the child who could not explain his feelings, but only affirm them, the glittering vane on the house-top was as true a symbol of his preference as any other pleasing object which he might happen to see.

And what Wordsworth learnt from him and wished to teach was not only the folly of obtruding adult ideas of cause and effect into the premental experience of the child, but also that such abstract and logical thinking was in fact less real and necessary than the child's apparent caprice, in so far as it was divorced from immediate feeling. This, indeed, was the essential lesson which he acknowledged in the lines —

> O dearest, dearest boy! my heart
> For better lore would seldom yearn,
> Could I but teach the hundredth part
> Of what from thee I learn.

The poems devoted to the simple affections of the countryman revealed the same fidelity to feeling preserved unbroken into middle and old age. In the old huntsman, 'Simon Lee,' he drew a character who equally in his youth, his prime, and his decline gave himself, like a child, to life. Both the primitive ecstasy which he had enjoyed in the chase and the pathetic gratitude which he showed in old age for a small service done to him, were conditioned by his innate selflessness. It was a selflessness akin to that of the hounds whose voices he so dearly loved, and he was as little capable as they of resenting the neglect and poverty which fate had brought him or the social callousness which tolerated it. Indeed, there can be few who have not in some measure felt as Wordsworth did in the

last stanza, when they have looked into the eyes of an old and
faithful dog —

> The tears into his eyes were brought,
> And thanks and praises seemed to run
> So fast out of his heart, I thought
> They never would have done.
> —I've heard of hearts unkind, kind deeds
> With coldness still returning;
> Alas! the gratitude of men
> Hath oftener left me mourning.

Once again, therefore, the contrast implied was between the
premoral goodness of those who instinctively resigned themselves to life and the impoverished virtue of the mentally self-
conscious. And in *The Last of the Flock* we have another
moving example of the poor man's submission to fate. But the
sturdy farmer of this poem, who had fallen upon evil times and
wept in the public road, was not so simple and undifferentiated
a being as Simon Lee. He had accumulated a flock of sheep
and a family of children, and the bitter conflict between these
two tenacious attachments is of course the subject of the poem.
And it was a subject which Wordsworth was particularly
qualified to realise with a simple depth of feeling. His admiration of the 'Statesmen,' the small free-holders, of his northern
dales has been remarked, and it sprang not only from observance of their virtues, their industry, capacity, and self-respect,
but from a real affinity with them. For despite his Revolutionary enthusiasms, he was essentially a tenacious individualist.
Consequently he felt the anguish of a man who was thus
pitifully deprived of his hard-earned possessions quite as
intensely as the gratitude of the old huntsman who had never
sought to possess anything.

Few of course can fail to share his feelings, or deny that the
farmer's attachment to his flock was a 'great and simple

affection of our nature.' Yet it was an affection which, unlike Simon Lee's for the voice of the hounds, had become to some extent possessive. Doubtless family affection, so far as it is self-centred and exclusive, is of the same order. But what Wordsworth failed to realise was that such instincts, however immediate and rooted in Nature, exposed the ultimate inadequacy of the naturalistic philosophy which he was developing.

The Last of the Flock has been described by Professor Beatty as 'a counterblast to Godwin's attack on property as the great evil of society,' and it is significant as the first of several such counterblasts of which *Michael* was to be the most notable, and as portending an attitude to life which was to be more and more characteristic of Wordsworth. For while Godwin's attack on property was facile because he disregarded the primary instinct in which it was rooted, Wordsworth's acceptance and even sanctification of that instinct was no less misleading.

The problem which both the individual and society in their development had to solve was how to recover the creature love of a Simon Lee on the higher level of conscious disinterested-ness. In sanctifying, therefore, 'the love of property, including the feelings of inheritance, home and personal and family independence,' Wordsworth was obeying a very natural and powerful impulse. But he was also denying the vision which he had once had of a humanity liberated from self, even more fatally than by his too insistent backward glances to the status of the child and the primitive.

But in *The Old Cumberland Beggar* the virtues of the primitive and the 'propertied' were significantly contrasted. In the earlier part of the poem he described the old beggar's service as being to remind more favoured people of the necessity of giving, to afford them the after-joy of patronage, to teach them to appreciate their better fortune and to encourage them, by the contrast his own state presented, in habits of prudence and thrift. Wordsworth, however, while approving such 'virtuous decency,' realised at this time that there was a truer charity, which transcended self-respect and prudence and even 'the moral law established in the land,' and which was found chiefly among the dispossessed and so unpossessive poor—

> But of the poor man ask, the abject poor,
> Go, and demand of him, if there be here
> In this cold abstinence from evil deeds,
> And these inevitable charities,
> Wherewith to satisfy the human soul?
> No—man is dear to man; the poorest poor
> Long for some moments in a weary life
> When they can know and feel that they have been,
> Themselves, the fathers and the dealers-out
> Of some small blessings; have been kind to such
> As needed kindness, *for this single cause,*
> *That we have all of us one human heart.*

Here, then, once again Wordsworth showed that 'the simple affections' were only manifested purely on the most primitive and passive level. Just as the hero of *The Last of the Flock* was relatively an egoist, compared with the improvident and childlike Simon Lee, so the more prosperous patrons of the old Cumberland beggar were only self-concerned philanthropists compared with the abject poor, whose charity was life-inspired and unthinking.

And in this study of the human relationship existing between working peasants and wandering beggars Wordsworth was objectifying anew his own moral dilemma. His heart approved the unqualified generosity of the 'abject poor,' but his head the 'virtuous decency' of their social superiors. Neither class, however, could teach him how to pass through self-consciousness to a renewed fullness of life. He could only feel that there was more essential virtue in the resignation of the very poor and simple and that such passivity as theirs was a corrective of which he was in need.

But with the renewal of his physical vitality in the spring of 1798 an instinctive return to Nature seemed to offer a simple solution of his problem, and in four lyrics he celebrated such a return with particular felicity. Yet it was significant that in each of them he stressed the contrast between Nature and man, and the opposition between the instincts that affirmed and the mind that denied. In *Lines Written in Early Spring* he told how, as he sat by the side of a water-fall made by a brook in the grounds of Alfoxden, he felt the least motion of the hopping birds or of the budding twigs trembling in the breeze, like 'a thrill of pleasure.' Every flower, he was convinced, enjoyed the air it breathed, and at the moment so did he: yet not so completely that he could quite forget his all too human mind which lurked, as a destructive principle, in the background, denying 'Nature's holy plan,' and giving him

> reason to lament
> What man has made of man.

And in the lines addressed *To My Sister* the same opposition between thought and sensation was emphasised. The Love which Wordsworth there acclaimed was indistinguishable from the Life that stirred expansively in the soil and the sod. Just as the bare trees sensed 'the blessing in the air,' so all that was hard and sterile in man melted in this 'hour of feeling.'

> One moment now may give us more
> Than years of toiling reason:
> Our minds shall drink at every pore
> The spirit of the season.
>
> Some silent laws our hearts will make,
> Which they shall long obey:

P

> We for the year to come may take
> Our temper from to-day.

> And from the blessed power that rolls
> About, below, above,
> We'll frame the measure of our souls:
> They shall be tuned to love.

In *Expostulation and Reply* he rejoiced in the same instinctive rejuvenation. To his good friend Matthew's complaint that he was idling in the open air instead of improving his mind with books, he replied that his idleness was only apparent. In truth he was being actively receptive.

> The eye—it cannot choose but see;
> We cannot bid the ear be still;
> Our bodies feel, where'er they be,
> Against or with our will.

> Nor less I deem that there are Powers
> Which of themselves our minds impress;
> That we can feed this mind of ours
> In a wise passiveness.

And in the sequel, *The Tables Turned*, he reaffirmed the lesson, bidding his friend to quit his books,

> Come forth into the light of things,
> Let Nature be your teacher.

> She has a world of ready wealth,
> Our minds and hearts to bless—
> Spontaneous wisdom breathed by health,
> Truth breathed by cheerfulness.

> One impulse from a vernal wood
> May teach you more of man,
> Of moral evil and of good,
> Than all the sages can.

We have quoted so much from these four lyrics because they represent the earliest and clearest expression of the naturalistic creed by which Wordsworth was to live, with modifications, for ten years.

Of their charm and freshness as poetry it is not necessary to speak. What we are concerned with here is the degree of their life-wisdom. Wordsworth preached in them a gospel of feeling. For three years he had almost lost the gift of feeling, of melting into life and becoming a conductor for powers that flowed in waves through him as they did through the trees and flowers. He had been insulated by the mind that murdered to dissect.

Inevitably, therefore, as life revived in him, he spurned the faculty which through misuse seemed to him an agent of death. He did not wish, like Whitman, to turn and live with animals, because he feared and was ashamed of his animal nature. But he longed to become one with earth; with the green fields and the budding woods, and to live intensely in the moment like the redbreast that sang from the tall larch.

And these poems are sufficient proof that he realised his longing in the moment. Unfortunately, however, he translated his satisfaction into a doctrine, which was so seductively near a true one as to be the more misleading. From Rousseau to D. H. Lawrence men stricken with the disease of thought have striven to cure themselves, as Wordsworth did here. And always they have failed, because they have chosen a descent into the primitive instead of an ascent into real enlightenment.

It is true that a necessary condition of such an ascent is a 'wise passiveness,' 'a heart that watches and receives.' The error lies in attempting to regain touch with life by the short-cut of feeling and the senses. Admittedly Wordsworth appeared in these poems to acknowledge in some measure the demands of the mind. 'Our minds,' he wrote, 'should drink at every pore the spirit of the season,' and it was 'our minds' which the 'Powers' might impress, and that we might feed 'in a wise passiveness.'

Yet the whole burden of the poems shows that this recognition of the mind was little more than verbal. He felt the mind to be the enemy of the heart, as, indeed, in his divided state it was, and he exultantly acclaimed a relapse into the mindless state of Nature. The divided consciousness must always be sorely tempted to seek to return thus to an earlier condition. For on its elementary level the natural world is spiritually unified, as the rationalist is not. Nevertheless it is only by going forward, by regenerating the mind and will as well as the heart, that there can be any true return to Nature.

The sensationalist may, indeed, feel the divine in Nature in a succession of vivid moments, but he is tied to the transitory forms through which it manifests itself, and, having no established spiritual centre in himself, is as much at the mercy of the ebb and flow of life as the sea is at the mercy of the moon. The mood of melting acquiescence passes, and the unresolved discord remains.

Certainly Wordsworth qualified his sensationalism by a characteristic moral appendix in the lines,

> Some silent laws our hearts will make,
> Which they shall long obey:

But the love to which his soul was to be attuned for the year to come was the expansive energy of Nature which, as the spring season passed, inevitably contracted. It was a love, therefore, which might temporarily flush the heart and senses with life, but could not fulfil the soul in freedom. To 'come forth into the light of things' demanded, in fact, a more fundamental transformation of the self than Wordsworth suggested in these poems. It required a submission of the whole being to what Boehme called 'the eternal and intellectual sun,' the creative Reason which irradiates the darkness of Nature. Only when a man has thus identified himself with God, the primal unity, and by so doing risen above the dualistic conception 'of moral evil and of good' can he afford to dispense with the teaching of the sages.

But the 'narrow way' to reintegration taught by the sages is obviously far more difficult to tread than the path into the vernal wood which Wordsworth invited his fellows to follow when he wrote, 'Let Nature be your Teacher.' And it was the same with his doctrine of 'passiveness.' Every great mystic has stressed the necessity of quelling the surface activities and the selfish tyranny of the mind and the senses, if a man is to gain contact with a deeper reality. But, unlike the mystic who would still both the mind and the senses that the spirit or true self might draw upon its divine source, Wordsworth would feed the mind 'in a wise passiveness' by merely opening the gateways of sense to the life-stream which flowed through the natural world. And although by so doing a sick man might regain

> Spontaneous wisdom breathed by health,
> Truth breathed by cheerfulness,

his health of mind was left dependent upon his bodily condition.

While, therefore, Wordsworth's gospel of feeling with Nature might seem to offer a true way of salvation from arid rationalism and life-denying morality, it was essentially delusive and invited a reaction into the very condition which it claimed to cure. Twenty years later Keats was to write that Wordsworth was one 'who would exist partly on Sensation, partly on thought—to whom it is necessary that "years should bring the philosophic Mind." ' And in these four poems in which he renewed his bond with the Nature of his boyhood we have the first clear expression of that fatal separation between the feeling and the thinking faculties. It was a separation which was inevitably to leave his mind spiritually starved and stunted when he ceased with the years to be able to share so ecstatically with tree and flower on a spring morning a succession of 'thrills of pleasure.'

§ 2

Whether, therefore, in the poems in which he 'thought into the human heart' of the peasant or the child or in those in which he celebrated his own re-immersion in the natural world, the *Lyrical Ballads* showed Wordsworth recoiling from the mental and moral complexities in which he had been so painfully entangled towards the blessed Nirvana of childhood and the lap of Mother Earth.

And in another poem which did not appear in *Lyrical Ballads*, but which was among the earliest composed in this new spring of 1798, he described unmistakably in terms of primitive drama and melodrama the conversion from sin which he believed himself to be experiencing at the hands of Nature, as he wrote. We have shown elsewhere[1] that Coleridge projected into *The Ancient Mariner* his own sense of sin and desire for atonement; and in *Peter Bell*, which is also a tale of sin, remorse and conversion, Wordsworth, in his own distinctive way, did the same.

In the 'Prologue' to the poem he confessed, indeed, his dislike of all unearthly aspects of the supernatural. And in the following lines he doubtless had Coleridge in mind and his own inability and unwillingness to vie with him in 'the wonders of a wild career.'

[1] *Samuel Taylor Coleridge*, pp. 162-166.

> For, restless Wanderer! I, in truth,
> Am all unfit to be your mate.
>
> Long have I loved what I behold,
> The night that calms, the day that cheers;
> The common growth of mother earth
> Suffices me—her tears, her mirth,
> Her humblest mirth and tears.

To stray along 'that lowly way' with 'sympathetic heart' and with 'a soul of power,' finding or creating 'in life's daily prospect' nobler marvels than the magician brought back from the realm of Faery, was the aim which he had set before himself. And although after listening to Coleridge chanting his *Ancient Mariner*, he was almost as stunned as the Wedding Guest of the poem, feeling

> like one
> Not wholly rescued from the pale
> Of a wild dream, or worse illusion,

he was determined himself to be faithful to fact and to prove it an even more effective medium of moral and spiritual revelation.

Peter, the hero of the poem, was doubtless in many ways an invented character, who owed some of his traits to the vagrants with whom Wordsworth had associated in his schooldays, but he had also recognisable affinities with his creator. For Wordsworth, too, had been essentially for ten years a vagrant. And for the latter of them he had been alienated both from Nature and his kind. Of these later years it was almost true to say that

> He travelled here, he travelled there;—
> But not the value of a hair
> Was heart or head the better.

Whether he 'roved among the vales and streams' or 'in the green wood and hollow dell,' Nature, from the time that he was thrown 'out of the pale of love,' had failed to find the way into his heart, as into that of Peter Bell. He, too, had observed the primrose without feeling its beauty or life-mystery. He, too, had ceased to feel, as Peter had never felt, 'the witchery of the soft blue sky.' And if he had not, like Peter, 'a dozen wedded wives,' he had one unwedded. And she was particularised in the

> sweet and playful Highland girl,
> As light and beauteous as a squirrel,
> As beauteous and as wild,

whom Peter had deserted when 'a mother's hope' was hers, who died of a broken heart and who, more than all of his victims, affected him later with 'strong compunction and remorse.'

Hazlitt's description of Wordsworth as he saw him at Alfoxden shows, too, how near to self-portraiture were the lines —

> There was a hardness in his cheek,
> There was a hardness in his eye,
> As if the man had fixed his face,
> In many a solitary place,
> Against the wind and open sky!

Peter, in short, was an elementary representation of Wordsworth himself during the years of his alienation from life, and the account which followed of Peter's conversion was also, apart from its elements of melodrama which were appropriate to Peter's primitive status, an approximate rendering of what Wordsworth conceived to be his own restoration at the hands of Nature.

The passive agent of Peter's conversion was an ass, a

creature for which Wordsworth confessed in his introduction much affection, and which symbolised for him in its most elementary form that patient submission to life in which the virtue of the simple peasant also consisted. The ass was the prototype of virtue which Peter was at last to recognise after Nature, considerably assisted by chance, had broken through the hard crust of his egotism. But the ass was only incidental to his conversion by a demonic power which worked through a succession of unusual but mundane events.

These incidents were the horrible braying of the ass, echoing 'among the rocks and winding crags,' and rendered more eerie by the moonlight; the discovery of the drowned man's face in the river and his ghastly uprising to the surface (an incident borrowed, as will be remembered, from Wordsworth's experience as a boy); the cry of the boy who was searching for his father, that rang along the silent wood; the rumbling of an explosion in a mine twenty fathoms underground; and the voice of the Methodist preacher crying repentance to his flock in a tabernacle near by. The effect of these incidents upon Peter was one of increasing terror, culminating in a sudden dissolution of all that was hard and resistant in his being. 'He melted into tears,'

> Sweet tears of hope and tenderness!
> And fast they fall, a plenteous shower!
> His nerves, his sinews seemed to melt;
> Through all his iron frame was felt
> A gentle, a relaxing, power!
>
> Each fibre of his frame was weak;
> Weak all the animal within;
> But, in its helplessness, grew mild
> And gentle as an infant child,
> An infant that has known no sin.

Peter's conversion is, in fact, a typically revivalist one. It is fitting that the Methodist preacher should complete the work of Nature. For they employ exactly the same sensational method and effect the same sensational conversion. They work upon Peter's credulous nature, they terrify him until his nerves are overwrought, until he sees blood upon a stone and a rustling leaf whispers to him of his wickedness, they assure him that God's vengeance is at his heels, and then, when sweat is pouring down his face, they offer him salvation from his terror and he falls exhausted and utterly submissive into their arms.

We do not doubt that such a conversion as Wordsworth described in *Peter Bell* is true to life, although the succession of events is a little too well organised to be quite within the compass even of poetic probability. But although such conversions have doubtless often occurred and even proved permanent, they could only occur with very simple and credulous natures. Admittedly Wordsworth was dealing here, as in *Lyrical Ballads*, with 'the humblest departments of daily life,' but since in some measure at least he dramatised in Peter the history of what he believed to be his own conversion, it is necessary to examine rather more closely what it implied.

'Let good men,' he wrote in two of the best known lines of the poem,

> feel the soul of nature
> And see things as they are.

But bad men, as he went on to show, were best brought to feel the soul of Nature by seeing things as they are not. For in the following stanza he addressed certain 'potent Spirits,' begging them to show their empire on the heart of Peter Bell. 'Your presence,' he wrote,

> often have I felt
> In darkness and the stormy night;
> And, with like force, if need there be,
> Ye can put forth your agency
> When earth is calm, and heaven is bright.

These 'Spirits,' however, were of a peculiar nature. They were 'Spirits of the Mind' which, taking advantage of the moonlight and other eerie circumstances, were soon

> busy with poor Peter Bell;
> Upon the right of visual sense
> Usurping with a prevalence
> More terrible than magic spell.

Peter Bell, in short, was afflicted as Wordsworth had been after his return from France, when his mind had wrought phantoms out of his remorse and despair, working incessantly in an awful vacuum. His senses were first terrified, then his conscience began to work, and finally through the hallucination effected by 'the Spirits of the Mind' he realised imaginatively all his past sins and even fancied he saw himself 'not four yards from the broad highway,' and the most pathetic of his victims, 'The Highland Girl,' in her death agony.

A necessary and strong element, therefore, in Peter's conversion was hysteria. It was in fact less a conversion than a convulsion of self-horror which tore open the barred gates of his being so that the generous and expansive stream of life (the 'soul of Nature'), could flow in. In this stream all that was hard in him is dissolved; his heart opens more and more and at the spectacle of the widow's anguish

> He feels what he for human kind
> Had never felt before. . . .

> And now is Peter taught to feel
> That man's heart is a holy thing;
> And Nature, through a world of death,
> Breathes into him a second breath,
> More searching than the breath of spring.

Such is Peter's rebirth from sin into virtue. It was followed, we are told, by ten months' melancholy, but there was no relapse. He who had been 'the wildest of his clan' became henceforth 'a good and honest man.'

And it can hardly be doubted that Wordsworth claimed such a conversion as valid not only for primitive natures, but for himself. If we strip the story of all its primitive circumstance, it embodies in essence the stages by which he had lost and renewed his contact with Nature and his fellow-men. His senses had also terrified him; remorse had consumed him; he had tried to defy it, but it had slowly sapped his self-confidence and isolated him from life. Imprisoned in himself, the 'Spirits of the Mind' had come from 'the wayword world' in which they dwelt and assailed him with dreadful visions.

And he, too, had emerged from this world of death by surrendering his senses to the gentle relaxing power of Nature, until his nerves and sinews seemed to melt, and as life flowed again through each fibre of his frame, his heart grew warm towards all created things, and his chilled mind was steeped in feeling. Once again, therefore, in *Peter Bell*, Wordsworth affirmed his belief in the sufficiency of a rebirth which assured to man the calm of 'the well-deserving brute' whose 'peace hath no offence betrayed.'

Yet although Time was to prove the inadequacy of his belief, such a gospel of Nature seemed now to be justified in his own experience. For his revival had all the freshness and richness of a spring that had been unseasonably delayed. Once again, as in boyhood, he seemed to share with the world of Nature an inpouring and outpouring of life. But he shared, too, the life of his fellow-men in a far greater measure than before he had passed into the vale of disillusionment. For if the mental sufferings which he had endured there had left behind a crippling fear of passion, they had also taught him to sympathise with the pain and perplexity of struggling humanity. He did not feel 'the miseries of the world' with that selfless intensity which Keats' 'High Prophetess' described as the condition of ascent to the heights of ultimate vision. But he had brooded over his own misery intensely enough to feel deeply for all who were desolate and deprived of joy as he had been. And while 'the still, sad music of humanity' chastened and subdued the pleasure he derived from Nature, it also enriched it, as the shadow enriches the sunlight, and was itself a source of poignant gratification.

His sympathy for human pain was, therefore, intimately bound up with instinctive pleasure. Consequently, as we shall find, it was, even while his instincts were still vital, limited somewhat narrowly within the range of his own personal preferences. Yet within this range of humble life his sentiments and his instincts were so deeply in accord, that his insight was profound. And of that insight *Lyrical Ballads* was the first memorable fruit.

§ 3

The lease of Alfoxden expired on 24th June 1798, and two days later Dorothy and her brother were homeless wanderers. They spent one week with Coleridge and another with Cottle at Bristol, and then set out towards the banks of the Wye. They crossed the Severn Ferry and walked ten miles further to Tintern Abbey.

The scene, as he came upon it, stirred Wordsworth profoundly, recalling as it did the delirium of five years before, which had been so intense but so transient and from which he had passed into a sort of death of the senses prolonged over four wretched years. And now he was risen from the dead and the scene was no longer merely a memory poignantly associated with 'sensations sweet' with which he had tried to restore himself 'in hours of weariness' and impotence.

It was a new scene. He saw and felt it differently. And by so doing he could measure the change in himself and believe that he had come through the shadow into mellow sunlight, which lacked maybe the wild radiance of his morning hour, but which was warm and steady and promised to grace his future years with a pleasure at once sober and benign.

Little wonder, then, that he could write of the poem which he began upon leaving Tintern, and concluded just as he and Dorothy were entering Bristol in the evening, that no poem was ever composed under more pleasant circumstances.

And if the *Lines Composed a Few Miles above Tintern Abbey* betrayed the characteristic limitations of the 'egotistical sublime,' they contained, too, lines which come nearer than any which he had yet written to expressing an ultimate vision. He acknowledged in the poem a threefold debt to the beauteous forms of Nature cherished by the memory through five long years and reinvoked in silent hours. He owed to them firstly

> sensations sweet
> Felt in the blood, and felt along the heart;
> And passing even into my purer mind,
> With tranquil restoration.

Secondly, feelings

> Of unremembered pleasure: such, perhaps,
> As have no slight or trivial influence
> On that best portion of a good man's life,
> His little, nameless, unremembered, acts
> Of kindness and of love.

In thus deriving the moral virtues of kindness and love from feelings of pleasure originally generated through intercourse with the natural world, Wordsworth was expressing the same belief in Nature as an all-sufficient teacher as in the other *Lyrical Ballads* we have noticed.

But in acknowledging the third gift, 'Of aspect more sublime,' he expressed a mystery which, if he could have recognised its significance, transcended the limits of his own sensationalism and the philosophy of Hartley in which he had come to rationalise it. The gift was

> that blessed mood,
> In which the burthen of the mystery,
> In which the heavy and the weary weight
> Of all this unintelligible world,
> Is lightened:— that serene and blessed mood,
> In which the affections gently lead us on,—
> Until, the breath of this corporeal frame
> And even the motion of our human blood
> Almost suspended, we are laid asleep
> In body, and become a living soul:
> While with an eye made quiet by the power
> Of harmony, and the deep power of joy,
> We see into the life of things.

This experience was the most real and profound which Wordsworth ever had. All his greatest moments of which he has left a record are associated with it. To him, however, it was no more than the crowning glory and satisfaction of that natural process which Hartley had defined in such detail, by which the primary sensations were transmuted in turn into feelings, into the 'purer' forms of thought, and into the moral sense. Yet the words,

> we are laid asleep
> In body, and become a living soul

expressed a reality which transcended Hartley's naturalistic economy, and is only to be explained as the mystics have explained it.

So long as a man is bound within the limits of his ordinary sense-perceptions, whether of the mind or the feelings, the world is 'unintelligible.' It is either felt without being known, however transiently 'sweet' the 'sensations,' or it is known in such a way that the feeling heart is agonised by the spectacle of apparent cruelty, injustice, and waste.

But there come moments, such as that recorded here by Wordsworth, when the ordinary faculties are overruled. They are caught up and reconciled in a spirit which is eternal; the bodily faculties of sense-perception and thought no longer exist as such. They are laid asleep as organs of self-consciousness; they reawake as organs of spiritual consciousness. The inevitable discord of thought and feeling has been resolved. The divided self has been made whole in the eternal unity.

Such an experience cannot be explained as merely a happy consequence of the association of sense and reason. It is not a mental state derived from sensation, an 'intellectual pleasure deducible ultimately from a sensible one,' as Wordsworth, clinging to Hartley's philosophy and his own physical being, wished to believe in defiance of his positive intuition which compelled him to write that in such a moment a living soul had taken possession of the stilled organs of bodily sense.

This third gift was in fact essentially of a different order from the two previous ones with which Wordsworth connected it. It was a state in which the spiritual no longer derived from or was dependent upon the sensations, except in so far as the divine, in the language of the mystics, had risen out of the grave of the body. But the divine which was thus quickened was the spiritual self whose faculty is not instinct or the discursive intellect or moral judgment, but imagination.

By such imagination a man experiences the spiritual reality in the forms of Nature, because he is no longer either sensuously immersed in Nature or mentally detached from her. He has become one with the Creative Spirit which manifests itself through the world of Nature without being tied to any of her transient forms and forces.

But Wordsworth failed to realise that in such moments he was living from another centre than that of the divided natural self, and so such moments passed without giving a new direction to his life. In them alone did he really transcend his egoism and enter into a new order of consciousness. But because he did not realise what this involved, he could never build upon them, but only accept them as blessed and inexplicable moods, of 'vain belief,' maybe, 'yet, oh!' how wonderfully restorative.

And the descent from the self-transcendent moment into the familiar ego-centric mood is apparent enough in the *Tintern* poem. For with the exception of one short and memorable passage the mood throughout the rest of the poem is one of anticipatory self-gratification. As he stood gazing on the beautiful landscape the last faint shadows of his 'sad perplexity' faded from his consciousness. They were dissolved in his 'sense of present pleasure' and in 'pleasing thoughts'

> That in this moment there is life and food
> For future years.

The troublesome mind was immersed 'in nature and the language of the sense.' The time of pure instinctive appetite with all its aching joys and dizzy raptures might be past. But in this, he could aver, there was no cause for regret. For the sensuous intimacy with Nature was still preserved intact, was still his to enjoy with a richer gratification because it was no longer wild and uncontrollable. It was tempered and refined; it had acquired the plaintive overtones of human sympathy,

Q

and at moments vouchsafed to him a sublime feeling of the demiurgic spirit working in all things,

> A presence that disturbs me with the joy
> Of elevated thoughts; a sense sublime
> Of something far more deeply interfused,
> Whose dwelling is the light of setting suns,
> And the round ocean and the living air,
> And the blue sky, and in the mind of man;
> A motion and a spirit, that impels
> All thinking things, all objects of all thought,
> And rolls through all things.

Such pantheistic moments he had enjoyed instinctively in his boyhood, but now they were overlaid with 'elevated thoughts.' The mind, the heart, the senses, were all satisfied; they were associated as pleasurably as the philosopher Hartley could desire, and they owed all their pleasure in its ascending scale to 'nature and the language of the sense,'

> The anchor of my purest thoughts, the nurse,
> The guide, the guardian of my heart, and soul
> Of all my moral being.

The defect in such a scheme of salvation lay in the fact that the three faculties were momentarily associated, but not creatively reconciled. And the direct consequence of this was that each faculty was regarded as a means to personal gratification. Admittedly it was highly moral gratification, the pleasure of feeding on Nature's forms and colours, of sympathising with human suffering, and of feeling the sublime. But at the centre of it was a quest of self-enhancement kindred to that which Oswald in *The Borderers* had pursued when he submitted his 'intellectual being' to the exhilarating effects of majestic natural objects.

Wordsworth had rightly exposed Oswald's misuse of Nature as a tonic to his own mental pride and sense of personal omnipotence. But although by now submitting himself *feelingly* to Nature, his mental egoism was temporarily 'chastened and subdued,' it still persisted unchanged as a determining factor in his being and only awaited the inevitable cooling of his ardent instincts to reassert itself. Not even Dorothy herself, who completed by her presence his happiness, could secure his 'genial spirits' against the physical processes of growth and decay. In her voice he caught

> The language of my former heart, and read
> My former pleasures in the shooting lights
> Of thy wild eyes.

And those pleasures, sobered by thought and softened by sympathy, might still, he argued, be his. And, indeed, they were to be his for another ten years to the lasting enrichment of English poetry.

Yet in the light of his own and Dorothy's after life we cannot but feel a pathetic irony in the moving lines in which he attested at Tintern the faith which he deemed sufficient,

> Knowing that Nature never did betray
> The heart that loved her; 'tis her privilege,
> *Through all the years of this our life, to lead*
> *From joy to joy*: for she can so inform
> The mind that is within us, so impress
> With quietness and beauty, and so feed
> With lofty thoughts, that neither evil tongues,
> Rash judgments, nor the sneers of selfish men,
> Nor greetings where no kindness is, nor all
> The dreary intercourse of daily life,
> Shall e'er prevail against us, or disturb

Our cheerful faith, that all which we behold
Is full of blessings. Therefore let the moon
Shine on thee in thy solitary walk;
And let the misty mountain-winds be free
To blow against thee: and, in after years,
When these wild ecstasies shall be matured
Into a sober pleasure; when thy mind
Shall be a mansion for all lovely forms,
Thy memory be as a dwelling-place
For all sweet sounds and harmonies: oh! then,
If solitude, or fear, or pain, or grief,
Should be thy portion, with what healing thoughts
Of tender joy wilt thou remember me,
And these my exhortations!

Never was there a heart which loved Nature more ardently than Dorothy's. Yet Nature was to betray even her, and wasting melancholy, not healing thoughts of tender joy, was to be her later portion. And if Wordsworth preserved himself more effectively against the sad necessity of Nature's physical betrayal, it was only because his mind was tough enough to stake out a claim for itself amid the decay of his instinctive faculties.

PART VII

RELAPSE AND RECOVERY

§ 1

WITH his inner conflict assuaged rather than really resolved Wordsworth had now entered upon his great productive period as a poet. And although he was, for the next eight years, to draw heavily on his vital capital, he was able, so long as it lasted, to bring to a perfect flowering in poetry all that had been sown in him so generously in the past.

But before he settled down to reap this harvest, a six months' interlude occurred in Germany. With Dorothy and Coleridge he sailed for Hamburg on 16th September 1798. His intention was to spend two years in Germany acquiring the language, and 'a tolerable stock of information in natural science.' He hoped by thus acquiring some scientific knowledge to equip himself the better for producing poetry which should be a 'history or science of the feelings.' But it is doubtful whether he added anything to his own native powers of introspection and observation and to the knowledge which he had derived from Hartley by his sojourn in a country in which intellectuals were beginning to study the 'facts of the soul' in a scientific manner.

His contact, indeed, with Germans during his stay was slight and unimportant. For unlike Coleridge, who was expansively sociable, Wordsworth, particularly when he was companioned by Dorothy, kept much to himself. A foreign country intensified the love of solitariness, which had now become a settled disposition, and the English provincialism which was his strength and weakness. It is true that at Hamburg he had several lengthy talks with the aged poet Klopstock, but this, so far as we know, was the only occasion on which he enjoyed any intercourse with a German of distinction. It was characteristic, too, that one of the first steps which he took at Ham-

burg was to visit an English bookseller and buy Percy's
Reliques. And certainly the remarkable group of poems which
he was to compose in Germany owed far more in spirit to
Percy than to any acquisition of scientific knowledge.

The Wordsworths, however, did not stay long at Hamburg,
and realising that they could never learn German, so long as
Coleridge was there to talk in English, they decided to part
from him. He set out for Ratzeburg to expand joyously in the
sunshine of German sentiment and speculation, while Dorothy
and her brother travelled for two days by diligence over wretched
mountain roads to Braunschweig and thence to Goslar.

Their manner of life here during the next three months was
in direct contrast to that of Coleridge. Wordsworth retired
more and more into himself and that other self which was
Dorothy. Goslar, a dull and dreary town, lay remote among
the hills, and apart from the family with which they lodged and
from whom they tried to learn the language they saw no one.
Wordsworth walked daily on the ramparts or in a sort of
public ground or garden in which was a pond, his only companion a kingfisher that used to glance at him. A very bitter
winter intensified his sense of isolation and numbed the feelings
which six months before had been so miraculously quickened.
For a short time, indeed, he could draw upon the resources of
feeling which he had accumulated at Alfoxden. And doubtless
it was during this period that he composed the two poems
which were later incorporated in *The Prelude*, *Influence of Natural
Objects* and *There Was a Boy*, and also another recollection of
childhood, entitled *Nutting*. Two lines, in fact, in *Nutting*,

> In that sweet mood when pleasure loves to pay
> Tribute to ease,

were an echo from the first stanza of *Lines Written in Early
Spring*, and the passage in which he described how he stood

> Breathing with such suppression of the heart
> As joy delights in,

no less than his final divination of 'a spirit in the woods,' recall the mood of *Tintern*.

But 'among unknown men in lands beyond the sea' the virtue which he had drawn from Nature in her spring efflorescence quickly drained away. He was uprooted from his native soil from which alone he could draw strength, and under such stark conditions it was hardly surprising that he should relapse into his earlier morbid state. In an attempt to avoid this he lashed his mind into activity, but by so doing only overwearied himself and suffered from pain and weakness in the side; and he made little progress in the language.

Sometime, however, in February he and Dorothy left Goslar for Nordhausen. Coleridge had constantly expressed his longing to be with them, exclaiming with typical ardour 'how you are incorporated into the better part of my being; how, whenever I spring forward into the future with noble affections, I always alight by your side.'

And in April they paid him a brief visit at Göttingen. They found him more eloquent than ever, but he was shocked at the change the winter had wrought in his friends, who, he wrote, were 'melancholy and hypp'd. Wordsworth was affected to tears at the thought of not being near me—wished me, of course, to live in the North of England near Sir Frederic Vane's great library . . . he deemed the vicinity of a library absolutely necessary to his health, nay to his existence.' 'I still think,' he added, 'Wordsworth will be disappointed in his expectations of relief from reading, without society . . . my many weaknesses are of some advantage to me; they unite me more with the great mass of my fellow-beings—but dear Wordsworth appears to me to have hurtfully segregated and isolated his being. Doubtless his delights are more deep and sublime, but he has likewise more hours that prey on his flesh and blood.'

Coleridge divined his friend's condition, and the defects of his temperament, with his usual insight. And it is not difficult to perceive what had happened to Wordsworth during these six months to explain his new and surprising attachment to books as a mental antidote to inward wretchedness, and his intensified sense of dependence upon Coleridge.

The gospel of Nature which he had preached so happily in the previous spring had already failed him when put to the test of a bitter winter in a strange land. So long as there was 'a blessing in the air' and the throstle sang blithely, his heart had seemed to be renewed within him. But when his cheeks were 'struck by the air as by cold iron,' when all the homely and familiar comfort of the English country-side was withdrawn from him, the prison doors had closed again upon him, and the self-lacerating pain returned. He seemed once again to be an outcast from his kind and disowned by the Nature whom he had embraced as his teacher.

Under these conditions he was inevitably haunted once more by thoughts of Annette. It has been suggested that after his visit to Coleridge at Göttingen he and Dorothy may have ventured into France. They were certainly lost to view for some weeks. But whether this was so or not, the fact that he was no longer separated from France by the sea must have brought Annette, as a once warm and beloved presence, appreciably nearer to him, and intensified his awareness that the 'hour of feeling' had ebbed and left him desolate once more.

But Dorothy remained; and the fact that she alone, in the absence of Coleridge, could out of the ardent resources of her nature melt his reserve and persuade him that 'Mother Earth' only withheld her life from him for a season, made her unbearably dear to him. Unbearably, because death might take her, as, in another sense, it had taken Annette. In his low moods of hypochondria the thought came to haunt him, and, as five years before at Keswick when she had consoled him in his utter disillusionment, Dorothy's image and to a less extent that of Annette, became blended in a series of poems which are perhaps the most exquisite and haunting that he ever wrote.

On 6th April Coleridge wrote that some months before Wordsworth had sent him 'a most sublime epitaph.' He could not say 'whether it had any reality,' but he conjectured that in some gloomier moment Wordsworth had 'fancied the moment in which his sister would die.' The 'sublime epitaph' was contained in the famous lines,

> A slumber did my spirit seal;
>   I had no human fears:
> She seemed a thing that could not feel
>   The touch of earthly years.
>
> No motion has she now, no force;
>   She neither hears nor sees;
> Rolled round in earth's diurnal course,
>   With rocks, and stones, and trees.

That Dorothy primarily inspired the last two lines of the first stanza of this exquisite poem can hardly be doubted. But Coleridge's description of the poem as an 'epitaph' was in some ways misleading. And certainly it expressed something far more essential than a morbid and momentary fancy that Dorothy was dead. For into the second stanza he distilled that feeling of the elemental, as a 'motion and a spirit' that 'rolls through all things,' of which he had written in *Tintern*. Just as in the Lyrics composed in the previous spring, he had proclaimed how man might live through Nature with quickened sensibility, so here he expressed most movingly his experience of dying into Nature, of becoming insensible to all human feeling and obeying, like rocks, and stones, and trees, only the unconscious rhythm of cosmic forces.

The bitter winter at Goslar which had numbed his heart and stripped from him all the expansive joy that the spring at Alfoxden had called forth, conditioned the lines quite as much as his passionate attachment to Dorothy. But behind both was a haunting apprehension of death as a force in Nature which reduced all human identity, however apparently secure in its unearthly perfection and grace, to nothingness.

That the individual should return at death to the womb of Nature, losing all that gave him or her distinctive beauty, a whirling atom in a dance of atoms, was in fact the logical issue of the return to Nature of which he had sung so gleefully in the previous spring. But although he could derive a certain satisfaction from contemplating this final denudation of the ego, in which the ache both of desire and desirelessness was for ever stilled in the majestic but insentient circling of the earth through space, all his deepest and tenderest feelings rebelled against it.

The only imaginative escape he could discover from his frozen and frustrated self was into this subhuman world. And there was a cosmic grandeur in his realisation of it which did enlarge and assuage. But to enter that world was to die as a spiritual being into the elemental. And if in the despondency of these winter months he could almost welcome such a death for himself, the thought that one so intensely living and so deeply loved as Dorothy must submit to it haunted him with a peculiar poignancy. And in the 'Lucy' poems which he wrote in Germany he crystallised with an exquisite simplicity and tenderness his love of her as a pure flower of Nature, doomed like all such flowers to die into the Nature in which they have lived so beautifully.

Whether, as has been suggested by Professor Harper and

M. Legouis, there was another memory behind these poems, that of some girl whom Wordsworth had loved in youth and who had died young, we cannot know. There is no real evidence for it, although both these writers have striven most ingeniously to discover some and even to locate 'the untrodden ways beside the spring of Dove.' But we do know that the earlier poem *Louisa* which, as we have shown, was almost certainly inspired by Dorothy, is closely akin both in its substance and metre to 'Three years she grew in sun and shower.' Moreover the lines written two years later and originally entitled *The Glow-worm* — 'Among all lovely things my love had been' — described, as Wordsworth himself admitted, an incident that took place between himself and Dorothy. And in this poem she was named 'my Lucy.'

Those, indeed, who argue that since Wordsworth almost always drew upon actual experience, he must have in the 'Lucy' poems recorded, 'in the delicate distillation of memory,' to quote Professor Harper's words, 'a real experience of youthful love and bewildering grief,' fail to realise how actual and real his love for Dorothy was and how in a strange way it was associated with and intensified by his earlier passion for Annette. In *Ruth*, as we shall see, the two loves were clearly intermingled. But even in the 'Lucy' poems it was to some extent Annette, who in a real sense had died to him, leaving an inescapable

> memory of what has been
> And never more will be,

who lay in Lucy's grave, while Dorothy was the Lucy who 'lived unknown' in her exquisite natural perfection.

The two sources of feeling were, of course, too intimately blended to be arbitrarily separated in this way, but if Dorothy was the primary and vital one, the ghost of Annette haunted Wordsworth's mind as he passionately cherished the living

presence of his sister, and whispered that death might claim
even her and leave him desolate.

How much his love for Dorothy transcended the normal
attachment of a brother and a sister, these 'Lucy' poems reveal
even more clearly than his earlier letters. For no woman elsewhere in his poetry was drawn with such an intensity of personal feeling. 'Strange fits of passion,' indeed, had he known,
judged by conventional standards. For the love which had
been turned back upon itself when he awoke with dismay
from the sensational dream in which he had wooed and
won Annette, had poured itself into this pure channel of
adoration.

And it was an adoration which engaged his whole being both
as a poet and a man. For in Dorothy he perceived one who
exquisitely personified his belief in Nature, who was in all her
eager motions and ardent responses a 'first-born birth' of
Mother Earth, and who most intimately embodied from day to
day the organic life which he sought to recover.

Into 'Three years she grew in sun and shower' he concentrated in fact all he meant by letting 'Nature be your teacher.'
He reaffirmed his creed while drawing a devoted picture
of one who lived it, of one to whom Nature said, as she had
once said to him—

> Myself will to my darling be
> Both law and impulse: and with me
> The Girl, in rock and plain,
> In earth and heaven, in glade and bower,
> Shall feel an overseeing power
> To kindle or restrain.
>
> She shall be sportive as the fawn
> That wild with glee across the lawn,
> Or up the mountain springs;

And hers shall be the breathing balm,
And hers the silence and the calm
Of mute insensate things.

The floating clouds their state shall lend
To her; for her the willow bend;
Nor shall she fail to see
Even in the motions of the Storm
Grace that shall mould the Maiden's form
By silent sympathy.

The stars of midnight shall be dear
To her; and she shall lean her ear
In many a secret place
Where rivulets dance their wayward round,
And beauty born of murmuring sound
Shall pass into her face.

And vital feelings of delight
Shall rear her form to stately height,
Her virgin bosom swell;
Such thoughts to Lucy I will give
While she and I together live
Here in this happy dell.

The essence of Wordsworth's youth was in the lines, the youth
that had died, but to the memory of which he clung. And in
mourning 'how soon my Lucy's race was run,' he was mourning
not only a Dorothy who might die or an Annette who lay dead
in his heart, but the primal joy which he had once drunk fresh
at its source but which he felt during these frozen months at
Goslar could never more be his.

And other poems which he wrote in Germany show how
much he was preoccupied with this quality of joy and with all

that in his own experience dimmed and quenched it. In *Poet's Epitaph*, for example, he brought a moralist and a poet to a humble grave-side and contrasted their manner of thinking upon the dead. The one

> has neither eyes nor ears;
> Himself his world, and his own God;

> One to whose smooth-rubbed soul can cling
> Nor form, nor feeling, great or small;
> A reasoning, self-sufficing thing,
> An Intellectual All-in-all!

The other—

> In common things that round us lie
> Some random truths he can impart,—
> The harvest of a quiet eye
> That broods and sleeps on his own heart.

> But he is weak; both Man and Boy,
> Hath been an idler in the land;
> Contented if he might enjoy
> The things which others understand.

The vagrant poet of these last two stanzas was of course himself so far as he had fed upon life with a wise passiveness, while in the moralist of the earlier lines he sketched the Godwinian he had tried to be. But although he knew full well at this time the spiritual paralysis which crept over those who 'slept in their intellectual crust,' the problem of living from a vital centre and at the same time ordering his life aright continued to perplex him.

To

> murmur near the running brooks
> A music sweeter than their own

brought an inward contentment so long as Nature favoured the mood. But his moods, as Goslar had bitterly shown him, were at the mercy of place and season, and beneath even the happiest of them, he was uneasily conscious of being 'an Idler in the land,' who fed his sensibility, but left his rational and moral faculties unexercised. Consequently he was absorbed more and more in contemplation of those who seemed to justify the belief in Nature as a sufficient inspiration. By appreciating their virtue, he hoped maybe to make their secret his own. And again and again in the poems which he wrote in Germany he reaffirmed his love of her in whom Nature

> hath tempered so her clay,
> That every hour thy heart runs wild,
> Yet never once doth go astray.

The poem in which these lines occur was entitled *Matthew*, and something in the personality of his old schoolmaster at Hawkshead entered into it. But the immediate prototype of all such 'favourite children' of Nature was Dorothy. She it was who in *The Two April Mornings*

> seemed as happy as a wave
> That dances on the sea.

And through the Matthew of this poem and of its successor, *The Fountain*, he expressed his own saddened realisation that the secret of purely instinctive happiness was no longer his. The sense of having ceased to be a 'favourite child' of Nature himself, and the hopeless longing to be taken once again into her arms, which was never to leave him, dictated the lines —

> 'Thus fares it still in our decay:
> And yet the wiser mind
> Mourns less for what age takes away
> Than what it leaves behind.

> 'The blackbird amid leafy trees,
> The lark above the hill,
> Let loose their carols when they please,
> Are quiet when they will.

> 'With Nature never do *they* wage
> A foolish strife; they see
> A happy youth, and their old age
> Is beautiful and free:

> 'But we are pressed by heavy laws;
> And often, glad no more,
> We wear a face of joy, because
> We have been glad of yore.'

A naturalist might well have questioned the claim that Nature's creatures, if they survive to old age, are always 'beautiful and free.' But at least they were not conscious of their loss of joy. And it was this consciousness which haunted Wordsworth whenever his instinctive life, that was at the mercy of circumstances, languished. And then he could only keep death at bay by renewing in words the joy that he had known or by experiencing imaginatively the natural integrity of primitive people or the ecstatic spontaneity of the lark or the blackbird.

Yet the sense of death at this time so constantly weighed upon him that it transformed almost all he wrote into elegies. For deep within himself he felt that the perfection of innocence could not survive into maturity, that the flower must be plucked and embalmed before it faded, if it was to remain unviolated by time, a pure and perfect memory. And so in *Lucy Gray* he drew with a lovely tenderness and simplicity the immortal child, a being whose primal freshness was unsoiled even by social contact, who drew her virtue from the wild moor upon which she flowered in solitude,

> The sweetest thing that ever grew
> Beside a human door,

whom Nature gathered again to herself before the bond
between mother and child could be weakened, and who still,
for the imaginative vision, tripped along the 'lonesome wild'
in which she had been cradled, blithe and trustful, and singing

> a solitary song
> That whistles in the wind.

Thus by her death 'Lucy Gray' was saved from life. The
heaven that had lain about her in her infancy, the celestial
light that apparelled her, never faded into the light of common
day. She remained a dream child for whom there was no fall
from Nature into human conflict, but who died into the
supernatural element in which she had lived.

It was an exquisite dream, and the poignancy of Wordsworth's delineation of it was due to the fact that in his own
personal life it was a shattered dream. He could only recreate
it imaginatively in moments of inspired memory, and the
inspiration he drew from past experience made more grievous
the intervening periods of despondency.

And in *Ruth* he dramatised once again the facts which in his
own experience had shattered the dream. Ruth in childhood
was another Lucy Gray, if less ethereal, an infant of the woods,
herself her own delight. She, too, was drawn from Dorothy.
But her history was Annette's. For the lover who deserts her
was Wordsworth himself. 'The tumult of a tropic sky,' which
proved 'a dangerous food' for

> a Youth to whom was given
> So much of earth—so much of heaven,
> And such impetuous blood,

R

was only an exotic rendering of the tumult of Revolutionary France as Wordsworth had thrilled to it. Once again he was confessing and exorcising his sins in the stanzas—

> Whatever in those climes he found
> Irregular in sight or sound
> Did to his mind impart
> A kindred impulse, seemed allied
> To his own powers, and justified
> The workings of his heart.
>
> Nor less, to feed voluptuous thought,
> The beauteous forms of nature wrought,
> Fair trees and gorgeous flowers;
> The breezes their own languor lent;
> The stars had feelings, which they sent
> Into those favoured bowers. . . .
>
> And yet he with no feigned delight
> Had wooed the Maiden, day and night
> Had loved her, night and morn:
> What could he less than love a Maid
> Whose heart with so much nature played?
> So kind and so forlorn!

And so Ruth, like her predecessors, is deserted and goes mad, but, becoming a vagrant, is restored to reason by the ministrations of Nature. The poem ends, indeed, on a note of conventional sanctity, and Ruth is honoured in old age with a respectable funeral, while 'all the congregation sing a Christian psalm.' But the stanza which contains these lines was probably composed in 1802, when Wordsworth was beginning to be at ease in Zion. At this time he was still bitterly aware that the heart might run wild with Nature and yet go astray. He himself had put his trust in Nature and had been betrayed. He could not forget this. And however much he might dream of natural perfection and embody his dream in 'Lucy Grays' the fear of life's treachery remained.

§ 2

But with the conclusion of his exile in Germany a period in his life opened when everything favoured the realisation of that fertile contentment which he had promised himself at Tintern. Restored to his native lake-country, companioned by Dorothy, and later finding in marriage and fatherhood a way of escape from the ghost of Annette, he could give himself undistracted to those past emotions recollected in tranquillity from which his greatest poetry took its origin.

He returned to England in the early summer of 1799, and went at once with Dorothy to the north. Mary Hutchinson's brother Thomas rented a farm at Sockburn on the banks of the Tees, living there with his three sisters. And here the two travellers stayed for nearly six months. The presence of Mary, however, did not raise his spirits as it had done at Alfoxden. Her nearness may, indeed, have proved tantalising. For he was in no position as yet to marry. *Lyrical Ballads* had been little noticed; few copies had been sold and the reviews had been on the whole depreciatory. Wordsworth was reasonably disappointed, but his suggestion to Cottle that the *Ancient Mariner* had been an injury to the volume and that in any possible second edition its place should be taken by 'some little things which would be more likely to suit the common taste' was strangely ungenerous to Coleridge.

Yet the apparent failure of *Lyrical Ballads* only provoked him to a prouder independence. 'My aversion from publication,' he wrote to Cottle, 'increases every day, so much so, that no motives whatever, nothing but pecuniary necessity, will, I think, ever prevail upon me to commit myself to the press again.' Fortunately his love for Dorothy was so satisfying that he was drawn by no urgent impulse towards marriage with Mary Hutchinson. And so long as he was content to live with Dorothy, he was faced by no immediate pecuniary necessity.

He could thus afford to scorn the world and patiently concentrate his powers upon that task of self-exploration and remembrance to which he had dedicated himself on that morning four years before when he travelled from Bristol to Racedown. The 'creative breeze' which he had felt that day had not in fact broken up the 'long continued frost' as effectively as in a moment of new expansion he believed it had. But if even the 'vernal promises' of Alfoxden had been blighted by a German winter, there still remained beneath his immediate sense of bafflement and melancholy

> the hope
> Of active days, of dignity and thought,
> Of prowess in an honorable field,
> Pure passions, virtue, knowledge, and delight,
> The holy life of music and of verse.

He had determined, in fact, to devote himself to a long philosophical poem which was to deal with 'Man, Nature, and Society,' and to be entitled *The Recluse*. By thus developing his 'most interesting feelings concerning Man, Nature, and Society,' he hoped to obtain relief from himself, to objectify his convictions, and in the process of composition to recover the inspiration of Alfoxden.

And in this endeavour he received inevitably great encouragement from Coleridge, whose speculative mind was fired by the thought of a philosophical poem and who generously overrated his friend's qualifications for the task. 'My dear friend,' he wrote to him from Germany in the summer of 1799, 'I do entreat you to go on with *The Recluse*; and I wish you would write a poem in blank verse, addressed to those who, in consequence of the complete failure of the French Revolution, have thrown up all hopes of the amelioration of mankind, and are sinking into an almost epicurean selfishness, disguising the same under the soft titles of domestic attachment and contempt for visionary *philosophes*. It would do a great good, and might form a part of *The Recluse*, for in my present mood I am wholly against the publication of any small poems.'

In writing thus Coleridge diagnosed with remarkable foresight the reaction from a too hasty and effusive Romantic idealism which was actually to occur. For the Victorian compromise was to represent just this relapse into selfishness, disguised under the soft titles of domestic attachment and contempt for the visionary. But Coleridge underestimated the degree to which disillusionment had maimed Wordsworth when he called upon him to plead the cause of idealism in spite of the Revolution. Certainly Wordsworth had not yet sunk 'into an almost epicurean selfishness, disguising the same under the soft titles of domestic attachment and contempt for visionary *philosophes*.' Nor, indeed, was his selfishness ever to be Epicurean. But there had been suspicious symptoms that he was tending in this direction. And both the intensity of his revulsion from the Revolution and his despairing flight from abstract rationalism to Nature and the natural man might have suggested to one less ready than Coleridge to identify his own visionary faith with that of his friend, that he was hardly qualified to reassure the doubting and the discouraged that 'the world's great age' might begin anew.

Coleridge, however, was still in Germany, and when he returned in July, he was in such wretched health and so addicted to opium that three months passed before he saw his friend. But in a letter early in October he renewed his encouragement, writing that he longed to see what Wordsworth had been doing. 'O let it be the tail-piece of *The Recluse*! for of nothing but *The Recluse* can I hear patiently.' Meanwhile Wordsworth had already invited him and Cottle to join him in a tour of Cumberland and Westmorland. And sometime later in the month he did so. Cottle soon dropped out of the tour, but Wordsworth's brother John took his place. They walked along Haweswater, and crossed the mountains to Windermere. From there they went on to Hawkshead, and through Rydal to Grasmere. And here John Wordsworth left them.

It was a fitting place for the two friends to be left alone. And the consequences to Wordsworth were considerable. For in the first place Coleridge fell in love with Grasmere and its neighbourhood, and infected Wordsworth with his enthusiasm. So much so that he thought at once of building a house by the lake side, or of taking a small empty cottage which they discovered at Grasmere. But Coleridge's enthusiasm had spiritual as well as material effects. Wordsworth had not recovered from the melancholy and hypochondria which had settled upon him in Germany. He had remained depressed and doubtful of his own powers, alternating in an uncertain fashion between work on *The Recluse* and a poem describing his earlier life which was to be a mere preamble to the philosophic poem, but which later grew into *The Prelude*.

There had been, indeed, according to Coleridge, 'alarming accounts of his health.' And deeply as he loved Dorothy, her minute faculty of observation and her intense instinctive vitality may well have proved devitalising to one in whom the faculty of analysis had gone dangerously far, whose vitality was at a low ebb through inward friction, and who needed above all someone to stimulate his synthetic powers.

Coleridge proved once again, as at Alfoxden, the saviour who was needed. 'You can feel, what I cannot express for myself,' he wrote to Dorothy, 'how deeply I have been impressed by a world of scenery absolutely new to me. At Rydal and Grasmere I received, I think, the deepest delight. Yet Haweswater, through many a varying view, kept my eyes dim with tears; and, the evening approaching Derwentwater . . . it was to me a vision of a fair country! Why were you not with us?'

That he should infect Wordsworth with the vision of a promised land, dissolving, in his own effusive warmth, the frozen reaches of his friend's heart and mind, was as inevitable as it had been at Alfoxden. And in so doing he not only renewed Wordsworth's faith in his own powers without which he could not have dedicated himself whole-heartedly to the long poem that he contemplated; but he helped to determine that return to and residence in the lake-country which harmonised so inevitably and for a time so fruitfully with his longing to recover the instinctive joy of his boyhood.

For within a month of parting with Coleridge, Wordsworth and Dorothy set out for Grasmere. They travelled on foot and on horseback to Kendal. There they ordered furniture and continued their journey in a post-chaise. The weather was wild and bleak, but the frosty wind was behind them. It helped them on their way, and they drew a feeling of strength and exultation from the stern face of Nature. For winter did not numb the heart here as it had in Germany. Its starkness was part of Wordsworth's very self. The naked trees and icy brooks spoke with a dearly familiar voice, and when at last they entered the vale of Grasmere and approached the small stone and plaster cottage which was to be their home, a 'bright and solemn sky' faced them with what seemed 'a passionate welcoming.'

The strongest tie of Wordsworth's life, his attachment to the hills and lakes of his boyhood, was re-established. He was in immediate contact once again with the primal source of his strength and joy. The years of exile were over; the distracted wanderer had come home. And although the two months

which followed his arrival on 20th December were continuously
dark and stormy, his spirits were unaffected. For he was safe
from the world that had bruised and bewildered him. He and
Dorothy shared with the lonely pair of swans, who had found
a safe retreat in the island at the centre of the lake, 'a still and
placid way of life, and constant love inseparable.' He had been
driven from Eden but miraculously he had been allowed to
return to it. Or so it seemed. And as he luxuriated in his sense
of restoration and security, the poet in him awoke from the
troubled sleep of doubt and indecision and began to mutter

> his prelusive songs
> With cheerful heart, an unknown voice of joy
> Among the silence of the woods and hills.

PART VIII

THE RETURN OF THE NATIVE

§ I

DOVE Cottage stood several hundred feet back from the north-east shore of Grasmere Lake. In front of it ran the old road that connected Grasmere village and Ambleside; behind it was a little orchard that rose so sharply that shrubs and flowers growing at its higher end pressed against the upper windows and shaded a tiny spring that tumbled down the rocky hillside in their midst. The cottage was almost the only one beside the lake which it overlooked. Beyond were the heights of Silver How and Loughrigg Fell, while at the back the first slopes of Rydal Fell began a stretch of green-turfed hill and rock-scarred mountain upon which nought but a few black-faced sheep would be met with in a day's wandering. Amid these reaches of wide and lofty solitude lay the vale and the lake, richly wooded on one side along its margin, on the other bordered by a small expanse of level meadowland.

To Wordsworth it was all exquisitely familiar and inspiringly new. Grasmere was only a three hours' walk from Hawkshead, a full day's walk from Cockermouth or Penrith. Once, as a roving schoolboy on a golden summer holiday, he had come upon this vale and as he overlooked it, its secluded beauty had halted his hasty footsteps and held him in a sudden stillness. He had thought with a sigh that few fortunes could be more happy than to live and die in this place, if indeed death could enter such a paradise. It was at the time no more than a fancy, the momentary reaction of a tired body that craved rest and found in the soft, green spot,

> Not giddy yet aerial, with a depth
> Of vale below, a height of hills above. . . .
> All that luxurious nature could desire.

Yet as he rested there, in touch with earth and yet cradled in the upper air, his spirit had become wonderfully volatile. He had seemed to share the liberty and joy of sailing clouds and sportive breezes, 'of sunbeams, shadows, butterflies and birds.' Yet even while he had yielded to the illusion of unfettered freedom, a deeper instinct within him had whispered that it could only truly be enjoyed within limits. And what limits could afford so much of height and depth and rich diversity as the bound of the huge concave upon which he gazed?

It had been but a pleasing and a passing fancy, but the tired boy had foreshadowed the disillusioned man. The boy on that summer day had wandered far, and knew the momentary contentment of relaxed muscles and the purified calm of exhausted energies. The man had wandered far too, but his wanderings had almost killed his desire for new or daring adventure. To nurse his creative impulse within limits familiar enough to shut out a world of fear and doubt, grand enough to uphold and enrich his spirit and to disperse the 'self-cherished sadness' which had clouded his faculties, was all the freedom that he craved. It was enough that Grasmere should 'be his home, this valley be his world.'

Until the spring came, he and Dorothy could anticipate its delights, building in imagination 'a seat, with a summer shed, on the highest platform' in their 'little domestic slip of a mountain,' which should command a view over two-thirds of the vale, or planning to enclose the two or three yards of ground between the house and the road and to plant flowers there. His inner thankfulness was such that, as he told Coleridge in a letter, he felt himself a debtor to the little cottage itself, despite its smoking chimneys, and took a solitary pleasure in doing something gratuitously for it, as for an individual to whom he owed so much.

But when the spring came and the clouds lifted from the hills, his gratitude flowed out into the dear vale, which now

was his, 'perchance for life.' At last he was easy in his conscience. Or he could persuade himself that he was, could
answer resolutely the voice which had so persistently whispered
that he was an idle and worthless dreamer. In such a humble
cottage and with such modest needs to satisfy, no one could
suggest that he was taking from life more than he would give.
He had paid for his present peace in years of uncertainty and
self-reproach, but now he blushed that he should have allowed
the judgment of the world to weigh so heavily with him. And
yet now that its power over him was surely past, he could bless

> the realities of life so cold,
> So cowardly, so ready to betray,

for all that they had taught him and for enriching by contrast
his present sense of security. And to be no longer troubled by
indecision, to be sure that the step which he had taken was
not only deeply gratifying but right and reasonable too, was
an immeasurable relief.

Yet a hint of self-defence still sounded in the lines in which
he justified his happiness and delighted in the fact that Dorothy
shared it.

> On Nature's invitation do I come,
> By Reason sanctioned. Can the choice mislead
> That made the calmest fairest spot of earth
> With all its unappropriated good
> My own; and not mine only, for with me
> Entrenched, say rather peacefully embowered,
> Under yon orchard, in yon humble cot,
> A younger Orphan of a home extinct,
> The only Daughter of my Parents dwells.
> Ay, think on that, my heart, and cease to stir,
> Pause upon that and let the breathing frame
> No longer breathe, but all be satisfied.

—Oh, if such silence be not thanks to God
For what hath been bestowed, then where, where then
Shall gratitude find rest? Mine eyes did ne'er
Fix on a lovely object, nor my mind
Take pleasure in the midst of happy thoughts,
But either She whom now I have, who now
Divides with me this loved abode, was there
Or not far off. Where'er my footsteps turned,
Her voice was like a hidden Bird that sang,
The thought of her was like a flash of light,
Or an unseen companionship, a breath
Of fragrance independent of the wind.
In all my goings, in the new and old
Of all my meditations, and in this
Favourite of all, in this the most of all.

A lover lives only in the present, and Wordsworth, as he wrote
these lines, could forget the years when he had taken pleasure
apart from Dorothy both at Hawkshead as a boy and in
France, when another voice than hers had been 'like a hidden
Bird that sang.' But the past had ceased to exist for him
except as a homeless background. And doubtless the fact
that he had been from such an early age an 'Orphan of a
home extinct' conditioned to some extent his need of a
domestic sanctuary, as it did the abnormal intensity of his
love for his sister.

And now that he was in fact as well as spirit at home with
her and with the Nature of his childhood, now that he held
in his hand the good for which he had sighed through homesick
years and his dearest Imaginations were realised, he was convinced that no being, since the birth of man, had ever more
abundant cause to be thankful. And in the fragment, entitled
The Recluse, from which we have already quoted, he poured out
his thanks in the spring of 1800 with a warmth and a freedom

from the sententious which outshone even the lyrical rapture of Alfoxden a year before.

In doing so he transgressed his original conception of *The Recluse*, as a long philosophical poem, in which his own personal history would play a subsidiary part. He obeyed instead the necessity of his being and resumed his true vocation which was that of one who could only delight and instruct mankind as a poet, when he was intimately personal.

And so, forgetting the ambitions and impersonal schemes which he had elaborated in the shadow of creative impotence, he began what was to be one of his most prolific years by calling on Verse 'to aid him and in song resound his joy.' Nor was he again to attempt to divorce the philosophical from the personal until he had almost drained the resources of autobiography and the shadow of poetic impotence lay once more upon him.

Meanwhile to concentrate himself within the safe world that he knew was his only thought. This world of crags and woody steeps, of the lake with its one green island and its winding shores, of little rocky hills and church and cottages of mountain stone, was already part of himself. He had assimilated it from childhood days. And so when he cried—

> Embrace me then, ye Hills, and close me in;
> Now in the clear and open day I feel
> Your guardianship; I take it to my heart;
> 'Tis like the solemn shelter of the night,

he was in a real sense returning to his past and shutting the future out. He was accepting the protection of the known against the dangers of the unknown. In the circle of these hills he had experienced the joy and faith that sprang from an inward unity. He had lost that unity and lost it so disastrously that he had given up hope of renewing it in any other place.

> Nowhere (or is it fancy?) can be found
> The one sensation that is here; 'tis here,
> Here as it found its way into my heart
> In childhood, here as it abides by day,
> By night, here only; . . .
> —'Tis, but I cannot name it, 'tis the sense
> Of majesty, and beauty, and repose,
> A blended holiness of earth and sky,
> Something that makes this individual spot,
> This small abiding-place of many men,
> A termination, and a last retreat,
> A centre, come from wheresoe'er you will,
> A whole without dependence or defect,
> Made for itself, and happy in itself,
> Perfect contentment, Unity entire.

The move to Grasmere was, indeed, 'a termination and a last retreat.' It not only involved Wordsworth finally in what Coleridge was later to lament as 'this inferred dependency of the human soul on accidents of birth-place and abode,' but also in the hopeless attempt to recover and possess a past state of virtue. Yet for seven or eight years his retreat almost seemed 'a whole without dependence or defect.' His creative impulse had found the 'local habitation' which it needed. Too content with his lot to be much disturbed by fear or doubt, those demons of the self-preserving mind, which, because they had not in fact been exorcised, were only waiting to renew their destructive work, he could relive imaginatively his past and translate it, through the very intensity of his reflective self-absorption, into great poetry. For although outwardly he might seem to have deserted the world of life and motion, inwardly the creative stream was flowing and, he was convinced, would 'never cease to flow.' To float upon that stream, in entire forgetfulness of all the surface agitations, filled his soul with beatitude. But that it was still contingent upon the same happy circumstances as had blessed his boyhood is revealed in the lines in which again he poured out his thanks to the

> Delightful valley, habitation fair,
> And to whatever else of outward form
> Can give an inward help, can purify,
> And elevate, and harmonise, and soothe,
> And steal away, and *for a while deceive*
> And lap in pleasing rest, and bear us on
> Without desire in full complacency,
> Contemplating perfection absolute,
> And entertained as in a placid sleep.

The joy of the true mystic who has risen to that plane of being in which reality is experienced beyond the temporal alternations of pleasure and pain, is as little dependent upon any act of self-deception as upon sublime scenery. He has achieved his inward radiance, not by turning away from the apparent pain and discord of the world to indulge for a while 'in pleasing rest,' but by bringing the creative spirit in himself into such perfect and assured union with Life that he perceives the eternal essence of all things and so has no need to flinch before their temporal impurities.

And although in *The Recluse* Wordsworth sang a very moving hymn of praise to the Providence which had brought him, as he believed, creative liberation, he had escaped rather from the prison of depressing circumstance than from the prison of himself. Beneath the melting mood which the temporary satisfaction of his desires had induced, the old dualism persisted. We see it in the alternations of his attitude towards his fellow dalesmen. In moments of emotional expansiveness he could believe that

> They who are dwellers in this holy place
> Must needs themselves be hallowed.

They must, he felt, be possessed, like himself, by an overflowing love

> Not for the creature only, but for all
> That is around them; love for everything
> Which in their happy Region they behold.

But then the realist would rebuke the sentimentalist, insisting that

> not betrayed by tenderness of mind
> That feared, or wholly overlooked the truth,
> Did we come hither, with romantic hope
> To find in midst of so much loveliness
> Love, perfect love: of so much majesty
> A like majestic frame of mind in those
> Who here abide, the persons like the place.

There was of course truth in both these attitudes and the greatness of his achievement as a poet of humble life was to spring from the fertile collaboration of the realist and the man of feeling in

> An act, a music, and a strain of words
> That shall be life, the acknowledged voice of life,
> Shall speak of what is done among the fields,
> Done truly there, or felt, of solid good
> And real evil, yet be sweet withal,
> More grateful, more harmonious than the breath,
> The idle breath of softest pipe attuned
> To pastoral fancies.

Yet it was not wholly true, as he asserted, that

> pleased with the good
> I shrink not from the evil with disgust,
> Or with immoderate pain.

There was one very considerable reservation. Where the Labouring Man preserved 'his rosy face' and was a 'Freeman sound and unimpaired,' where he was favoured by the 'noble privilege' of living in a lovely vale, Wordsworth could observe without dismay the flaws in human nature. But from those who were immured in 'the vast metropolis,' who toiled in

> the living and dead wilderness
> Of the thronged world,

he shrank, if not with disgust, at least with a despairing distaste. He wished, in short, to part 'with all remembrance of a jarring world,' and his belief in man, like his renewed and fertile faith in himself, was only secure so long as he shut his eyes against all the life that was fermenting for good and evil in cities and devouring the green country-side in the dark track of Industrialism.

But meanwhile his roots drew once more upon their native source of nourishment, and the idea that his own discord and the world's could be resolved by a return to primitive integrity seemed valid enough amid men and women who had never lost such integrity. The dale folk had long, indeed, outgrown the early communal stage of primitive life. They had a staunch and independent individuality. But the conditions of their life had prevented self-consciousness with all its attendant ills from eating into their integrity, as it had done into Wordsworth's. And in associating with them he could so successfully forget that he had ceased to be as they, that for a time he could return to their condition, and by becoming their voice release the deepest springs of his nature and his poetry.

s

Thus sustained by his native earth and his native folk he could feel as the spring advanced that

> the inward frame,
> Though slowly opening, opens every day.

The low-hung mists had broken up both in the dale and in himself. The primrose peeped forth, the blackbird sang, the fountains sparkled in the sun. Everywhere in Nature there was a calm revelry that passed into himself, breeding delight and confidence and a gleeful anticipation of the whole year that was to come. His previous despondency seemed now to belong to another life. The world over which he had brooded so despairingly was well lost. One hope was sufficient now,

> that we shall neither droop
> Nor pine for want of pleasure in the life
> Scattered about us, nor through want of aught
> That keeps in health the insatiable mind.

Yet he had hardly affirmed the sufficiency of personal pleasure as an end before his conscience awoke and reproved the hedonist.

> Yet 'tis not to enjoy that we exist,
> For that end only; something must be done.

He remembered his mission in life. He was a poet, and although he eschewed 'ill-advised Ambition' and Pride, he felt as strongly as ever that he had been vouchsafed 'an internal brightness . . . that must not die.' 'Possessions have I,' he wrote,

> that are solely mine,
> Something within which yet is shared by none,
> Not even the nearest to me and most dear,
> Something which power and effort may impart;

I would impart it, I would spread it wide:
Immortal in the world which is to come—
Forgive me if I add another claim—
And would not wholly perish even in this,
Lie down and be forgotten in the dust,
I and the modest Partners of my days
Making a silent company in death;
Love, knowledge, all my manifold delights,
All buried with me without monument
Or profit unto any but ourselves!
It must not be, if I, divinely taught,
Be privileged to speak as I have felt
Of what in man is human or divine.

Certainly it was no 'ill-advised Ambition' which he voiced in these lines. And it is only in the light of his earlier devotion to the cause of humanity, a devotion more impulsive and invested with so much less of the 'egotistic sublime,' that this determination to achieve a memorable name among the mankind over whom he now assumed the privilege of a seer and inspired instructor, suggests a decline to a lower level.

He himself was not unaware of the change. But he justified it as being in the course of nature. Just as the wild appetites and blind desires of childhood had passed, so the longing to participate in forlorn enterprises or to lead a crusade had been outgrown. Nature had tamed him, bidding him to seek for other agitations or be calm. But where he deceived himself was in insisting that there was no 'want of inspirations that have been,' that

                         the love,
The longing, the contempt, the undaunted quest,
All shall survive, though changed their office, all
Shall live, it is not in their power to die.

Alas! it was not possible to bid farewell to 'the forwardness of soul,' while remaining true to the creative impulse which for a short time in youth had urged him to embrace the heroic adventure of selflessness.

Nevertheless for one who wished above all to try to understand and explain his own experience, it was a positive advantage to emphasise the rights of

> the individual Mind that keeps her own
> Inviolate retirement, subject there
> To Conscience only, and the law supreme
> Of that Intelligence which governs all.

And as long as he was too happy in himself and his lot to remember the unclosed gulf which had opened between him and life in the days of his wretchedness he could convincingly proclaim

> How exquisitely the individual Mind
> (And the progressive powers perhaps no less
> Of the whole species) to the external World
> Is fitted—and how exquisitely, too—
> Theme this but little heard of among men—
> The external World is fitted to the Mind.

Certainly the external world of Grasmere was perfectly fitted to his individual Mind at this time, but the fact hardly proved the truth of his 'high argument.' For self-satisfaction derived from 'grateful haunts' was obviously a very insecure basis for a life-philosophy. That the individual Mind is exquisitely fitted to the external world is, indeed, a profound truth. But it can only be realised as a truth by one who has gradually learnt to surrender the exclusive claims of his individuality, and whose happiness, in consequence, does not depend upon privileged circumstances.

The 'high argument,' however, to which Wordsworth now dedicated himself as a Bard 'in holiest mood' was not based upon this truth. The fact was not to prevent him from giving 'utterance in numerous verse,'

> Of Truth, of Grandeur, Beauty, Love, and Hope
> And melancholy Fear subdued by Faith;
> Of blessèd Consolations in distress;
> Of moral strength, and intellectual Power;
> Of joy in widest commonalty spread.

But it was to separate him fatally from the 'prophetic Spirit,' upon which he called,

> that inspir'st
> The human soul of universal earth,
> Dreaming on things to come.

For eventually he was bound to rediscover an external world to which his individual Mind was not so exquisitely fitted as he could believe while nothing threatened his security and all things were so kindred to himself that it was a pleasure to love them.

§ 2

During the next seven years, however, Wordsworth's deep-rooted individuality expanded sympathetically to its extreme limits. The fragment of *The Recluse* was completed before the end of April 1800, and from it he turned to the composition of *The Prelude*, the first two books of which, treating of his childhood and school-time, were completed before the end of the year. It was then put aside and was not continued until the summer of 1804. It was natural that at this time, when he had regained so fully his sense of self-contentment, he should devote himself to this poem on his early life. But he still regarded it as no more than a comparatively short introduction to the complete philosophical poem in three parts which he had planned.

But meanwhile in the intervals of work upon *The Prelude*, he continued to express his views of Nature, Man, and Society in the only way which his personality allowed, by projecting his own feelings into the peasant folk and children who imaged in such circumstantial detail his ideal of individual and social integrity. For, as he wrote in *Hart-Leap Well*,

> Grey-headed Shepherd, thou hast spoken well;
> Small difference lies between thy creed and mine:

and again in the same poem,

> The moving accident is not my trade;
> To freeze the blood I have no ready arts:
> 'Tis my delight, alone in summer shade,
> To pipe a simple song for thinking hearts.

And among the earliest poems which he wrote in the summer shade of 1800 were two domestic tales that concerned the life of shepherds and owed their impressiveness to the strength of simple human feeling which he discovered in the apparently ordinary and matter-of-fact.

Both *The Brothers* and *Michael* are transcribed so directly from human life, that a reader might suppose that they cost Wordsworth little creative effort. Yet in fact he wrote them both and particularly the former with difficulty, constantly revising what he had written as he strove to concentrate emotion by simplifying diction. This painful process of revision was indeed to be always characteristic of him even when in later years it had become only a craftsman's labour. But during his great creative period the technical effort quickened his emotional powers, which in turn reacted upon and dictated his technique.

To achieve the bare narration of *The Brothers* and *Michael* he had, in fact, to strip his feeling of every inessential, to return to the simple core of his being, and unlive his years of mental unrest. It cost him pain to do so, but there was nothing which he so much desired or which, when he had succeeded, brought him more content.

He lived himself in the subjects of both poems. For the Leonard of *The Brothers* is, like himself, one whose 'soul was knit to this his native soil,' who in foreign places had seen with feverish vision the forms of sheep that grazed on the mountains, and who as a returned traveller walks through fields, which once had been well known to him, with unspeakable joy. And in the old Priest who could help him to the history of half the graves in the churchyard where they talk, Wordsworth drew an early sketch of the Pastor of *The Excursion*, that reverend personification of his middle-age, whose counterpart in actual life was probably Mr. Sympson, the clergyman at Wythburn, at whose house, midway between Keswick and Grasmere, he used often to break his journey during this summer.

The theme of the poem, too, the deep attachment which bound the two brothers together, and the fate which parted them, was doubtless suggested by the presence during most of the summer months of his sailor brother John. In the poem it is Leonard who goes to sea and returns to find his brother dead. In life it was John Wordsworth who was to be drowned at sea, and his brother who survived to lament 'the happy warrior' whom he loved. But in writing the poem Wordsworth clearly grafted on to a tragic local incident, described to him at Ennerdale, his own reawakened feelings for the brother who after Dorothy was nearest to him in temperament and dearest of any of his family — 'the *silent* Poet' and 'Cherished Visitant,' whom he described with such tender admiration in the lines, entitled *When to the Attractions of the Busy World*, written later in the summer after his brother had left them to set out on his last voyage.

But in *Michael*, which he wrote about the same time as *The Brothers*, he identified himself far more profoundly with the shepherds whom he loved. Michael is the owner-shepherd of *The Last of the Flock*, drawn over again in a full-length picture. The details of his history are somewhat different, but his essential character and the pathos of his situation are the same. With his stout heart and bodily frame, his keen, intense, and frugal mind, and above all his deeply rooted love for the hills which he had so often climbed and the fields and flocks which he had acquired by long years of unrelaxed toil, he was brother to Wordsworth himself. And his love for his wife, who equalled him in thrift and industry and for his only son, was of a like tenacious quality. Hence the deep pathos of the old man's words, when disaster through no fault of his own threatens him—

> I have been toiling more than seventy years,
> And in the open sunshine of God's love
> Have we all lived; yet if these fields of ours
> Should pass into a stranger's hand, I think
> That I could not lie quiet in my grave.

Equally affecting is his parting with his son, the struggle in his heart between his desire to keep him and his hope that by sending him to an industrial town he may redeem the family's fortunes. In both impulses the possessive instinct was involved, but this made them only the more agonisingly true to life as Wordsworth read it and as most men live it. And in the son's ultimate corruption by 'the dissolute city,' his surrender to evil courses and his eventual flight across the seas, Wordsworth drew of course again upon his own experience and dramatised his belief that the only hope for man lay in a return to rural virtue.

The partiality of this belief does not, of course, lessen the truth or pathos of the poem, as 'a faithful copy from Nature,' nor the impressiveness of its conclusion, told with masterly brevity and directness, in which the old Man endures the loss of all he held most dear with the same staunch, though inwardly stricken, self-sufficiency, the same 'stern, unbending mind,' as in the days when instinctive love and pride of possession enhanced each other.

As a picture, indeed, 'of a man, of strong mind and lively sensibility, agitated by two of the most powerful affections of the human heart—the parental affection and the love of property,' 'Michael' is a wonderfully true and moving poem. But in its relation to Wordsworth himself it reveals even more clearly than *The Last of the Flock* that in his views of man, Nature, and society he had turned his back upon the future. Doubtless he had every excuse in the conditions of his time. For up to a certain point in human development the acquisitive instinct is necessary to life and even beneficent. Michael within his limits was whole and admirable, while the manufacturing towns were full of men who had lost his primal virtues. Nor did these towns with their airless factories and smoke-grimed hovels promise anything but increasing deterioration, while the palliatives which Liberal men with a conscience sought to apply were, in the workhouse for example, almost as vicious as the disease.

Little wonder, therefore, that Wordsworth saw nothing but an endless prospect of demoralisation in the drift of the rural population to the manufacturing towns and turned from it to concentrate all his love and admiration upon those proprietors of small estates in his own North Country, whose 'little tract of land serves as a kind of permanent rallying-point for their domestic feelings, as a tablet upon which they are written, which makes them objects of memory in a thousand instances, when they would otherwise be forgotten. It is a fountain fitted to the nature of social man, from which supplies of affection, *as pure as his heart was intended for*, are daily drawn.'

Looking back indeed upon the social and economic history of the last century, with its increasing sacrifice of the individual to the heartless forces of financial greed and the machine, we cannot but admit that Wordsworth's mistrust of the catch-cry of 'progress' was justified. But it was not, as Professor Harper asserts, 'perfectly in harmony with his earlier Revolutionary zeal.' It was rooted in the local attachments of his boyhood, but it denied the ideals of Beaupuy.

For the virtues which he rightly applauded in the Cumberland 'Statesmen' depended upon a limited and working ownership of property in land. They were the beneficent fruit of a self-interest, so disciplined by circumstance, that it was prevented from destroying the balance of give and take which is essential to healthy life. The manufacturing towns, however, were the fruit of the same self-interest unrestrained and swelling to monstrous proportions. And however suggestive as a pattern of ancient virtue the integrity of the northern dalesman was, the disease of selfishness which was spreading through the world, and of which the inhumanities and ugliness of industrialism were only the most obvious symptoms, could not be arrested or cured by pointing to the staunch excellencies of proprietors of small estates 'now almost confined to the North of England.'

In all men the creative and the destructive motive, the lust for personal gain, and the disinterested love of life, exist in varying degrees. Up to a point in human development they are fruitfully balanced, as they were in Michael and his kind. But once this point is passed, once the acquisitive impulse has come to dominate, virtue can only be recovered by a spiritual advance. The self which has lost its roots in Nature and consequently its natural balance, but which in the process has acquired an increasingly mental awareness, must be enlarged until it embraces through sympathetic understanding the world to which it was once instinctively attached but from which it has become alienated.

Inevitably, perhaps, Wordsworth could not see in the industrial movement a world travailing towards a new birth. Indeed it is only to-day after a century and more of human suffering, culminating in the agony of the war, that we can begin to see the meaning of what on the face of it must be regarded as a prolonged process of waste and deterioration.

But by recoiling from his Revolutionary belief that mankind was entering upon a new age of selfless devotion, however credulous at the time it was, to a belief in the peasant and the small proprietor as the ultimate expression of human virtue, he betrayed his own inability to outgrow his past. And as his belief in the virtues of property increased, his creative power inevitably declined.

But that was not yet, and Coleridge, who was never to lose his belief in the excessive evils of property and his aversion to the Rich, helped to delay the process. On his return from Germany he had accepted work on the *Morning Post*, but this he had abandoned in the spring to translate Schiller's *Wallenstein*. Before this he had been more than once a guest at Dove Cottage, and on 29th June he came with his family for a month until they moved into Greta Hall at Keswick.

From midsummer, therefore, he and Wordsworth were constantly together, and his influence can be felt in *Hart-Leap Well*, a poem which also originated in local lore, but was not, like *The Brothers* and *Michael*, unenriched by strange event. The 'pleasure-house' of this poem, and the curse which fell on the spot where it was built, because of the hart that was hunted to its death there, are redolent of Coleridge. The pulse of *The*

Ancient Mariner beats to a soberer measure in the lines—

> The Being, that is in the clouds and air,
> That is in the green leaves among the groves,
> Maintains a deep and reverential care
> For the unoffending creatures whom he loves.
>
> . . . One lesson, Shepherd, let us two divide,
> Taught both by what she shows, and what conceals;
> Never to blend our pleasure or our pride
> With sorrow of the meanest thing that feels.

And in the pastoral fable, *The Oak and the Broom*, we hear again the voice of Coleridge, confirming his friend's readiness to believe, so long as he was reasonably secure, that there is more wisdom in the humble joy and love that trusts in Providence than in the pride of self-complacent prudence. For 'the little careless Broom' that gently murmured

> Frail is the bond by which we hold
> Our being, whether young or old,
> Wise, foolish, weak, or strong.
>
> Disasters, do the best we can,
> Will reach both great and small;
> And he is oft the wisest man,
> Who is not wise at all,

reflected Coleridge's native spirit of benevolent improvidence. Once again Wordsworth could sun himself in the light of this spirit and under circumstances far happier even than at Alfoxden.

For, two months before Coleridge moved to Keswick, Wordsworth had gone on a visit to Mary Hutchinson in Yorkshire. His means were still very limited, but he was now at least sufficiently secure to contemplate marriage. That Dorothy knew of his intentions is clear from the first entry in her Grasmere *Journal*, in which she recorded that her brother set off into Yorkshire at half-past two o'clock with cold pork in his pocket, and continued, 'My heart was so full that I could hardly speak to W. when I gave him a farewell kiss. I sate a long time upon a stone at the margin of the lake, and after a flood of tears my heart was easier. The lake looked to me, I knew not why, dull and melancholy, and the weltering on the shores seemed a heavy sound.' Two days later her spirits were still low. 'Grasmere very solemn,' she noted, 'in the last glimpse of twilight. It calls home the heart to quietness. I had been very melancholy in my walk back. I had many of my saddest thoughts, and I could not keep the tears within me. But when I came to Grasmere I felt that it did me good. I finished my letter to M. H. . . .'

Warmly attached as Dorothy was to Mary Hutchinson she could not but approve her brother's choice. But because he was to her so much more than a brother, she inevitably suffered, too, the pangs of a supplanted lover. The dream which she had cherished from girlhood days of being all in all to William had been realised. But hardly were the cottage, garden, and little orchard theirs, than they were to be taken from her, or at least shared with another. All her brother's assurances that their life together would continue unchanged could not alter this. He no longer needed her exclusively as it had been her joy to know that he did. And doubtless it was to some extent this sense of baffled devotion which deepened her attachment to Coleridge who more and more as the months went by, and sickness and domestic unhappiness weighed upon him, needed and accepted all that she could give. Nevertheless her devotion for her brother was always to come first, but the ecstasy was to go out of it, until at last it took the form of ungrudging domestic service and the endless occupation of copying his poems.

But for Wordsworth, when he returned late at night three

weeks later and found his sister sitting up for him and wild with joy to have him home again, there was no painful conflict of feeling. He was secure in the love of two women. And if he was drawn to the one who was to be his wife with less than a lover's passion, Dorothy was something more than a sister. And with both he was safe from what he secretly feared most, from what haunted him whenever he remembered Annette. How deeply he felt the fatality of passion breathes through the poem he wrote at this time, entitled *'Tis Said, That Some Have Died for Love*. He had known too bitterly the love that brought self-destruction in its train to risk again the love which brings joy and completion in perfect self-surrender. His love for Annette had been 'such a grievous pain' that all he desired from woman now was the comfort of quiet affection. And the concluding lines of this poem were clearly addressed to Mary Hutchinson —

> Ah gentle Love! if ever thought was thine
> To store up kindred hours for me, thy face
> Turn from me, gentle Love! nor let me walk
> Within the sound of Emma's voice, nor know
> Such happiness as I have known to-day.

But with Mary Hutchinson any such fears, as he must have known, were groundless. He could even recommend her to his friend Francis Wrangham as 'a most amiable and good creature, with whom you could converse with great pleasure.' And in one of the *Poems on the Naming of Places* which he wrote this summer and dedicated to her, he drew a charming picture of her personality, retiring, restful, and selflessly kind. He described how a hidden track

> brought us to a slip of lawn,
> And a small bed of water in the woods.
> All round this pool both flocks and herds might drink

On its firm margin, even as from a well,
Or some stone-basin which the herdsman's hand
Had shaped for their refreshment; nor did sun,
Or wind from any quarter, ever come,
But as a blessing to this calm recess,
This glade of water and this one green field.
The spot was made by Nature for herself;
The travellers know it not, and 'twill remain
Unknown to them; but it is beautiful;
And if a man should plant his cottage near,
Should sleep beneath the shelter of its trees,
And blend its waters with his daily meal,
He would so love it, that in his death-hour
Its image would survive among his thoughts.

It was hardly necessary to give the name of 'my sweet Mary' to this 'still Nook.' She was the pool of limpid water, the calm recess, the one green field, unknown to other men, but ideally fashioned to share his cottage and blend her benevolence with his daily meals.

But two years were to pass before he made 'this calm recess' his own. At times, indeed, he felt still 'the trouble of the Wanderer in his soul.' But unlike the Wandering Jew of his poem he had now an established home and haven. Beneath the outward harmony of his life there remained, indeed, an inward distraction which was never really to be appeased, but which he relieved by his daily wanderings along the country roads that still, as in childhood, beckoned 'to things unknown and without bound' and also afforded many a chance converse with men who were real characters, if lowly and obscure. He relieved it, too, by the poetry which he composed so often aloud without pencil or paper in the open air. For in this way he was able to listen to his own poetry as if it were the creation of another, while at the same time appreciating the fact that it was his own. And whenever exhaustion followed a prolonged spell of concentration, Dorothy was at hand to minister to him, and Coleridge to renew his faith.

Coleridge's dream of a domestic haven was, indeed, already shattered. He had become in spirit the Wandering Jew, just when his friend had found

> a home to enter
> In some nook of chosen ground.

But for the time his wanderings took him no farther than Dove Cottage, and although he was often ill and a source of deep concern to his friend, his presence was a constant stimulus and delight. Dorothy, too, was making the most of the last period in which she would have her brother to herself. And with her to quicken his observation and Coleridge to quicken his ideas he was ideally companioned.

The walk along the eastern shore of Grasmere Lake on a calm September morning, of which he left a record in verse, was typical of many. And doubtless it was she in particular who frequently bid her brother and Coleridge, as they strolled along, playing with their time,

> stop to watch some tuft
> Of dandelion seed or thistle's beard,
> That skimmed the surface of the dead calm lake,
> Suddenly halting now—a lifeless stand!
> And starting off again with freak as sudden;
> In all its sportive wanderings, all the while,
> Making report of an invisible breeze
> That was its wings, its chariot, and its horse,
> Its playmate, rather say, its moving soul.

But it was, we can believe, neither Dorothy nor Coleridge who exclaimed 'improvident and reckless,' as later in the same walk they approached a poor peasant fishing in the lake instead of helping with the harvest. Nor was the moral which Words-worth derived from the incident theirs, when on a nearer view they discovered that the idling peasant was a sick man using his best skill to gain a pittance from the dead, unfeeling lake.

For Dorothy and Coleridge had no need to be admonished to 'temper all their thoughts with charity.'

> The happy idleness of that sweet morn
> With all its lovely images

was enough for them, and possibly their presence quickened beneficially Wordsworth's sense of regret for his censorious-ness. Certainly Dorothy's pity for the poor and unfortunate, of which her *Journal* provides so much moving evidence, must have proved a constant spur, if any was needed at this time, to her brother's sympathies, and the more so because it was so wholly devoid of moralising.

It was on another walk a week or two later that they met the old man, bent almost double, who was later to be immortalised in Wordsworth's *Leech-Gatherer*. And the account which Dorothy gave of him in her *Journal* is such a perfect example of her disinterested objectiveness that we may be forgiven for quoting it in full. 'He had on a coat,' she wrote, 'thrown over his shoulders, above his waistcoat and coat. Under this he carried a bundle, and had an apron on and a night-cap. His face was interesting. He had dark eyes and a long nose. . . . He was of Scotch parents, but had been born in the army. He had had a wife, and "she was a good woman, and it pleased God to bless us with ten children." All these were dead but one, of whom he had not heard for many years, a sailor. His trade was to gather leeches, but now leeches are scarce, and he had not strength for it. *He lived by begging*, and was making his way to Carlisle, where he should buy a few godly books to sell.

T

He said leeches were very scarce, partly owing to this dry season, but many years they have been scarce. He supposed it owing to their being much sought after, that they did not breed fast, and were of slow growth. Leeches were formerly 2s. 6d. per 100; they are now 30s. He had been hurt in driving a cart, his leg broken, his body driven over, his skull fractured. He felt no pain till he recovered from his first insensibility. It was then late in the evening, when the light was just going away.'

There can be few better ways of measuring the difference between Dorothy and her brother or of understanding the workings of the creative process in him than by comparing this account with the poem written two years later. In Dorothy we have here the pure and impartial observer with a gift for seizing upon all the salient facts in a situation. So far as any sympathetic emotion entered into her record, it served only to bring out the significant details. There was no attempt to penetrate beneath the surface or explore the human mystery. But neither was there any moralising or sententious comment.

But when the incident came to birth in a poem after two years of inward gestation, it was transformed in two ways. By projecting himself and his own needs into it, Wordsworth modified the facts. *His* 'Leech-Gatherer' was not driven even by misfortune to begging. He continued to gain an honest, if hazardous, maintenance. He personified that 'independence' which was such a cherished tenet of his creator's creed. But if Dorothy's account was more objectively true, her brother's poem was charged with an inward reality with which she had no concern. His relation to the old man was not disinterested. But by identifying him with himself he invested him with his own sense of the mystery and meaning of human life.

The new and enlarged edition of *Lyrical Ballads* which he was preparing for the Press during the summer and autumn of 1800 showed, indeed, not only in the new poems added but in the revision of the old, how much closer his fidelity to actual life had become. He had almost outgrown his earlier tendency towards the abnormal or the grotesque, while the last vestiges of the social theoriser, and also the social rebel, had disappeared. He had found the facts upon which his imagination could feed.

And it was doubtless this growth in himself which explained, if it does not justify, his somewhat ungenerous attitude to Coleridge's poetry, despite the ungrudging help and encouragement which his friend gave in the compiling of the new volume. Coleridge's contributions to it were very slight, and although he himself accepted Wordsworth's reasons for not including *Christabel* as quite adequate, they were not impressive. Still less was the patronising criticism of *The Ancient Mariner* contained in a note to the new edition. 'The Poem of my Friend,' Wordsworth wrote, 'has indeed great defects; first, that the principal character has no distinct character, either in his profession of Mariner, or as a human being who, having been long under the control of supernatural impressions, might be supposed himself to partake of something supernatural; secondly, that he does not act, but is continually acted upon; thirdly, that the events, having no necessary connection, do not produce each other; and lastly, that the imagery is somewhat too laboriously accumulated.'

We have commented elsewhere[1] upon the critical crassness of this indictment and need not do so here. It was a characteristically honest judgment. But in fact Wordsworth was complaining that Coleridge's poetical powers worked differently from his own. And not only his poetical powers, but his whole nature. For it was not merely the Mariner, but Coleridge himself, who 'does not act, but is continually acted upon.' Doubtless Wordsworth was unconscious at this time that he was criticising his friend as well as his friend's poem. Yet the

[1] *Samuel Taylor Coleridge*, p. 168.

first symptom of the rift which was to widen between them is perhaps to be found here.

It was because Coleridge was so continually acted upon that he had such a vivid sense of the supernatural and the enchanted, while Wordsworth had lost much of his sympathy for his friend's unearthly experiences because his own feet were now firmly enough set in the earth that he loved for him to shape actively his experience. For better and for worse he was now, except at certain abnormal times, the master of his will as he was of his circumstances. But Coleridge was still as ever beatifically and disastrously at the mercy of the fluctuations of life. Hence the delight he took in prostrating himself before his friend's virtues, revealed in a letter to Godwin in which he wrote that if he died and the booksellers offered anything for his Life, 'be sure to say, "Wordsworth descended on him like the γνῶθι σεαυτόν from heaven; and by showing him what true poetry was, he made him know that he himself was no poet." '

Wordsworth cannot, of course, be blamed for having this effect upon Coleridge, but it was curiously characteristic that he should at the same time complacently accept and draw strength from his friend's appreciation and depreciate him in print for failing as a poet to write as he himself did.

§ 3

The book appeared in January 1801, and the degree of self-assurance to which Wordsworth had now attained may be gauged by the fact that he sent a copy of it to Charles James Fox with a letter in which he affirmed his confidence that he had performed one of the noblest functions of a poet. To some extent the pomposity which he was always to affect in writing or speaking of his own poems was, as Charles Lamb suggested, less due to vanity than to humourlessness, although the two were of course connected. Profundity and a light touch are seldom found together and only the spiritually emancipated man can carry the burden of his understanding with a smile and be the more humble for his greater insight.

Wordsworth had penetrated deeply into life because he had accepted a narrow province. It was doubtless true, as he had claimed, at the beginning of his original Preface to *Lyrical Ballads*, that 'it is the honourable characteristic of poetry that its materials are to be found in every subject which can interest the human mind.' But although he had looked passionately and searchingly into his own heart, the subjects which appealed to his mind were proportionately circumscribed. Fortunately for English poetry his self-interest attracted him to a class of people whose lives had never previously been intimately explored and whose integrity he was peculiarly qualified to appreciate. And because this subject was new to poetry, it demanded a new language. Augustan poetry had become conventional and formalised because it had almost lost its roots in instinctive life. There was little creative necessity in the rationalised good sense which it reflected. The faculty of vivid sensation had become dulled and with it the possibility of spiritual vision. For the two are intimately related.

Yet in reaffirming in his new preface the necessity of vivid sensation Wordsworth characteristically over-simplified the problem. For neither the imaginative language of poetry nor the experience of reality which it embodies spring exclusively from sensation. Poets and men speak a real language when their whole being is quickened. They create out of a creative unity in themselves. And although with Blake we may describe this condition as spiritual sensation, it needs to be clearly distinguished from those lower forms of sensationalism which reflect disunity rather than unity.

Wordsworth, in his most creative moments, had enjoyed this experience, but he failed to understand fully its significance.

Hence the ambiguity of his association of reality with 'a state of vivid sensation.' Hence, too, his own tendency as a poet to indulge in the merely matter-of-fact and to confuse the prosaically actual with the real. His literalism and his sententiousness were in fact the by-products of his imperfect sensationalism. At its extreme false sensationalism represents a temporary absorption into an entirely selfish state of feeling. The individual uses life to increase his own private sense of pleasure, until gradually his ability to draw life into himself contracts and he reaches a state of impotence.

The 'states of vivid sensation' in which Wordsworth spoke the real language of men and of poetry were, of course, far from being so exhaustingly subjective as this. For he had in a rich measure at this time the faculty of entering into the Nature and the humble lives which he loved. And all his greatest poetry is the fruit of this true marriage between himself and the external world. Nevertheless poetry for him was never quite disinterested creation, and there was something more than the weariness incidental to all creative effort in the nervous agony and exhaustion which Dorothy recorded so often in her *Journal*.

For in some measure at least he always sought and found in poetry a compensation for the passionate satisfaction that ever since his experience with Annette he had shrunk from seeking from life. Poetry need not be the less real for being an expression of some inhibited instinct. And for seven more years this inward frustration was to condition Wordsworth's greatest poetry. Yet his fear of passion, so far as it prevented him from breaking through the crust of his egoism, was at least one of the causes which led to a final frustration.

The marriage which he contemplated with Mary Hutchinson was a similar means of self-defence. She was intimately associated with the happiness of his youth, and would thus link him more securely to his past. She would supply his need of affection and strengthen his sense of domestic stability, without for a moment endangering through passion his nervous determination to keep himself intact. And because the same recoil from complete self-surrender characterised the marriage with life of which his poetry was the issue, the harmony which he realised in verse was uncertain and dependent on his moods.

But his poetical theory betrayed more clearly than his poetical practice at this time the limitations of his egoism. He wrote in the Preface to the new edition of *Lyrical Ballads* that the principal object proposed in them was 'to choose incidents and situations from common life, and to relate or describe them, throughout, as far as was possible in *a selection of language really used by men, and, at the same time, to throw over them a certain colouring of imagination, whereby ordinary things should be presented to the mind in an unusual aspect.*'

The surprising thing is that this conception of the poetic act should ever have been considered revolutionary and romantic, when in fact it reflected so clearly the traditional dualism of a one-sided classicism. In this sentence Wordsworth reduced imagination from an essentially creative faculty which divined the real in the actual to a merely subordinate and decorative one. Admittedly he observed the facts which he chose to describe in his poems with deep sympathy. And in the finest of them his sympathy was so deep that he did imaginatively identify himself with such facts and so recreate them from within. To this extent his practice belied his theory. But his theory betrayed the detachment which was habitual to him except in moments of vivid sensation. Fidelity to fact, at least as a concept, meant more to him, despite his appreciation of the limits of scientific observation, than any surrender of himself to reality. Hence his interest in the unusual aspect of ordinary things and his ambition to make his poetry a systematic illustration of mental science.

The reality which the poet apprehends either in ordinary or

extraordinary things, is, indeed, always unusual, because it is newly perceived. But it is not merely an unusual aspect but the inward meaning, which is new and unforeseen. In the sentence which followed that already quoted Wordsworth did, indeed, attempt a more creative definition of his purpose. He wrote that his object was 'above all to make these incidents and situations interesting by tracing in them, truly though not ostentatiously, *the primary laws of our nature*: chiefly, as far as regards the manner in which we associate ideas in a state of excitement.'

But if we examine this rather ambiguous statement in the light of his practice, we find that 'the primary laws of our nature' were for him those tenacious instincts which he had known as a child and rediscovered in the peasant. That a complete surrender of the individual to the group might be a primary law of human nature antecedent to the emergence of the independent and to some extent acquisitive self which he admired in the peasant, he never sought to inquire. He believed that 'those first affections' which, both in time and strength, underlay human feeling, were inevitably strongly egoistic, that their preservation was a condition of all healthy life, and that in a 'natural' environment they would never degenerate into selfishness. And his aim as a poet was to illustrate and exalt these feelings.

By so doing he justified the compromise with life which he himself had accepted. It was easier to believe and preach that the primary laws of our nature allowed development only up to a certain point, the point reached by the estimable, but comparatively unenlightened peasant.

And his further contention in the same Preface that our thoughts are 'the representation of all our past feelings' was dictated quite as much by the fact that he was now living as a poet and a moralist on his past as by his reading of Hartley. So far as Hartley stressed in his philosophy the necessity of a vital relationship between feeling and thought and of grounding all knowledge in experience, he was enforcing a truth to which many eighteenth-century rationalists, such as Godwin, were blind. And doubtless it was because his philosophy seemed to restore the broken unity of human nature and consciousness that Coleridge, who recognised that 'there had been, in some sense, a Fall,' was at first so enthusiastically attracted to him.

But Wordsworth was far more inevitably and unalterably Hartley's disciple because his *Observations on Man* fitted so exactly his history. The stages in individual development which Hartley traced corresponded perfectly with his own. His earliest pleasures had been those of sensation, arising from impressions of external objects. As he grew to manhood he had known the intellectual pleasure derived from simple ideas of sensation, or from those complex ideas which were compounded from simpler ideas under the power of association. And now, in his maturity, he had discovered the moral pleasures which were in turn generated out of the intellectual ones and completed the vital association of thought and sensation in sympathetic judgment and observation.

Hartley's scheme of organic development through three stages was, indeed, true to life so far as it went. And it went exactly as far as Wordsworth wished to go. The fundamental proposition underlying Hartley's philosophy and Rule of Life was that 'God sent us into the world to make ourselves happy.' By pursuing that aim through the orderly stages which he laid down, we should best succeed in making others happy. The appeal of such a philosophy to Wordsworth is obvious. It seemed to justify both his egoism and his insistence on the 'grand elementary principle of pleasure.' Nevertheless it was a dangerous half-truth and conflicted with the facts of human nature and the deeper laws of life as they had been observed by the most spiritually enlightened of mankind.

The early stages of human growth are self-centred from the complete and unified egotism of the infant to the tempered but uneasy egotism of the adult who has been compelled to adjust his claims in some measure to the claims of others. But the possibilities of growth do not end here, and to attempt to fix them at this point leads inevitably to deterioration and sterility. The 'grand elementary principle of pleasure,' which is, indeed, when truly conceived, the touchstone of life, can only be preserved active and vital after a certain stage in development is reached, if it is transformed into creative delight. The creative self, freed from all personal acquisitiveness, experiences such delight. It lives in what it contemplates. It passes out of the circumscribed life of sense and knows the joy of union in place of the pleasure of possession. The hunger of egotism is appeased because the individual is no longer prevented by fear or thought of private advantage from participating purely and wholly in the Universe which he perceives. His identity with life is as complete as that of the day-old infant, but it is an identity of freedom instead of bondage. The journey from pure egotism to that pure selfhood which is also selfless has been completed.

In few men is it completed, but a striving towards the goal is essential, as every religious teacher has insisted, to continued growth. And Hartley's blindness to the necessity of the imaginative redemption of instinct, his acceptance of a purely natural economy, and his claim that every one who obeyed the dictates of self-interest and the guidance of association would arrive at the highest reaches of the moral sense, merely confirmed Wordsworth in his delusive self-esteem. If he could have turned to Blake instead of to Hartley he would have found a scheme of human development which in its first two stages was close to Hartley's, but which in its definition of 'Threefold' and 'Fourfold Vision' revealed how true imagination must be born out of the suffering of the heart and the knowledge of the mind, and how it must grow within a man until all his faculties of sense minister to spiritual insight.

But such a scheme of life would have demanded a going forward instead of a going back. It would have made *The Prelude* a real prelude to a new advance instead of a premature last will and testament.

And so although he could justifiably claim for his own *Lyrical Ballads* what he claimed for 'all good poetry, that it is the spontaneous overflow of powerful feeling' in men 'possessed of more than usual organic sensibility' who have 'thought long and deeply,' and although he could scorn those poets who 'separate themselves from the sympathies of men, and indulge in arbitrary and capricious habits of expression, in order to furnish food for fickle tastes and fickle appetites, of their own creation,' the organic sensibility upon which he drew was already threatened from within.

For a time he could preserve it as a source of vital poetry by conforming to Hartley's system. He could cherish those moments of vivid sensation which had been so frequent in earlier years and which he still experienced when the moralist and rationalist in him were subdued by the instinctive forces of his nature. He could recollect and contemplate such experiences in tranquillity 'till, by a species of reaction, the tranquillity gradually disappeared, and an emotion kindred to that which was before the subject of contemplation, was gradually produced, and itself actually existed in the mind.' And by bringing all his faculties to work upon this emotion, by qualifying and enriching it with ideas associated with it in a state of pleasurable excitement, he could 'by slow creation' impart to it 'outline and substance,'

> till it has given
> A function kindred to organic power,
> The vital spirit of a perfect form.

In such composition his conscious mind and self were truly subdued to the creative will. They gave form and meaning to experiences which were received immediately from life. He acted out of a wise passiveness. But the province of life to which he could be truly passive was narrowly limited by his instinctive preferences. It was limited to the world of his childhood and boyhood, in which he felt so safe that his selfish fears were stilled. And so when he wrote that the best measure of human nature was to be found 'by stripping our own hearts naked, and by looking out of ourselves towards men who lead the simplest lives and most according to Nature,' he was measuring human nature by his own desires.

No one will deny the virtue of such men or their native superiority to those whose integrity is sapped by 'false refinements, wayward and artificial desires, false criticisms, or effeminate habits of thinking and feeling.' And admittedly Wordsworth also included in his 'best measure' those who 'having known these things, have outgrown them.' But to the real significance of this outgrowing he was blind. He approved the virtues of the peasant and of the aristocrat, because both were dignified, capable and responsible individualists, as he now felt himself to be. But he could not conceive a way of life even more 'according to nature' than this, an integrity in which the instincts of self were not merely disciplined and morally elevated, but redeemed and fulfilled in pure being.

There was nothing in Hartley's writings to encourage him to strip his own heart naked to this extent, and he had suffered too much from his one youthful attempt to do so. It was more gratifying to exploit the 'unusual organic sensibility' which he still possessed, and disregard the law of diminishing returns which governs every self-consuming activity.

§ 4

Thus the end of the first year of the new century found Wordsworth firmly established in the convictions and the secluded way of life which were to remain essentially unchanged. He had recovered his stability, and henceforth his primary concern was to preserve it by strengthening his defences. Grasmere, Dorothy, a marriage devoid of dangers, and the philosophy of Hartley were all to minister to his need of self-defence. But as a poet he needed inspiration too, a quickening of the spirit which neither Dorothy nor Mary Hutchinson could fully supply. He was to cherish a deep affection for both of them, but so far as his feelings had been diverted towards his future wife, they had, as Dorothy foresaw, diminished somewhat in their intensity towards her. And as the years passed and affection settled into domestic attachment, the passionate love which had bound the brother and sister together in such an unusual relationship inevitably faded. Deep down, maybe, it persisted even through the long years of Dorothy's later decline. But already it had become in some measure an emotion to be recollected in tranquillity.

It was fitting, therefore, that two out of the three short original poems which were all that he composed in this year, should have been tributes to the happiness which she radiated, whether in *The Sparrow's Nest*, as the 'little Prattler among men' and enchanted companion of his childhood, or, in *There is a Little Unpretending Rill*, as the tireless walker of his restless years.

But for new inspiration he henceforth was soon to depend almost wholly upon Nature and Coleridge. Nature, indeed, was always new as she was always old. And it was not she that was to fail him but he who, despite his longing to rise out of himself on the ecstatic wings of the skylark, was to deny her deepest purpose, the urge to new creation. And to some extent the same was to be true of his relationship with Coleridge.

We have already suggested that the first symptom of a rift between them is to be found in the preface to the new *Lyrical Ballads*. The conditions of their associations had in fact perceptibly changed. Wordsworth had now recovered his stability and determined the boundaries beyond which he would not adventure. Coleridge, on the other hand, was more than ever a sick soul. The brief but magical spring, which he had known as a poet, was over. His marriage was a proved failure, and his spiritual distress was reflected in ill-health, nervous suffering, and a feverish mental activity which he at once relieved and aggravated by narcotics. Yet his suffering had proved a pathway to a deeper knowledge. And because he had not hardened himself against his disillusionment, as Wordsworth to some extent had done, he had, despite all his wretchedness, outgrown, in vision at least, his past. His eyes were opened to the inadequacy of the Hartleian philosophy which he had once enthusiastically embraced. He had 'overthrown the doctrine of association as taught by Hartley, and with it all the irreligious metaphysics of modern infidels — especially the doctrine of necessity.'

In this he now differed from Wordsworth, and it was more than a difference in philosophical opinion. For Hartley's system was for Wordsworth, as we have shown, the philosophical justification of his egoism and his whole scheme of life, while Coleridge's rejection of it sprang from a recognition of religious values which transcended the personal self.

On the surface, of course, Wordsworth seemed and was always henceforth to seem in the right. For as a good Hartleian he was to preserve his self-respect, to be a prudent husband and father, and an industrious poet, while Coleridge was to neglect all his responsibilities and float painfully down his life on a tide of opium and eloquence. Yet because Coleridge was so lamentably incapable of self-regard, his vision and ultimately, perhaps, even his influence upon the thought and aspirations of the future were to outlast Wordsworth's.

And already the inevitable opposition between so tenacious an individualist and so irresponsible an altruist had begun at least faintly to be felt. They were still, of course, deeply attached to each other. But Wordsworth was now sufficiently complacent to be capable of moral disapproval, to criticise inwardly, even while he commiserated. And although Coleridge was far too conscious of his own weaknesses to question the strength and virtue of his friend, he had already ceased to share his provincial view of human nature. Like him, he deplored 'our pestilent commerce and our unnatural crowding together of men in cities.' But he still deplored, too, 'our government by rich men,' and he read in all this not a mere transgression of rural economy. It was to him the fruit of sin, 'the manifestation of offended Deity.' And he saw no reason for supposing that the purposes of God and the possibilities of living in accordance with His Will were finally demonstrated in the persons of Westmorland 'Statesmen.' Consequently, although he had accepted orthodox Christianity some years earlier than Wordsworth was to do, he never ceased to discover new meaning in it and indeed was to play a notable part in reaffirming and interpreting its spiritual truth.

But if Coleridge had ceased to believe in Hartley, he still believed unreservedly in his friend's poetic powers. He was still, therefore, an inspiration, but his distracted way of life made him a very uncertain one, and the bond between them had begun imperceptibly to weaken. It had even weakened a little between Coleridge and Dorothy. For he had found another and dearer comforter in the person of Mary Hutchinson's sister, Sara. And his affection for her was in fact later to aggravate, to some extent at least, Wordsworth's moral disapproval.

Whether then, through some decline in Coleridge as a source

of inspiration or because his thoughts were engrossed by his coming marriage, Wordsworth wrote little in 1801. He laid aside *The Prelude* and occupied his leisure in the gratuitous task of rewriting Chaucer. In the later summer he visited Scotland, and during almost the whole of the last three months of the year Mary Hutchinson was a guest at Dove Cottage.

But on 28th December she returned to her relatives at Penrith and Wordsworth and Dorothy went on a visit to Thomas Clarkson, the abolitionist, who lived at the northern end of Ullswater. Three weeks later they came back to Grasmere, once again through rain, hail, and snow, and Wordsworth entered on his period of greatest productiveness, a period which lasted with little interruption until 1807, when the harvest richly sown in boyhood and youth was so thoroughly reaped that only a few gleanings of poetic reality remained to reward the persevering industry of his later years.

PART IX

THE HARVEST

§ 1

ALTHOUGH politics were soon again to influence considerably Wordsworth's poetical activity, they had ceased for some time either to absorb or distract his mind. But this was, perhaps, as much due to the fact that there was a lull in the world storm as to the remoteness of Grasmere from public events or to his own domestic contentment. Preliminaries of peace with France had been signed in October 1801, and for the year and a half during which the peace lasted, it seemed even possible that the Republic might restore in some measure the stricken hopes of idealists. Disillusionment was soon to return, when in August 1802 Napoleon was made Consul for life with power to appoint his successor. But meanwhile there was a breathing-space. The retreat at Grasmere was untroubled by even the distant menace of external events, and Wordsworth was at liberty to concentrate wholly upon poetry and himself.

The heart-rending letters which Coleridge sent from London until he returned in March were the only serious distraction, and it was Dorothy who chiefly suffered from them. Wordsworth, of course, shared her concern, but he was too absorbed in sufferings of his own to be agitated like her. He was in travail as a poet, and the pains of labour were incessant. Day after day in Dorothy's *Journal* we read of his being worn to death after a period of composition, of nervous headaches and insomnia. Dorothy devoted herself wholly to him, reading him to sleep, copying his verses and writing his letters. And since the tension under which he was working could best be relieved by constant bodily exercise, she was incessantly stepping by his side. Yet she gives no hint in her *Journal* of ever being exhausted herself. For she was fulfilling her genius for love more harmoniously than her brother his genius for poetry.

A fine morning in February tempted him to flee from his creative obsession and seize a couple of hours with Mary Hutchinson near Penrith, but even this journey bore poetical fruit, since he brought back with him the story of *Alice Fell*, which was told him on his way by a friend of Mr. Clarkson's, and which he retold in verse to illustrate how the imagination of a child can take such possession of a humble fact that the whole tragedy of life and death can be contained in it.

Later in March he went to Keswick for several days to stay with William Calvert. But these were the only diversions during three months of almost frenzied composition. During January and February he devoted some of his time to revising and completing *Peter Bell*, but it was upon *The Pedlar*, later to be incorporated in *The Excursion*, that during the early months of the year he concentrated all his powers, torn between the demands of his craft, the contraction of his thought, and the intensity of his feeling.

§ 2

It is unknown how much of *The Excursion* was composed at this time. *The Pedlar*, which Wordsworth arranged and Dorothy wrote out in July, was on her own confession only two hundred and eighty lines long. On the other hand, the poem which he finished early in March is supposed to have been comparable in length to *The White Doe of Rylstone*, or about nineteen hundred lines. And this accords much better with the length of time which we know that he devoted to the task. The first book of *The Excursion*, as it ultimately appeared, was nearly a thousand lines in length. But it also included the tale of *Margaret*, or *The Ruined Cottage*, which had been written in 1798, and hailed by Coleridge as 'superior to anything in our language which anyway resembles it.' In the second book of *The Excursion*, The Pedlar also figures, if chiefly as a guide to The Solitary. And it runs to nine hundred lines. It seems probable, therefore, that much of the material of these first two books was composed in the early months of 1802, although there are clearly passages which were later additions.

The character at least of The Pedlar, or The Wanderer, as he was later called, was certainly drawn at this time. He had actually been conceived, according to the testimony of Coleridge, a year and a half earlier. And he was, in fact, the consummation of such characters as Wordsworth had dramatised in some of the *Lyrical Ballads*. Freed from domestic ties and the struggle for survival, he lacked the pathos of those earlier figures. But he was the better qualified thereby to personify Wordsworth's ideal of the complete man and to be the voice of his mature convictions.

For each of the chief characters of *The Excursion* embody their creator at a certain stage in his development, although obviously they overlap. Speaking summarily we may say that the 'I' of the poem represents the still vital and unsubdued lyrical element in Wordsworth's personality. The Solitary is the disillusioned and embittered man who retired to Racedown. The Wanderer is the poet of Grasmere who believed that he had recovered his integrity. The Pastor is the later moralist and pietist into whom the poet through his fatal compromise inevitably degenerated.

We shall consider later the extent to which the books in *The Excursion* which treat of 'despondency' and 'despondency corrected' were to reveal this fatal compromise. Here we are only concerned, as Wordsworth was at this time, with The Wanderer and The Solitary.

The history of The Wanderer from boyhood to early manhood is almost identical with the personal history which Wordsworth had begun to trace in *The Prelude* two years earlier. Certainly we are told that he had been taught from childhood

> Stern self-respect, a reverence for God's word,
> And an habitual piety.

But such lines as these were almost certainly added later when *The Prelude* had been completed and the earlier parts of *The Excursion* were transposed as much as possible into the key of religious orthodoxy. In 1802 Wordsworth's Pedlar was not so much 'a man of reverend age' with affinities to the worthy Pastor, but an idealised version of one of those vagrants with whom he had so happily associated as a schoolboy. And the Pedlar's early experiences were Wordsworth's own.

> He, many an evening, to his distant home
> In solitude returning, saw the hills
> Grow larger in the darkness; all alone
> Beheld the stars come out above his head,
> And travelled through the wood, with no one near
> To whom he might confess the things he saw.

> So the foundations of his mind were laid.
> In such communion, not from terror free,
> While yet a child, and long before his time,
> Had he perceived the presence and the power
> Of greatness; and deep feelings had impressed
> So vividly great objects that they lay
> Upon his mind like substances, whose presence
> Perplexed the bodily sense. He had received
> A precious gift; for, as he grew in years,
> With these impressions would he still compare
> All his remembrances, thoughts, shapes, and forms;
> And, being still unsatisfied with aught

> Of dimmer character, he thence attained
> An active power to fasten images
> Upon his brain; and on their pictured lines
> Intensely brooded, even till they acquired
> The liveliness of dreams.

This is pure autobiography, as is the description which follows of the manner in which The Wanderer incessantly turned ear and eye on all things which the moving season brought, feeding his senses and discovering a power to trace, even in the apparent solidity of naked crags, 'an ebbing and a flowing mind.'

Like his creator too, The Wanderer had small need of books, although he had a taste for supernatural tales, and fed his imagination upon folk legends and traditions. Up to a certain age he was physically possessed and overawed by Nature, and was thus prepared to receive, as his faculty of conscious recognition developed, the deep lesson of love, which he

> Whom Nature, by whatever means, has taught
> To feel intensely, cannot but receive.

Such was The Wanderer in boyhood, and such was Wordsworth. And his identification of himself with The Wanderer as a rising youth was equally complete.

> What soul was his, when, from the naked top
> Of some bold headland, he beheld the sun
> Rise up, and bathe the world in light! He looked—
> Ocean and earth, the solid frame of earth
> And ocean's liquid mass, in gladness lay
> Beneath him:—Far and wide the clouds were touched
> And in their silent faces could be read
> Unutterable love. Sound needed none,
> Nor any voice of joy; his spirit drank

The spectacle: sensation, soul, and form,
All melted into him; they swallowed up
His animal being; in them did he live,
And by them did he live; they were his life.
In such access of mind, in such high hour
Of visitation from the living God,
Thought was not; in enjoyment it expired.

The passage in *The Prelude* in which Wordsworth was to
describe his early morning return from a dance during his first
vacation was identical in spirit with this.

And we can understand why the writing of *The Pedlar* cost
him such creative agony at this time. For to reconceive these
youthful moments of liberation from self, of spiritual recognition through sensational self-surrender, demanded a breaking
of those bonds of prudent self-regard in which he had begun
to tie his genius. To return to his past was not always to
recollect pleasing emotions in tranquillity. For the highest
moments of his youth had been moments of ecstatic self-
abandonment, of bodily and mental dissolution as a condition
of the influx of the spirit. And to renew those moments when
his ego had become so much more fixed, his faith in life so
much more contracted, and his mind and senses so much more
cautious, involved a rending of the tomb which had begun to
close about him.

But the sense of release and enrichment, when such moments
in which 'his existence' had been 'oftentimes possessed,' were
imaginatively reborn, must have been correspondingly great.
As The Wanderer exclaimed,

O then how beautiful, how bright, appeared
The written promise!

And in similar words Wordsworth was to describe his experience when crossing the Alps as a visiting 'of awful promise.'

The best of his poetic endeavour during these crowning years of his life was, indeed, directed towards recapturing that miraculous sense of promise. But in his portrait of The Wanderer he made his first considerable attempt since the *Lines at Tintern* to convince himself that the 'promise' of his youth was a guarantee of an assured creative maturity, that, having early learned

> To reverence the volume that displays
> The mystery, the life which cannot die,

he could never forget the lesson but would preserve an openness of heart and mind into a kindly and dignified old age.

Unfortunately, however, The Wanderer's history differed from his own in one essential respect. There had been no break in his organic development. He had never known a Fall. Wordsworth created another character, The Solitary, to personify his own Fall from unity. And in this way he was able to preserve the ideal character of The Wanderer. The Wanderer's history was, in short, his own without the break which invalidated his whole theory of the sufficiency of a merely natural growth.

He himself in early youth had read Milton and yet secretly resented everything that tended to separate him from the immediate influence of Nature. He, too, before his eighteenth year, had known

> the first virgin passion of a soul
> Communing with the glorious universe,

had sought in Nature's tempestuousness repose from 'the stillness of abstracted thought,' while his moral being had been strengthened and braced by breathing the wholesome air of poverty and drinking from the well of homely life. And he, too, had found it impossible to settle down to any task and had pursued a wandering life in defiance of anxious relatives.

But his wanderings had taken him much further from his native source than did The Pedlar's. He had not confined himself to 'the simpler forms of rural life' or kept among the fields

> In solitude and solitary thought
> His mind in a just equipoise of love.

In The Wanderer's steady course

> No piteous revolutions had he felt,
> No wild varieties of joy and grief.
> Unoccupied by sorrow of its own,
> His heart lay open.

How different it had been with Wordsworth! Yet the later Wanderer who, after obtaining enough provision for his wants to enable him to give up his trade as pedlar, still

> loved to pace the public roads
> And the wild path,

was a man such as Wordsworth conceived and wished himself to be after his retirement to Grasmere. His very appearance was that of his creator as De Quincey and others have drawn him —

> Plain his garb;
> Such as might suit a rustic Sire, prepared
> For sabbath duties; yet he was a man
> Whom no one could have passed without remark.
> Active and nervous was his gait; his limbs
> And his whole figure breathed intelligence.

The religious piety with which The Wanderer was finally invested, his remembrance in his riper age 'with gratitude' and 'reverential thoughts' of the influence of the Scottish Church was doubtless a later addition. Yet it, too, was closely linked with his natural wisdom. It sometimes 'seemed self-taught,'

> as of a dreamer in the woods;
> Who to the model of his own pure heart
> Shaped his belief, as grace divine inspired,
> And human reason dictated with awe.

This after-thought of a 'grace divine' was not provided for in Hartley's system. But it was to prove for Wordsworth a very helpful addition by which the limitations of a naturalistic philosophy might be concealed. We do not question, however, its appropriateness to The Wanderer, who had preserved his native purity of heart and thereby his faculty to be truly inspired by 'grace divine.'

But Wordsworth had not remained from youth to maturity a pure and humble channel for creative life or kept his mind 'in a just equipoise of love.' And so although the humanising virtue of Nature, which he illustrated in the history of The Wanderer, was apparent also in his own history and in his receptiveness to those sympathies

> That steal upon the meditative mind,
> And grow with thought,

The Wanderer's life-story could not be fitted, except in its early chapters, to his own.

§ 3

Wordsworth, however, wrote both *The Excursion* and *The Prelude* to convince himself that the fissure in his being had been closed, and to show how it had been closed. To do this, however, it was necessary to describe the disease of which he believed that he had discovered the cure. And in *The Excursion* he personified it in The Solitary.

The temporary cessation of hostilities between England and France had brought him into touch once again with Annette. We read in Dorothy's *Journal* of letters written to her in January 1802 and received from her in February. The thought of her and his daughter Caroline could no longer disturb him greatly. But for one who re-lived so intensely his past, even the sight of her handwriting must have awakened sleeping memories and the pain associated with them. And since the best way of relieving such pain was to express it in poetry, it is the more probable that his work on *The Pedlar* at this time included some of the history of The Solitary.

For The Solitary's history is as clearly that of the disastrous years in his own life, as The Wanderer's is of his happy boyhood and youth. The Solitary who lives in a lonely and lost seclusion among the mountains, was rural born. As a young man he left the humble ground of social life in which he had been nurtured to be called to the ministry. Wordsworth himself, it will be remembered, had gone up to Cambridge with the idea of taking Orders. But, like Wordsworth, The Solitary had little real religious vocation, and his position as an army chaplain was not calculated to strengthen any which he possessed. It led him into 'haunts of social vanity,' in which he affected a graceful gaiety, became lax and buoyant and lived and roamed where Fortune led. Eventually Fortune led to a 'blooming Lady' of sweet disposition whom he married. Relinquishing his office he retired

> From the world's notice to a rural home.
> Youth's season yet with him was scarcely past,
> And she was in youth's prime. How free their love,

> How full their joy! Till, pitiable doom!
> In the short course of one undreaded year
> Death blasted all.

The passages in which Wordsworth described the love and domestic happiness of these two, while a boy and a girl were born to them, may well have owed some of their ardour to the fact of his approaching marriage. But essentially the 'blooming Lady' of the poem was Annette, not Mary Hutchinson. Only once again, in *Vaudracour and Julia*, was he to dare three years later to recall the ecstasy of young love in kindred tones. And Julia was Annette. It was this love, which death had blasted no less effectively, although Annette survived the dangers of child-bed, that he recalled here.

The Solitary's after-history, too, differed only in points of chronology from his own. He experienced first anguish, then 'an uncomplaining apathy,' when

> indifferent to delight,
> To aim and purpose, he consumed his days,
> To private interest dead, and public care.

Wordsworth's disillusionment as a lover, however, had been intimately associated with his faith in the Revolution. And so was The Solitary's with the unimportant difference that his response to

> the unlooked-for dawn,
> That promised everlasting joy to France,

succeeded his private tragedy and temporarily restored his hopes.

> Her voice of social transport reached even him!
> He broke from his contracted bounds, repaired
> To the great City . . .

And from the pulpit, zealously maintained
The cause of Christ and civil liberty,
As one, and moving to one glorious end.
Intoxicating service!

Wordsworth himself had repaired to the great City after his
return from France, not indeed to maintain the cause of Christ,
but to find a transient solace from the disillusionment which
was descending upon him, in Godwinian rationalism. But
these lines and the account of the Revolution which follow
them were undoubtedly written eight or ten years later, when
The Solitary's history, as we shall see, was continued in a
different key by a Wordsworth who had become a good
Churchman and Conservative.

The Solitary, however, whose history he sketched up to this
point, probably during the early months of 1802, embodied
himself during the most painful years of his life. They were the
years which he wished to forget, not only because they had
contained so much of suffering and self-reproach, but because
even the memory of them suggested that the deep wound which
he had received in youth was not so perfectly healed as he
professed or the philosophy in which he had taken refuge so
secure and sufficient as he had believed.

In describing the early disillusionment of The Solitary, he
began the process of sealing up his past, as it really was, which
he completed in The Prelude; while in The Wanderer he conceived the equable character, upon which he wished henceforth
to model his life in defiance of the facts of The Solitary's history
and the deep fissure in his being which those convulsive years
had wrought.

§ 4

As the days lengthened, however, Wordsworth became less
engrossed in The Pedlar. Another spring was approaching, and

once again it was to quicken miraculously his lyrical powers. The short visit, too, he paid to William Calvert early in March made a break. Dorothy, after eight weeks of intensive devotion felt his absence deeply. 'I *will* be busy,' she wrote in her *Journal*. 'I *will* look well, and be well when he comes back to me. O, the Darling! Here is one of his bitter apples. I can hardly find it in my heart to throw it into the fire.'

On the morning of the day of his return she copied out *Ruth*, that poem composed in Germany three years before, of which she herself was the primary, and Annette the secondary inspiration. And Wordsworth curiously enough brought two new stanzas back with him, including, probably, the one which was to conclude with such bathos, as we have noticed, the published version of the poem. For in its reference to the funeral bell and the Christian congregation it recalls the funeral incident in the second book of *The Excursion* upon which Wordsworth may well have been working before he went away.

But during the next few weeks he was to throw off temporarily the mantle of The Wanderer, and renew the fresh lyrical note of previous springs. And three of the earliest poems which he wrote enshrined memories of Dorothy—the two lyrics entitled *To a Butterfly*, in both of which he recalled those

> summer days, when we were young
> Sweet childish days, that were as long
> As twenty days are now.

and the lines *Among All Lovely Things my Love Had Been* in which he recorded how seven years before he had brought home a glow-worm for her to see, and named her for the last time, 'my Lucy.'

Two other poems, also composed at this time, *The Beggars* and *The Leech-Gatherer*, dealt with incidents which he had shared with Dorothy and which she had minutely related in her *Journal*, while the lovely lines, 'I wandered lonely as a cloud,' were to owe something to her account of the walk which they took along the lake through the woods beyond Gowbarrow Park on a mild mid-April day, and of the daffodils they saw there.

'I never saw daffodils so beautiful,' she wrote. 'They grew among the mossy stones about and about them; some rested their heads upon these stones, as on a pillow, for weariness; and the rest tossed and reeled and danced, and seemed as if they verily laughed with the wind, that blew upon them over the lake; they looked so gay, ever glancing, ever changing.'

The exquisite lyrical feeling crystallised in her words here was more calculated to help Wordsworth to renew his feelings in tranquillity than her account of the Leech-Gatherer. Yet there is the same fidelity to detail in both. It is impossible to say how much Wordsworth's later vision of golden daffodils

> Fluttering and dancing in the breeze

was strengthened by a reference to his sister's *Journal*, or how much he owed it entirely to

> that inward eye
> Which is the bliss of solitude.

But there can be little doubt that the fact of sharing such experiences with her quickened and deepened his original response to them, while her detailed accounts of such homely incidents as that, recorded in *The Beggars*, of the young vagrants, so joyously impervious to moral reproof, must at least have served to focus his mind upon events which had often occurred some years before.

And on 18th March Coleridge returned. The effects of

opium were visible in his face, and he stayed only two days. His presence agitated Dorothy very much, but it was still an inspiration to Wordsworth, as he walked with him in the orchard and later read aloud *The Pedlar*. In the same orchard two days after he left, the lines *To the Cuckoo* were composed. And it is not perhaps fanciful to feel that when Wordsworth wrote,

> Thou bringest unto me a tale
> Of visionary hours,

he had subconsciously the 'wandering voice' of his friend in mind as well as that of the bird. And the Cuckoo, like the Butterfly, recalled him to his childhood—

> And I can listen to thee yet;
> Can lie upon the plain
> And listen, till I do beget
> That golden time again.

> O blessèd Bird! the earth we pace
> Again appears to be
> An unsubstantial, faery place;
> That is fit home for Thee!

In each of these short lyrics he sounded the note which was soon to swell into the great chorale of the *Intimation Ode*. For as the spring advanced, the argument which he had begun to build up in *The Pedlar* in proof that he had recovered from his fears and sense of decline, and that the years which bring the philosophic mind could bring also a deeper joy, carried less conviction. He hungered once again for visionary ecstasy, and the moral sympathies of The Wanderer seemed a poor substitute for that participation in the mystery which he had known in schoolboy days.

And it was while still working at *The Cuckoo* that he wrote the lines which were to lead on directly to the *Intimation* Ode, the lines in which he made the rainbow the touchstone of his poetic vitality through the years. That, however, he was far from certain that the Man and the Child were inevitably bound together in a beneficent scheme of organic development, is shown by the Ode which he began to write at breakfast on the following morning, a 'divine morning,' as Dorothy described it. For it opened ominously with the words—'There was a time'—the very words which Coleridge was to repeat to him three weeks later, when he read aloud the completed Ode, *Dejection*.

Coleridge wrote his Ode for Sara Hutchinson, and since he was some time working on it, it is very possible that he had repeated these saddest of all his lines, when he was walking with Wordsworth in the orchard just a week before. But whether or not the first line of what was to be the *Intimation* Ode was an unconscious echo of his friend's poignant confession of poetic defeat, the obvious and heart-rending fact that Coleridge's 'genial spirits' were failing, and with them his beauty-making power, cannot but have deepened Wordsworth's own haunting sense that the bond of natural piety was an insecure one, and that in growing old he might indeed die to the rainbow's glory.

How much of the Ode was written on this 'divine morning' is unknown. But internal evidence suggests the first two stanzas which hang inevitably together—

> There was a time when meadow, grove, and stream,
> The earth, and every common sight,
>> To me did seem
>> Apparelled in celestial light,
> The glory and the freshness of a dream.
> It is not now as it hath been of yore;—

> Turn wheresoe'er I may,
> By night or day,
> The things which I have seen I now can see no more.
>
> The Rainbow comes and goes,
> And lovely is the Rose,
> The Moon doth with delight
> Look round her when the heavens are bare,
> Waters on a starry night
> Are beautiful and fair;
> The sunshine is a glorious birth;
> But yet I know, where'er I go,
> That there hath past away a glory from the earth.

This, it is reasonable to suppose, is all that he wrote on this morning. And when he added the next two stanzas in May, the spring was at full flood, the birds were singing, the lambs bounding and he again was strong. His heart held festival with the season, and he poured its joy and florescence into the lines he wrote. Yet even then the fullness of his bliss was haunted by an afterthought. There was something lacking,

> something that is gone:
> The Pansy at my feet
> Doth the same tale repeat:
> Whither is fled, the visionary gleam?
> Where is it now, the glory and the dream?

Four years were to elapse before he was to continue this Ode, and in completing it acknowledge the loss but find strength and reassurance, as he believed, 'in what remains behind.'

But in the spring of 1802 his doubts were at least temporarily swept away by the abounding force of reawakened life. Early in April he had spent a fortnight with the Hutchinsons, and on

x

the days immediately following his return he wrote the lines beginning 'The Cock is crowing,' in which the pure magic of April's alternating sun and shower was distilled in a series of direct and staccato statements, and the lyric *To a Butterfly*, to which we have already referred. The two poems, *To the Small Celandine*, ushered in beneath cloudless skies the month of May, both of them ' hymns in praise' of the natural innocence which he loved; and later on the same day he turned from the 'unassuming Spirit' of flowers to pay a tribute to the same spirit as he remembered it in the Leech-Gatherer whom he and Dorothy had met on one of their walks two years before.

The next day was very hot, and after writing several new stanzas of his poem in bed in the morning, he and Dorothy started to walk to Wythburn, several times resting on the way and repeating what he had written. Near Wythburn they met Coleridge, and spent the afternoon with him, lying in the shade on a moss-covered rock at the foot of a waterfall.

It was one of Coleridge's happy days; he looked well, and parted at sundown from his friends cheerfully, hopping upon the side stones of the beck. Yet they, who only ten days before had heard him repeat his *Dejection* Ode, knew that behind such transient flickerings of happiness, lay

> A grief without a pang, void, dark, and drear,
> A stiffled, drowsy, unimpassioned grief,
> Which finds no natural outlet, no relief,
>   In word, or sigh, or tear.

Three days later, however, Wordsworth, feeling strong after sleeping uncommonly well, fell to work on the poem again, and on 11th May he finished it. It exhausted him as much as anything which he wrote, and it is significant that on the day when he particularly wearied himself to death, he received bad news of Coleridge, and, to relieve the tension of his feelings, began to compose the *Stanzas* in the manner of Thomson's *Castle of Indolence*, in which he drew an admiring and compassionate portrait of Coleridge, and another of himself.

These *Stanzas*, *The Leech-Gatherer*, and the first four stanzas of the *Intimation* Ode, are indeed intimately connected. For in writing each of them Wordsworth was haunted by the shade of Coleridge, and the ghost of his friend troubled his heart so deeply because it was in some measure the ghost of himself.

In the *Stanzas* and *The Leech-Gatherer* he strove to lay that ghost. Of Coleridge, sick with the malady of the ideal, he wrote,

> Ah! piteous sight it was to see this Man
> When he came back to us, a withered flower, —
> Or like a sinful creature, pale and wan.
> Down would he sit; and without strength or power
> Look at the common grass from hour to hour.

But although he himself, too, had once roamed 'out of our Valley's limits' and had returned, also, in a measure maimed, power had returned to him. And so he could draw his own portrait in the same poem, as if he had never known his outcast hour—

> Noisy he was, and gamesome as a boy;
> His limbs would toss about him with delight
> Like branches when strong winds the trees annoy.
> Nor lacked his calmer hours device or toy
> To banish listlessness and irksome care.

But these lines were true of his happy, not of his hypochrondriac hours. Even spring could not deliver him from these or make him a boy again. Indeed he paid for the intense pleasure which the season brought by hours of deeper gloom, that bore an alarming resemblance to that of Coleridge.

And in *Resolution and Independence* he faced the fact and sought in the old Leech-Gatherer a solvent for his fears. The poem opens with a picture of just such another spring morning following a night of rain as he had sketched in 'The Cock is crowing.' And momentarily he is a boy again. The world of Nature only exists for him; 'the ways of men, so vain and melancholy,' are utterly forgotten. He lives in the hare 'running races in her mirth,' and the 'pleasant noise' of woods and waters. But the familiar reaction follows. From the heights of joy he sinks into the abyss of dejection,

> And fears and fancies thick upon me came;
> Dim sadness—and blind thoughts, I knew not,
> nor could name.

He tries to reason the mood away. Was he not, like the skylark and the hare, a happy Child of Earth? Was he not, as they, free from care and the pressure of the world? It might seem so in the moment. But, unlike them, he had the fatal gift of foresight—

> there may come another day to me—
> Solitude, pain of heart, distress, and poverty.

But not only material anxieties intruded. A deeper fear underlay these. Was not this alternation of mood written large in the lives of poets, in that of Chatterton or of Burns? And did it not portend an ultimate eclipse?

> By our own spirits are we deified:
> We Poets in our youth begin in gladness;
> But thereof come in the end despondency and madness.

Must he, in short, read in the wan and heartless mood of Coleridge the writing on the wall?

It was a question which he was never successfully to silence, but which for the next ten years he was to devote himself to answering. He answered it here through the Leech-Gatherer. The old Man of his poem differs in some essential points, as we have shown, from the man whom he and Dorothy had met. He was created to satisfy Wordsworth's own needs, to represent as The Pedlar had done, the natural virtue in which he would fain believe that he might share. Haunted by 'the fear that kills,' 'perplexed and longing to be comforted,' he assails him with the question which in different ways he was to ask again and again—

'How is it that you live, and what is it you do?'

And the answer which the old Man gives, without putting it specifically into words, is that he lives by patience, humility, and resignation, that while he has never rebelled against the will of life or asserted any personal claim upon it, he has preserved his dignity and independence as a man. And so, although he seemed

like a man from some far region sent,
To give me human strength, by apt admonishment,

his figure was in essence familiar enough. He imaged once more the peasant integrity to which Wordsworth so fruitlessly aspired, because he had outgrown the peasant. And so the cheerfulness and resolution which contemplation of such a character induced could not but be transitory. The fear that kills remained; the question was not truly answered.

And in the days that followed, the coming and going of

Coleridge and his melancholy letters could not but revive his former thoughts of

> Cold, pain, and labour, and all fleshly ills;
> And mighty Poets in their misery dead.

On the 15th Dorothy was so distressed by what she heard that she resolved to go to Keswick alone for two days. But her efforts at conciliation proved fruitless, and on the morrow of her return she received a letter from Coleridge asking her and Wordsworth not to come to Greta Hall. No efforts of friends could now disperse the cloud of dispathy which had been for long gathering between him and his wife, and any attempt to do so could only embarrass.

And if Coleridge's private affairs were foreboding, so now were public events. The uneasy peace between France and England had lasted seven months. But already the hopes that it had revived were beginning to fade. It was not until August that Napoleon became Consul for life. But his imperialistic and reactionary tendencies were already apparent.

That Wordsworth was aware of this is clear in the sonnet on Bonaparte which he wrote on a warm moist morning two days after Dorothy's return, when she read him Milton's sonnets. And in explaining in it why his grief for Bonaparte was vain and unthinking, he affirmed characteristically the doctrines of 'association' and 'necessity.' It was vain to hope anything of Bonaparte because of his nurture and upbringing. A man brought up in such a harsh environment and from youth apprenticed to war could never prove a 'wise and good' Governor,

> And temper with the sternness of the brain
> Thoughts motherly, and meek as womanhood.

Certainly the social virtues may well spring most happily from a homely soil, but it is doubtful whether Napoleon would have possessed a tenderer or a less dominating mind, if he had been brought up in the wilds of Westmorland instead of the wilds of Corsica, or as a young man had walked the courts of St. John's College instead of a barrack square.

And the defect of all such philosophies as Hartley's was that, in attributing almost everything to environment and favourable upbringing, they made the human soul the slave of circumstance. A Napoleon, for Wordsworth, was irretrievably doomed to spread ruin over Europe because he 'fed his first hopes' on a vicious diet. A peasant was bound to be a pattern of virtue, because he was reared in circumstances that humbled his pride.

Both assertions were half-truths, and because they underestimated the intrinsic qualities of men, they were essentially fatalistic. In a Napoleon the original force of the ego was immeasurably stronger than in the peasant. And it was for that reason, and not merely in view of his upbringing, vain to grieve for him.

But behind Wordsworth's explanation of his character as determined by his upbringing was the assumption that the egoism of the thousands of petty Napoleons or self-seeking men, who overran human life then as they do to-day, was similarly and exclusively determined by violations at some stage in their upbringing of the laws of natural necessity and could only be cured by a return to primitive virtue, and, by implication, to conditions of life which fostered such virtue.

That such a return was in fact impossible was to be best proved by his own unavailing attempts, even under the most favourable conditions, to achieve it. But he was to devote his best endeavours during the next few years to demonstrating that he had succeeded.

A month, however, after writing this sonnet on Bonaparte he received some news which must have assuaged the material anxieties to which he had confessed in The Leech-Gatherer. The new Lord Lowther had agreed to pay the debts with interest which had been owing for nineteen years to the Wordsworth family. Wordsworth's and Dorothy's share of this money was not considerable, but it assured a modest security, and may well have proved more lastingly effective in generating a sense of 'independence and resolution' than the memory of the Leech-gatherer.

A cloud was lifted and the fortnight which followed the receipt of this news proved 'a happy time.' We hear no more of sleepless nights, but of financial consultations with Clarkson at Eusemere, and of a quickened sense of the blessings of life and of Nature. 'We were in the orchard a great part of the morning,' Dorothy wrote in her *Journal* two days later. 'After tea we walked upon our own path for a long time. We talked sweetly together about the disposal of our riches. We lay upon the sloping turf. Earth and sky were so lovely that they melted our very hearts.'

But while this change in their fortunes enabled Wordsworth to complete without any further delay the scheme of life upon which he had decided, it meant for Dorothy the end of the dream of lover-like intimacy which she had cherished as a girl and realised with such single-minded devotion for seven happy years.

For her brother was free at last to marry Mary Hutchinson. Their days of unqualified intimacy together at Grasmere were already numbered, and the fact gave to this last week of June and first week of July a peculiar poignancy. How happy Wordsworth was himself can be felt in the light-hearted lines, entitled *The Sun Has Long Been Set*, which he threw off beneath a 'beautiful soft half-moon' with Dorothy at his side. But he cannot but have shared in some measure her feeling, and in the *Farewell* which he composed shortly before they left Grasmere for Gallow Hill and the Hutchinsons, he dwelt on the past rather than the future. Mary was to be no more than a tender addition to the 'little Nook of mountain-ground' and the cottage, which was essentially and by right of first tenure his and Dorothy's.

> We go for One to whom ye will be dear;
> And she will prize this Bower, this Indian shed,
> Our own contrivance. Building without peer!
> —A gentle Maid, whose heart is lowly bred,
> Whose pleasures are in wild fields gatherèd,
> With joyousness, and with a thoughtful cheer,
> Will come to you; to you herself will wed;
> And love the blessed life that we lead here.

From these lines one ignorant of the facts might suppose that Mary was to wed, not the poet, but the country-side of his adoption and the shed of his contrivance. And possibly Wordsworth was as anxious to reassure himself as Dorothy that the life at Grasmere would continue just as it had been.

But for himself he needed little reassurance. He knew his Mary well enough to be certain that she would amiably acquiesce in all that he desired, would listen with a smile to those

> tales of years gone by,
> And this sweet spring, the best beloved and best,

and would never rekindle the fever which he feared. And so he could end his poem with a calm prophecy of unruffled continuity—

> Two burning months let summer overleap,
> And, coming back with Her who will be ours,
> Into *thy* bosom we again will creep.

But although Dorothy knew as certainly as her brother that Mary, who embodied the unassuming spirit of peace, could never prove a disturbing rival, she knew, too, that bounds must henceforth be imposed upon the rapture of her devotion. And the knowledge hurt no less because she accepted it without a touch of bitterness.

On the night before they left Grasmere she and Wordsworth walked backwards and forwards on the White Moss path. 'There was,' she wrote in her *Journal*, 'a sky-like white brightness on the lake. The Wyke cottage light at the foot of Silver How. Glow-worms out, but not so numerous as last night. O, beautiful place! Dear Mary, William. The hour is come. . . . I must prepare to go. The swallows, I must leave them, the well, the garden, the roses, all. Dear creatures! They sang last night after I was in bed; seemed to be singing to one another, just before they settled to rest for the night. Well, I must go. Farewell.'

To the tender-hearted every parting is a death. And never did a tenderer heart beat in a woman's breast than Dorothy's. To lavish tenderness was a necessity of her nature, and in her devotion to her brother and later to Coleridge she had satisfied that need. But now both seemed to be slipping from her. Mary and Sara Hutchinson, through their very quiescence, could give something which was less in her power to give through the very ardency of her nature. They could soothe, she could quicken. They could comfort in its gradual decline the poetic genius which she had helped to fan into flame.

And although her own genius for experiencing life with a caressing intimacy was to remain active for some years, yet it, too, was gradually to decline. Engrossed more and more in tireless domestic service, the creative inspiration of love in its fullness was to fade out of her life as out of her brother's. But while in him the cause was a contraction of the self, in her it was the lack of any being to whom she could give herself with a wholeness of devotion that would alone have relieved the wearing tension of her feelings.

§ 5

On the following morning they set out for the Hutchinsons' at Gallow Hill, near Scarborough. They travelled slowly, spending two nights at Keswick, where they had a melancholy parting with Coleridge, and, after lingering and loitering to make the most of their time alone together, two nights at Clarkson's at Eusemere. They met Mary and Sara, who had come to meet them, on the evening of 15th July.

But there was a duty yet to perform before Wordsworth could marry with an easy conscience. No fears of disturbing passion troubled his outlook on the future. But he had yet to settle up his account with the passion of the past. Four months before he and Dorothy had resolved to see Annette, while circumstances still allowed. And after ten days at Gallow Hill they started off on their journey to France.

As they left London by the Dover coach at six o'clock on a beautiful morning, Wordsworth composed the noble sonnet, *Upon Westminster Bridge*, the deep and radiant calm of which was unruffled by any tremor of prospective agitation. They reached Calais, where Annette had agreed to meet them with Caroline, on 1st August. And they spent the whole month with her. The situation might well have proved embarrassing. But Annette's good sense, Dorothy's sympathy, and Wordsworth's own power of investing his past with a solemn dignity, combined to make everything easy.

The presence of Dorothy and the child was a safeguard against undue intimacy, and although the brother and sister walked some evenings by the seashore alone, we do not hear of any solitary walk with Annette. Caroline accompanied them on at least one night, as the sonnet, *It is a Beauteous Evening, Calm and Free*, testifies. For she was the 'Dear Child' who appeared 'untouched by solemn thought,' but whose nature was 'not therefore less divine.' But the whole tone of this sonnet shows what a sublime refuge Wordsworth had discovered in his poetic philosophy from the shame and remorse which had once devoured him. The child with whom he walked on the seashore at Calais was no longer his natural daughter. She was a consecrated personification of the genius of childhood to which he had paid his tribute in such poems as *Anecdote for Fathers*, and was to immortalise when he completed the *Intimation Ode*. Remote from mortal failings and his own past indiscretions, she lay 'in Abraham's bosom all the year.'

This capacity to forget the embarrassing fact in the sublime idea did not at this time prejudice his powers of expressing the sublime in great poetry. But it involved a certain self-deception which was slowly but surely to shut him off from the truth. More than forty years later, when describing to an American pilgrim and admirer his experiences at the outbreak of the Revolution, and particularly in Orleans at the time of the September Massacres, he was to turn to his wife with the words, 'I wonder how I came to stay there so long, and at a period so exciting.'

But if self-deception had by that time become as ingrained as the incident suggests, he had already begun to practise it when he wrote *It is a Beauteous Evening*. Indeed, the fact that he now first adopted the sonnet form has a personal significance. He had recourse to the most stately and dignified of metrical forms in a situation most calculated to humble his dignity. The form of the verse, like the religious solemnity of its feeling, was an additional means of protecting himself against memories that secretly preyed upon his mind. The feeling was still real and powerful enough to animate the form, but because it had in it an element of hypocrisy, it was bound ultimately to be paralysed by convention.

Yet we may be grateful that circumstances encouraged Wordsworth at this time to find refuge from mundane embarrassments in the poetically sublime. For the immediate result was a series of sonnets unrivalled of their kind in depth of feeling and Biblical solemnity. And Annette contributed very helpfully to the event, not only by her sensible refusal to revive painful or affecting memories, but by the fact that she herself appeared habitually as untouched by solemn thought as her daughter.

Her sociable good sense was very comforting to Wordsworth. It transformed her from the 'Forsaken Woman' of his remorseful fancy into a woman of the world and it strengthened his conviction that he had acted rightly in forsaking her. He was alive to her excellent qualities, but they were quite clearly not of a kind to harmonise with his own or conduce to poetic contentment. Her Gallic liveliness, which had once entangled his senses, would have fatally disturbed the contemplative peace of Grasmere, and even her political opinions were now quite alien to his own.

For while he grieved over Napoleon for proving false to the original ideals of the Republic, she, as an ardent monarchist and Catholic, hated him for failing to restore the Bourbons. Thirteen years later Wordsworth himself was to desire such a restoration, and if he had been as free from self-deception as she was, he might even at this time have recognised that he had already embarked on the road which led to such a standpoint. But fortunately for English poetry he still clung to the belief that a compromise might be effected between his early Radicalism and his growing Conservatism.

Just as in the sonnet to his French daughter he sought to dignify and consecrate the fruit of his early recklessness as a lover, so in the sonnets which he wrote after Napoleon's proclamation on the 15th of August of his Consulship for life, he strove to evade the fact that his early Revolutionary zeal for humanity was indeed dead within him, by restating it in terms of a lofty individualism.

In a sonnet composed a week before the proclamation he recalled how twelve years before he and his friend Jones had set out from Calais on that festive journey southward, when the road 'streamed with the pomp of a too-credulous day,' and 'faith was pledged to new-born Liberty.' It all seemed to him now a delusive dream. 'Yet Despair,' he ended,

> Touches me not, though pensive as a bird
> Whose vernal coverts winter hath laid bare.

And he was immune from despair, as the sonnet he wrote on the 15th of August shows, because of his new-found self-sufficiency. He could look back with a pitying smile upon his youth and that 'prouder time' when 'the senselessness of joy' seemed sublime. For his feelings were no longer entangled in the future or in any progressive cause. He no longer wished to believe in the dawn of a new age, and the triumph of Napoleon was deplorable only because it heralded a more selfish kind of reaction than that which he himself had come to consider as right and necessary. 'Happy is he,' he wrote,

> who, caring not for Pope,
> Consul, or King, can sound himself to know
> The destiny of Man, and live in hope.

The true destiny of man was to live as he hoped to live himself, to be staunch and self-respecting, like the Lakeland peasants. His hope and faith were centred in such men and such a mode of life and could not be seriously affected by the strutting ambition of a little Frenchman. Grasmere would abide unchanged, though Napoleon overran Europe. And when he had passed, like a hurricane, the same virtues would be found blossoming in the same homely soil.

And Grasmere was the heart of England. No longer was

there any conflict in his mind between his own country and a France that should lead the world into new and higher paths. Standing on the shore at Calais one evening he watched the evening star hanging on the brink of the western horizon, and seeming to sink on the bosom of his native country. And he hailed it as the emblem of her beauty and her ordered freedom, 'a glorious crest conspicuous to the Nations.'

And in view of the naked tyranny and autocracy to which France was succumbing, his feelings were justified. For if England had never aspired so high as the idealists of the Revolution, she had never fallen so low. Insensitive as she might be to humanitarian causes, she still on the whole cherished a spirit of individual independence. That such a spirit, translated into the economic terms of *laisser-faire*, was compatible with the worst kinds of human enslavement was already becoming apparent, in her multiplying mills and mines. But to Wordsworth, to whom England had become Grasmere, the Industrial Revolution was as vain and transitory a horror as the French Revolution. The England which he cherished was a counterpart of himself. She stood by the old ways; she, too, was self-sufficient, and although it was from her that the intellectual pioneers of the French Revolution had originally derived much of their inspiration, she had been typically embarrassed by France's attempt to carry her ideas to a logical and actual extreme, had been alarmed and outraged by the brutal excess in which that attempt had culminated, and was now equally disgusted by the inevitable reaction to autocracy.

Such Continental extravagance was utterly alien to her slow and solid character. And the fact that it endangered her security strengthened her innate tendency to withdraw into herself. Soon, indeed, she was to be engaged in active self-defence. But for a few more months she held herself in disapproving reserve.

And in all this, apart from that first delirious year or two of young enthusiasm, Wordsworth had reflected the mood of his country. He, too, now cherished above all things the ideals of security and self-sufficiency, and that hardy independence which was the dominating characteristic of the average Englishman and which renewed itself from generation to generation in the rural life from which his country still drew her virtue.

To-day, in the sad decline of rural life and in our servitude to industrialism and the machine, we cannot but recognise how real that virtue was. But the loss of it has also taught us its limitations. And if, for the average Englishman, an interested self-sufficiency was at the time and by comparison with the predatory ambition of a Napoleon, a political and social virtue, it was bound eventually to sap the creative power of such a poet as Wordsworth.

Yet in this summer of 1802 it enabled him to concentrate himself in verse of a noble eloquence, as in the sonnet *To Toussaint L'Ouverture*, in which he invoked the elemental powers of Nature to vindicate the inviolable rights of man to independence and to confirm his hatred of 'the intoxicated despot.' The mantle of Burke had, indeed, fallen upon him, and whether he deplored in other sonnets the extinction of the Venetian Republic, applauded the manifesto of the young King of Sweden, or execrated the decree which drove all the negroes from France, he felt himself to be a voice of England. She, the mother and nurse of temperate Reason and Liberty, was behind him, approving his vindication of her ancient and ingrained traditions. No longer were the poet in him and the patriot at conflict, and he could almost be grateful to Napoleon for thus sealing their union.

And his final break with France confirmed the necessity of his break with Annette. He could associate neither her nor his daughter with England. They were alien to him in tastes and habits. They spoke another language; they would always be deaf to his poetry and indifferent to his creed. And so at the end of August he bid farewell to all that shamed him in his past. He settled with Annette and with France. He had loved both with passion, and passion was dead. He hated passion because he had suffered for it, and because for a time it had destroyed his self-sufficiency. It should never do so again.

And Annette made it easy. She approved his retirement to the safe level of kindly consideration. They parted as friends, and although on the day of his return to England Dorothy noted in her *Journal*, 'We sat upon the Dover cliffs, and looked upon France with many a melancholy and tender thought,' the sonnet which he wrote on the same day reveals with what relief he landed on his native soil—

> All, all are English. Oft have I looked round
> With joy in Kent's green vales; but never found
> Myself so satisfied in heart before.
> Europe is yet in bonds; but let that pass,
> Thought for another moment. Thou art free
> My Country! and 'tis joy enough and pride
> For one hour's perfect bliss, to tread the grass
> Of England once again, and hear and see,
> With such a dear Companion at my side.

It was his own freedom, as well as his country's, which he celebrated in this sonnet, his freedom to forget his past in the kind company of Dorothy and Mary and to tread the grass of the Lake Country down a vista of years, recollecting emotions in tranquillity.

But had he really exorcised the past by truly settling his account with it? Was he really free from the fear that kills and the haunting conscience? Two days later, when through the clearness of the atmosphere the coast of France was 'drawn almost into frightful neighbourhood,' he 'shrunk' from it. He felt his security to be precarious, and he was never to escape

Y

that feeling, however tenaciously he strove to protect himself against it. He comforted himself on this September day with the thought of the power that lay sleeping in the waters that stretched so placidly between him and France.

> Even so doth God protect us if we be
> Virtuous and wise. Winds blow, and waters roll,
> Strength to the brave, and Power, and Deity;
> Yet in themselves are nothing! One decree
> Spake laws to *them*, and said that by the soul
> Only, the Nations shall be great and free.

But if he could believe himself to be virtuous and wise enough to merit God's protection, the week or two which he spent in London before setting out for Gallow Hill seriously shook his faith in the soul of England.

In France it had been easy to be a lofty patriot, for whom England breathed the virtues of Milton and of Grasmere. But the vanity and parade of the London streets, typical as he supposed they must be of other towns and cities, contrasted painfully with the quiet and even 'the desolation, that the Revolution had produced in France.' All his fear and hatred of Industrialism returned. Far from being loyal to her old traditions, as he had assumed too easily in France, England was already in danger of forgetting them. And in five weighty sonnets he strove to recall her from the idolatry of wealth and cheap display.

There was a commanding ring in his voice, but his heart was heavy. For it seemed at the moment as if all he cherished, all he meant to build his life upon, was already in process of dissolution.

> Plain living and high thinking are no more:
> The homely beauty of the good old cause
> Is gone; our peace, our fearful innocence,
> And pure religion breathing household laws.

And to strengthen his wavering faith he summoned the great moralists of the past to confirm his admonitions.

> Milton! thou should'st be living at this hour:
> England hath need of thee: she is a fen
> Of stagnant waters: altar, sword, and pen,
> Fireside, the heroic wealth of hall and bower,
> Have forfeited their ancient English dower
> Of inward happiness. We are selfish men;
> Oh! raise us up, return to us again.

And not only Milton, with whom the Puritan in him was so much akin, was called to testify against the laxness and avarice of the times, but also

> The later Sidney, Marvel, Harrington,
> Young Vane, and others who called Milton friend.
> These moralists could act and comprehend:
> They knew how genuine glory was put on;
> Taught us how rightfully a nation shone
> In splendour: what strength was, that would not bend
> But in magnanimous meekness.

It is difficult, however, to preserve 'magnanimous meekness' untainted by false pride. And with each sonnet that Wordsworth wrote his doubts diminished and his sense of patriotic exultation increased.

There was little of 'magnanimous meekness' in the lines which followed his acclamation of that virtue.

> France, 'tis strange
> Hath brought forth no such souls as we had then.
> Perpetual emptiness! unceasing change!
> No single volume paramount, no code,
> No master spirit, no determined road;
> But equally a want of books and men!

And the fact that France could boast no Milton in her history convinced him of his country's essential soundness. She might at times spurn 'the check of salutary bands,' but her genius for ordered freedom was indestructible.

> We must be free or die, who speak the tongue
> That Shakespeare spake; the faith and morals hold
> Which Milton held. *In everything we are sprung*
> *Of Earth's first blood*, have titles manifold.

There was more of proud magniloquence in these lines than of 'magnanimous meekness.' And in the sonnet that followed the inevitable martial note entered.

> When I have borne in memory what has tamed
> Great Nations, how ennobling thoughts depart
> *When men change swords for ledgers*, and desert
> The student's bower for gold, some fear unnamed
> I had, my Country! am I to be blamed?

But now 'of those unfilial fears,' which he had in fact named most unequivocally, he confessed himself ashamed. Possibly he had left London before he wrote these two last sonnets, and, no longer vexed by the vanity and parade of her streets, he could once again regard his country as 'a bulwark for the cause of men.'

But although he had achieved a splendid utterance in these sonnets, he had taken one more step along a path that was fatal to his true genius. Events had made it almost inevitable. But the patriotic sublime was ultimately to prove as stultifying as the egotistic sublime of which it was a large expression.

Half a century later, at the time of the Crimean War, Tennyson was to stress the same contrast between the virtues of the soldier and the vices of the business man, and to com-

plain that nations degenerate 'when men change swords for
ledgers.' And to those who turned their eyes to the past
instead of the future there was no alternative. For the 'armoury
of the invincible Knights of old' did shine with a true lustre.
The selflessness of the soldier put the greed of the industrialist
to shame.

Yet the future was to be with the industrialist, and it might
have been a far less ugly future, if such men as Wordsworth,
who prized the ancient virtues, had recognised the need of
co-operating with all that was true and vital in the new movement, instead of merely acclaiming the past in their reasonable
recoil from all that was false and deathly in the present. Those,
too, who, disgusted by the commercialism of the ledger, strove
to revive the chivalry of the sword, were particularly dangerous
sentimentalists. They could not foresee how fatal war was to
prove in an industrialised and mechanised world. But if they
had listened to the spirit of the future instead of the past they
would have known that war, however picturesque its trappings
or beneficial its discipline upon the individual soldier, was
fundamentally as much a denial of humanity as child-labour in
the factories.

Eight years earlier, when he wrote *Guilt and Sorrow*, Wordsworth had known this and voiced his protest in no uncertain
terms. And it was the pacific ideals of the early Revolution
which had appealed to him most strongly. But France had
proved false to her ideals and essentially he had too. Constituted
as he was, it could hardly have been otherwise. Yet his
acceptance of the moral compromise which was to characterise
the nineteenth century and bear its inevitable fruit in the Great
War of the twentieth is no less tragic.

For a poet who accepts the role of moral teacher has great
responsibilities. He can foster the false pride which is the
converse of a false timidity. He can sanction with a lofty
rhetoric that clinging to personal security which is always the

index of a secret weakness and which always leads ultimately to alarmed aggression. Or he can persuade men that the only true morality is imaginative understanding, and that only the disinterested man or nation is really free.

The poet who sixteen years later wrote the lines *Among the Euganean Hills* devoted all his powers to the communicating of this truth, and we have only to compare Shelley's poem with Wordsworth's sonnet *On the Extinction of the Venetian Republic* to know who was the truer moralist.

But Wordsworth's sympathies were now too irretrievably tied to 'the shade of that which once was great' to feel 'the prophetic soul of the world dreaming on things to come.' And certainly the immediate aspect of the world gave him much excuse. It would have required a remarkable faith and vision to see in the middle-class industrial movement the painful travail of a new world that was coming to birth, a world which, despite all its ugliness, was to condition a new order of thought and consciousness. The 'progressive' claims of this movement must, indeed, have seemed a hollow mockery to one whose criterion of virtue was Milton and the Grasmere peasant. Yet all that was left of the Revolutionary ideals and enthusiasm belonged to it. And inadequate as those ideals were to leaven the lump of materialism and a rampant individualism, they were the creative forces of the future.

The belief in reason and the perfectibility of man, the conception that both nations and individuals should serve as members of one harmonious society, and the consequent conviction that war was a moral anachronism, were, indeed, to be obscured for a century by an orgy of acquisitiveness. But they have been vindicated by the very ruin which that acquisitiveness has brought. To-day they are increasingly recognised as necessary truths, even if the machinery for expressing them has yet to be constructed.

Wordsworth might have clung to those truths in the face of

his country's disillusion, had he not been so deeply disillusioned himself. Instead he inevitably gravitated to the timid and negative Tory side, sharing its panic, its concern for rights and privileges, its anxiety to preserve the past as long as it could against the inroads of the future. He had come as a poet to live in and sanctify his own past. It was inevitable that as a patriot he should also live in and sanctify his country's past.

And behind both reactions lay the same refusal really to accept the meaning of suffering. Revolutions, when they occur either in national or in a private life, are ordeals which can be truly or falsely experienced. If truly, the result is new spiritual growth. As Nicholas Berdyaev has written of the Russian Revolution of our own day — 'When a revolution has happened in the destiny of a nation, when it has suffered that misfortune, there is only one way out of it. One must accept the event as sent by Providence, accept it like all the sufferings and misfortunes of life, like all great trials, must be accepted . . . bearing the misfortune in a religious spirit as an expiation; one must help the life-giving currents through which the revolution evolves into its opposite, into positive creation. It is morally false to seek the source of evil outside myself, and imagine that I am a vessel of holiness. That sort of disposition gives birth to spiteful fanaticism. . . . No, the source of evil is in me too, and I must take my share of blame and responsibility. . . . That is the only way of coming through a revolution which . . . can give any spiritual light.'

These brave and humble words by one who has been expelled from his country by the Bolshevists reveal the true path of organic development from which Wordsworth had turned aside in his attempt to return to a pre-revolutionary state. It is true that England had not experienced a violent revolution. But Wordsworth himself had, both in his private life and as a sympathiser with France. He had refused, however, to go through the interior purification which such an experience demands if it is to prove creative. He sought instead to recover the self-respect and security of his pre-revolutionary days, like the dispossessed landowner who longs to recover his lost property. And such reaction is fatal to true regeneration. It merely perpetuates the disease of which Revolution was at once the violent expression and the attempted purge.

In Wordsworth the disposition of self-righteousness never, if we except one deplorable sonnet to be quoted later, gave birth to spiteful fanaticism, because he had up to a point accepted suffering and humbled himself before it. But it was very soon to give birth to narrow and even violent prejudice. For beneath the assumption of recovered health, the disease persisted.

¶ PART X

JOURNEY'S END

§ 1

WORDSWORTH reached Gallow Hill again on 22nd September, and on 4th October he and Mary Hutchinson were married. Thus the process of re-establishment which had begun at Racedown six years before was completed, and the event which for most men is a prologue was for him an epilogue. The drama of love had been played out in another place and time, and if the catharsis had been imperfectly experienced, he could feel, after his settlement with Annette, that he had been dismissed 'with peace and consolation'

And calm of mind, all passion spent.

It was not he, but Dorothy, who was deeply moved on the day of the wedding. A few days before she had written to her friend Jane Pollard—'I have long loved Mary Hutchinson as a sister, and she is greatly attached to me; this being so, you will guess that I look forward with perfect happiness to this connection between us; but, happy as I was, I half dread that concentration of all tender feelings past, present, and future, which will come upon me on the wedding morning.'

And of that morning she wrote in her *Journal*—'At a little after eight o'clock I saw them go down the avenue towards the church. William had parted from me upstairs. . . . I kept myself as quiet as I could, but when I saw the two men running up the walk, coming to tell us it was over, I could stand it no longer, and threw myself on the bed, where I lay in stillness, neither hearing nor seeing anything till Sara came upstairs to me, and said, "They are coming." This forced me from the bed where I lay, and I moved, I knew not how, straight forward, faster than my strength would carry me, till I met my beloved William, and fell upon his bosom. He and John Hutchinson led me to the house, and there I stayed to welcome my dear Mary. As soon as we had breakfasted we departed. It rained when we set off.'

The journey back to Grasmere, too, was full of affecting reminders, since for part of the way they followed the same route as she and William had done three years before. Passing through the village of Wensley her heart 'melted away with dear recollections—the bridge, the little waterspout, the steep hill, the church. They are among the most vivid of my own inner visions, for they were the first objects that I saw after we were left to ourselves, and had turned our whole hearts to Grasmere as a home in which we were to rest.'

Wordsworth's calm, however, was unruffled by the feelings either of his sister or his bride. On the first evening of the journey he composed a sonnet on the sunset, and on the following morning another on the captivity of Mary Queen of Scots in Bolton Castle, in which the captive Queen was made to cry—

> Just Heaven, contract the compass of my mind
> To fit proportion with my altered state!

But if the compass of his own mind was, indeed, to be contracted by his altered state, it was due to what Harriet Martineau was to describe as the perfect 'aptitude of Mary Hutchinson to his own needs.' She served him equally as a capable housewife and as an amanuensis, and she offered him that unquestioning devotion and admiration which he craved as a narcotic against his secret sense of failure.

That such narcotics are ultimately demoralising and that her very submissiveness tended to enhance his complacence is probably true. But when he married her his state was in fact so firmly fixed that only some convulsion in his life could have altered it. Certainly she sustained and sweetened his dying life for nearly fifty years. Nor is there any question of the deep and deepening affection which he felt for her, even if it was to be associated, as indeed his affection for Dorothy was to be, with a certain autocratic lack of consideration in domestic matters. But as a domestic partner, so mild and kind that she was even glad to be exploited, she was in the practical province of life, as Coleridge had been in the spiritual, the perfect feminine complement of his too masculine self.

She could not, however, give what Coleridge had given. And there was a pathetic irony in the fact that Coleridge printed his *Dejection* Ode in the *Morning Post* on Wordsworth's wedding day. It was his wedding present to his friend. Out of the depths of his own despondency he prayed for Wordsworth's happiness. Homeless himself, like a child that 'upon a lonesome wild' had lost his way, he blessed the fate which had brought his friend the contentment and security of a home. Never did a more generous tribute blossom out of a sense of failure. These lines and those which he wrote four years later after hearing Wordsworth read *The Prelude* were the final expression of that beautiful self-abasement before his friend which had always characterised their relationship.

He himself seemed now a joyless outcast in the world, Wordsworth joyfully at home in it. Yet because in his weakness he was without pride or self-righteousness, Coleridge was, it may be, even now nearer to the infinite heart of creation. And there was to come a time when even he was to feel that his tribute was no longer appropriate to one whose sympathies had become narrowed by the 'anxious dread' that underlay his lofty affirmations of 'the good and fair.' And then he was to give his poem back again to Sara Hutchinson.

But at this time, although he was aware that a hypochondriac strain underlay Wordsworth's apparent stability and self-possession, and even commented upon it to his friend Wedgwood, he did not see in it a symptom of a deeply rooted organic discord or realise how crippling it was to prove. 'I was much pleased,' he had written to W. Sotheby in July 1802, 'with your description of Wordsworth's character as it appeared to you. . . . The word "homogeneous" gave me great pleasure, as most accurately and happily expressing him.'

Yet, in the same letter, he first declared his disagreement with certain tenets in Wordsworth's poetic creed, admitting that 'we have had lately some little controversy on the subject, and we begin to suspect that there is somewhere or other a radical difference in our opinions.' A fortnight later in a letter to Southey he was even more explicit, criticising not only 'the extreme elaboration and almost constrainedness of the diction' of the latter half of the Preface to *Lyrical Ballads*, but some of Wordsworth's more recent poems in which he had been startled to find here and there 'a daring humbleness of language and versification, and a strict adherence to matter of fact, even to prolixity.'

'The radical difference' which he had begun to suspect, concerned at present only 'our theoretical opinions respecting poetry' and particularly the matter of diction. But behind their differences concerning diction lay in fact two radically opposed conceptions of the nature of imagination. And these two conceptions were not merely theories. They reflected the personalities of the two men, one of whom was convinced not only mentally but physically of the essential insufficiency of Nature, as the other conceived it, to the demands of the human spirit. And time and circumstances were to show how irreconcilable they were.

For the first nine months of his married life, however, Wordsworth saw little of Coleridge. Later in the year he

resumed work upon *The Prelude*. Far from Coleridge having
sowed any seeds of doubt in his mind concerning the sufficiency
of Hartley's scheme of life, he was convinced that his own
history from childhood to his present maturity confirmed its
truth. And if there were moments in that history which broke
the perfect continuity of natural law, the fracture had surely
been healed. Even his parental instinct was now to be tran-
quilly satisfied. For Mary was with child. As he was to write
later in *The Excursion*—

> O happy time! still happier was at hand;
> For Nature called my Partner to resign
> Her share in the pure freedom of that life,
> Enjoyed by us in common.—To my hope,
> To my heart's wish, my tender Mate became
> The thankful captive of maternal bonds;
> And those wild paths were left to me alone.
> There could I meditate on follies past;
> And, like a weary voyager escaped
> From risk and hardship, inwardly retrace
> A course of vain delights and thoughtless guilt,
> And self-indulgence—without shame pursued.
> There, undisturbed, could think of and could thank
> Her whose submissive Spirit was to me
> Rule and restraint—my guardian—shall I say
> That earthly Providence, whose guiding love
> Within a port of rest had lodged me safe;
> Safe from temptation, and from danger far?

He was safe and he was soothed. In that lay the essence of
his happiness, which not even the renewal of war between
England and France in May 1803 could at first disturb. And
once again the spring quickened his lyrical impulse, recreating
for him a world 'where life is wise and innocent.' As he

watched the six-year-old Hartley Coleridge he entered that world again,

> O blessed vision! happy child!
> Thou art so exquisitely wild.

But lovely as was this child's 'season of delight,' it was haunted by the shadow of his father—

> I think of thee with many fears
> For what may be thy lot in future years.

No shadow, however, haunted that 'Child of the Year,' that 'unassuming Common-place of Nature,' the humble daisy. Contemplating it the tension of his nature was relaxed. He read in it a symbol of pure friendliness, 'unchecked by pride or scrupulous doubt.' Life became a pleasant thought. He demanded nothing for himself, he exacted nothing from others, and melancholy seemed as superfluous as the lofty moral rhetoric in which he had recently indulged as a poet.

> If stately passions in me burn,
> And one chance look to Thee should turn,
> I drink out of an humbler urn
> > A lowlier pleasure;
> The homely sympathy that heeds
> The common life, our nature breeds;
> A wisdom fitted to the needs
> > Of hearts at leisure.

In such moments Wordsworth knew that to be happy is to be humble and his greatness as a poet derived from that knowledge. Yet it was only when he was untroubled by any sense of personal insecurity that he could scatter his gladness without care, like the green linnet which he also celebrated in a lyric at this time.

And there were moments, too, when even the natural world kindled a desire for something more than unassuming simplicity. Such a moment occurred one evening when Sara Hutchinson called him to the window, saying, 'Look how beautiful is yon star! It has the sky all to itself.' The star's self-sufficiency seemed more sublime than any flower's. He had the sky to himself,

> 'tis all his own.
> O most ambitious Star! an inquest wrought
> Within me when I recognised thy light;
> A moment I was startled at the sight;
> And, while I gazed, there came to me a thought
> That I might step beyond my natural race
> As thou seem'st now to do; might one day trace
> Some ground not mine; and, strong, her strength above,
> My Soul, an Apparition in the place,
> Tread there with steps that no one shall reprove!

It was not, however, merely after a heavenly eminence that he aspired, judging by a variant reading in which he described the thought as 'a startling recollection'

> Of the distinguished few among mankind,
> Who dare to step beyond their natural race.

'Thy soul,' he had recently written in his sonnet on Milton, 'was like a star.' And the sublimity of which he dreamed was that of being another Milton. The 'stately passions' which the daisy had reduced, the star renewed.

But as a holiday season the spring and early summer of 1803 were happy enough. And in June Mary gave birth to a son, who, in Dorothy's words, had 'a very prominent nose, which *will be* like his Father's, and a head shaped upon the very same model.' 'Smoothly,' indeed, as he wrote later in *The Excursion*,

> did our life   .
> Advance, swerving not from the path prescribed.

But when Mary had been churched and the baby christened, he took the path to Scotland. The plan may have originated with Coleridge, who for months had had thoughts of escaping from his tortured self to Portugal, Malta, the West Indies, or Hungary, but had been baulked by want of funds. He could at least flee to Scotland and ease in some measure his restlessness and irresolution by physical activity. And the Wanderer in Wordsworth welcomed the idea of leaving for a season the 'port of rest' and domestic propriety in which he was now lodged so safe. For months his state had seemed paradisaical, but, in his own words,

> The gentlest shade that walked Elysian plains
> Might sometimes covet dissoluble chains. . . .

The poet in him was in fact a little restive. He felt the dangers of a too placid contentment. The power might fail, the folded wings cease to grow. He was established as a husband and a father. With Dorothy and Coleridge in a strange wild country he might quicken the flame of his genius.

§ 2

The poetical fruit of the Scottish tour certainly justified his expectations. But it brought appreciably nearer the inevitable break with Coleridge. The good spirits with which the three of them set out with one horse and an Irish jaunting-car rapidly declined. Indeed, if it had not been for Dorothy, the party could hardly have preserved its cohesion for as long as it did. Coleridge talked about poetry almost all the time, and if his metaphysics passed over Dorothy's head like a driving mist,

they must at times have disturbed Wordsworth, whose duty
it was to drive the horse, and who drove it so badly that he let
it back down hillsides and tangle itself in the harness. At
frequent intervals Coleridge led the horse and then Dorothy's
intense and vital absorption in the nuances of the landscape
and her frequent and detailed comparisons of Scots lochs
with English lakes must have proved somewhat disturbing to
him. Yet her companions would have been lost without her
practical capacity for discovering cottages where they could
get refreshment or pass the night or for seeing that the horse
was fed and littered. Even so, they had to endure much physical
hardship, for which Coleridge was in poor condition. Moreover, his habitual refuge from painful actuality, the laudanum
bottle, was probably closed to him.

Under these conditions he struggled on to Glasgow, but
during the following fortnight when 'it rained all the way, all
the long, long day,' his misery became unendurable, and on
29th August, by the shore of Loch Long, he fled. Rheumatism
was his excuse, and he told his friends that he would return to
Edinburgh by the shortest route. But in fact, when he had
left them, he, too, went north as far as Inverness, walking
nearly three hundred miles in eight days according to his own
account, in a desperate attempt to escape the inward anguish
that he recorded in *The Pains of Sleep*.

And some at least of this anguish was, perhaps, due to his
realisation that there could never again be real harmony between
himself and Wordsworth. He was an outcast even from his
friend, or at least their relationship was no longer easy and vital.
'To live beloved,' he wrote

is all I need,
And whom I love, I love indeed.

And Wordsworth's response to that love, he felt, was now
qualified. There was constraint, where before there had been

z

freedom. 'Wordsworth's hypochondriacal feelings,' he wrote later, 'kept him silent and self-centred. . . . Somehow or other I had not been quite comfortable.' Wordsworth voiced later a similar complaint. 'Poor Coleridge,' he remarked, 'was too much in love with his own dejection.'

And it would be unfair to blame him for a want of sympathy. For Coleridge was no fitting companion for such a tour. And there is little wonder that the exactions of metaphysical talk combined with the severe physical demands of travel reduced Wordsworth to silence. Nevertheless the experience must have deepened his sense of the gulf which was opening between him and his friend. Coleridge had begun to be less a source of inspiration than of exasperation.

The tour, however, was not spoilt by Coleridge's secession. Wordsworth could now give his undivided attention to the country and to the manners and talk of the humble folk whose cottages they frequented and whose food they shared. And the wildness both of the country and the people harmonised with the deepest strain in his being. In the Highlands he was under no restraint. He and Dorothy, true to the gipsy nature which both of them in part possessed, could trudge through mud and rain, across desolate moors and over dangerous ferries, exulting in their freedom from all conventional ties and relishing even storms and privations because they brought them nearer to the starkly primitive. They could

> cull contentment upon wildest shores,
> And luxuries extract from bleakest moors.

And under such conditions the elemental depths in Wordsworth were stirred. With 'Nature's freedom at the heart,' the balance between his expansive instinct and his contracting mind was readjusted, and the poems which he wrote, even although some of them were not completed until months after his return, reflected the vital tension.

The truth of this is particularly apparent if we compare the lines which he wrote *At the Grave of Burns*, with those that he addressed many years later to the sons of the poet. Certainly the feeling behind the second poem originated at this time. For Dorothy noted in her *Journal* that 'the grave of Burns's son, which we had just seen by the side of his father, and some stories heard at Dumfries respecting the dangers his surviving children were exposed to, filled us with melancholy concern, which had a kind of connexion with ourselves.' But in the years which elapsed before Wordsworth put this feeling into words the moralist had taken command of the poet, and Burns's life, dismally embellished by Dr. Currie, had become a subject for reverent admonishment.

But the lines written under an immediate stress of feeling were very different. In them Wordsworth was at one with his subject in his grief, pity, and admiration. He wrote at once with a noble dignity and an impulsive intimacy, untroubled by the thought that Burns had at times composed 'seductive lays' and followed a light which was not 'from Heaven.' It was enough that Burns had opened up a path along which he himself was treading, that he had

> showed my youth
> How Verse may build a princely throne
> On humble truth.

And his heart went out to him as to a kindred soul.

> Neighbours we were, and loving friends
> We might have been; . . .
> True friends though diversely inclined;
> But heart with heart and mind with mind,
> Where the main fibres are entwined,
> Through Nature's skill,
> May even by contraries be joined
> More closely still.

And well, indeed, might he and Burns in kinship of genius

> Have sate and talked where gowans blow,
> Or on wild heather.

For beneath the moralistic crust which was beginning to form over Wordsworth's genius, the same 'genuine springs' of natural impulse and homely affection flowed, as had coursed through the heart and mind of Burns. And in the last stanza of his tribute to one whose generous humanity kindled all that was generous in himself, he experienced for a moment the unity which transcends all cautious self-regard—

> Sighing I turned away; but ere
> Night fell I heard, or seemed to hear,
> Music that sorrow comes not near,
> A ritual hymn,
> *Chaunted in love that casts out fear*
> By Seraphim.

Echoes of that ritual hymn sounded in almost all the poems which he wrote during this tour in Scotland. For Earth was once again apparelled in a celestial light, in which the homely was limitless and the every-day magical. So it was with the Highland Girl whom he met at Inversneyde upon Loch Lomond in a perfect setting of rocks and trees and waterfall, where the lake curved into a little bay.

> In truth together do ye seem
> Like something fashioned in a dream;
> Such Forms as from their covert peep
> When earthly cares are laid asleep!
> But, O fair Creature! in the light
> Of common day, so heavenly bright,
> I bless Thee, Vision as thou art,
> I bless thee with a human heart.

And if in the perfect innocence and spontaneity of the Highland Girl he saw and accepted the absolute goodness of life, by Ossian's grave in Glen-Almain he felt the perfect happiness of death, of a tranquillity more deep and entire than any temporal quiet or ease. And the same certainty that all was right in life and death, and that within each was a heavenly home of harmony, came to him one evening when he and Dorothy were walking beside Loch Ketterine, facing the afterglow of sunset, and a passer-by greeted them with the words, 'What, you are stepping westward?'

The words seized his imagination. For in that lonely place, in a strange land and far from home, to be stepping westward did seem a '*wildish* destiny.' Yet with such a sky to lead him on, who could stop or fear to advance into the unknown? He no longer yearned to retrace his steps in life; the future beckoned:

> The dewy ground was dark and cold;
> Behind, all gloomy to behold;
> And stepping westward seemed to be
> A kind of *heavenly* destiny;
> I liked the greeting; 'twas a sound
> Of something without place or bound;
> And seemed to give me spiritual right
> To travel through that region bright.

It was not merely a passing fancy quickened by the sunset, the 'solitary place,' and a chance encounter, that he expressed in these lines. It was the mystic in him gladly affirming his conviction that

> Our destiny, our nature and our home
> Is with infinitude, and only there.

And because this realisation, when it comes to a man, frees him from the servitude of time, from regrets for lost youth or fear of death and the unknown, Wordsworth wished in this moment no longer to preserve his life but to spend it, no longer to retreat but to adventure. He saw the future not as a decline from the past, but as an eternal present, in which his spirit, though a pilgrim on earth, was with every step he took essentially at home, and intimately linked with his fellow pilgrims in a heavenly destiny. The woman who had greeted him was such a pilgrim. Her voice had an eternal significance, but its echoes 'enwrought,' too,

> A human sweetness with the thought
> Of travelling through the world that lay
> Before me in my endless way.

And on another day the voice of a girl 'reaping and singing by herself in a field' cast the same spell upon him, as he paused to listen.

> No Nightingale did ever chaunt
> More welcome notes to weary bands
> Of travellers in some shady haunt,
> Among Arabian sands:
> A voice so thrilling ne'er was heard
> In spring-time from the Cuckoo-bird,
> Breaking the silence of the seas
> Among the farthest Hebrides.
>
> Will no one tell me what she sings?—
> Perhaps the plaintive numbers flow
> For old, unhappy, far-off things,
> And battles long ago:
> Or is it some more humble lay,
> Familiar matter of to-day?
> Some natural sorrow, loss, or pain,
> That has been, and may be again?

Here again he was lifted out of time. The maiden sang, 'as if her song could have no ending.' The earthly and the unearthly, the far-off and the near, the fabulous and the familiar, were reconciled in an enchanted moment. He had mounted above the plane of moral judgment and repressed instincts, and in the joy of such pure affirmation he had entered a realm in which the conflict of sense and reason was resolved in a transcendent harmony. And in his *Address to Kilchurn Castle Upon Loch Awe* he affirmed the same experience—

> Oh! there is life that breathes not; Powers there are
> That touch each other to the quick in modes
> Which the gross world no sense hath to perceive,
> No soul to dream of.

And although these lines were written some years later they record what he felt at this time as he had not felt it, perhaps, with such certainty of illumination, since the days of his youth. For a few weeks he experienced, if but intermittently, the power of harmony and saw into the life of things, not through imaginative recollection, but as a new and present realisation.

The experience wrought no deep change in his being. It depended too much upon the accident of physical and mental freedom. But temporary as the emancipation from inward conflict was, it was a link between his youth and his maturity. The gulf between them seemed less deep, and he could bridge them, when he came to complete *The Prelude*, with a greater confidence.

And this was the real importance to him of the tour in Scotland. He had experienced once again a creative freedom of spirit with a fullness of joy that would remain a fertile memory even 'if Care with freezing years should come.' There were, of course, many other secondary pleasures to remember, chief among them a meeting with Scott, whose vigour, frank cordiality, and entertaining conversation were as exhilarating as the air of his own hills.

Here at least was a poet who was not stricken with the disease of romanticism, who could be both a genius and a man of property and of the world. And if as he listened to his host reciting the first four cantos of the *Lay of the Last Minstrel*, Wordsworth missed the enchantment of *The Ancient Mariner* or *Christabel*, he may well have felt too, the poignant contrast between this active, resolute poet and the dispirited companion who had parted from him in such distress a few weeks before.

But as September advanced he began to feel that his rambling disposition had been sufficiently indulged. Grasmere beckoned and as he approached it on a beautiful autumn day the joy of 'sweet return' flowed into a few lines of greeting to the Mother and the Child, composed as he walked. He found Mary in perfect health, and little John asleep in the clothes-basket by the fire, and the cup of his contentment was full.

And a few evenings later it found expression in another poem. The story of *The Blind Highland Boy* was told him by the parish-clerk of Grasmere, who had been an eye-witness of a small boy's adventure in a washing-tub on the tidal waters of Loch Leven. And Wordsworth's re-telling of it may be read and enjoyed simply as one of his characteristic tales of humble life.

But it has a personal significance too. For behind the simple humour and pathos of this 'tale told by the fireside, after returning to the vale of Grasmere,' was Wordsworth's own recent experience. His own exultant sense of recovered freedom in Scotland informed the lines describing the blind boy's surrender of himself to 'the great Sea-water' whose coming and going he had sensed so eagerly.

> He launched his vessel—and in pride
> Of spirit, from Loch Leven's side,

Stepped into it—his thoughts all free
As the light breezes that with glee
   Sang through the adventurer's hair.

A while he stood upon his feet;
He felt the motion—took his seat;
Still better pleased as more and more
The tide retreated from the shore,
   And sucked, and sucked him in.

The boy's joy, however, is short-lived. He senses the approach of his rescuers, and cries to them to keep away. But their hands are on his 'dancing shell,' and

     all his dreams—that inward light
With which his soul had shone so bright—
All vanished;—'twas a heart-felt cross
To him, a heavy, bitter loss,
   As he had ever known. . . .

Thus, after he had fondly braved
The perilous Deep, the Boy was saved;
And, though his fancies had been wild,
Yet he was pleased and reconciled
   To live in peace on shore.

There is more in this poem than a homely tale or even the feelings of a returned traveller. It is an unconscious allegory of Wordsworth's life, of his own blind adventure into ecstasy, and his recoil into domestic security.

But his experience in Scotland gives it a particular significance. For his ecstasy there had not been blind. It had been luminous and liberating. It had fulfilled his being and his vision. Yet although he loved and longed to preserve it, he feared it too. There was danger to his finite self in its infinite demands. It was safer to preserve his life in peace on shore, even if

> that inward light
> With which his soul had shone so bright

should slowly vanish until only the haunting memory of it remained.

§ 3

The consequences of preferring security to reality were not slow to appear. Indeed the deterioration of Wordsworth's public sentiments during the months which followed his return from Scotland was as sudden and emphatic as his creative revival during the tour itself.

The chief external cause was the threat of invasion by Bonaparte. The pride in his country and the fear for her which he had felt and expressed in a series of sonnets a year before returned upon him, but his patriotism now was far less a stately passion than a rabid sentiment. It was not merely that every Frenchman was

> One of a Nation who, henceforth, must wear
> Their fetters in their souls,

while England was

> the only light
> Of Liberty that yet remains on earth!

Not only 'British reason' but 'the British sword' were now for him the sole instruments of divinity left in the world. And he even exulted and bid little children and infants exult in the sanguinary prospect—

Shout, for a mighty Victory is won!
On British ground the Invaders are laid low;
The breath of Heaven has drifted them like snow,
And left them lying, in the silent sun,
Never to rise again!—the work is done.
Come forth, ye old men, now in peaceful show
And greet your sons! drums beat and trumpets blow!
Make merry, wives! ye little children, stun
Your grandame's ears with pleasure of your noise!
Clap, infants, clap your hands! Divine must be
That triumph, when the very worst, the pain,
And even the prospect of our brethren slain,
Hath something in it which the heart enjoys:—
In glory will they sleep and endless sanctity.

Even those who experienced the blood-lust of civilian patriots during the Great War cannot but be shocked that a poet once so sensitive to humane causes and so uncompromising in his independence should have written these lines. That Wordsworth should have shared the common fear of his countrymen at this time and sought to strengthen their determination, was reasonable enough. But only an utterly demoralising personal panic could have brought him to gloat over slaughter, and sanctify it, as he did in this sonnet.

Fear, in fact, had momentarily deadened his sensibility when he wrote these lines, and it was undermining his independence, as the relationship which he now formed with Sir George Beaumont clearly showed.

Sir George was a most agreeable man of fifty, a landed proprietor, an accomplished amateur artist, and a patron of letters. He was living at Greta Hall, and shortly before Wordsworth had set out for Scotland he had bought and presented to him a piece of land near Keswick in the hope that he would build on it and so be able to live near Coleridge.

Wordsworth did not acknowledge the gift until after his return, and there was a hint of uneasiness in the manner of his acceptance. But it is significant that he enclosed with his letter of acceptance three sonnets, all bellicose in tone and including the one quoted.

For Sir George had military interests, and had raised a corps of infantry in various places. Perhaps, therefore, thoughts of what would please Sir George and of making some return to him for his gift entered into their composition. And shortly afterwards Wordsworth tendered also the gift of himself by becoming a volunteer. 'At Grasmere,' he wrote to Sir George, 'we have turned out almost to a man. We are to go to Ambleside on Sunday to be mustered, and put on, for the first time, our military apparel.'

Possibly, therefore, the ferocity of his political verses at this time was to some extent assumed in order to please Sir George, who sent them to the newspapers. Yet Dorothy herself testified to the intensity of his feelings. 'Surely,' she wrote in a letter to her friend Mrs. Clarkson, regretting her brother's precipitate enrolment as a volunteer, 'there never was a more determined hater of the French, nor one more willing to do his utmost to destroy them if they really do come.'

But the extent to which patriotism or patronage dictated his feelings is of minor importance. For behind his surrender to both of them was a woeful denial of his true self. Under the stress of a time of public alarm his love of ancient virtues had degenerated into the reactionary's hate, his austere independence into social servility. And the poet who had cherished the cause of human brotherhood could write to a gratified Sir George—'The nation would err grievously if she suffered the abuse which other states have made of military power to prevent her from perceiving that no people ever was or can be independent, free, or secure, much less great, in any sane application of the word, without martial propensities and an assiduous cultivation of military virtues!'

Thus does fear don the mask of self-righteousness and preach the virtues of Prussianism. It had not of course poisoned the deeper springs of Wordsworth's nature. For more than a year later, when the public tension was somewhat relaxed and death had taken one who was near and dear to him, he could write to Southey—'Oh! it makes the heart groan that, with such a beautiful world as this to live in, and such a soul as that of man's is by Nature and gift of God, we should go about on such errands as we do, destroying and laying waste; and ninety-nine of us in a hundred never easy in any road that travels towards peace and quietness. And yet, what virtue and what goodness, what heroism and courage, what triumphs of disinterested love everywhere, and human life, after all, what it is! Surely, this is not to be for ever, even on this perishable planet!'

That was the voice of his true self, of the self that bowed down before the mystery and received from it the vision of disinterested love and the secret of creativeness.

Yet although that vision survived the petty ferocities of this time or *The Prelude* would never have been written, its eventual darkening was already foreshadowed. Wordsworth was now thirty-three. He had reached an age which is crucial in spiritual development, when a poet must either grow imaginatively through giving himself to life, or by clinging to what life has given him decline inevitably to death. The fire-eating patriot and 'humble servant' of Sir George had irrevocably chosen the path of decline.

§ 4

The presence of Coleridge, however, during the early weeks of 1804 diverted Wordsworth's thoughts somewhat from the menace of invasion, even if it depressed his spirits. For

Coleridge had come to Dove Cottage late in December on a farewell visit before starting, as he hoped, for Malta in search of health. There he fell ill, and was devotedly nursed by Dorothy and Mary for three weeks. He was an amiable but trying patient, and even Dorothy was a little fretted by his continual demands for 'coffee, broth, or something or other.'

His irregular habits must have tried Wordsworth's pity and patience too, and although he still hoped that a change of climate might do something to restore his friend and generously lent him a hundred pounds to take him to Malta, it must have been with more relief than hope that he heard of his sailing early in April.

Coleridge on his part believed that he had during those weeks convinced Wordsworth that the doctrine of Necessity was 'pernicious.' He had in reality done no such thing. The truth was that Wordsworth in his religious, as in his political and social views, was becoming an orthodox Conservative. The poet in him still remained a Necessitarian and was fortunately to remain such until after *The Prelude*, in its original form, was completed. But the patriot and the friend of Sir George had already come to appreciate the stability and security of the Established Church. And such conformity brought him in fact no nearer to Coleridge. For it was not the result of any real spiritual conversion. There had been a necessary correspondence between the creed of Hartley and his most vital experiences. But in Anglicanism he sought only a dignified retreat from the dangers of life.

The Christianity to which Coleridge had become converted was not such a retreat. For it not only commanded his assent as one stricken and humbled by a sense of sin, but offered in its fundamental dogmas a mould into which he could pour a stream of new metaphysical meaning. But what drew Wordsworth to the Church was its fear of new life and its moral

propriety. And no respectable Churchman could credit
Coleridge with these qualities.

But there was another poet who had come to live at Keswick
who did possess them. And this was Southey. He had written
a malicious review of *Lyrical Ballads* on the morrow of its
appearance, possibly under the impression that they were all
the work of Coleridge with whom he had quarrelled. But that
was past history, and neither his conservatism nor his censorious
attitude to Coleridge, for which indeed he was to have considerable excuse, divided him any longer from Wordsworth.

They were in fact henceforth to be drawn more and more
together, and the dying poet was as inevitably the friend of
Southey as the living poet had been of Coleridge. But death
had not yet struck at his roots, and during the next two years
he was to complete the testament of his life, which he had
actually begun in 1795, and of which he had composed the first
two books during 1799-1800.

It would seem that soon after his return from Scotland he
had returned to the task, which he had taken up for a short time
earlier in the year. For Coleridge noted with characteristic
enthusiasm in October 1803 — 'But now he is at the helm of a
noble bark; now he sails right onward; it is all open ocean and
a steady breeze, and he drives before it, unfettered by short
tacks, reefing and unreefing his sails, hauling and disentangling
the ropes. His only disease is the having been out of his
element; his return to it is food to famine; it is both the specific
remedy and the condition of health.'

Coleridge, however, spoke too soon. Political panic, as we
have seen, supervened, but early in 1804 the fever abated its
violence, and he wrote that he had 'great things in meditation'
and that he was at present engaged on a poem on his own
earlier life, which would take five parts or books.

He still, however, conceived of *The Prelude* as a mere
tributary to a far larger and more important work, the moral and

philosophical poem treating of what he found most interesting
in Nature, Man, and Society, to which he meant to devote the
prime of his life and the chief force of his mind, and which was
to be followed by a narrative poem. The poem on his own
life was to be the least important of the three and was not to
amount to more than 4000 or 5000 lines.

During January and February, however, he worked continuously upon *The Prelude*, not only writing but taking out the
umbrella, according to Dorothy, and standing stock still under
it, during many a rainy half-hour, in the middle of road or field.
And early in March he reported that he had finished another
book of it, that which described his residence at Cambridge,
including presumably the summer vacation described in Book
IV of the poem as it now stands. Only one more book, he then
supposed, remained to be written, the fifth, now entitled *Books*.
And this was apparently completed before the end of the month,
since Mary and Dorothy made a copy of the five books, which
were then regarded as the completed poem, for Coleridge to
take with him when he sailed for Malta on 2nd April.

But the steady breeze, of which Coleridge wrote prematurely,
had now got hold of Wordsworth's sails. He had become too
absorbed in his own early history to conclude it at his eighteenth
year. Moreover, it was not the right stopping place. For his
youth really ended, as he knew only too well, in his twenty-
first year, before he took that fatally enthusiastic journey to
France. And so during April he added another book to the
poem, which completed his account of his Cambridge days and
described his tour with Jones in Switzerland. And he wrote
also a third of the seventh book, treating of his residence in
London, and this was probably completed during the summer.

He still, however, held to his intention to confine *The
Prelude* to the years before 'the Fall.' And in describing the
progress of the poem in a letter to a friend he confessed that
'It seems a frightful deal to say about myself; and, of course,

will never be published—during my lifetime, I mean—till another work has been written and published of sufficient importance to justify me in giving my own history to the world.'

The other work was, of course, the philosophic poem on Nature, Man, and Society, for which in fact he had little real qualification, but which, as a prospective idea, served admirably to counterbalance any uneasy feeling that he was writing too much about himself.

And for a time he seems to have intended to end *The Prelude* with Book VIII. For early in September he wrote to Sir George Beaumont—'You will be glad to hear that I have been busily employed lately. I wrote one book of *The Recluse*, nearly a thousand lines, then had a rest. Last week I began again, and have written three hundred more, and hope all tolerably well, and *certainly with good views*.'

He had in fact taken up again the story of The Wanderer and The Solitary. What he had already written of it was, as we have shown, essentially little less personal than *The Prelude* itself. Nevertheless it was his project of a philosophic poem, even if the views on Nature and Society which it was to contain were already restricted within the safe limits of Sir George's approval.

Fortunately, however, he could not still the voice of his vital past. In his work on *The Prelude* he had reached the threshold of his manhood and the crisis of his life. He could not stop there. All that he now was depended on that fateful visit to France and the bitter revulsion of the following years. And the urge to re-live those years, and by expressing all that they were and meant to him, put them in a sense from him, was overpowering.

And so, although he still insisted that *The Recluse* was the chief object upon which his thoughts were fixed, he turned again to the poem on his own life. No longer was it to be in

2 A

reality a mere 'prelude.' In all essentials it was to describe the whole course of his poetic life to the highest point which he had reached.

Through the autumn of 1804 and the early months of 1805 he worked steadily on, and in May the end was in sight. Early in that month he wrote to Sir George, 'It is not self-conceit, as you know well, that has induced me to do this, but real humility. I began the work because I was unprepared to treat any more arduous subject, and diffident of my own powers. Here, at least, I hoped that to a certain degree I should be sure of succeeding, as I had nothing to do but describe what I had felt and thought; therefore could not easily be bewildered.'

He still in fact felt apologetic about his great poem. It was still a task to be finished as soon as possible, so that he could fall to his 'principal work.' His genius compelled him to this protracted task of self-contemplation, but he was a little ashamed of the self-absorption which it involved. And when he finished it a fortnight later, he suffered the inevitable reaction. 'I had looked forward to the day,' he wrote to Sir George, 'as a most happy one; and I was indeed grateful to God for giving me life to complete the work, such as it is. But it was not a happy day for me; I was dejected on many accounts: when I looked back upon the performance it seemed to me to have a dead weight about it—the reality so far short of the expectation. It was the first long labour that I had finished; and the doubt whether I should ever live to write *The Recluse*, and the sense which I had of this poem being so far below what I seemed capable of executing, depressed me much. . . . This work may be considered as a sort of *portico* to *The Recluse*, part of the same building, which I hope to be able, ere long, to begin with in earnest; and if I am permitted to bring to a conclusion, and to write, further a narrative poem of the epic kind, I shall consider the task of my life as over.'

He still hoped, therefore, to realise the ambitious plan which

Coleridge had encouraged him to project. But, in fact, the task of his life, so far as it was one of vital poetry, was already nearly over. *The Prelude* was the fine fruit and eternal justification of his self-engrossment. But to be tied to a self which was rapidly becoming narrower in its sympathies and withdrawn from life by its fears and prejudices, was hardly favourable to the creation of a great philosophical poem.

And when he returned to *The Recluse* a month later he made but slow progress. Coleridge had assured him that he was destined to write the philosophical poem of the century, but apart from the philosophy which he had wrung from his personal history, he had little to give except the 'good views' of worthy Sir George. He could only hope that Coleridge, who had a genius for philosophy, might supply his deficiencies. 'Should Coleridge return,' he wrote to Sir George in August, 'so that I might have some conversation with him on the subject, I should go on swimmingly.'

Alas! Coleridge, in Malta, was in the depths of despair, and when a year later he struggled back to England he was in no condition to renew Wordsworth's waning powers.

And so the philosophical poem, to which Wordsworth was to devote the prime of his life and the chief force of his mind, was to hang heavily on his hands, like a depreciating investment, for nine years, and little more of it was written until after 1810. He had in fact almost exhausted the vital resources of his past in writing *The Prelude*. And he had ceased as a poet to invest anything in the future.

PART XI

THE TIME OF TRIAL

§ I

WORDSWORTH had written in his great poem of

> The time of trial, ere we learn to live
> In reconcilement with our stinted powers,

but in its concluding passages he had proclaimed with a noble fervour that that time was passed, that the years which had taken something away had given more in return and that his real powers, far from being stinted, were being fulfilled in a rich maturity. 'Oh, who is he,' he had cried

> that hath his whole life long
> Preserved, enlarged, this freedom in himself?
> For this alone is genuine Liberty:
> Witness, ye Solitudes! where I received
> My earliest visitations, careless then
> Of what was given me, and where now I roam,
> A meditative, oft a suffering Man,
> And yet, I trust, with undiminish'd powers,
> Witness, whatever falls my better mind,
> Revolving with the accidents of life,
> May have sustain'd, that, howsoe'er misled,
> I never, in the quest of right and wrong,
> Did tamper with myself from private aims;
> Nor was in any of my hopes the dupe
> Of selfish passions; nor did wilfully
> Yield ever to mean cares and low pursuits;
> But rather did with jealousy shrink back
> From every combination that might aid
> The tendency, too potent in itself,

> Of habit to enslave the mind, I mean
> Oppress it by the laws of vulgar sense,
> And substitute a universe of death,
> The falsest of all worlds, in place of that
> Which is divine and true. To fear and love,
> To love as first and chief, for there fear ends,
> Be this ascribed; to early intercourse
> In presence of sublime and lovely forms,
> With the adverse principles of pain and joy,
> Evil as one is rashly named by those
> Who know not what they say. By love, for here
> Do we begin and end, all grandeur comes,
> All truth and beauty, from pervading love,
> That gone, we are as dust.

In these lines he reached the goal of those wanderings 'to eternal truth' of which *The Prelude* was so singularly honest and searching a record. Yet although his whole life, as we have read it, justified his claim to have preserved his independence, his conviction that he had never pursued a private aim or been the dupe of selfish passion revealed a certain blind-spot in his self-knowledge, if not, indeed, a defensive self-complacence. In a later version of the lines he did, in fact, confess to

> lapse and hesitating choice,
> And backward wanderings along thorny ways;

but he still insisted that he had never disobeyed his conscience. And this was doubtless true. Yet a laudable superiority to 'mean cares and low pursuits' may not be innocent of private aims.

But it was in his celebration of 'fear and love' that he touched the heart of his problem. And although he proclaimed love so truly and eloquently as the source of all truth and the solvent of all fear, the lines which follow in which he

examined the nature of this love and its workings both in the
Universe and in the creative activity of the poet, revealed the
characteristic limits of his conception. He found love's earliest
manifestation in the heart· that went out to the 'fields, in
balmy spring-time, full of rising flowers,' and to the tender
ways of the lamb and its mother. And linked with this love,
but of a higher order, was the love which proceeded

> More from the brooding Soul, and is divine.
> This love more intellectual cannot be
> Without Imagination, which, in truth,
> Is but another name for absolute strength
> And clearest insight, amplitude of mind,
> And reason in her most exalted mood.
> This faculty hath been the moving soul
> Of our long labour: . . .
> Imagination having been our theme,
> So also hath that intellectual love,
> For they are each in each, and cannot stand
> Dividually.—Here must thou be, O Man!
> Strength to thyself; no Helper hast thou here;
> Here keepest thou thy individual state:
> No other can divide with thee this work,
> No secondary hand can intervene
> To fashion this ability; 'tis thine,
> The prime and vital principle is thine
> In the recesses of thy nature, far
> From any reach of outward fellowship,
> Else is not thine at all. But joy to him,
> Oh, joy to him who here hath sown, hath laid
> Here the foundations of his future years!

This then was the love by which Wordsworth hoped henceforth
to live as a poet and a man, and of which he could write that

> he whose soul hath risen
> Up to the height of feeling intellect
> Shall want no humbler tenderness.

In this love he believed that he had truly adjusted the two impulses of love and fear, faith and prudence, of which his adult life had been the battle-ground.

We need not retrace the pattern of his growth as he had drawn it through the thirteen books of his poem. For that has already been done in the course of this narrative. It is enough to say that within the conceptual framework of Hartley's 'three ages' he had described the gradual encroachment of thought and self-consciousness upon the unconscious life of feeling, the crisis of dislocation which threatened death, and the gradual return to life through a true co-ordination of reason and selfhood with the basic commands of natural feeling. This co-ordination he had proclaimed as his in the *Lines Composed Above Tintern Abbey*, but in the passage which we have just quoted he defined it more precisely than ever before. In the 'intellectual love' which he here described as the crown and blessing of maturity man came, he claimed, to completion. Reason which had in turn transformed the sensation of childhood into the feeling of youth and then for a season falsely denied the vital feeling out of which it grew, was now truly incorporated in 'feeling intellect.'

But beneath this 'feeling intellect' and sustaining it was the sensation from which feeling and thought had progressively derived. He did not, however, call it now 'sensation,' but 'imagination.' It was the faculty which had been the 'moving soul' both of childhood and youth, but which only became wholly expressive in the mind of man, in 'reason in her most exalted mood.' For man was the centre of the Universe and his mind was the culminating point of that 'something' which rolled 'through all things.'

In many splendid and moving passages of his poem Wordsworth had recorded his experiences of that 'something.' In
his early years he had felt it simply as an elemental sensation,
but later, and when he looked back upon such moments of
strange possession and usurpation as that which occurred on
his crossing the Alps, it had seemed a Power which overrode
the ordinary channels of sense, which, infinite in itself,
quickened directly what was infinite in the individual and
revealed an 'invisible world,' where greatness made abode.

And finally, as his own reason had developed, Nature
appeared to him as

> The perfect image of a Mighty Mind,
> Of one that feeds upon infinity,
> That is exalted by an underpresence,
> The sense of God, or whatsoe'er is dim
> Or vast in its own being.

And this Mighty Mind imaging itself so powerfully in Nature
was

> the express
> Resemblance, in the fulness of its strength
> Made visible, a genuine Counterpart
> And Brother of the glorious faculty
> Which higher minds bear with them as their own
> That is the very spirit in which they deal
> With all the objects of the universe;
> They from their native selves can send abroad
> Like transformations, for themselves create
> A like existence, and, whene'er it is
> Created for them, catch it by an instinct;
> Them the enduring and the transient both
> Serve to exalt; they build up greatest things
> From least suggestions, ever on the watch,

Willing to work and to be wrought upon . . .
Such minds are truly from the Deity,
For they are Powers; and hence the highest bliss
That can be known is theirs, the consciousness
Of whom they are habitually infused
Through every image, and through every thought,
And all impressions. . . .

Here, if anywhere, we have the culmination of Wordsworth's experience, and the most confident affirmation of his creed. Happiness, he insisted, was assured to the man

> that hath his whole life long
Preserved, enlarged, this freedom in himself.
For this alone is genuine Liberty.

And, as he wrote, calling the mountain Solitudes, in which he had been reared, to witness, he believed that through good fortune and native perseverance he had preserved and enlarged this freedom in himself, and that, therefore, all the consequent blessings which he had assumed, the unquenchable vitality, the sovereignty within and peace at will, the feeling devoid of fear, the truth in moral judgments and unfailing delight in the external universe, must be indefinitely his.

Was it then due to some flaw in his creed or in himself that this happy prospect was not to be realised? Few would deny the truth of his claim that the Power which animated the forms of Nature was 'the prime and vital principle' of all creation. But although it was centred in the recesses of the individual's being, could it be truly realised by 'higher minds' so intent on preserving their 'individual state'? And if the Creative Spirit, which he called 'Infinity and God' evolved in man the intellect as a special function of Itself, did the 'Intellectual Love' which he conceived as its highest human expression bear any true resemblance to the Love which in a ceaseless outpouring of itself sustained and replenished the life and the forms of Nature?

Although, in fact, the last two books of *The Prelude* may convince the reader at first that Wordsworth had at last truly reconciled the life of instinct and of thought, of Nature and of Man, it becomes clear on a closer examination that he had not, and that his conception equally of the creative process in Nature and in the poet was prejudiced by his imperfect realisation in his own being of the creative demands of life. Upon the mysterious and intangible 'something,' which he had sensed instinctively as a child and a boy, he had imposed the features of his own divided manhood.

The 'Mighty Mind' of which Nature was the perfect image, feeding upon an infinity in itself, upon the '*sense* of God,' was a magnified replica of his own 'higher mind' feeding on the infinity of his own sensations. God Himself, in short, was governed by Hartley's laws of association. In Him, too, on a cosmic level 'continued influxes of feeling' were 'modified and directed by thoughts, which were the representatives of all past feelings.' And far from Imagination being the 'esemplastic' faculty which Coleridge was to name it, the creative principle which moulded all the elements of life into one, it remained merely the sensational source of all life, a dim, vast reservoir of primal energy from which the Deity and himself equally replenished their consciousness.

This was, indeed, a more profound conception of Imagination than that which Wordsworth had advanced in the preface to *Lyrical Ballads*. But the two conceptions were essentially kindred. And both reflected the dualism in himself. Those who have really humbled themselves to reality have discovered in God not a 'Mighty Mind' feeding upon sensations, but a creative Spirit that for ever in a divine ecstasy goes out from and returns upon Itself, eternally self-sufficient, yet eternally self-transcendent, intimately personal, yet infinitely impersonal, a Spirit at once of pure intelligence and of pure creation. And in the expression of this Spirit both in natural and human life they have known a love of a different order from the 'intellectual love' which Wordsworth conceived as its highest attribute.

The essence of this Spirit lies in its unity. And Nature is its 'perfect image' because on her own unconscious level she expresses its wholeness. 'All things,' in the words of a Chinese sage, 'are the imagination of the Universal Soul.' And the poet's imagination is 'truly from the Deity,' so far as it reflects this unity of Spirit, which resolves the conflict of thought and feeling in the creative harmony of pure being.

Wordsworth had expressed this harmony in different degrees in his poetry and he had had glimpses of it in his most ecstatic moments. But these had been abnormal moments either of sensational possession or of intense and trancelike self-absorption, of which we shall have more to say when we consider the *Intimation* Ode.

And so, although he wrote that 'intellectual love' and 'imagination' could not 'stand dividually,' he had not truly reconciled them. For to do so it was necessary that even 'higher minds' should become as submissive to the Creative Spirit as the instincts had been in childhood; it was necessary that Imagination should take up into itself the lower faculties of sense instead of being reduced to a sensational 'something' which the intellect exploited.

Wordsworth's conception, therefore, of the correspondence between the life of Nature and of the poet, with which *The Prelude* culminated, was a subtle perversion of that unified act of eternal self-expression and self-contemplation which the true mystic has divined in the mystery of Creation. And although so sublimely expressed a conception may well have filled him with a sense of exaltation as he wrote, his assurance that all was well with him was ill-grounded. Certainly he was enough of a mystic to know that the grandeur of human life consisted in something more than the ability of lofty minds to display its grandeur. He knew that love was the beginning and the end. He had risen from the plane of sensation to that of feeling, and from feeling 'up to the height of feeling intellect.' But the 'Love that moves the sun and the other stars' is of a purer and simpler order than 'feeling intellect.'

Once again the 'three ages' of Hartley, which Wordsworth had adopted as his own, fatally curtailed the possibilities of imaginative growth. To divide human life into such ages was, indeed, no new idea, although it was to be particularly characteristic of Wordsworth's time. Lessing, Comte and Fichte, Schelling and Hegel, all concerned themselves with the Ages of Humanity and its progressive self-realisation. But centuries before, Joachim of Flora had developed his mystical theory of the three world Ages of the Father, the Son and the Holy Spirit, and the German idealists who conceived of human life as passing through the Ages of Faith and Reason were but elaborating his idea without, however, truly realising, through an excess of abstract intellectualism, the nature of the third age of spiritual freedom and wholeness in which human life should culminate.

And the weakness of Hartley, to whose philosophy Wordsworth was now irretrievably bound, was his far more pronounced failure to conceive truly a third age, which represented something more than a precarious balance between unconscious instinct and active reason.

The greatness of *The Prelude* as a poem and as a magnificent piece of self-exploration was in no way prejudiced by this fact. For it was a true and vivid record of the growth of a poet's mind and being up to a certain point. But the poet who thought to find in 'intellectual love' sustained by infinite

sensations the firm 'foundations of his future years' had little
reason to proclaim the assured perpetuation of his joy.

<h2 style="text-align:center">§ 2</h2>

Three months, however, before he completed *The Prelude*
in 1805, an event occurred which more than any other put
Wordsworth's philosophy to the test.

During 1804 nothing had happened to ruffle the calm
surface of his domestic life except the birth of a daughter in
August, an event which he and Dorothy once again celebrated
by a walking tour. But this time they went no further than
Ennerdale and Wasdale. He found time, however, during this
year to compose one or two of his best lyrics, in which, as in
The Prelude, he was renewing before it was too late the inspiration of an earlier day.

And in several of them he betrayed the anxiety lest the
power to live and enjoy was already slipping from him. He
watched a kitten sporting with some fallen leaves to the
delight of his infant daughter and the spectacle quickened his
resolve to preserve his capacity for such thoughtless transport
against the encroaching years —

> And I will have my careless season
> Spite of melancholy reason,
> Will walk through life in such a way
> That, when time brings on decay,
> Now and then I may possess
> Hours of perfect gladsomeness.

But the threat of 'Life's falling leaf' was not always so easily
or light-heartedly defied. And in *The Small Celandine* he
revealed very movingly that stoical resignation into which his
earlier faith in a 'wise passiveness' was beginning to decline.

He too, like the flower, had in past years shrunk from cold and rain and then renewed his joy and opened himself to life when the sun of happier circumstances came out again. He, too, had survived the days of disillusionment by being

> muffled up from harm
> In close self-shelter, like a Thing at rest.

But the Celandine could not always thus withdraw. There came a time when in its decay it stood exposed to the blast.

> I stopped, and said with inly-muttered voice,
> 'It doth not love the shower, nor seek the cold:
> This neither is its courage nor its choice,
> But its necessity in being old.
>
> 'The sunshine may not cheer it, nor the dew;
> It cannot help itself in its decay;
> Stiff in its members, withered, changed of hue.'
> And in my spleen, I smiled that it was grey.
>
> To be a Prodigal's Favourite—then, worse truth,
> A Miser's Pensioner—behold our lot!
> O Man, that from thy fair and shining youth
> Age might but take the things Youth needed not.

The fear that the self-defence which he had practised so successfully hitherto was powerless against withering age, was in these lines. He, too, had been in youth a 'Prodigal's Favourite.' Life had been lavish with him. But was he not already becoming a Pensioner, drawing upon a dwindling account?

Earlier in the year, however, he was less troubled by autumnal thoughts and in two of his loveliest lyrics he distilled some of the essence of his past experience. In *I wandered Lonely as a Cloud* it was the daffodils which he had seen with Dorothy two years before and which had often 'in vacant and in pensive mood' flashed

> upon that inward eye
> Which is the bliss of solitude,

that he remembered. *She was a Phantom of Delight* was on the surface connected with a more recent experience. For its germ was, on his own confession, four lines from the poem on the Highland Girl composed on the tour in Scotland. And probably the lines were these —

> But, O fair Creature! in the light
> Of common day, so heavenly bright,
> I bless Thee, Vision as thou art,
> I bless thee with a human heart.

For *She was a Phantom* developed inevitably from these lines. In it he expressed with a more reasoned concentration that blending in a woman's being of the angelic and the actual, of heavenly innocence and home-bred sense, which he perceived in the Highland Girl.

To argue, therefore, whether or not the lines were inspired by his wife is quite irrelevant. Doubtless he had her in mind when he wrote of

> A Creature not too bright or good
> For human nature's daily food.

But the woman who inspired the poem was the ideal woman of his dreams, substantiated by the women of his actual experience. There were elements of Annette in her and of

Dorothy, of the Highland Girl and of his wife. And in this woman he embodied his dream of life, of a perfect unfoldment of spirit in matter and a perfect expression of it in character. For in her the vision splendid did not fade into the light of common day but only assumed a more palpable form and substance. The 'lovely Apparition' clothed itself in a body. The 'dancing shape,' the 'Image gay' became a woman moving light and free about her household tasks. And then as experience began to inform innocence and the breath of her being became more charged with thought, her character developed with the same necessary grace as her body,

> The reason firm, the temperate will,
> Endurance, foresight, strength, and skill.

But there was no dimming of the original light within her. Finely moulded and tempered by experience she remained in her maturity as in her maidenhood

> a Spirit still, and bright
> With something of angelic light.

In this lyric, therefore, Wordsworth imaged the same organic growth of being through three stages which he was demonstrating as his own at such length in *The Prelude*. And it was probably while his thoughts and feelings were carried back once again, in writing *The Prelude*, to Annette, that he composed the two lyrics, entitled *The Affliction of Margaret* and *The Forsaken*, in both of which he expressed again the grief of a deserted woman. But if he betrayed the fact that the old wound could still pain him in the lines —

> Heaven grants even to the guiltiest mind
> An amnesty for what is past;
> When will my sentence be reversed?

he received early in 1805 a new wound which temporarily at least brought forgetfulness of the old.

On the night of 5th February his brother John was drowned when his ship, the *Abergavenny*, went down off Weymouth. It was almost as shattering a blow to Wordsworth as if Dorothy had been taken from him. On the day when the news arrived he wrote to Sir George — 'I can say nothing higher of my ever-dear brother than that he was worthy of his sister who is now weeping beside me, and of the friendship of Coleridge — meek, affectionate, silently enthusiastic, loving all quiet things, and a poet in everything but words!'

Alone of his brothers, John had encouraged him to persist as a poet, when it seemed least justified. He had helped, too, materially. 'He would work for me,' wrote Wordsworth '(that was his language) — for me and his sister; and I was to endeavour to do something for the world . . . and I shall never forget him, never lose sight of him. There is a bond between us yet, the same as if he were living — nay, far more sacred — calling upon me to do my utmost, as he to the last did his utmost, to live in honour and worthiness.'

The very tenacity of Wordsworth's affections exposed him to the full force of such a blow, and his own naturalistic faith and philosophy which was rooted in earth and subjected man, even at his highest stage of development, to physical law, involved also the assumption of the finality of physical death.

He may not, indeed, have previously realised that his creed of nature and Hartley's philosophy inevitably implied this. For he had been too absorbed in the problems of life to ponder seriously the problem of death, and had been content merely to profess no strong belief in human survival. But now death had struck home, and the thought that a sentient being, so noble and so lovable as his brother, should be annulled, like any leaf that a chance wind tossed into a ditch, was intolerable.

'A thousand times,' he wrote to Sir George, 'have I asked myself "Why was he taken away?" And I have answered the question as you have done. In fact, there is no other answer which can satisfy and lay the mind at rest. Why have we a choice and a will, and a notion of justice and injustice, enabling us to be moral agents? Why have we sympathies that make the best of us so afraid of inflicting pain and sorrow, which yet we see dealt about so lavishly by the Supreme Governor? Why should our notions of right towards each other, and to all sentient beings within our influence, differ so widely from what appears to be His notion and rule, if everything were to end here? Would it not be blasphemy to say that, upon the supposition of the thinking principle being destroyed by death, however inferior we may be to the Great Cause and Ruler of things, we have more of love in our nature than He has? The thought is monstrous; and yet how to get rid of it, except upon the supposition of another and a better world, I do not see.'

How deeply Wordsworth was moved and shocked by his brother's death is clearly shown by this letter. Although it might be that so long as a man lived, 'Nature never did betray the heart that loved her,' she could apparently hurry the fondest and most loyal of her children to their death without the least concern. Like countless men before and after him Wordsworth's human sensibility was outraged by the callousness of physical forces. But his reaction was typically limited. He first protested, and then he sought to console himself for his hurt and his loss by fancying 'another and a better world' in which such cruel chances could not happen and all that was lost could be found again.

This other and better world was for him a supposition, not a conviction. It was the world in which good Churchmen like Sir George believed. Previously Wordsworth had not believed in it. The world of Nature sufficed him. And in truth he did not believe in it now. For such a world can only become real to a man who has experienced it, and knows that it exists independently of the bodily senses. In his most exalted moments, when the light of sense went out, Wordsworth had glimpsed this reality in ecstatic, if uneasy, flashes. But scarcely had the Sun of the Infinite broken through, before the clouds of his finite being closed again. He still hungered for the Sun, but the clouds were growing thicker, and the illumination of such abnormal moments could not prevail against the pressure of his normal experience.

Consequently the 'other and better world' which he postulated to supply the deficiencies of the Natural world in which he lived was no more than an anxious assumption. The Church assured him that it existed and so he was inevitably drawn towards the Church. But it was a quite unreal world to him.

When six years before in Germany the thought of death had oppressed him, he had nevertheless felt it as a great liberator of man from his vexed individuality, as a dark gate through which he returned to unity with the primal spirit that rolled through all things. And although there was more of dying into nature in his conception of it than of being reborn in the spirit, he did then experience and express something of the true mystery of death. For since the meaning of death can only be apprehended by dying to the personal self, even the man who abandons himself to the elemental in Nature can realise something of life's deathless essence.

Wordsworth had so abandoned himself when he wrote *A Slumber did my Spirit seal*, but although at this time he could confess that suffering 'has the nature of infinity' he could not, in suffering his brother's death, sufficiently renounce his own instinctive claims on life to discover any new and real meaning in it. The ingenuous desire for merely personal happiness typical of the child and the childlike man was too deeply grounded in him. Nature had so richly gratified him in the past that he wished to preserve as long as he could the life which he derived from her against the creeping or the sudden death that she indifferently decreed. And he sought to evade the grim fact of death, which ultimately rendered such a philosophy of life inadequate and which shocked his humanity, by taking refuge in the 'other and better world' of conventional piety, which was altogether separated from the order of Nature and so had no roots in his real experience.

This false separation of the natural and the supernatural reflected the division in himself, but it was also approved by organised religion, which had fallen into the very dualism that its Founder came to disprove. The Church, too, directed men's gaze to a Kingdom of Heaven hereafter because it had become too spiritually sluggish to believe that the Kingdom might be realised on earth within the heart of every man who had the strength and humility to bring his true self to birth and live his life from a new centre. It, too, by transferring the possibilities of perfection to an unreal 'better world' of the future separated the natural world from its true source in the supernatural.

Inevitably, therefore, although in defiance of his deepest and most compelling experiences, Wordsworth began to approve its teaching. For it justified his inability to change himself and his consequent abandonment of his earlier belief in the perfectibility of man. That belief in its earlier form had undoubtedly been emotional and credulous, but so far as it entailed recognition of the truth that man is essentially a spiritual being born into a natural body, who can, therefore, while still in that body, realise his true nature, it was of all beliefs the most vitalising. And by abandoning it Wordsworth had tied himself not only to the conventional creed of a Churchman and a Tory, but to a 'universe of death.'

Yet how fertilising sorrow and suffering can be even if it is only partially accepted, was clearly shown by the immediate effect upon him of his brother's death. We have already quoted from the letter that he wrote to Southey at the time, in which he deplored the waste and destruction apparent in a world that could show, too, so many triumphs of disinterested love. And after the first shock had passed, and he had ceased to be too numbed by grief to continue his writing, his creative powers were strikingly renewed. His heart was softened, his pride humbled alike by the mystery of death and by the remembrance of his brother's unassuming selflessness. And it is a significant fact that the concluding books of *The Prelude*, in which he testified so eloquently to love and the heart's tenderness, were composed during the next three months.

But a number of shorter poems, written during the summer and autumn, were the direct fruit of this sorrow, as in some measure was the *Intimation* Ode which he completed in the following year. This tragic death of one dear to him enriched, indeed, if it did not generate, his last period of vital activity as a poet.

And he himself would seem to have felt at first that the event had changed his being. For in the *Elegiac Stanzas Suggested by a Picture of Peele Castle in a Storm* he contrasted his early indolent dreams of life, as an Elysium 'without toil or strife' with his experience of it now.

> So once it would have been—'tis so no more;
> I have submitted to a new control:
> A power is gone, which nothing can restore;
> A deep distress hath humanised my soul.
>
> Not for a moment could I now behold
> A smiling sea, and be what I have been:
> The feeling of my loss will ne'er be old;
> This, which I know, I speak with mind serene. . . .

> Farewell, farewell the heart that lives alone,
> Housed in a dream, at distance from the Kind!
> Such happiness, wherever it be known,
> Is to be pitied; for 'tis surely blind.
>
> But welcome fortitude, and patient cheer,
> And frequent sights of what is to be borne!
> Such sights, or worse, as are before me here.—
> Not without hope we suffer and we mourn.

He had of course expressed the same conversion from self-engrossed pleasure to sympathetic understanding in the *Lines Composed Above Tintern Abbey*. And those lines, too, were written at a time when pain and self-contrition were humanising his soul. But in the intervening years good fortune had fortified his self-assurance and in the process weakened his sympathies.

Temporarily, however, the death of his brother arrested the process. He submitted to a new control, which was in fact the old control of life overruling his stubborn individualism and compelling him to identify himself with humanity. Yet although he could assert in these lines that his submission was complete, the last stanza betrays the fact that the mystic in him had not swallowed up the stoic, and that he had not really learnt the secret of that ultimate acceptance in which even the pain of life is known to be necessary and right. And in the *Elegiac Verses In Memory of My Brother* the Stoic spoke more clearly, bidding him,

> With calmness suffer and believe,
> And grieve, and know that I must grieve,
> Not cheerless, though forlorn.

But it was in the *Ode to Duty* that he revealed most clearly how he hesitated between the pure affirmation of love and a prudent dependence upon morality.

Certainly the 'Stern Daughter of the Voice of God' whom he invoked in the first line was something far more real than the standards of any conventional moral code. Duty was not only 'a rod to check the erring,' but 'a light to guide,' not only a law and a surety against temptation, but a 'victory' of the higher self.

Yet his conception of duty had a markedly negative side to it and it is just in this negative emphasis that the moralist differs from the mystic. For the true mystic duty consists in obedience to the creative will of life. Such obedience involves of course a conditioning of the self to reflect truly the creative will. But the mystic knows that he can only express the creative will truly by purging himself of every negative thought or impulse. His self-discipline, therefore, is always positive. In it his will is directed towards a more perfect self-surrender and self-fulfilment in the Whole.

Wordsworth, however, as the subsequent stanzas of this Ode show, felt the need of such pure surrender, but for want of faith wished also to safeguard himself. In the second and third stanzas he wrote with wistful appreciation of those who, untroubled by any thought of duty, obeyed the inspiration of life,

> who, in love and truth,
> Where no misgiving is, rely
> Upon the genial sense of youth:
> Glad Hearts! without reproach or blot
> Who do thy work, and know it not.

And although he admitted that the confidence even of these might be misplaced, he could imagine a time when the inspiration of love and joy would be sufficient.

But that time was not yet, and he defined the compromise
which he hoped to achieve himself when he wrote that

> they a blissful course may hold
> Even now, who, *not unwisely bold,*
> Live in the spirit of this creed;
> Yet seek thy firm support, according to their need.

And as the Ode advanced the conflict in his being between
faith in life and the warnings of experience became more
apparent. He wished to affirm life as the innocent did and to
obey its inspiration. But alas! love had not proved for him 'an
unerring light' nor 'joy its own security.'

> I, loving freedom, and untried;
> No sport of every random gust,
> Yet being to myself a guide,
> *Too blindly have reposed my trust.*

It was the old canker at his heart, the ghost of his Youth's
reckless self-abandonment that he could not lay and which
blocked his path to creative maturity. He had paid in suffering
for the joy of love, and not only in his passion for Annette but
even in his affection for his brother. Love was dangerous. It
exposed those who surrendered to its power equally to the
wilful impulses of their own nature and the cruel chances of
life. And so he fell back upon Duty. He craved the control of
an unalterable moral law.

> Me this unchartered freedom tires;
> I feel the weight of chance-desires:
> My hopes no more must change their name,
> I long for a repose that ever is the same.

He tried, indeed, to reconcile his conception of Duty as a

stern Lawgiver' with the joyous creative power of life, 'the Godhead's most benignant grace.'

> Flowers laugh before thee on their beds
> And fragrance in thy footing treads;
> Thou dost preserve the stars from wrong;
> And the most ancient heavens through Thee are
>   fresh and strong.

But he had not really reconciled the moral and the creative impulses in himself. The one sprang from his fear of life, the other from his love of it. And his love of life was still the instinctive appetite of his youth. He was still at the mercy of physical nature, and it was because he felt and feared this that he commended himself to the 'awful Power' of Duty, 'sent from God,' as he wrote in an early version of the poem,

> To enforce on earth his high behest,
> And keep us faithful to the road
> Which Conscience hath pronounc'd the best.

Yet how close he was to a disinterested conception of Conscience and to accepting its creative guidance is revealed in the concluding lines of the Ode —

> Oh, let my weakness have an end!
> Give unto me, made lowly-wise,
> The spirit of self-sacrifice;
> The confidence of reason give;
> And in the light of truth thy Bondman let me live!

The words tremble on the edge of ultimate truth. We are almost convinced by them that the death of his brother had loosed the chains which held him back from that dying to the self and rebirth into new life which Keats was to image in *The Fall of Hyperion*. Yet we have only to compare the two poems to know that Wordsworth had not crossed the gulf between a self-conscious and a real dedication of the whole being to life as Keats had done. Both, indeed, approve the beauty and the inspiration of innocence, of those who, in Keats' words,

> seek no wonder but the human face,
> No music but a happy-noted voice.

But Keats knows that for those who have lost their innocence, it is not enough to preserve as much of 'the genial sense of youth' as possible within the limits of prudent experience.

And that in essence was all that Wordsworth could bring himself to do. The 'Stern Lawgiver' to whom he commended himself for guidance embodied his own dual nature, the elemental power in life upon which he still drew in his creative moments and the negative force of fear which was gradually transforming him into a self-regarding moralist. Duty for him had, indeed, still a cosmic significance, but it was only a short step from bondage to it to conformity to a conventional and reactionary code.

Yet there was one more poem inspired by memories of his brother in which he came somewhat nearer perhaps reconciling reason and conscience with fidelity to life. In the *Character of the Happy Warrior* he embodied his ideal of sensitive and sagacious manhood. In writing this he drew equally upon the ardour of his youth and the circumspection that the years had brought. For it was a tribute to Beaupuy as well as to his brother John, and it expressed that vital balance between natural impulse and rational self-control, which he himself was to find it impossible to preserve. For although the 'Happy Warrior' was one 'whose law is reason,' he was, too,

> the generous Spirit, who, when brought
> Among the tasks of real life, hath wrought
> Upon the plan that pleased his boyish thought:

Whose high endeavours are an inward light
That makes the path before him always bright.

The self-dedication was in fact by no means complete. For
the 'Happy Warrior' of Wordsworth's conception, although
he strove daily to surpass himself and sought on earth only
the rewards of an easy conscience, drew

His breath in confidence of Heaven's applause.

Yet Wordsworth went as far in this poem as it was in his
nature to go towards harmonising the inspiration of youth
and the rationality of age, the 'sudden brightness' that attired
the selfless lover of mankind and the self-command of the
active and discriminating moralist. As a boy he had wanted
to be a soldier; as a youth he had dedicated himself to poetry.
And in the 'Happy Warrior' he blended the two impulses,
earnestly desiring that he too should keep faithful to them both
'with a singleness of aim.'

But when shortly after writing the *Character of the Happy
Warrior* he resumed and completed the *Intimation* Ode of which
he had composed the first three stanzas four years before, he
wrought, not upon the plan which pleased his boyish thought,
but upon the planless ecstasy of his childhood. And in the
light of those early magical recollections the compromise of
stoicism seemed indeed insufficient.

The poem as he had put it aside in 1802 ended with the question,

Where is it now, the glory and the dream?

He had tried to answer it again and again, to convince himself
that if that peculiar glory had faded, something even more
satisfying had taken its place. Yet he continued to be haunted
by a sense of declining capacity for joy. He had already
affirmed in *The Prelude* that all was well with him, that in his

imaginative maturity he was a living proof of the truth and
virtue of Hartley's philosophy. But still in his heart he felt
that he had lost something which was infinitely precious and
without which his life must be unfulfilled.

And so in completing the *Intimation* Ode he made what was
perhaps his last really compelling attempt to reason that fear
away. As in *The Prelude* he divided human life into the three
ages which he felt that he had experienced himself. But in
reconceiving his childhood and the celestial light which he
associated with it, his imagination penetrated further into the
mystery of man's primal being than it had done before. He
wrote the famous lines,

> Our birth is but a sleep and a forgetting:
> The Soul that rises with us, our life's Star,
>   Hath had elsewhere its setting,
>   And cometh from afar:
>   Not in entire forgetfulness,
>   And not in utter nakedness,
> But trailing clouds of glory do we come
>   From God, who is our home.

These lines did not mean that he had come to accept the
doctrine of reincarnation or even of a pre-existent state, although
we know that it appealed to Coleridge who had possibly discussed it with him. Probably, indeed, he could not have
defined what his belief was. He only knew that in his childhood there had been 'the glory and the freshness of a dream,'
and that Heaven had seemed then to lie about him. Now he
could only recollect that Heaven, and since his whole life, so far
as it was still creative, depended upon recollection, he attributed
the same condition to childhood. The child had glimpses of a
miraculous past as the ageing man of a miraculous childhood.

Moreover, as we have shown, he had recently argued the

necessity of 'another and a better world' hereafter, because the pantheism which had sufficed him before could not console him for his brother's death. And so he assumed a similar world behind the enchanted state of childhood. Behind it, too, surely, lay another and a better world and a 'God who is our home.' His recent acknowledgment of the necessity of individual survival after death was paralleled here by his assumption of individual pre-existence.

But the intimations of reality which he had experienced not only in early childhood but in such later moments of strange possession and illumination as he had recorded in *The Prelude* had not in fact brought with them any real conviction either of individual pre-existence or survival. It was only now, when he had begun to feel the need of such a belief, that he super-imposed a God and a Heaven upon the earth which he had previously accepted as all sufficient.

We need not, then, suppose from these four stanzas, inserted into the middle of the *Intimation* Ode, either that Wordsworth had come to believe in reincarnation, or that his attitude to Nature had undergone any real change. The youth, 'who daily further from the east must travel' still was 'Nature's Priest,' and it was to her that he owed 'the vision splendid,' even if behind her there lurked a conjectural God and heavenly home.

Yet Wordsworth did betray in these stanzas a new conflict of view concerning Nature. The Nature who granted 'the vision splendid' to the child and youth was directly contrasted with the Mother Earth who did all she could

> To make her Foster-child, her Inmate Man,
>   Forget the glories he hath known,
>   And that imperial palace whence he came.

Wordsworth had of course often before proclaimed his belief, based upon his own experience, in the child's inability to conceive of death. But he had associated it with the child's perfect at-onement with natural life. Certainly he had suggested that this identity was not one merely of physical instinct. It was the spirit of the child that was at one with the spirit of Nature. But in these stanzas he insisted that the spirit of Nature in its earthly workings was directly opposed to the unearthly spirit of the child. He confirmed, in fact, in the language of great poetry the doctrine of the Fall.

And doubtless one explanation of it was his new inclination to accept the tenets of the Established Church. But there was another and a deeper one, that of his own experience in those moments of which he wrote in his introduction to the Ode, that 'I was often unable to think of external things as having external existence.' And in the stanza which followed he gave immortal expression to that experience which in its various recurrences from childhood to manhood was the most strange and the most real which he had known, raising a song of thanks

> for those obstinate questionings
> Of sense and outward things,
> Fallings from us, vanishings;
> Blank misgivings of a creature
> Moving about in worlds, not realised,
> High instincts before which our mortal Nature
> Did tremble like a guilty Thing surprised.

In this experience we have the core of Wordsworth's imperfect mysticism. The sense of the numinous, belongs equally to the poetical and the religious genius. Every artist who breaks through the conventional ways of looking at things and unveils the reality within possesses it in some measure. He divines, if only in glimpses, the Eternal in and beyond the temporal and penetrating it.

But the experience which Wordsworth described here was

peculiar to himself. In these moments which at once thrilled and terrified him, the actual world was not revealed to him in its eternal reality. It was dissolved into nothingness. Only he himself remained real, floating in intense self-consciousness, over an immeasurable void. As he wrote in his Introduction, 'I communed with all that I saw as something not apart from, but inherent in my own immaterial nature,' or more simply in the words of his old age, 'I was sure of my own mind; everything else fell away and vanished into thought.' Hence the 'blank misgivings' which accompanied the experience and which he attributed to the abasement of his mortal Nature before a reality so much purer than itself.

And certainly all the great mystics have acknowledged this feeling of awe in their moments of intense illumination. But their awe has had no element in it of creature fear. And it is in this significant respect that their experience differs from Wordsworth's. Wordsworth was troubled by a sense of fear and guilt, not so much because he was abashed by a reality greater and purer than himself, but because he was cut off from any reality but himself.

For the true mystic, who really sees with the eye of spirit, the things of sense are transformed. He sees them as they subsist in essence and knows that the mortal aspect both of them and of himself is illusory. But far from being separated from the actual world, he is then only really at home in it, and he is sure not of his own mind, but of his own spirit and its union with the creative spirit in all things. Wordsworth, as a boy, had experienced something of this union in an elementary way, when in the early morning, sitting on the hillside, he had been caught up in a *holy calm* and seemed no longer to view a world outside himself with bodily eyes, but rather 'a dream, a prospect of the mind.' But, as he grew to manhood, the dream had less and less in it of 'holy calm,' and became more and more subjective. For that tenacious self-consciousness which we have traced through all his less intense experiences reached its extreme in these moments of introverted ecstasy.

Certainly he was possessed in them by spiritual forces which surged upwards from his subliminal self. His physical senses were consumed by a purifying fire, as in some ritual of atonement. But the purification remained incomplete because he clung mentally with all the force of his deep-rooted fear of self-surrender to his separate individuality. Consequently his mind was bedazzled and bewildered, but it was not truly illuminated, and the trance condition which he experienced was nearer to that of hysteria than of mystical vision.

Yet a similar condition has frequently preceded the attainment of true liberation, as the inner history of many mystics shows. They have called it 'the dark night of the soul' in which the ego is stripped naked and, aghast at its awful aloneness, is compelled to abandon the last of its selfish defences. And it is for this reason that it is of such importance in an understanding of Wordsworth's life. For in these moments, as he shuddered over an abyss of nothingness and felt at once denuded and invaded by some infinite Power, he approached as near as he ever did to the rebirth which might have renewed his genius. But while his physical being was dissolved and 'the light of sense' went out in flashes, his mind continued to resist, and to assert its own isolated identity. And so the perfect union with creative life remained unrealised.

Yet it was upon these experiences that he based in this Ode his belief in immortality and his new interpretation of childhood in agreement with the doctrine of the Fall. For he had known in such moments something which transcended utterly and alarmingly all temporal conditions and at the same time existed only in himself. Surely, therefore, the self was eternal. And because the 'mortal Nature' of the self trembled 'like a guilty thing surprised' before the high instincts of this eternal self, surely natural life was a prison-house that closed upon the heaven-born child. Surely those 'first affections' of his childhood which he had once attributed to the beneficence of Mother Nature were really 'shadowy recollections' of a purer and unearthly state. And so, surely, they were not dependent upon any earthly circumstance, or at the mercy of encroaching years or any physical decay. They were

> truths that wake
>   To perish never;
> Which neither listlessness, nor mad endeavour,
>   Nor Man nor Boy,
> Nor all that is at enmity with joy,
> Can utterly abolish or destroy!
>   Hence in a season of calm weather
>   Though inland far we be,
> Our Souls have sight of that immortal sea
>   Which brought us hither,
>   Can in a moment travel thither,
> And see the Children sport upon the shore,
> And hear the mighty waters rolling evermore.

Thus his intense longing to regain the joy and innocence of his childhood and the necessity which his brother's death had forced upon him of believing in 'another and a better world' were miraculously reconciled in this great Ode. But, they were not reconciled in himself. Indeed by thus accepting the orthodox view that the child was a blest but irretrievably fallen being, he had given up all hope of really becoming 'as a little child.' For although it was profoundly true that the radiance of childhood faded as self-consciousness encroached upon the unconscious play of instinct, the whole secret of the child's happiness lay in the fact that he was not a fallen being, that he did not live on memories of another state, but in an eternal 'now.'

2 C

That he was a Spirit come 'from God, who is our home' was true. But he was, also, perfectly at home in his natural being. And the problem facing the full-grown man was how to regain the unity of the spiritual and the natural, which the child enjoyed unconsciously, after self-consciousness had asserted itself and brought the inevitable division.

And he could not solve it by merely returning imaginatively in seasons of calm weather to an eternal holiday resort where Children sported upon the shore. For by thus seeking to recover a state which preceded the Fall, he did nothing to alter the fact of the Fall in himself.

Behind, therefore, the poignant beauty of this Ode, there was the same fundamental evasion which characterised all Wordsworth's attempts to convince himself that he had resolved his inner discord. And in adding a celestial home of origin to the natural Eden of childhood he had only extended the region of recollection in which he could take refuge, while to make that region more blissfully habitable by a full-grown man he had tended to ascribe to children powers of vision which they did not possess.

For although the child may be 'haunted by the eternal mind,' he is unconscious of the creative will which he obeys. He is not, therefore, except symbolically, a 'Mighty Prophet! Seer Blest!' In *The Prelude* Wordsworth had been content to see 'in simple childhood *something of the base*,' on which the greatness of Man stood. But his tribute to the child in this Ode went far beyond that, and although doubtless the words were not meant literally, they were those of one who found it increasingly easier to sentimentalise childhood than to grow into the perfect stature of a man.

Although, therefore, the two concluding stanzas of his Ode, with their triumphant summons to Birds and Lambs, Fountains, Meadows, Hills and Groves, to join in the song and dance of spring, rang convincingly enough, there was an

undertone in them of uneasiness and sadness, more marked
than in those other songs of lyrical affirmation which successive
springs in the past had called forth.

'In thought' he could join with them. But 'the radiance
which was once so bright' was dimmer. Yet if nothing could

> bring back the hour
> Of splendour in the grass, of glory in the flower

he insisted that he would not grieve, but

> rather find
> Strength in what remains behind;
> In the primal sympathy
> Which having been must ever be;
> In the soothing thoughts that spring
> Out of human suffering;
> In the faith that looks through death,
> In years that bring the philosophic mind.

It was an impressive list of substitutes for instinctive rapture.
But on examination they may well have seemed less convincing. For was it certain that 'the primal sympathy must
ever be,' since it, too, was an instinct? Was it either safe or
tolerable to regard human suffering as a source of 'soothing
thoughts'? Did he really possess a faith which looked through
death, as he had once possessed a faith in natural life? And
could 'the philosophic mind' coexist with the poetic genius?

In the concluding stanza, with a sublime forgetfulness of
the fatal gulf between earth and heaven which he had proclaimed earlier in the Ode, he swept his doubts aside. There
was no need to doubt or to forebode any severing of his love
for nature. In his heart of hearts he still felt her might, and
felt it more deeply and poignantly for the thought which had

seemed to divide him from her. Now surely it only enriched
their relationship —

> I love the Brooks which down their channels fret,
> Even more than when I tripped lightly as they;
> The innocent brightness of a new-born Day
> > Is lovely yet;
> The Clouds that gather round the setting sun
> Do take a sober colouring from an eye
> That hath kept watch o'er man's mortality;
> Another race hath been, and other palms are won,
> Thanks to the human heart by which we live,
> Thanks to its tenderness, its joys, and fears,
> To me the meanest flower that blows can give
> Thoughts that do often lie too deep for tears.

It was a magical song of victory, in which all that was deepest
and tenderest, gravest and gayest in his nature blended in an
exquisite harmony. But 'the philosophic mind' and the poetic
genius cannot be lastingly reconciled on such easy terms. And
the song of victory was but a second prelude to a long decline.

§ 3

The first three stanzas of the *Intimation* Ode had been
written four years before in the shadow of Coleridge's distress.
And 'the gladness of the May' in which it was concluded was
tempered by anxiety on his account. No letter had been
received from him for two and a half years, but it was known
that he had left Malta and had been at Naples and Rome. In
April Dorothy had written, 'We look forward to Coleridge's
return with fear and painful hope, but indeed I dare not look
to it. I think as little as I can of him. Oh, my dear friend, my
heart seems to be shut against worldly hope!'

Wordsworth had little hope for Coleridge himself. He had judged his weakness of character now only too well. But he still hoped to benefit from the visionary mind which went so exasperatingly with moral incapacity. The philosophic poem which was to be his masterpiece and the final justification of that growth to maturity which he had traced in *The Prelude* had still to be written. And Coleridge, surely, who had so ardently insisted upon his undertaking it, could help him to write it, if only by rekindling an inspiration and a self-confidence which were flagging. And so he waited through the summer of 1806, excusing himself for his inability to settle to any serious employment by the plea that 'the expectation of Coleridge not a little unhinges me.'

But although Coleridge reached Portsmouth in the middle of August, he neither sent word nor came himself. Rumours concerning him, however, were ominous. It was said that he was very ill and in miserable spirits, and the fact that he made no attempt to return to Keswick confirmed the supposition that he was as far from being reconciled to living with his wife as when he went away.

Yet Wordsworth needed his help so much that he even thought of leaving Dove Cottage and going anywhere to be near him. He could not believe that a relationship which had once been so miraculously fertile might not be renewed with equal benefit to them both. For although his own need was paramount, he still believed that he might give something in return, and Dorothy encouraged his belief by hoping 'everything from the effect of my brother's conversation upon Coleridge's mind.'

He himself, however, hoped everything from the effect of Coleridge's conversation upon his own mind and trusted only to do something in the way of overruling his friend's lamentable indecision. Yet he had little real hope even of this, writing to Sir George—'What shall I say of Coleridge? or what can I say? My dear friend, this is certain, that he is destined to be unhappy. . . . In fact, he dare not go home, he recoils so much from the thought of domesticating with Mrs. Coleridge, with whom, though on many accounts he much respects her, he is so miserable that he dare not encounter it. What a deplorable thing! I have written to him to say that if he does not come down immediately I must insist upon seeing him somewhere. . . . I believe, if anything good is to be done for him, it must be done by me.'

Coleridge had once admired the resolute will-power of his friend. And doubtless he still did. But if Wordsworth wrote to him in the tone which this letter suggests, it can have given him little comfort. He shrank from meeting the Wordsworths for obvious reasons. His last hopes of renovation had been invested in the Malta venture, and with them a hundred pounds from Wordsworth. It had proved a complete failure. He had derived no benefit from it in health. He was more than ever the slave of opium, and at the moment he felt himself to be spiritually bankrupt.

To reveal the fact to Wordsworth, whose views were becoming as respectable as Southey's, another of his creditors, was too painful to contemplate. There is little wonder that he hid himself in London. But Wordsworth's letter seems to have shocked him into action. And in November he announced that he was coming North. Wordsworth was then about to move to Coleorton, where he was to help Sir George in laying out an estate, but on his way there he learnt that Coleridge was at Penrith, which was as near as he could bring himself to approaching Keswick. Sara Hutchinson was sent to persuade him to come to Kendal, where Wordsworth, his wife, and Dorothy awaited him.

The messenger was well chosen and he consented. He reached an inn there about seven in the evening and sent for Wordsworth, who with his three companions at once went to him. They were prepared by many distressing meetings in the past to find him in great affliction of mind and body. But what they found exceeded their worst expectations. In Dorothy's words — 'Never, never did I feel such a shock as at first sight of him. We all felt exactly in the same way — as if he were different from what we had expected to see; almost as much as a person of whom we had thought much, and of whom we had formed an image in our own minds, without having any personal knowledge of him. . . .'

Doubtless Dorothy felt the change more intensely than her brother, but he, too, must have known in that moment that the concord between him and Coleridge upon which he had still counted, was in any vital sense at an end.

It was not only that, as Dorothy put it, 'the divine expression of his countenance was lost,' except now and then for a gleam, faint and transitory. For that might return. But he seemed as if he wished to withdraw himself from them, refusing any personal confidences and offering no inquiry about them or their common friends. And that had never happened before.

This recoil of Coleridge was inevitable. He knew that Wordsworth was sincerely concerned about him. But he knew, too, that Wordsworth was a just man and an upright, and that with his sympathy went an element of judgment. It could not be otherwise, but out of his own hopeless sense of self-abasement he recoiled morbidly from anything in the nature of an inquisition. Wordsworth's aim was to soothe him and then get him to apply himself to 'some grand object connected with permanent effects.' The intention was excellent, but Coleridge was in no state to benefit by it. Some degree of self-esteem, such as Wordsworth himself possessed, as he planned his philosophic poem, was necessary for the undertaking of grand objects connected with permanent effects.

And Coleridge had lost the little self-esteem which he ever possessed. He had given up the struggle with life and his own nature, and he shrank sensitively from anyone who sought to prevail upon him to renew the battle or reminded him of obligations which he wished to forget.

Wordsworth, in fact, with the best intentions, made demands which Coleridge had no power to meet. And he was not wholly disinterested in the demands which he made. Coleridge was a sick soul, sick even to death he felt at that time; and he craved in his weakness an unqualified sympathy such as Wordsworth could not give him. Wordsworth was firmly established within the pale of respectability, and he was an outcast. Between such there is a great gulf fixed. And Coleridge knew it. He could turn in his distress to Sara Hutchinson, because she was kind and uncritical as good women are. But in Wordsworth he felt the menace of that moral judgment the whispers of which in his own conscience he had to stifle if life was to be at all endurable.

And so he retired into himself, as he had never done before, not in positive unfriendliness, but behind a blank wall of misery and shame. And Wordsworth, who had counted so much upon a renewal of their intercourse, was deeply hurt and disappointed. 'There is a change,' he wrote,

> —and I am poor
> Your love hath been, not long ago,
> A fountain at my fond heart's door,
> Whose only business was to flow;
> And flow it did: not taking heed
> Of its own bounty, or my need.
>
> What happy moments did I count!
> Blest was I then all bliss above!
> Now, for that consecrated fount
> Of murmuring, sparkling, living love
> What have I? shall I dare to tell?
> A comfortless and hidden well.

> A well of love—it may be deep—
> I trust it is,—and never dry:
> What matter? if the waters sleep
> In silence and obscurity.
> —Such change, and at the very door
> Of my fond heart, hath made me poor.

Doubtless his heart had been fond towards Coleridge and still was in a great measure. Nevertheless the man who wrote this 'complaint' was more intent upon taking than giving; more concerned with his own loss than his friend's manifest distress. The withdrawing of Coleridge's outflowing love was so grievous because he needed it to replenish the shrinking springs of his own being.

Yet the fountain of Coleridge's generosity had not, in fact, ceased to flow. And two months later it poured forth in a final rhapsody of admiration. In December he had joined the Wordsworths at Coleorton, bringing with him his son Hartley. And there his spirits began to revive. He had been homeless for so long, that to be once again one of a household which cared for him was infinitely consoling. He was in love, too, with Sara Hutchinson in his mild and melting way. And there in January,

> eve following eve,
> Dear tranquil time, when the sweet sense of Home
> Is sweetest,

Wordsworth read aloud *The Prelude*, and as Coleridge listened, all that he had felt and shared with his friend and all that he had become himself returned upon him in a wave of joy and pain,

> Sense of past youth, and manhood come in vain;
> And all which I had culled in wood-walks wild,

> And all which patient toil had reared, and all,
> Commune with *thee* had opened out—but flowers
> Strewed on my corse, and borne upon my bier,
> In the same coffin, for the self-same grave!

But deeply moving as this personal confession was, it served only to heighten by contrast the tribute of admiration which he paid in the same poem to his friend, the friend whom he named here 'Friend of the wise! and Teacher of the Good!', as a 'great Bard in the choir of ever-enduring men, strong in thyself and powerful to give strength.'

It was the last gift of poetry and praise which he made to Wordsworth. Yet it was, also, an elegy upon what had been and could never be again. And the 'long sustained Song' which Coleridge named

> an orphic song indeed,
> A song divine of high and passionate thoughts,
> To their own music chanted,

was in a sense an elegy too. It too enshrined a 'sense of past youth and manhood,' not indeed come in vain, but halted in mid-career and already drawing upon its last reserves of poetic strength.

Wordsworth himself was dimly conscious of this, despite his exultant affirmation in the last book of the poem. Hence his eagerness to renew communion with the fertilising spirit of Coleridge. But these weeks at Coleorton shed only a sunset pathos upon the memory of their creative partnership. And there was to remain but an afterglow prolonged indeed, and with occasional radiations from the sun that had set, but becoming each year more colourless, as prosaic propriety extinguished what remained of the poetic ardour which Coleridge had fanned and fed.

PART XII

THE LAST RETREAT

WORDSWORTH had concluded his *Song at the Feast of Brougham Castle*, composed in 1807, with the lines —

Alas! the impassioned minstrel did not know
How, by Heaven's grace, this Clifford's heart was
    framed,
How he, long forced in humble walks to go,
Was softened into feeling, soothed, and tamed.

Love had he found in huts where poor men lie;
His daily teachers had been woods and rills,
The silence that is in the starry sky,
The sleep that is among the lonely hills.

In him the savage virtue of the Race,
Revenge, and all ferocious thoughts were dead:
Nor did he change; but kept in lofty place
The wisdom which adversity had bred.

Glad were the vales, and every cottage hearth;
The Shepherd-lord was honoured more and more;
And, ages after he was laid in earth,
'The good Lord Clifford' was the name he bore.

And in this account of Lord Clifford's 'restoration to the estates and honours of his ancestors' he expressed what he conceived to be his own past, present, and future. And certainly with the publication of his Poems in two volumes in the same year the shepherd-lord was to be honoured more and more and before long, for the visitors who came on pilgrimage

to Grasmere, 'the good lake-poet' was the name he bore.
Certainly, too, from this time he did not change, but kept in
lofty place the views which he had already formed about life.
Unfortunately, however, life gradually ceased to inform his
views, as they hardened into the fixed dogmas and prejudices
which he donned as an armour against the radical tendencies
in his age and the disintegrating tendencies in himself. For
then, although the common range of visible things and the
self-sufficing power of solitude were still dear to him, he could
no longer lose and find himself in them. The 'silent inobtrusive sympathies,' which had once been as inevitable as
breathing, had to submit to a moral censorship, and, so far as
he could, he resolutely refused those 'gentle agitations of
mind' by which wisdom grows and insight deepens from day
to day.

And behind the discourse, that was soon to be rather
pompous than lofty, with which he edified his visitors there
lurked an insidious consumption of the soul. Already, during
Coleridge's absence abroad, he had aged rapidly and now
looked far older than his thirty-seven years. Indeed a traveller,
according to De Quincey, took him about this time for sixty.
The passion to which he had denied outward expression had
wasted him inwardly, and despite his sanguine complexion
and an increasing air of solemn benignity, he looked, with his
lean body, grizzled hair and narrow drooping shoulders, a
stark, but ravaged man, as much the victim of 'a self-consuming
style of thought' as his wife was blessed with a 'luxurious
repose of mind.'

Yet for six more years at least he could preserve the illusion
that he had brought wisdom and feeling into a rich alliance,
and that although Nature no longer haunted him like a passion,
she had become a dear and inexhaustible 'Mother of fresh
thoughts and joyous health.' Of his domestic peace and
security there could be no doubt. With Mary and Dorothy to

minister to his needs he was almost glutted with 'homefelt
delight' and with 'sober certainty of waking bliss.' And in a
lyric which he wrote in 1807 he contrasted the nightingale,
that creature of a 'fiery heart' with the stock-dove who 'cooed
—and cooed.' He acknowledged the tumultuous harmony of
the one, but it was of the other that he cried, 'That is the song
—the song for me!'

But it was in a longer and more ambitious poem, completed
in the same year, *The White Doe of Rylstone* that he approved
more fully and sanctified his own resignation. Of its heroine he
wrote,

> *Her duty is to stand and wait:*
> In resignation to abide
> The shock, AND FINALLY SECURE
> O'ER PAIN AND GRIEF A TRIUMPH PURE.

And the whole poem was a celebration of this passive virtue
which he deemed himself to have realised 'through force of
natural piety.' Though ostensibly historical it was quite as
personal in its reference as any of its predecessors. The Emily
who had hoped for the success of the Catholic cause, who had
been heart-broken by its failure, but had escaped

> that most lamentable snare
> The self-reliance of despair,

was of course the poet who had survived the French Revolution
and conceived himself now to be

> worthy of the grace
> Of God . . .
> A Soul, by force of sorrows high,
> Uplifted to the purest sky
> Of undisturbed humanity!

And the fact that the era of imaginative adventure had come to an end was fittingly signalised in 1808 by his removal from Dove Cottage to a larger house, known as Allan Bank. His growing family (and two more children were born to him in 1808 and 1810) necessitated the change, but it was certainly appropriate in a deeper sense to his changed condition.

So far, however, as Liberty meant the inviolate right of the individual to independence he could still be passionately moved, as the two sonnets he wrote on the subjugation of Switzerland and the final passing of the Bill for the abolition of the slave trade had proved. Yet even in these the didactic and the dogmatic note had begun to sound ominously. And the reason was not merely that he had altered his aim as a poet.

'Every great poet,' he wrote to Sir George, 'is a teacher: I wish either to be considered as a teacher or as nothing.' And certainly every great poet does instruct mankind, but he does so implicitly through his deep fidelity to his experience and his disinterested expression of it. Wordsworth himself had been such a teacher when he wrote *The Prelude*, but because he had ceased to accept experience disinterestedly, he was coming to use poetry for the conscious illustration and enforcing of preconceptions. He could describe his aim as being 'to direct the attention to some moral sentiment, or to some general principle, or law of thought, or of our intellectual constitution.' But these moral sentiments and general principles coincided conveniently with his own interests, while any which threatened his own security could be dismissed as transgressing the 'law of thought.'

It was, however, in two prose pamphlets composed in 1809 that he revealed best his capacity and his limitations as a teacher. The first was called forth by events in Portugal and was a trenchant protest against the treaty at Cintra by which the French army had been allowed to return to France after

its defeat by Wellesley. The passion which dictated Wordsworth's pamphlet had its roots in his fear and hatred of
Napoleon. He shared to the full the panic of the time, and
during the expedition to Portugal he often walked in the dead
of night to the top of Dunmail Raise to anticipate the post and
get the newspapers. His feelings, too, in writing the pamphlet
were so intense that it left him completely exhausted.

He devoted much of it to a defence of 'this just and necessary
war,' to insisting that as a champion of Liberty his principles
were consistent with his earlier opposition to war with France,
and to a sublime attack upon the British leaders for their
'utter want of *intellectual* courage.' Yet while he was doubtless
justified in deploring the want in practical statesmen of 'that
fixed and habitual principle which implies the absence of all
selfish anticipations, whether of hope or fear, and the inward
disavowal of any tribunal higher and more dreaded than the
mind's own judgment upon its own act,' he was magisterially
blind to any similar deficiency in himself. For he was honestly
convinced that his moral judgment sprang inevitably and
without prejudice from 'the instincts of natural and social
man, the deeper emotions, the simpler feelings, the spacious
range of the disinterested imagination,' and that his pride in
his country was that of a man who had not been called to
serve her professionally and whose mind was, therefore, 'left
in a state of dignity only to be surpassed by having served nobly
and generously.'

Self-complacency, however, detracted little from the force
and sagacity of his pamphlet, but in writing the second one he
was less concerned with being the Milton of his age or with
preserving the state of dignity which he enjoyed, and so
could combine the assurance of a 'superior mind' with at
times a becoming humility.

Coleridge was to some extent responsible for its appearance.
Early in 1809 he had planned to launch a weekly periodical,

entitled *The Friend*. The first number did not actually appear until June, but between that time and the following March twenty-seven numbers were issued. During all these months Coleridge was a guest at Allan Bank, and undoubtedly a somewhat trying guest, who depended almost wholly on Sara Hutchinson to transcribe the paper for the press.

Late in the year, when *The Friend* was already showing symptoms of collapse, it is supposed that he received a contribution in the form of a letter addressed to Wordsworth from John Wilson (Christopher North) who signed himself 'Mathetes.' It was published in the middle of December with part of Wordsworth's reply. And this was completed in the following number.

Wilson, who had been living at Windermere, had met Wordsworth some months before, and certainly, judging by his letter, he had identified himself perfectly with his history and his personality. For 'Mathetes'' letter is so exactly in the style of Wordsworth's reply to it that it is difficult to believe that he did not compose it in collaboration with Coleridge. It not only asked the particular questions which he wished as a teacher of the young to answer, but in describing the perplexities of enthusiastic youth it seemed to draw upon his history as only one who had written or read *The Prelude* could have done.

Who, for example, was more likely than he to write of the powerful causes that inflame the credulous disposition of youth that 'to trace these causes it will be necessary to follow the history of a pure and noble mind from the first moment of that critical passage of seclusion to the world, which changes all the circumstances of its intellectual existence, shews it for the first time the real scene of living men, and calls up the new feeling of numerous relations by which it is to be connected with them. To the young adventurer in life, who enters upon this course with such a mind, everything seems made for delusion. He comes with a spirit, the dearest feelings and highest thoughts of which have sprung up under the influences of nature. He transfers to the realities of life the high wild fancies of visionary boyhood: he brings with him into the world the passions of solitary and untamed imagination, and hopes which he has learned from dreams . . . To love and to admire has been the joy of his existence . . . there is an unconscious determination that his soul shall be satisfied; an obstinate will to find good everywhere. And thus his first study of mankind is a continued effort to read in them the expression of his own feelings. He catches at every uncertain shew and shadowy resemblance of what he seeks; and unsuspicious in innocence, he is at first won with those appearances of good which are in fact only false pretensions.'

If John Wilson wrote such passages as these he possessed an uncanny insight into the history of the 'teacher, conspicuous above the multitude in superior power, and still more in the assertion and proclamation of disregarded truth,' from whom he sought guidance for the young. And Wordsworth was very happy and, up to a point, peculiarly well qualified to respond. For although a film of fear and prejudice was beginning to cloud his eyes, his youth, as he looked back upon it, was still vivid and real. Indeed, tamper as he might through the long years that lay before him with passages of *The Prelude* in an attempt to transpose his earlier pantheism into the key of Christian orthodoxy, he never falsified the essential truth of that record.

And so although he addressed himself to youth with all the superiority and dignity of a 'more advanced mind' which overlooked its subject and commanded it from centre to circumference, he candidly admitted that Youth had virtues which age lacked, and that an insistent preceptor might well prove an oppression and even a fatal hindrance. This admission was, of course, based upon his own experience, upon that happy immunity from meddling elders which he himself had

2 D

enjoyed. And it was bound up with his true conviction that all real growth springs from the individual's own immediate experience of life. 'Nature,' as he wrote, 'has irrevocably decreed, that our prime dependence in all stages of life after infancy and childhood have been passed through (nor do I know that this latter ought to be excepted) must be upon our own minds; and that the way to Knowledge shall be long, difficult, winding, and oftentimes returning upon itself.'

Consequently he insisted that the prime necessity for the young was to be true to themselves. 'To expect from youth these virtues and habits, in that degree of excellence to which in mature years they may be carried, would indeed be preposterous. Yet has youth many helps and aptitudes for the discharge of these difficult duties, which are withdrawn for the most part from the more advanced stages of life. For youth has its own wealth and independence; it is rich in health of body and animal spirits, in its sensibility to the impressions of the natural universe, in the conscious growth of Knowledge, in lively sympathy and familiar communion with the generous actions recorded in history, and with the high passions of poetry; and, above all, youth is rich in the possession of time, and the accompanying consciousness of freedom and power . . . Hence, in the happy confidence of his feelings, and in the elasticity of his spirit, neither worldly ambition, nor the love of praise, nor dread of censure, nor the necessity of worldly maintenance, nor any of those causes which tempt or compel the mind habitually to look out of itself for support; neither these, nor the passions of envy, fear, hatred, despondency, and the rankling of disappointed hopes . . . have power to preside over the choice of the young, if the disposition be not naturally bad, or the circumstances have not been in an uncommon degree unfavourable.'

That Wordsworth was describing his own youth when he wrote this passage is obvious, and he was no less remembering

it when he contended that a young man's opinions 'could nowhere deceive him beyond the point up to which, after a
season, he would find that it was salutary for him to have been
deceived.' And this again was based upon a true recognition
that disillusionment is necessary to advance on to a new level
and that suffering may fertilise the soul.

But how was the 'disinterested and free condition of the
youthful mind' to be recovered when once the instinctive
faith of youth had been maimed or shattered? To this question
Wordsworth confidently replied — 'He cannot recall past time;
he cannot begin his journey afresh; he cannot untwist the
links by which, in no undelightful harmony, images and
sentiments are wedded in his mind. Granted that the sacred
light of childhood is and must be for him no more than a
remembrance. He may, notwithstanding, be remanded to
nature, and with trustworthy hopes, *founded less upon his
sentient than his intellectual being*; to nature, as leading on
insensibly to the society of reason, but to reason and will, as
leading back to the wisdom of nature. A reunion, in this
order accomplished, will bring reformation and timely support; and the two powers of reason and nature, thus recipro-
cally teacher and taught, may advance together in a track to
which there is no limit.'

It was his last clear statement, uncompromised by orthodox
piety, of the creed of Hartley. And doubtless, as he wrote, he
believed that the creed did suffice him and that it represented
'the confirmed wisdom of manhood.' How reason and will,
once embarked upon their own self-determined course, should
lead back to the wisdom of nature and recover her inspiration,
he did not inquire. It was enough to suppose that, like errant
children, who had learnt the folly of their ways, they would
come to suitable terms with their kindly mother, that 'teacher
of truth through joy and through gladness,' that 'creatress of
the faculties by a process of smoothness and delight.'

And so the reply to 'Mathetes,' however eloquent as an appreciation of youth, threw no new light on the problem of how age might recover the 'inward sense of absolute and unchangeable devotion,' which youth unconsciously enjoyed. Wordsworth might insist that the maturing man admonished by reason and relying upon this newly acquired support, would find a world of fresh sensations gradually opening upon him as his mind put off its infirmities; and that by making it his prime business to understand himself, the precious feelings of disinterested and self-disregarding joy and love would be gradually regenerated and restored.

But if he could have examined himself more searchingly, he must have known that while this was true up to a certain point, the 'elevation, the absolute possession of the individual mind' which he described as the goal of human life, and thought to have achieved himself, had not brought with it in any true sense 'a consistency or harmony of the being within itself, which no outward agency can reach to disturb or impair.'

His own condition was, indeed, more truthfully symbolised in the striking image of the dying taper which he used to illustrate nature's method of teaching the young, 'It fades and revives, gathers to a point, seems as if it would go out in a moment, again recovers its strength, nay becomes brighter than before: it continues to shine with an endurance, which in its apparent weakness is a mystery; it protracts its existence so long, clinging to the power which supports it, that the observer . . . becomes sad and melancholy; . . . it is to him an intimation and an image of departing human life.'

§ 2

The reply to 'Mathetes' was Wordsworth's last precise definition in prose of the creed which he had affirmed so eloquently in the last two books of *The Prelude*. But the fact that despite his claim to the possession of 'undiminish'd powers' he had been unable to make any progress with the 'philosophic poem' which was to crown his maturity, was disturbing. For if his genius as a poet was failing, it was difficult to believe that the peace which he now desired above all things was as firmly founded in the fertile nature of things as he hoped.

Nor had Coleridge's presence quickened the flame. Indeed he had had rather the opposite effect, and when in October 1810 Basil Montagu stopped at Allan Bank to pick up Coleridge on his way to London, Wordsworth warned him what a troublesome guest his travelling companion was likely to prove. Montagu most inconsiderately repeated Wordsworth's remarks to Coleridge, and the result was a violent estrangement which was never really healed.[1] For this Wordsworth can hardly be blamed; his remarks were certainly justified and may well have been kindly meant. Moreover the public breach between himself and Coleridge, which he was perhaps unduly slow to close, merely proclaimed in a painful way the reality of their relationship as it had existed for some time.

Yet it was a deep grief to him to have to recognise how complete and final the estrangement was, and although he had known ever since the miserable interview at Kendal that Coleridge would never again be a source of inspiration, it made it more difficult to continue with any confidence the 'philosophic poem' for which the magnanimous and admiring friend of past days had insisted that he was so signally equipped.

He had, however, resumed work on it during 1809, incited to the task, if not inspired, by Coleridge's presence, and he continued the work uninterruptedly for five years until in 1814 he brought it to completion. His life during these years was not unshadowed by other troubles. For he lost in 1812

[1] For further details see the author's *Samuel Taylor Coleridge*, p. 265.

two of his children, but if the spirit of poetry within him was a dying taper, reason had taught him resignation. And perhaps his chief purpose in completing *The Excursion* was to convince himself that that resignation to what he then described as the will of God was as real and fertile as his original submission to the Spirit of Nature.

He took up the poem where he had laid it down seven years before in the middle of The Solitary's history. But it is clear that he first worked over what he had already written, adding for example a pietistic postscript to the tale of Margaret told by The Wanderer in the first book. This after-comment, however appropriate to the devout character of The Wanderer, was quite out of keeping with the suffering woman whose hopeless acceptance of her destiny he had previously described with such a deep fidelity to the truth of actual life.

But Wordsworth's fidelity to Nature was now compromised by his attachment to the creed of the Church. He wished to reinforce Hartley with Holy Writ, and in the third and fourth books of the poem in which in turn The Solitary proclaims and laments the inevitability of his despondency and The Wanderer seeks by argument and exhortation to correct it, he strove with an ardour that transcended any conventional prejudice to reconcile natural and orthodox piety in a convincing synthesis, to be at once faithful to life as he had known it and to 'repose upon the breast of Faith.'

It was, indeed, his final attempt to persuade himself and others that the re-establishment of his being after his fall was a reality. Previously he had been content to claim that he had by his own efforts and adaptability reconciled reason and feeling in conformity with natural law. The closed order of Nature had sufficed him and he had dispensed with any divine sanction, any God outside this order. And so far as in this he had rejected the false dualism of conventional religion, he had been right. For in his immediate experience of Nature he had known a God who was at home in the natural world, even if He transcended it. But since he himself was now neither instinctively nor spiritually at one with Nature, it was inevitable that he should accept a God who was similarly divided from the physical world of His creation. And so he enthroned above his earlier self-sufficient naturalism and as a final guarantee of grace, security and respectability, the God of the devout.

For to one who had already begun to feel the chill of autumn in his blood a spirit so rapturous but so faithless as Nature's, so tender in its cherishing but so ruthless in its destruction, could offer no ultimate satisfaction. And it was finality that he craved even at the cost of fixity, a shelter for his anxious soul within which he could still enjoy the Nature that he loved, but which would stand firm and stable against the fluctuations and impermanence of all natural life. In the words of The Solitary,

> Ah! what avails imagination high
> Or question deep? what profits all that earth,
> Or heaven's blue vault, is suffered to put forth
> Of impulse or allurement, . . .
>   —if neither in the one,
> Nor in the other region, nor in aught
> That Fancy, dreaming o'er the map of things,
> Hath placed beyond these penetrable bounds,
> Words of assurance can be heard; if nowhere
> A habitation, for consummate good,
> Or for progressive virtue, by the search
> Can be attained,—a better sanctuary
> From doubt and sorrow, than the senseless grave?

This was the assurance which Wordsworth now sought above all else. To quote The Solitary again,

Slight, if you will, the *means*; but spare to slight
The *end* of those, who did, by system, rank
As the prime object of a wise man's aim,
Security from shock of accident,
Release from fear; and cherished peaceful days
For their own sakes, as mortal life's chief good,
And only reasonable felicity.

In wishing, therefore, to satisfy 'the universal instinct for repose,' Wordsworth was seeking an absolute refuge from the bane of Nature's mutability, from the 'fear, doubt and agony' which she dealt out so capriciously with her favours. Nor do we question the necessity of his quest. For the ultimate goal of human life must always be an absolute serenity of spirit. But this vital peace, in however small a measure, is only given to the man who has cast down the last of his personal defences, who out of his deep faith in the creative will of Life and through freedom from attachment to things, has dared to be insecure and in that insecurity discovered a perfect safety. The absolute independence, in short, which Wordsworth now sought was only to be found in an absolute dependence.

How nearly he came to perceiving this, while at the same time contriving to cling inwardly to the compromise which was fatal to both his peace and his poetry, these two books of *The Excursion* show. Once again in The Solitary's description of his youth, he recalled the happy state in which he rested 'upon earth's native energies,' enjoying both peace and 'life's genuine inspiration.' For 'the serene was also bright.' It was not the uneasy or stagnant calm of a beleaguered city, such as the man who recoiled from life in search of a private satisfaction knew.

This was the course upon which The Solitary had embarked when in his disillusionment he

                                     began to feel
That, if the emancipation of the world
Were missed, I should at least secure my own,
And be in part compensated.

And Wordsworth's present search for a personal recompense
in tranquil meditation for the dizzy raptures of his youth was
merely the final stage of that recoil.

But the eloquent harangue which The Wanderer 'poured
forth with fervour in continuous stream' throughout the
fourth book of *The Excursion* is so full of aspiration and
sagacity that Wordsworth might seem to have discovered at
last a self-forgetful faith by which he could live and in which
his earlier naturalism was truly reconciled with and completed
in a religion of the spirit. There could hardly be, for example,
a more fervent or unqualified expression of the necessity of an
absolute dependence than that contained in its opening passage.
'One adequate support,' The Wanderer says,

> For the calamities of mortal life
> Exists—one only; an assured belief
> That the procession of our fate, howe'er
> Sad or disturbed, is ordered by a Being
> Of infinite benevolence and power;
> Whose everlasting purposes embrace
> All accidents, converting them to good.
> —The darts of anguish *fix* not where the seat
> Of suffering hath been thoroughly fortified
> By acquiescence in the Will supreme
> For time and for eternity; by faith,
> Faith absolute in God, including hope,
> And the defence that lies in boundless love
> Of his perfections; with habitual dread
> Of aught unworthily conceived, endured

Impatiently, ill done, or left undone,
To the dishonour of his holy name.
Soul of our Souls, and safeguard of the world!
Sustain, thou only canst, the sick of heart;
Restore their languid spirits, and recall
Their lost affections unto thee and thine!

It was nobly said, and doubtless, as Wordsworth wrote these lines, he did so long for the support of this 'absolute faith' that he believed that he possessed it, and that he who had been constituted by heaven a priest of Nature might now also be the poet of religion. He could even invoke the very spectres that he dreaded —

—Come, labour, when the worn-out frame requires
Perpetual sabbath; come, disease and want;
And sad exclusion through decay of sense;
But leave me unabated trust in thee —
And let thy favour, to the end of life,
Inspire me with ability to seek
Repose and hope among eternal things —
Father of heaven and earth! and I am rich,
And will possess my portion in content!

Yet the very grandiloquence of the language and the undertone of insistent demand upon the 'dread source, prime, self-existing cause and end of all' to give him the satisfaction which Nature was ceasing to render, showed that at heart he was still unchanged and that his claims were far more absolute than his faith.

For despite all the noble eloquence of the fourth book of *The Excursion* Wordsworth had not really experienced the God whom he enthroned over life and whose 'infinite benevolence and power' he acclaimed, as he had once experienced the spirit of Nature. His very language betrayed him.

For the capacity to give the self away and thereby rediscover it as an organ of Creation itself, is the essential condition equally of all true religious experience and all true poetical expression. And it is clear from the quality of the verse that Wordsworth's 'Father of heaven and earth' was too unreal to command any such devotion.

Consequently his devotional eloquence and moral affirmations command only an external assent. He wrote truly enough, for example, that

> by the storms of circumstance unshaken,
> And subject neither to eclipse nor wane
> Duty exists.

But Duty for him was now, even less perhaps than when he wrote the *Ode to Duty*, the directing voice of an overruling Creator to whom he had surrendered his will. It was rather a code of self-defence against the pain and danger of fluctuating passions, a substitute for the creative sensibility which he had denied.

And his failure to recognise the apostasy from life falsified throughout the claim which he made through The Wanderer to the achievement of a full maturity. The Wanderer, indeed, recognises how hardly won and still more hardly held is such maturity. But the sacrifices which he claims as easy were for Wordsworth the hardest of all. In speaking of his later life he says—

> Those fervent raptures are for ever flown;
> And, since their date, my soul hath undergone
> Change manifold, for better or for worse:
> Yet cease I not to struggle, and aspire
> Heavenward; and chide the part of me that flags,
> Through sinful choice; or dread necessity
> On human nature from above imposed.

> *'Tis , by comparison, an easy task*
> *Earth to despise;* but to converse with heaven —
> This is not easy: — *to relinquish all*
> *We have, or hope, of happiness and joy,*
> *And stand in freedom loosened from the world,*
> *I deem not arduous;* but must needs confess
> That 'tis a thing impossible to frame
> Conceptions equal to the soul's desires;
> And the most difficult of tasks to keep
> Heights which the soul is competent to gain.

Nothing in fact was more difficult for Wordsworth than to relinquish all he had or hoped of happiness and joy and stand in freedom loosened from this world. All his greatest achievements as a poet was due in the past to the deep tenacity of his attachment to earth and his intense pursuit of instinctive and self-centred happiness. And to this was also due the almost hysterical excess of his 'soul's desires,' the frightening sense of instability associated with them, and his consequent longing for

> that state
> Of pure, imperishable, blessedness,
> Which reason promises, and holy writ
> Ensures to all believers.

The desire was a true and necessary one. But not all the assurances of holy writ could guarantee him such a state, so long as he failed to realise the conditions which governed it. And he did not realise them. He could write of the man who had lost the visionary powers of his youth that he

> feels too vividly; and longs
> To realise the vision, with intense
> And over-constant yearning; — there — there lies
> The excess, by which the balance is destroyed.

But the excess did not lie in the intensity of the yearning but in its acquisitiveness. It was because even in the 'passion of the soul that leads to ecstasy' he could not outgrow an avid craving for self-satisfaction, that he could not experience real illumination, but was for ever baffled and troubled by a sort of vertigo. Disdaining 'the crooked paths of time and change' he projected his 'limitless desires' into eternity itself. But in so doing he experienced only a dizzy unrest.

Consequently he fell back upon a settled peace and creed which lacked all the transforming vitality of creative life. He might think to rest in it,

> not fearing for our creed
> The worst that human reasoning can achieve,
> To unsettle or perplex it.

Yet he had also to acknowledge 'with pain and grievous self-reproach,' that 'the endowment of immortal power' was matched unequally with 'custom, time, and domineering faculties of sense' and, 'in the private region of the mind,' with

> Ill-governed passions, ranklings of despite,
> Immoderate wishes, pining discontent,
> Distress and care.

Instead, therefore, of recovering on a higher level and through the achievement of a full personality the unity of his childhood, he had accepted the dualism of orthodox religion without really believing in its creed. For all his most vital experiences in childhood and boyhood disproved the ultimate truth of such a dualism. And through this false resignation he had ensured the death of his genius as a poet.

Already in the discourse of the 'venerable sage,' in his lofty pronouncements upon conscience or upon the wisdom of

cultivating a rational mean between the two extremes of blind
hope and despondency, 'whereon to build sound expectations,' we feel that the original virtue of poetry is almost
submerged in the conventionally edifying. And when he
spoke of

>   rejoicing secretly
> In the sublime attractions of the grave,

the words were equally false to the true spirit of religion and
of poetry.

But in the latter part of this fourth book of *The Excursion*
Wordsworth did for the last time recover something of his
earlier inspiration when, turning from his poetical exposition
of the creed of an orthodox Churchman, he recalled once
again the true source of his inspiration, the 'bountiful Nature'
which he delusively supposed that he was reconciling with
religion. When he emphasised the vassalage that binds the
heart to earth, and cried:

> Take courage, and withdraw yourself from ways
> That run not parallel to nature's course,

he was no nearer to realising what a complete fidelity to
Nature involved. But at least he was vindicating the truth and
necessity of the instinctive relation that had been so richly
his, when he had roamed 'an equal among mightiest energies.'
He could still cherish the remembrance of vitality, and hope
for its recurrence, even if it defied the tranquillising power
of time with 'a noble restlessness.' And forgetting his previous
appreciation of 'the sublime attractions of the grave,' he could
ask,

>   who thinks, and feels,
> And recognises ever and anon
> The breeze of nature stirring in his soul,

> Why need such man go desperately astray,
> And nurse 'the dreadful appetite of death?'

And later, in recalling the time in human history before the
rational creature felt the weight of his own reason, and when
'the imaginative faculty was lord of observations natural' he
could affirm with vital conviction the SPIRIT that hung over
the towns and farms, the statues, temples and memorial
tombs of Greece, a spirit that was immortal and yet 'in Nature's
course' and which assured the Votary

> Of Life continuous, Being unimpaired;
> That hath been, is, and where it was and is
> There shall endure.

Indeed the faith of Paganism

> Exemplified by mysteries, that were felt
> As bonds,

appealed to the depths of his nature far more compellingly
than the pseudo-Christian faith which he had assumed but
which left his Being impaired. He had exclaimed three or four
years before in one of the noblest of his sonnets —

> Great God! I'd rather be
> A Pagan suckled in a creed outworn;
> So might I, standing on this pleasant lea,
> Have glimpses that would make me less forlorn . . .

And if his protest in that sonnet had been against a worldliness
given over to getting and spending, the tribute which he made
The Wanderer pay to the religion of Paganism was no less
a protest of his vital being against a Christian orthodoxy

which left him fundamentally forlorn. For in the Pagans there
had been no conflict between nature and spirit, instinct and
imagination.

> They felt,
> And did acknowledge, wheresoe'er they moved,
> A spiritual presence, oft-times misconceived,
> But still a high dependence, a divine
> Bounty and government, that filled their hearts
> With joy, and gratitude, and fear, and love;
> And from their fervent lips drew hymns of praise,
> That through the desert rang. Though favoured less,
> Far less, than these, yet such, in their degree,
> Were those bewildered Pagans of old time.
> Beyond their own poor natures and above
> They looked; were humbly thankful for the good
> Which the warm sun solicited, and earth
> Bestowed; were gladsome—and their moral sense
> They fortified with reverence for the Gods;
> And they had hopes that overstepped the Grave.

All that was repressed in Wordsworth's nature by the creed in
which he had sought refuge went out in joyous affirmation of
such a faith. And although The Wanderer, 'raising his voice
triumphantly,' proceeds to insist upon the higher reward to be
obtained from sense and reason in conformity with Holy Writ,
the faith which he commends is that of a man lamentably
conscious that time has not only 'shorn his natural wings' but
crippled his imagination.

As in *The Prelude* Wordsworth attacked eloquently the pride
of intellect that kills the imaginative faculty by analysis. But
although he knew well the deadliness of prizing

> This soul, and the transcendent universe,
> No more than as a mirror that reflects
> To proud self-love her own intelligence,

he overlooked the subtler self-love which lurked behind
what seemed to be a sublimely moral renunciation. 'O blest
seclusion!' he wrote,

> when the mind admits
> The law of duty; and can therefore move
> Through each vicissitude of loss and gain,
> Linked *in entire complacence* with her choice;
> When youth's presumptuousness is mellowed down,
> And manhood's vain anxiety dismissed;
> When wisdom shows her seasonable fruit,
> Upon the boughs of sheltering leisure hung
> In sober plenty; when the spirit stoops
> To drink with gratitude the crystal stream
> Of unreproved enjoyment; and is pleased
> To muse, and be saluted by the air
> Of meek repentance, wafting wall-flower scents
> From out the crumbling ruins of fallen pride
> And chambers of transgression, now forlorn.
> O, calm contented days, and peaceful nights!

The power that 'abides in man's celestial spirit' as in 'the
deep stillness of a summer even,' the power by which Wordsworth had been a great poet, was denied in these lines. Comfort
was sanctioned in them by morality and self-complacence
adorned with humility. Wordsworth might congratulate himself that he had ceased to strive.

> To reconcile his manhood to a couch . . .
> Stuffed with the thorny substance of the past
> For fixed annoyance.

But in ceasing to struggle, not because he had resolved the
conflict, but because he desired peace at any price, he had
abandoned the creative adventure of life.

2 E

And the concluding passages of this fourth book of *The Excursion* in which he affirmed, as in the last book of *The Prelude*, his faith in the principle of love revealed the same stultifying evasion. 'For—the Man,' he wrote

> Who, in this spirit, communes with the Forms
> Of nature, who with understanding heart
> Both knows and loves such objects as excite
> *No morbid passions, no disquietude,*
> *No vengeance, and no hatred*—needs must feel
> The joy of that pure principle of love
> So deeply, that, unsatisfied with aught
> Less pure and exquisite, he cannot choose
> But seek for objects of a kindred love
> In fellow-natures and a kindred joy.
> Accordingly he by degrees perceives
> His feelings of aversion softened down;
> A holy tenderness pervade his frame.
> His sanity of reason not impaired,
> Say rather, all his thoughts now flowing clear,
> From a clear fountain flowing, he looks round
> And seeks for good; and finds the good he seeks:
> Until abhorrence and contempt are things
> He only knows by name.

Certainly by avoiding all objects which might excite disquietude, vengeance, or hatred through opposing his desires or inclinations, a man might ensure that in seeking for good he always found the good he sought. But the teacher who bid men set their affection on things above and not on things of the earth implied no such privileged and discreet retreat from evil. He knew that evil is as magnetically attracted to those who shrink from it as to those who desire it. The pure principle of love is not thus sheltered from objects or occasions which might put it to the test. It suffereth long, but is still kind. It grows

strong in battling against temptations to hatred, in rising above
the allurements of morbid passion, and in smiling in the face
of personal danger and disquietude. The love, however,
which Wordsworth professed in these lines and of which he
promised himself the enjoyment, had nothing heroic in it.
Far from bearing or enduring 'all things,' it consorted only
with pleasing objects.

Such love must inevitably lose the inspiration of life and
become weak and enervated. Instead of 'flowing from a clear
fountain' of inward faith and courage, it is poisoned by fear
at its source. Doubtless for those so agreeably instructed
every object might teach

> Some acceptable lesson to their minds
> Of human suffering, or of human joy.

Doubtless such love might foster

> The ability to spread the blessings wide
> Of true philanthropy.

It might even impel its votaries 'by strict necessity along the
path of order and of good,' until

> whate'er we see,
> Or feel, shall tend to quicken and refine;
> Shall fix, in calmer seats of moral strength,
> Earthly desires; and raise, to loftier heights
> Of divine love, our intellectual soul.

But behind this grandiloquent conclusion lay the sad truth
that Wordsworth had denied in its essentials the divine love
which he professed to vindicate. And although he could now
conceive himself to be one

> whom time and nature had made wise,
> Gracing his doctrine with authority,

one, in whom knowledge had ripened into faith,

> and faith become
> A passionate intuition; whence the Soul
> Though bound to earth by ties of pity and love,
> From all injurious servitude was free,

he had, in fact, lost that ultimate faith in life upon which all passionate intuition and all true poetry depends. By withdrawing from the conflict before he had brought it to a victorious issue and seeking sanctuary in a Churchman's and a moralist's creed he had lost both his integrity and the pearl of inward honesty that is beyond price. And in its place he had preferred a righteous unction beneath which, however much leavened by pity and philanthropy, the bright spirit of life dimmed and died.

And so the eloquent harangue of The Wanderer was succeeded by the protracted moralising in a graveyard of The Pastor, moralising in which there was much that did prove Wordsworth's claim to be bound to earth by ties of pity and love, but which was discursive and sapless. The Philosophic poem which was to have been the crown and glory of his life-work had become a mere amalgam of parochial reminiscence and moral anecdote.

§ 3

So pleasantly immersed, however, had he been in his task, and so considerably had self-complacence sapped his powers of self-criticism that it was only when *The Excursion* was published in 1814 and evoked cries of disappointment, if not of dismay, from every reputable critic, that the inner doubt against which the whole poem had been an elaborate defence, for a short time reasserted itself.

Could it be that time and Nature had made him wise only

to destroy him as a poet? He could dismiss the opinions of a Jeffrey, and even those of Lamb, Hazlitt and De Quincey would count for little if Coleridge approved. But Coleridge remained silent. The breach between them had never really been closed, but he needed his approval so deeply that after nine months he begged him for his opinion.

Coleridge's response was characteristically considerate, but it was resolutely and searchingly unfavourable. He frankly confessed his disappointment. He was far from being as ruthless as the young Keats was to be three years later, when he wrote to a friend that 'every man has his speculations, but every man does not brood and peacock over them till he makes a false coinage and deceives himself.' But he emphasised the same defect with a beautiful tact when he suggested that the inferiority of *The Excursion* to *The Prelude* 'might have been occasioned by the influence of *self-established convictions* having given to certain thoughts and expressions a depth and force which they had not for readers in general.'

Wordsworth's convictions, however, had by now become so self-established that even Coleridge's criticism could not shake them. He was deeply grieved, and doubtless what remained of the vital poet in him acknowledged the justice of Coleridge's conjecture and disappointment. But it was easy to assume that Coleridge who lacked so lamentably the moral dignity which *The Excursion* consistently upheld, was hardly qualified to appreciate its merits. As he had remarked to Crabb Robinson three years before, 'If men are to become better, the poems will sooner or later find admirers . . . But no one has completely understood me—not even Coleridge. He is not happy enough!'

And the more surely life was leaving him stranded within his own self-centred shell of propriety and prejudice, the more essential it was that he should believe that he was happy and that his claims as both a poet and a teacher of mankind were secured by the highest moral sanctions.

How much, however, conventional morality, and the self-deception and secret fear which had conditioned his acceptance of it, had already deadened the vital sensibility by which alone true happiness and true poetry could be secured was shown very clearly in *Laodamia*, which he wrote in the year in which *The Excursion* was published. It was perhaps the last poem in which he preserved something of the vitality of his prime together with that careful craftsmanship and lofty tone which were henceforth to be an inadequate substitute for it. It cost him, on his own confession, more trouble than almost any-thing of equal length he had ever written. And this, we can believe, was due not only to his anxiety to give the incident 'a loftier tone than, so far as I know, has been given to it by any of the Ancients who have treated of it,' but to a conflict of feeling in himself.

Laodamia, in fact, represents in his poetry the final defeat of the man of deep instinctive feeling by the censorious moralist. And although the poem proves how conclusive the defeat was, it also shows in places that his deeper emotional nature was still sufficiently alive to resent its defeat. He still craved, in fact, the instinctive joys and powers which were ebbing from him. But because he felt them to be failing, because the Nature which he had loved and in dependence upon which he had lived creatively was apparently betraying him, he was driven to deny her, and not only to deny but to accuse and condemn. In the person of Laodamia he arraigned and punished the instinctive life which had once been the source of his inspiration and also of his suffering.

Her husband, Protesiláus, killed at Troy, is through the pity of Jove restored to her for a brief three hours. As con-ceived by Wordsworth, however, he shows little celestial pity himself, since he comes first to tantalise and then to lecture. For it is not as a spectre or a vain shadow that he appears, but with the 'vital presence' and 'corporeal mould' that were his upon the beach of Troy. When, however, the 'impassioned Queen' seeks very naturally to clasp her lord, he eludes again and again her eager grasp. Laodamia pleads and protests. She appeals to her husband, whose ⋅ locks are as redundant in her sight, and

> lips as fair
> As when their breath enriched Thessalian air,

to love her, as he had been wont to do.

> 'Come, blooming Hero, place thee by my side!
> Give, on this well-known couch, one nuptial kiss
> To me, this day, a second time thy bride!'

The longing of her warm woman's nature might seem to be innocent and appealing enough to soften the heart of the Gods. But Jove, who had invited such a human appeal by restoring to her such a blooming and corporeal Hero, 'frowned in heaven' at her words;

> the conscious Parcæ threw
> Upon those roseate lips a Stygian hue,

and a spectral Protesiláus begins his harangue. The change in his appearance, he remarks, should not be mourned,

> even if the joys
> Of sense were able to return as fast
> And surely as they vanish. Earth destroys
> Those raptures duly—Erebus disdains:
> Calm pleasures there abide—majestic pains.

> Be taught, O faithful Consort, to control
> Rebellious passion: for the Gods approve
> The depth, and not the tumult, of the soul;
> A fervent, not ungovernable, love.
> Thy transports moderate; and meekly mourn
> When I depart, for brief is my sojourn.

But Laodamia's human longing is not appeased by this lofty homily. She cites the precedents of Alcestis and Æson who returned to earth and human life. And so Protesiláus continues his discourse. He speaks eloquently of love as being far mightier than strength of nerve and sinew. He admits that Love's favourite seat 'is often feeble woman's breast,' but he expatiates upon

>   such love as Spirits feel
> In worlds whose course is equable and pure;
> No fears to beat away—no strife to heal—
> The past un-sighed for, and the future sure;
> Spake of heroic arts in graver mood
> Revived, with finer harmony pursued.

He describes, in fact, the sort of love which Wordsworth promised himself in *The Excursion*, and he emphasises the moral condition of its achievement,

> Yet there the Soul shall enter which hath earned
> That privilege by virtue.

He then proceeds to laud the supremacy of his own virtue at Troy and to describe how

>   lofty thought
> In act embodied, my deliverance wrought.

And from this height of moral self-applause he looks down with stern disapproval upon the hapless Laodamia,

'And Thou, though strong in love, art all too weak
In reason, in self-government too slow;
I counsel thee by fortitude to seek
Our blest re-union in the shades below.
The invisible world with thee hath sympathised;
Be thy affections raised and solemnised.

'Learn, by a mortal yearning, to ascend —
Seeking a higher object. Love was given,
Encouraged, sanctioned, chiefly for that end;
For this the passion to excess was driven —
That self might be annulled: her bondage prove
The fetters of a dream, opposed to love.'

That Laodamia 'shrieked' on the conclusion of this homily is
understandable, quite apart from the appearance of Hermes to
remove her dear but didactic Shade. But Wordsworth had not
yet done with her. For the stress of her feelings was such that
it killed her.

Thus, all in vain exhorted and reproved
She perished; and, as for a wilful crime,
By the just Gods whom no weak pity moved,
Was doomed to wear out her appointed time,
Apart from happy Ghosts, that gather flowers
Of blissful quiet 'mid unfading bowers.

It is true that in the first version of the poem Wordsworth was
still too merciful to be so rigorous a moralist. He wrote,

Ah, judge her gently who so deeply loved!
Her, who, in reason's spite, yet without crime,
Was in a trance of passion thus removed;
Delivered from the galling yoke of time,
And these frail elements — to gather flowers
Of blissful quiet 'mid unfading bowers.

It was some years before he thought it necessary to inflict upon her an endless damnation, which he reduced in the relenting mood of old age to the lengthy sentence in purgatory, pronounced above.

But the poem, even as it stood in 1814, could only have been written by a man whose poetic instinct was stultified by a self-defensive and self-deceiving morality. If, as he claimed, he had succeeded in giving the subject a loftier tone than any of the Ancients, he had sacrificed in the process both simple human feeling and imaginative truth. He had denied equally the poignancy of human love that yearns for a bodily presence beyond the grave, and the beauty of spiritual love that is not tied to the things of sense but can enter into them and redeem them. The Laodamia, whom he condemned, had at least the gift of love, if she cherished too ardently the dear garment of the flesh, while the Protesiláus whom he approved and exalted, was not a spirit, but a moral prig.

Only one who had failed to fulfil the love-impulse in himself could have thus denounced the warmth of generous instinct. Wordsworth had, in fact, lost the generosity of the natural man without gaining the charity of the spiritual man, and in thinking to exalt the spiritual by condemning the natural he revealed the typical attitude of the censorious moralist, who is baulked of abundant life on either plane.

The poem revealed clearly that he still longed for those raptures which, to his dismay, 'earth destroys duly,' and was incapable of reconciling 'such love as Spirits feel' with his earthly nature. He had feared the senses even when they served him as channels of life, and now that the channels were running dry, he had begun to hate them. He concealed his hate behind a moral condemnation of the natural joy that men and women may take in one another, which was wholly different from a spiritual recognition of the ultimate inadequacy of the life of the senses. And he concealed his bitter feeling that life was leaving him stranded behind claims to 'deliverance' from 'old frailties.'

But he was so far from being delivered that his moral self-esteem was continually haunted and disproved by memories of a richer, if unregenerate, life. And in this poem he turned upon such memories and denounced them. In the person of Laodamia he brought Annette up for final judgment. She was no longer the 'forsaken woman' who had haunted his conscience and wrung his heart. Hers was 'the crime of lovers that in Reason's spite have loved.' Doubtless passion had once driven him, too, to excess. But in his own eyes he had now atoned by becoming a man of lofty probity, in whom the 'self had been annulled.' Frail and loving women, however, who never hardened into moralists, were inevitably criminals in the eyes of the just Gods whom no weak pity moved and of whom he himself, through Protesiláus, was the approved minister.

Wordsworth did not of course consciously condemn Annette in the person of Laodamia. But the instinctive love of woman for man and man for woman could never be dissociated in the deeps of his being from her. With her alone had he known it. She alone had driven him to excess of passion, and so she alone impugned in the secret places of his heart and mind the moral dignity which he had assumed.

And there could, perhaps, be no more conclusive evidence of the extinction of his imaginative life than that he should now reprove and condemn the 'forsaken woman' who had received from the poet that had been such tender tributes of pity, understanding and regret.

§ 4

Wordsworth's creative life was over, although he was to continue for thirty-five years to exercise his skill as a verbal craftsman. Doubtless the universe was still at moments to murmur to him like a shell of that native sea from which he had emerged into conscious life, but he could no longer travel thither or see the eternal children sport upon its shore. The deep bond with Nature by virtue of which he had been the voice of staunch and simple men, of forlorn womanhood, of mysterious powers and invisible elements, had ceased to replenish him with life. Instead it held him subject to the implacable forces of decay, from which he sought unavailingly to escape into the fortress of morality and the Established Church.

The very qualities which had made him a great poet, his stark independence, his intense self-absorption and his tenacity of feeling, became, now that life no longer inspired him, his chief defects. For it was because he had refused to come to easy terms with life, because he had had the strength to stand alone, to preserve his unique relationship with the universe, that he had been able to discover in the world of human experience so much that was both new and immemorial and to express it in a language that was peculiarly his own.

And it was for the same reason that he had always been something more than a nature mystic or expansive pantheist. Nature he had loved as few have loved her, but he had never allowed her to seduce him from himself. And in this he had been right. For the destiny of man is not to be submerged in Nature but to be reconciled with the Creative Spirit which is in and beyond her. And to achieve this he must preserve and perfect his human identity, that unique and inaccessible selfhood which is, when fully vindicated, the organ of the Godhead. He must realise the truth that in life, as in the hour of death, he is essentially alone with the mystery, that real life is every moment also a death, and that only by gladly accepting and acting out of this aloneness can he fulfil the purpose of the creative principle in himself and thereby come into true union with all creation.